THE
POLITICAL ECONOMY
OF
SOCIAL CLASS

PRENTICE-HALL SOCIOLOGY SERIES
NEIL J. SMELSER, Editor

THE
POLITICAL ECONOMY
OF
SOCIAL CLASS

CHARLES H. ANDERSON
Gothenburg University, Sweden

PRENTICE-HALL, INC., Englewood Cliffs, New Jersey

Library of Congress Cataloging in Publication Data

ANDERSON, CHARLES H
    The political economy of social class.

    (Prentice-Hall sociology series)
    Includes bibliographical references.
    1. Communism. 2. Social classes. 3. Marxian
economics. I. Title.
HX56.A57   335.43   73-12584
ISBN 0-13-685149-5

TO SUE, CHRIS, AND SIDSEL

© 1974 by Prentice-Hall, Inc.
Englewood Cliffs, New Jersey

Printed in the United States of America

10 9 8 7 6 5 4 3 2 1

PRENTICE-HALL INTERNATIONAL, INC., London
PRENTICE-HALL OF AUSTRALIA, PTY. LTD., Sydney
PRENTICE-HALL OF CANADA, LTD., Toronto
PRENTICE-HALL OF INDIA PRIVATE LIMITED, New Delhi
PRENTICE-HALL OF JAPAN, INC., Tokyo

CONTENTS

This book is an attempt to make sense out of widespread senselessness, and to see logic and reason behind illogic and irrationality. Phrased otherwise, it is a Marxist sociological critique of class-stratified capitalist society. The events of the past quarter century have forced concerned citizens to seriously re-examine the premises upon which their lives and their society are founded. Serious and critical thought requires the assistance of theory— a body of concepts and ideas, propositions and interpretations—to help organize the welter of fast-moving historical events. Modern sociology has cast about in many directions in search of valid and practical theory. While theories of a very limited range have been to various degrees successfully applied to very limited circumstances, taken together these limited theories help very little in organizing our thinking about the larger topics of society, about society as an overall system. General theories of society have themselves proved singularly impotent and have been largely boiled down into so much textbook jargon and neologism—capable of mystifying but unable to explain or clarify.

The restrictive force of capitalist society has been a major obstacle to unclouded thinking about itself as a system. Bourgeois ideologies cloaked in the garb of scientific social theory have been passed off on several generations of sociology students in the United States. Beginning with a revival of populist-type criticism in the early 1960s, social thought has progressively matured, and the maturation process has led increasingly toward Marxist theory. This book employs Marxist theory as an organizing tool to help clarify the social, political, and economic forces at work upon ourselves and our society. The test of any theory lies in the extent to which it aids in the comprehensive understanding of the concrete social and historical events both past and present, and in its ability to be a reliable guide in future practice. To a large extent, Marxist theory has stood the test of successful practical application, and the body of materials assembled in this volume should solidly attest to this conclusion.

The first three chapters set out the essentials of Marx's theoretical framework. The reader should always be aware of the important part played by Frederick Engels, Marx's closest friend and collaborator, in the development and presentation of Marxist theory. Dual authorship is frequently cited, and Engels himself is frequently cited as well. Chapter 4 takes up the question of inequality and the distribution of wealth, and Chapter 5 lays out a theoretical discussion of the concept of social class. Then, a pair of chapters delve into the working class and the several relevant issues that relate to it. Similarly, the ruling class is taken up directly in the subsequent two chapters. Chapter 10 confronts the rise of state capitalism as a political and economic solution to the problems facing the ruling class under advanced capitalism, and a brief Chapter 11 describes the imperialist solution to ruling class needs under the same advanced capitalist conditions. As should become clear in the reading of Chapters 8 through 11, the concepts of monopoly capitalism, state capitalism, and imperialism are separate referents of a single broad system. Chapter 12 focuses attention upon working class political posture and outlook as represented in the traditional working class, the black population, students and the left, and women, in an effort to discern the potential for radical change and the direction of current militance. A short final chapter probes into the nature of a socialist transition and suggests the kinds of concrete changes that might begin such a transition.

The initial draft of this volume contained chapters on the radical theories of Lenin and Veblen, on the impact of imperialism on underdeveloped countries, and on contemporary collectivisms as found in the Soviet Union, China, and Sweden. These topics warranted more lengthy treatment than this book would allow and departed in part from the central emphasis upon the United States class system. Stratification in contemporary advanced welfare and collectivist societies is, of course, a complete topic unto itself and offers valuable theoretical comparisons with the United States class structure. The same points apply to stratification within the underdeveloped countries.

Thus, although drawing from the relevant literature on comparative stratification whenever possible, the book is primarily a survey and analysis of the contemporary United States class system as viewed from a Marxist perspective. The purpose of the book is to bring together under a Marxist lens the pertinent issues and literature bearing upon the operation of social classes under advanced capitalism, particularly as it is found in the United States. The book has been written under the assumption that capitalism is a destructive human and environmental force and with the conviction that socialism represents a viable alternative to capitalist irrationality.

The reader will discover that the contents of this book are quite demanding. But so, too, are the practical issues and problems with which the book deals. My hope is that the students of social class who persevere in this study will find their efforts rewarded with a much firmer intellectual grip upon the social, political, and economic events that swirl around them, and that such a grip will serve them well as an effective asset in bringing about a more humane and equal society.

ACKNOWLEDGEMENTS

For taking their time to read, criticize, and offer a number of useful suggestions on an earlier draft of the manuscript, I would like to express gratitude to Lynda Ann Ewen, Jack Roach, Neil Smelser, and Al Szymanski. Bill Green performed an exceptional job of editing the manuscript, providing many improvements in composition and in content as well. Thanks are also due to Ed Stanford of Prentice-Hall for his encouragement, patience, and assistance in publishing this volume; and to Ann Torbert of Prentice-Hall for her help in the work of production.

I am grateful to Oxford University Press for permission to use their copyrighted material from *The Power Elite* and *White Collar* by C. Wright Mills.

one —————————————————————————

MARXIST THEORY: SOCIOHISTORICAL AND ECONOMIC FOUNDATIONS

MARXISM AND THE STUDY OF SOCIAL CLASS

The study of social class has resumed once again its classical position of centrality within sociology and the social sciences. The myths of a uniform "middle-class" society composed of universal common men, all standing equal to one another in status and opportunity, have been violently exploded once and for all. The latter part of the twentieth century portends the revival, though not the replication, of the kinds of class conflicts and struggles which swept through industrial society of the late nineteenth century. As the industrial system of competitive capitalism grew to maturity, the social upheavals which followed in its wake drew the attention, both apologetic and critical, of social theorists of the time. And prominent among their concerns were the rise and fall of social and economic classes, and the meanings of the various kinds of ties and relationships between such classes for the future course of the society. The theoretical ferment focused on the writings of Karl Marx. And Karl Marx was above all concerned with the class structure of the capitalist system. "Thus," writes S. M. Lipset, "if one were to award the title of father of the study of social class to any individual, it would have to be Marx." [1]

But as the capitalist class rose to unprecedented heights of power and prestige, particularly in America, the theoretical apologists of the capitalist system flourished as well in their own small world. In America, Marx and

---

[1] S. M. Lipset, *Revolution and Counterrevolution* (New York: Basic Books, 1968), p. 122.

1

Marxist theory were largely excluded from that world, and with them, the prominence and reality of class inequality and the radical analysis of social class. Notions regarding progress, mobility, equality, opportunity, and social status groups were pressed into service, while critical and probing study of the class antagonisms and socioeconomic irrationalities of capitalism largely faded from sight. The Great American Celebration, as C. Wright Mills referred to it, was begun and reached an efflorescence in the period following World War II. A complex of social and economic forces were at work undermining the sanctity of the status quo, but at the surface the chief event was the Vietnam War. This tragic historical event acted as a catalyst to the radicalization of a great number of people, including many social scientists, in a fashion that nothing short of another major depression could have done. Students of society were in ever-growing numbers led to a more incisive review of the sociopolitical role of the large corporation, the function of the state and the defense establishment, foreign economic and political involvements, and the status of social class and inequality. The study of social class pushed its way to center stage during the 1960s and early 1970s; and as the irrationalities and contradictions of corporate capitalism unfold themselves with still greater clarity, we might well anticipate the magnification of class inequities and the sociological coverage of them. What is more, this coverage will assume an increasingly Marxist form, for as we shall argue and endeavor to make clear, the Marxist theoretical model and orientation is the best suited, if not the only, framework within which to lay bare the economic, political, and social determinants of class and inequality.

To say as we have that Marxism has been pushed aside in the past as a serious theoretical instrument in the study of class and society is not to say that it has been totally neglected. Although tokenism and distortion have been the rule in American sociology's dealings with Marx, there have been significant exceptions prior to the more recent resurgence of interest. Most noteworthy for our purposes here have been the contributions of Thorstein Veblen and C. Wright Mills. In this context, the contributions of Paul M. Sweezy and Paul A. Baran should also be stressed, the latter two scholars being far more the orthodox Marxists than the former pair. Nevertheless, while both Veblen and Mills were variously critical of Marx, their major contributions to social class analysis clearly stem from the Marxist tradition, particularly those of Veblen.

What has been said, then, is that Marxism is a potent theoretical framework for the understanding of social class and for the entire field of political economy, i.e., the theoretical study of capitalism as a system.[2]

---

[2] Engels defines political economy as follows: "Political economy is the theoretical analysis of modern bourgeois society." In Karl Marx and Frederick Engels, *Selected Works,* vol. 1 (Moscow: Progress Publishers, 1969), p. 507.

Marxism is a powerful framework for the understanding of our society because such an understanding must be grounded in a thorough comprehension of class relations. This is, as we shall see, the message of Marxism. Certainly there are other scholarly approaches to the study of class and society, such as that of Max Weber, and we shall on occasion make some use of them. But such addendums and subsidiaries to the Marxian approach will be limited, for we are avoiding what Mills referred to as Sophisticated Marxism, in which revisions are so bulky that the theory becomes unrecognizable or useless.[3] Conversely, neither shall we be Dead Marxists, those who adhere to "the view that it [Marxism] is all true, and that it contains all that men need to know." [4] We shall strive for what Mills called Plain Marxism, to work as Marx did, openly and flexibly with his general social theory. The Marxism of Marx rejects the idea of forcing living realities into hard-and-fast patterns.[5] And while these other non-Marxist approaches may be useful within certain limited contexts, we shall concur with David Horowitz that the traditional Marxist model is the only model which "is capable of analyzing capitalism as an historically specific, class-determined social formation." [6]

The theoretical foundation of Marxism—that the way people relate to one another and organize the productive forces of a society gives shape to other social, cultural, and political institutions—has retained full sociological meaning.[7] A viable theoretical model provides its users valuable and indispensable advice, for it tells them where to begin the search for knowledge and understanding, leads them through a bewildering array of facts, and ultimately makes sense of the often seemingly senseless events of the world. In the realm of political economy a viable theory should tell a person not only why he or his neighbor is unemployed but why millions of others are too, why he is in an economic squeeze in a land of millionaires, why his son kills and is killed in an unknown land, and many other pressing concerns. And precisely such are the events that the Marxist theoretical framework is able to account for, as well as many more facts which routinely escape non-Marxist theoretical accounting. Events change and tend to be unique, but sound theory encompasses change and uniqueness. As Mills observes about Marx: "His model is what is great; that is

---

[3] C. Wright Mills, *The Marxists* (New York: Dell Publishing Company, 1963), p. 104.

[4] Ibid.

[5] Y. Zhukov et al., *The Third World: Problems and Prospects* (Moscow: Progress Publishers, 1970), p. 251.

[6] David Horowitz, "Marxism and Its Place in Economic Science," *Berkeley Journal of Sociology* 16 (1971–72): 57.

[7] See Samir Amin, "The Class Struggle in Africa," African Research Group reprint 2, Cambridge, Mass., p. 23.

what is alive in marxism. He provides a classic machinery for thinking about man, society, and history." [8]

This is not to say that the Marxist framework provides the theoretical machinery to understand all men, all societies, and all history; such would be Dead Marxism, and we are not here concerned with universal knowledge. Rather, our concern is with social class and with the major dynamics of class-stratified capitalist society. It is for such a purpose that Marxist theory is chiefly intended, and for which we shall apply it with considerable gain.

Marxism is thought by many sociologists to be mere political rhetoric and ideological dogma. Although aspects of the Marxist model have been vulgarized by opportunists to serve their own political purposes, taken as a whole the body of Marxist thought is an empirically grounded and testable approach to social science. As Osipov points out, Marx (and Engels his close associate as well) based his work on specific social research and used the results as an instrument for understanding reality: "Without specific social research Marxist sociology could neither have emerged nor continuously developed." [9] Dogma and doctrine provide ready-made answers without research. Marxist theory does nothing of the kind. In the words of Engels, who coauthored many of Marx's most important works, "our conception of history is above all a guide to study" rather than a lever for the a priori construction of reality. [10]

The scientific and empirical orientation of Marxist theory does not imply, however, that it is devoid of value orientation as well. Marxism embodies moral precepts at the same time that it is a guide to empirical research. Mills has stated the point succinctly: "Marxism is at once an intellectual and a moral criticism. In its documents, in its very conceptions, the two *are* often difficult to separate, but it *is* political philosophy *and* at the same time it is definitely social science." [11] Thus, Marx has made a major contribution to both humanism and social science. Arising out of Marxist social theory is a path leading toward a humanist utopia. "Marx did not abolish Utopia," writes Fromm. "On the contrary he rejuvenated it and enlarged its scope." [12] While involved in the process of dissecting the relationships (and pointing out the contradictions) within capitalist economy

---

[8] Mills, *The Marxists,* pp. 36–37. It should be pointed out, however, that Mills was a sharp critic of Marx. He wrote: "The model as Marx left it is inadequate. One can use it only with great intellectual clumsiness and wasted sophistication, and often only with doubletalk" (p. 130).

[9] G. Osipov, *Sociology: Problems of Theory and Method* (Moscow: Progress Publishers, 1969), pp. 179–80.

[10] Ibid.

[11] Mills, *The Marxists,* p. 102.

[12] Erich Fromm, ed., *Socialist Humanism* (London: Penguin Press, 1967), p. 194.

and society, Marxist theory simultaneously points the way to a more person-centered (i.e., humanistic) social order. Just as the present contains within it indications of the future, so does an understanding and grasp of the existing structure of social relations lead to an image of what is possible in the future.

While the Marxist model has long been underutilized as a guide to thought and action, indications are that social science is turning increasingly to Marxist theory and analysis as a guide to study. As Colfax has written, "there is reason to believe that a Marxist class-analysis of contemporary society holds the greatest promise for the transformation of sociological and social consciousness over the next decade." [13] Whether such a prognosis will be born out is unanswerable at the moment; what can and should be said is that the study immediately at hand is an endeavor in that direction.

Although this volume is foremost a study of social class, it is also an analysis of major social problems of capitalist society. The two areas are inseparably linked. This fact suggests an error in Blumer's assertion that "contrary to the pretensions of sociologists, sociological theory, *by itself*, has been conspicuously impotent to detect or identify social problems." [14] Blumer was correct in saying that not objective conditions but social definitions isolate problems. He was also correct regarding the impotence of established social theory to identify and explain social problems. The error was that of failing to recognize the potency of Marxist theory to identify the major problems of the day; indeed, this is its deep and abiding strength. It not only detects but sheds bright illumination on the conflicts and contradictions that rent most of Western society and the latter's activities in the Third World. [15] However, when a theory isn't used, as Marxist theory has not been by established American sociology, it obviously won't work for you.

SOCIAL REALITY AS SOCIAL RELATIONS

In the Marxian schema, the locus of social reality is to be found in the social relations of a group or society. The object of investigation can never

[13] J. David Colfax, "Varieties and Prospects of 'Radical Scholarship' in Sociology," in Colfax and Jack Roach, eds., *Radical Sociology* (New York: Basic Books, 1971), p. 84.

[14] Herbert Blumer, "Social Problems as Collective Behavior," *Social Problems* 18 (Winter 1971): 299.

[15] Paul Baran has phrased the point well in saying that "Marxism is nothing if not a powerful magnifying glass under which the irrationality of the capitalist system protrudes in all of its monstrous forms." (*The Longer View*, New York: Monthly Review Press, 1969, p. 41.)

be a single individual taken in isolation. To Marx "the human essence is no abstraction inherent in each single individual. In its reality it is the ensemble of the social relations." And for Marx "society does not consist of individuals; it expresses the sum of connections and relationships in which individuals find themselves." [16] As LeFebvre observes, "To Marx, the 'subject' is always social man, the individual viewed in his actual relationships with groups, classes, society as a whole." [17] Locating social reality in the individual is one kind of error; at the opposite extreme is the mistaken view of reality as existing independently of individuals in society. In Marx's words, "What is to be avoided above all is the re-establishing of 'Society' as an abstraction *vis-à-vis* the individual." [18] The *social* nature of the individual and the relational nature of society received subsequent articulate formulation in the works of American scholars such as Charles Horton Cooley and George Herbert Mead. Also worked out in the theories of these social psychologists is the Marxian assumption that the mind (or consciousness) and its contents arise from the individual's active participation in the social process, and that language comes into existence with human intercourse and serves as the medium of consciousness.[19] To cite Marx and Engels, "Consciousness is, therefore, from the very beginning a social product, and remains so as long as men exist at all." [20]

Marx, like Mead later, noted the importance to the human situation of imaginative preliminary construction of impending or possible social relationships. Extrapolating from his relational view of man and society, Marx was able to say that "a bee puts to shame many an architect in the construction of her cells. But what distinguishes the worst architect from the best of bees is this, that the architect raises his structure in imagination before he erects it in reality." [21] Potentially, this attribute permits people to plan, to act purposively, and to rationally control the course of their social life and history.

Marx stressed a further distinguishing aspect of human beings that subsequent sociology has tended to neglect or entirely ignore. It is the human ability to *produce* their means of subsistence upon which Marx lays the

---

[16] Karl Marx, *Theses on Feuerbach*, in Marx and Engels, *Selected Works*, vol. 1, p. 14; and Karl Marx, *The Grundrisse*, edited and translated by David McLellan (New York: Harper & Row, 1971), p. 77.

[17] Henri LeFebvre, *The Sociology of Marx* (New York: Vintage Books, 1969), p. 8.

[18] *Essential Writings of Karl Marx*, edited by David Caute (New York: Collier Books, 1967), p. 41. (From *Economic and Philosophic Manuscripts of 1844*.)

[19] See G. H. Mead, *Mind, Self, and Society* (Chicago: University of Chicago Press, 1934).

[20] Marx and Engels, *The German Ideology*, in *Selected Works*, vol. 1, p. 32.

[21] Karl Marx, *Capital*, vol. 1 (Chicago: Charles H. Kerr & Company, 1908), p. 198.

heaviest emphasis in his social psychology: "The first premise of all human history is, of course, the existence of living human individuals. The first *historical* act of these individuals distinguishing them from animals is not that they think, but that they begin to *produce their means of subsistence*." [22] ("This sole but cardinal difference alone," Engels adds, "makes it impossible simply to transfer laws of animal societies to human societies." [23]) Combining Marx's view on the relational nature of society with his emphasis on the human ability to produce the means of subsistence through labor, we are able to come to grips with the Marxist axiom that the production of a group's livelihood is a social relational endeavor, and that exactly *how* individuals relate to one another in the production process ultimately determines their social class position and with it their place and actions in society at large. As we shall later elaborate, Marx stressed that the development of capitalism increasingly places men's productive relations in a greater and greater *social* situation and setting until individual labor can no longer serve as a basis for the organization of economic institutions.

In summing up this brief excursion into the Marxist view of social reality and human life, we can with Ollman count productive work, self-consciousness and will, planned and purposive action, mental and physical flexibility, concentration, rationality, and social cooperation among the distinguishing traits of Marx's view of man.[24] Although human life regularly exhibits the opposite traits, it is only through their full realization that individuals can obtain the liberation or freedom they may desire.

PEOPLE MAKE HISTORY

"Despite all the criticism levelled by its enemies," write Makhov and Frish, "it is indisputable that Marxism is a genuinely humane theory in which the problem of the individual holds the central place." [25] Critics of Marxist theory often assert that it purports to be a theory of iron historical determinism, the laws of history inevitably grinding out their will, while individuals are mere puppets acting out a preconceived drama. Nothing could be further from the truth. Let Marxism speak for itself: "*History* does *nothing,* it 'possesses *no* immense wealth,' it 'wages *no* battles.' It is *man,*

---

22 Marx and Engels, *The German Ideology,* in *Selected Works,* vol. 1, p. 20.
23 Engels to P. L. Lavrov, 1875, in Marx and Engels, *Selected Works,* vol. 3 (1970), p. 478.
24 Bertell Ollman, *Alienation: Marx's Conception of Man in Capitalist Society* (Cambridge: Cambridge University Press, 1971), p. 118.
25 A. S. Makhov and A. S. Frish, eds., *Society and Economic Relations* (Moscow: Progress Publishers, 1969), p. 16.

real living man, that does all that, that possesses and fights; 'history' is not a person apart, using man as a means for *its own* particular aims; history is *nothing but* the activity of man pursuing his aims." [26] Thus, history has no more abstract reality than does society; both are the products of human action.

Yet individuals are not altogether free agents, for before them have lived other individuals who have established a structure of social relations tending to carry people along in a historical momentum. Just as interaction exists between individuals and society, so is there interplay between people and their history. Marx has stated the case plainly: "Men make their own history, but they do not make it just as they please; they do not make it under circumstances chosen by themselves, but under circumstances directly encountered, given and transmitted from the past. The tradition of all the dead generations weighs like a nightmare on the brain of the living." [27] History reveals that "circumstances make men just as much as men make circumstances." [28]

Here we again encounter the flexibility in Marx. At times a given set of social relations is determinate, quite consistently holding individual actors within the logic of its development. At other times individuals are capable of breaking this hold and reconstructing social reality. As we shall discuss, Marxist theory tells us that the possibility of breaking the hold of a given set of social relations is not at all times present, but rather is a real option only at certain historical junctures. The point to be emphasized is that the real job of remaking a society is wholly up to the participants and is not worked out by external historical forces. As Stojanovic has pointed out, in no other way could people be morally obligated to try to bring about change: "Only the kind of Marxism that conceives of socialism as an historical possibility, and not a necessity, is in the position to oblige people ethically to put their efforts into its realization." [29] That Marx would agree is clearly implied in his well-known aphorism, "The philosophers have only *interpreted* the world, in various ways; the point, however, is to *change* it." [30] Marx is saying that if people themselves don't make the effort to change their world, things will never get further than a philosopher's point of view of it. And by his own writings and actions on behalf of the working class of his day, Marx confirms his action-oriented view of the historical process.

---

[26] *Essential Writings of Karl Marx,* ed. Caute, p. 50. (From *The Holy Family.*)

[27] Marx, *The Eighteenth Brumaire of Louis Bonaparte,* in *Selected Works,* vol. 1, p. 398.

[28] Marx and Engels, *The German Ideology,* in *Selected Works,* vol. 1, p. 42.

[29] Svetozar Stojanovic, "Marxism and Socialism Now," *New York Review of Books,* July 1, 1971, p. 17.

[30] Marx, *Theses on Feuerbach,* in *Selected Works,* vol. 1, p. 15.

THE ECONOMIC PIVOT

We have just refuted the frequent criticism that Marxist theory deals with history as some autonomous, independent force. Next we turn our attention to a theoretical premise of Marxism which is also frequently misunderstood: that dealing with the role of material production. First, we have already taken note of Marx's social psychology and the origins of consciousness in the social process. Combining this idea with that of the active role individuals play in the historical process, we see it is hardly necessary to state that to Marx human consciousness is no mere reflection of material conditions. Quite to the contrary, Marx fought this kind of crude materialism current in his own day, and would be equally opposed to the crude psychological behavioralism of our own day. (Fromm points out that Marx himself never used the term *historical materialism*.[31]) To argue that human consciousness is a mere reflection of material environmental conditions reflects the same sort of passiveness Marx rejected in his larger view of the historical process. As Avineri points out, such a view would imply that people can never emancipate themselves, can never positively act upon the material world and change it.[32]

Now, Marx was also in reaction to the Hegelian view that reality is found in the realm of abstract ideas, and that the movements of these independent ideas govern human behavior and the course of history, ending in the consummation of the Idea of the State. Marx countered that individuals are not the embodiment of ideas but the producers of ideas, ideas produced within a definite, historical structure of social relations. In brief, there exist no ideas with lives of their own, nor do our ideas simply reflect their material surroundings; consciousness is firmly rooted in the on-going relations of the group and evolves from participation therein.

Society, of course, is composed of many different kinds of such relations—e.g., religious, familial, military, political, and economic. Is an individual's consciousness shaped equally by all of the relations he has with others in the group or society? Marxist theory argues that it is not. Economic relations, relations of production, are held to be the primary determinants of consciousness. Further, economic relations are taken to be the foundation upon which arise other modes of consciousness and conduct

---

[31] Erich Fromm, *Marx's Concept of Man* (New York: Frederick Ungar Publishing Company, 1961), p. 12.

[32] Shlomo Avineri, *The Social and Political Thought of Karl Marx* (Cambridge: Cambridge University Press, 1970), pp. 66–67.

in capitalist society. The words *shape* or *condition* are more accurate than *determine* when considering the linkages between economic and other cultural and institutional formations. But before pursuing finer questions of causation, let Marx speak for himself on the economic pivot:

> In the social production of their life, men enter into definite relations that are indispensable and independent of their will, relations of production which correspond to a definite stage of development of their material productive forces. The sum total of these relations of production constitutes the economic structure of society, the real foundation, on which rises a legal and political superstructure and to which correspond definite forms of social consciousness. The mode of production of material life conditions the social, political and intellectual life processes in general. It is not the consciousness of men that determines their being, but, on the contrary, their social being that determines their consciousness.[33]

As we shall discuss at greater length in Chapter 3, Marx subdivides the economic structure of the society into two parts: (1) the material productive forces, consisting of all the social and technological relations and knowledge that go into creating the goods that sustain life; and (2) the existing relations of production, consisting of the legal property relations within which productive forces operate. It is the eventual conflict and contradiction between these two dimensions of economic life that generate the conditions for social transformation as a whole, including that of the political order. Marx cautions that the economic conditions of production may change without rendering immediate alterations in the legal and political orders, and that ideological and political rhetoric should not be confused with the underlying social productive processes: "The social structure and the State are continually evolving out of the life process of definite individuals, but of individuals, not as they may appear in their own or other people's imagination, but as they *really* are; i.e., as they operate, produce materially." [34]

The distinction between the economic order of a society and other institutions is obviously not a distinction involving matter and machines versus conscious human life and activity (though this is a popular misconception). Rather, it is a distinction between conscious human economic or productive material life and the other cultural and social creations of society. It is a distinction, in Avineri's words, "between conscious human activity, aimed at the creation and preservation of the conditions of human

---

[33] Marx, Preface to *A Contribution to the Critique of Political Economy*, in *Selected Works*, vol. 1, p. 503.

[34] Marx and Engels, *The German Ideology*, in *Selected Works*, vol. 1, p. 24.

life, and human consciousness, which furnishes reasons, rationalizations and modes of legitimization and moral justification for the specific forms that activity takes." [35]

Returning to the nature of the relationship between economic productive relations and the rest of social structure, we may observe that Marx was no simple economic determinist: "It is not, as people try here and there conveniently to imagine, that the economic condition produces an automatic effect." Nevertheless, "the economic relations, however much they may be influenced by the other—political and ideological—ones, are still ultimately the decisive ones, forming the red thread which runs through them and alone leads to understanding." [36] Engels later clarified the position further:

> Political, juridical, philosophical, religious, literary, artistic, etc., development is based on economic development. But all these react upon one another and also upon the economic basis. It is not that the economic situation is *cause, solely active,* while everything else is only passive effect. There is, rather, interaction on the basis of economic necessity, which *ultimately* always asserts itself.[37]

Ollman has drawn our attention to the fact that Marx's relational conception of reality excludes the possibility of economic determinism, and that the impact of the economic structure of society has simply been assigned the greatest weight.[38] However, the economic weight, as Engels put it, is in the final analysis the determining one, even though within the final or ultimate limits of bourgeois society there exists widespread latitude for legal, political, ideological, and other factors to assert their influence.

From previous comments and citations it should be evident that Marx's empirical method can be carried over into the study of, for example, economic and political relations. Marx's comment that "the connection between production and the social and political structure must in every case be uncovered by empirical observation, without mystification or speculation," [39] should adequately dispose of the charges by those who claim Marxist theory closes the door on research of, say, relations between the economic order and the state. Marx himself was continuously examining precisely this relationship.

---

[35] Avineri, *The Social and Political Thought of Karl Marx,* p. 76.
[36] Cited in Osipov, *Sociology,* p. 18.
[37] Engels to W. Borgius, 1894, in *Selected Works,* vol. 3, p. 502.
[38] Ollman, *Alienation,* p. 26.
[39] Cited in Martin Nicolaus, "Proletariat and Middle Class in Marx: Hegelian Choreography and the Capitalist Dialectic," *Studies on the Left* 7 (January–February 1967), 24.

ECONOMY AND THE STATE

Without question, the factors of political power and the state weigh heavily in Marxist analysis. Regarding actual events of major societal change and revolution, the state assumes centrality. And even prior to revolution the state is of the utmost importance from the standpoint of both the dominant economic classes and the dominated ones. Far from being indifferent to political power, Marx devoted the bulk of his nontechnical economic analysis, at least after his early treatises, to conflicts in the political arena. There are many Marxist critics who, while granting this point, take issue with Marx's contention that political power in bourgeois society takes root within the economic structure.

Baldly stated, Marx held that the modern state was "nothing more than the form of organization which the bourgeois necessarily adopt for the mutual guarantee of their property and interests." [40] It is a committee for the administration of the consolidated affairs of the bourgeois class as a whole. Why is the state an instrument of the capitalist class and not some other group or class. Or: Why does it not serve as an arena for balancing off one class against another? Because power in capitalist society derives from wealth, and the capitalist class has a grossly disproportionate amount of the wealth. At the level of the personal exercise of power, Marx argues, "the power that each individual exercises over others' activity or over social wealth exists in him as the owner of . . . money. Thus both his power over society and his association with it is carried in his pocket." [41]

The organized power of the wealthy capitalist class takes as one of its chief forms, then, the political power of the state: "Political power, properly so-called, is merely the organised power of one class for oppressing another." [42] In Engels's words: "The cohesive force of civilised society is the state, which in all typical periods is exclusively the state of the ruling class, and in all cases remains essentially a machine for keeping down the oppressed, exploited class." [43] (Note that Engels refers to *"typical* periods," meaning that Marxist theory does not hold that the state is always the instrument of the dominant class, not even within the capitalist period itself; at times the state may exercise power as ostensible mediator,

---

[40] Marx and Engels, *The German Ideology* (Moscow: Foreign Language Publishing House, 1965), p. 78.

[41] Marx, *The Grundrisse,* p. 66.

[42] Marx and Engels, *Manifesto of the Communist Party,* in *Selected Works,* vol. 1, p. 127.

[43] Engels, *The Origin of the Family, Private Property, and the State,* in *Selected Works,* vol. 3, p. 332.

acquiring independence from conflicting but mutually balancing classes.[44])
However, Marx was well aware that in noncapitalist or precapitalist periods and areas of the world state monopolies or bureaucracies could and
systematically did crush capital or wealth-producing classes.

There is a second but related criterion, in addition to the control of
capital or wealth, that enters into the equation of state power. And this is
that the class representing and most concerned with advancing the productive forces of society, the class most crucial to achieving this goal,
stands as the eventual inheritor of political power. Otherwise, a wealthy
but economically and productively reactionary class could indefinitely suppress change. In Chapter 2 we shall deal in some depth with the economic
contradictions that place the ruling capitalist class in a position of declining power. Suffice it to note here Marxist theory argues that the ruling
class of our period has become reactionary with regard to the full and
constructive use of socially productive economic forces, and the working
class represents and is indispensable to the progressive advance and use of
these forces.

That such an objective economic situation exists does not mean that
the ruling class of bourgeois society will automatically be dethroned. We
have previously emphasized the human-action role in history, and fundamental change of bourgeois society necessitates political action and struggle. As Marx wrote, "To conquer political power has therefore become
the great duty of the working class." [45] The achievement of political power
is essential for accomplishing the transformation of the economic relations
of a society. Without political power people are, according to Marx, "incapable of enforcing their class interests in their own name, whether
through parliament or through a convention. They cannot represent themselves, they must be represented by . . . an unlimited governmental
power that protects them against the other classes and sends them rain
and sunshine from above." [46]

Among the political developments of late capitalism is the increasingly
direct economic role played by the bourgeois state. Owing to problems
arising from an irrational relationship between economy and society (see
Chapter 2), the state must assume the position of surrogate capitalist, or
state capitalist. Engels wrote: "In any case, with trusts or without, the
official representative of capitalist society—the state—will ultimately have
to undertake the direction of production." [47] Such measures result in state

---

[44] Ibid., p. 328.

[45] Marx, *Inaugural Address of the Working Men's International Association,*
in *Selected Works,* vol. 2 (1969), p. 17.

[46] *Essential Writings of Karl Marx,* ed. Caute, p. 75. (From *The Eighteenth
Brumaire of Louis Bonaparte.*)

[47] Engels, *Socialism: Utopian and Scientific,* in *Selected Works,* vol. 3, p. 144.

capitalism, or in more familiar Galbraithian terms, the new industrial state. From the standpoint of Marxist theory, state capitalism is but a technical step in the direction of a socialist economy; the former represents a development in economic relations which may immediately precede the institutionalization of socialist economic relations. Again from Engels we have: "State ownership of the productive forces is not the solution of the conflict, but concealed within it are the technical conditions that form the elements of that solution." [48] The solution consists, according to Engels, in recognizing the social nature of modern production and in harmonizing it with the control and utilization of productive forces.

CAPITAL AND CAPITALISTS

Owing to primacy of economic variables in the Marxist theory of social classes, we must build up to a full understanding of class and class relations on a foundation of economic analysis. Of initial importance is an acquaintance with the meaning of capital—and hence of capitalists, the key class in the development of capitalism in its early stages and one of the two pivotal classes of the current epoch. We shall meet the other class, the proletariat, soon enough.

We may begin by drawing an important distinction between something having a use-value and an exchange-value.[49] If something has a use-value it usually has been the creation of human labor, the exceptions being things of utility to man that are not due to labor such as natural supplies of air, water, soil, etc. (Marx reserved the term *value* to the achievements of human labor.) The use-value of something is realized in its consumption by or utility to its human user. If the producer of an object created it for the *direct* satisfaction of his or her own group's wants or needs, it never moves beyond its use-value status. However, when the product of labor has been created for the indirect consumption by others, it takes on the status of a commodity and is put up for exchange. What the object can bring in return, in the form of money or other products, is its exchange-value. Briefly here, an object's exchange-value is set by the amount of labor time used up in its creation. (Incidentally, and importantly for later discussions, not all products of labor are endowed with value, inasmuch as certain of these may be useless or wasteful, and hence the labor does not count as labor and the objects have no value.) Understandably, exchange-value will play a central role in the definition of capital and the emergence of a capitalist class.

---

[48] Ibid., p. 145.
[49] Marx, *Capital*, vol. 1, pp. 47–48.

Yet we readily see that the circulation of commodities as objects with exchange-values may follow two distinctive paths, one noncapitalist and the other capitalist. When objects with use-values are exchanged for one another, or through the medium of money (also a commodity for exchange and essential to the development of capitalism), the purpose of the exchange may be solely to consume the commodities. Say an artisan sells a piece of his pottery for a given sum of money in order to obtain shoes for his children. We have commodity-money-commodity as the form of circulation. This is the noncapitalist path. It consists of selling in order to buy. By contrast, a person may buy in order to sell, in which case the person's purpose in engaging in the activity is not to satisfy wants or meet needs, but to accumulate money as a commodity. If a person buys two thousand pounds of cotton for a given sum and subsequently sells it for a larger sum, he has, in effect, exchanged money for more money. Now we may, with Marx, define capital: "Money that circulates in the latter manner is thereby transformed into, becomes capital." [50] In the circulation process consisting of money-commodity-money we have the creation of capital: "We have here, therefore, a palpable difference between the circulation of money as capital, and its circulation as mere money . . . [In the former case,] its leading motive, and the goal that attracts it, is therefore mere exchange value." [51]

We may now define the capitalist and his motives of action. Again from Marx: "The simple circulation of commodities—selling in order to buy—is a means of carrying out a purpose unconnected with circulation, namely, the appropriation of use-values, the satisfaction of wants. The circulation of money as capital is, on the contrary, an end in itself, for the expansion of value takes place only within this constantly renewed movement. Thus the conscious representative of this movement, the possessor of money becomes a capitalist." [52] The distinction between commodities produced for exchange specifically for use-value and production of commodities for the purposes of the capitalist is very basic to later discussions in this book and cannot be overemphasized at this point. A further clarification from Marx is in order: "Use-values must therefore never be looked upon as the real aim of the capitalist; neither must the profit on any single transaction. The restless never-ending process of profit-making alone is what he aims at. This boundless greed after riches, this passionate chase after exchange-value, is common to the capitalist and the miser; but while the miser is merely a capitalist gone mad, the capitalist is a rational miser." [53]

---

[50] Ibid., p. 164.
[51] Ibid., pp. 166–67.
[52] Ibid., pp. 169–70.
[53] Ibid., pp. 170–71.

We shall further clarify the meaning of capital when we confront the problem of labor dealt with below. But first we shall look into the problem of how commodities receive their exchange-value and are sold at a profit.

LABOR THEORY OF VALUE

How can two use-values be compared in conducting an exchange? The answer lies in the concept that labor is the source of all value. Labor and value are interchangeable terms. Hence, the measurement of exchange-value is gauged by the amount of labor time needed to produce the commodities in question. The price of a commodity thus expresses only the "average amount of social labour necessary, under the average conditions of production, to supply the market with a certain mass of a certain article." [54] Or: "We see then that that which determines the magnitude of the value of any article is the amount of labour socially necessary, or the labour-time socially necessary for its production." [55]

Observe here the emphasis upon *"socially* necessary"—meaning that industrial production is a profoundly social and interdependent undertaking and that it is difficult or impossible to isolate the productive act of labor in the separate individual. The social nature of production becomes increasingly crucial to economic forces of change in the development of capitalism. Also, observe the emphasis upon the term *"average* conditions of production"; commodities of a given type cannot be individually gauged for value by the socially necessary labor time going into each. Rather, we are here referring to labor in the abstract, to the normal time requirements. Thus, slower production time for a given commodity is relatively penalized and workers thus labor longer to produce the same amount of value; conversely, rapid production time is rewarded with less work required or more items produced. We are here, then, speaking of labor *productivity,* which is determined by the skill of the workmen, the degree of technology and extent of application, the social organization of production, the capabilities of the means of production, and so on.[56] Nevertheless, variations in productivity, and hence normal or average socially necessary labor time of production, can only yield temporary gains and losses. For unless competitors in a given field utilize and adopt productive power similar to that of the more advanced producers, the former will soon be pushed or cut out of the market. One group of workers laboring twelve hours to produce a number of commodities cannot compete long with

---

[54] Marx, *Wages, Price, and Profit,* in *Selected Works,* vol. 2, p. 53.
[55] *Capital,* vol. 1, p. 46.
[56] Ibid., p. 47.

another group working an equal length of time but producing twice the number of same commodities. Nor can the latter producer long market products at a price above the average labor time required for production during that period as competitors remaining in the field reach equivalent productive capacities. As the use of machinery of a given type becomes general in a particular industry, temporary advantages in price gained from greater productivity sink down to the natural value, i.e., the socially necessary labor time to produce the commodity.[57] Thus, producers are driven by efficiency requirements to introduce the latest machinery and skills to remain in business, but in so doing the necessary production time per unit is lowered and likewise its value or price. This process could conceivably go on and on until commodity after commodity becomes cheaper and cheaper if it were not for one thing: the process of continually renovating the means of production overwhelms large numbers of aspiring capitalists, leaving the field to fewer and fewer. The remaining large producers find it healthier for all of them to come to an agreement regarding market prices rather than continue to play the game of cut-throat competition to the benefit of consumers. We have then reached the state of monopoly capital, of which we shall have much more to say throughout the book.

One further point regarding value: "Circulation, or the exchange of commodities, begets no value." [58] Thus, to Marx, labor is the sole source of value. Temporary fluctuations due to supply-and-demand influences may occur. Any arbitrary rise in price or selling too expensively can only render gain to a class that always sells and never buys. Such can clearly never be the case. Thus, arbitrary markups to achieve gain are always counteracted elsewhere in the system, leaving the original value relations the same. (There are, it should be noted, people who are hurt by this kind of inflation, i.e., unorganized and powerless groups on fixed sources of purchasing power who cannot play the game of markup.) Thus, although monopoly pricing distorts the labor theory of value, as theorists we may still analyze value in labor terms.[59]

LABOR-POWER AND SURPLUS VALUE

If it is true that commodities are sold at their value, how is it possible for the capitalist to realize a profit? To realize a profit from buying and selling commodities at their value (rather than from arbitrary markups

[57] Ibid., p. 444.

[58] Ibid., p. 182.

[59] On Marx's theory of value, see Paul M. Sweezy, *The Theory of Capitalist Development* (New York: Monthly Review Press, 1968), pp. 23–67.

or dishonest dealing), it is necessary to discover a commodity that is variable, i.e., that is capable of yielding greater value than it itself costs the buyer. In other words, there must be a use-value that has the quality of being able to produce value much in excess of the equivalent of its own exchange-value. Such a commodity is, in fact, labor-power. Labor-power has the capacity to create value over and above the cost of its own reproduction or exchange-value. In the process of consuming the labor-power that he has purchased, the capitalist is able to realize a gain in value beyond the exchange-value or wages paid the laborer. This is, then, *surplus* value, value beyond the value required to purchase the laborer. In Mandel's words "surplus value is nothing but *the difference between the value created by the worker and the cost of maintaining him.*" [60]

The labor time required to produce the exchange-value or wages of the laborer Marx called necessary labor time, while the value produced over and above this comes from surplus labor time and is surplus value. The rate of surplus value, then, is the ratio of surplus to necessary labor, or put otherwise, of surplus value (s) to variable capital (v). For example, if in an eight-hour day a laborer creates thirty dollars exchange-value and his own cost (wage) is fifteen dollars, the rate of surplus value is 100 percent; if his wage is twenty dollars the rate is 50 percent, and if ten dollars 200 percent. "The rate of surplus-value," writes Marx, "is therefore an exact expression for the degree of exploitation of labour-power by capital, or of the labourer by the capitalist." [61] Considering the rate of surplus value, or the relationship between necessary and surplus labor, Marx observes that the same idea can be expressed by saying that the laborer (assuming a 100 percent rate) works thirty seconds for himself and thirty seconds for the capitalist every minute.[62] To the worker, however, the time is not so divided, but rather all hours are thought of as applied to the wage, i.e., labor as worth three dollars an hour, etc.

An important note to keep in mind in this connection is that the laborer does not earn his wage in the process of creating value for the capitalist, but rather the capitalist purchases labor-power beforehand along with the other materials of production. These latter raw materials and instruments of production Marx terms constant capital (c). Such constant capital is the product of past labor, and, along with money profits, constitutes "stored-up labour." [63] Capital is stored-up, accumulated labor. Capital increases further only through the further application of labor-

---

[60] Ernest Mandel, *Marxist Economic Theory,* vol. 1 (New York: Monthly Review Press, 1970), p. 88.

[61] *Capital,* vol. 1, p. 241.

[62] Ibid., p. 161.

[63] *Karl Marx: Early Writings,* translated and edited by T. B. Bottomore (New York: McGraw-Hill, 1964), p. 85.

power: "Capital is dead labour, that vampire-like, only lives by sucking living labour, and lives the more, the more labour it sucks." [64] In less poetic terms, "Capital can only increase by exchanging itself for labour power, by calling wage labour to life." [65] Capital is "a live monster that is fruitful and multiplies" only through the exploitation of labor, and the higher the rate of exploitation the greater the rate of multiplication. The laborer, chides Marx, is "like one who is bringing his own hide to market and has nothing to expect but—a hiding." [66]

Before raising the question as to how the exchange-value of labor-power is determined and what factors influence it, we might early note here that Marx employed the term *revolution* in the economic sense to the continual increase in constant capital in relation to variable capital (labor) as a proportion of total capital employed.[67] Expressing this relationship as $c/(c + v)$, Marx stressed that the organic composition of capital (as he called it) is constantly increasing during the development of capitalism due to efforts toward increasing productivity and the rate of surplus value. The application of machinery to the production process steadily reduces the role of labor and by so doing increases the rate of surplus value; the labor time required to produce or maintain labor-power, necessary labor time, is constantly reduced in favor of surplus labor time and surplus value. Marx referred to such increases in surplus value as relative surplus value—value derived from the increased productivity of labor-power with the rising proportion of constant capital.[68] In addition to relative surplus value through mechanical advances, we may take note of two further methods of increasing surplus value: first, by lengthening the working day so as to add hours of surplus labor time (absolute surplus value), and second, by intensifying the production process (a very crude method of advancing relative surplus value). Frequently, the reduction of hours worked is accompanied by the speed-up to counteract the loss of absolute surplus value. Intensification of the work process is also a counterbalance to a stagnating technology and a capitalist class which envisions greater profits through speed-ups than through research.

WAGES AND THE SUBSISTENCE LEVEL

In this section we examine what it costs the capitalist to purchase the commodity of labor-power and factors that influence that cost. In the

---

[64] *Capital,* vol. 1, p. 257.
[65] Marx, *Wage Labour and Capital,* in *Selected Works,* vol. 1, p. 162.
[66] *Capital,* vol. 1, p. 196.
[67] Ibid., p. 234.
[68] Ibid., pp. 345–50.

following section we ask whether the laborers' situation grows better or worse in the development of capitalism. To purchase labor-power the capitalist must pay according to the same principle of value as determines the exchange-value of any other commodity: the cost of labor-power is equal to the socially necessary labor time to produce it, i.e., the labor time required to supply the laborer and his family (integral to the creation of the laborer's future replacements) with the commodities for a subsistence level of living. The point of reference here is not actually the individual laborer, but rather the entire class of laborers, the proletariat (which shall be fully defined in Chapter 3). This is an important point, since we shall discover the capitalist does not always need the labor-power of all workers.

So, to use Marx's words: "The value of labour-power is determined, as in the case of every other commodity, by the labour-time necessary for the production, and consequently also the reproduction, of this special article. . . . Therefore the labour-time requisite for the production of labour-power reduces itself to that necessary for the production of [the] means of subsistence." [69] But what is the subsistence level? Is it enough to barely keep a worker and his family alive, at a minimum level of comfort, or something above that level? In one passage, Engels defines the subsistence level as that "needed to make the worker fit to perform the labour and to prevent the working class from dying out. Thus, the worker will not receive more for his labour than is necessary for that purpose; the price of labour, or wages, will be the lowest, the minimum required to maintain a livelihood." [70] Elsewhere, however, Marx adds the following: "Besides this mere physical element, the value of labour is in every country determined by a *traditional standard of life*. It is not mere physical life, but it is the satisfaction of certain wants springing from the social conditions in which people are placed and reared up." And continuing: "By comparing the standard wages or values of labour in different countries, and by comparing them in different historical epochs of the same country, you will find that the *value of labour* itself is not a fixed but a variable magnitude, even supposing the values of all other commodities to remain constant." [71]

Thus, Marx clearly holds to a sociocultural definition of the subsistence minimum in the proletariat. Just as labor is itself the only commodity that has a variable and value-creating quality, so also does the purchase of labor-power vary according to both physical conditions and, especially, the kind of culture in which the working class has been formed. "In con-

---

[69] Ibid., pp. 189–90.

[70] Engels, *Principles of Communism*, in *Selected Works*, vol. 1, p. 83.

[71] Marx, *Wages, Price, and Profit*, in *Selected Works*, vol. 2, pp. 71–72.

tradistinction therefore to the case of other commodities," writes Marx, "there enters into the determination of the value of labour-power a historical and moral element." [72] Marx further observes, and importantly for our own purposes later on, that we also must consider the cost of training the workers as a part of the cost of labor-power, and "this amount varies according to the more or less complicated character of the labour-power." [73] We might expect from the above comments, then, that in an advanced industrial society both the culturally normative aspect and the nature of work would press *upward* the minimum subsistence level. We would also expect, with Marx, that "in proportion, therefore, as the repulsiveness of the work increases [and, we may add, as the skill and training requirements go down], the wage decreases." [74]

We next encounter a phenomenon upon which we shall comment briefly here, inasmuch as it bears on the question of subsistence wages, but will have considerably more to say about later: the industrial reserve army, in Marxist terminology, or the unemployed workers in current parlance. The industrial reserve army brings into play the forces of supply and demand, playing for the most part upon the side of supply or, in class terms, on the side of the capitalists. The presence of unemployed workers brings depressing wage pressures to bear on the active portion of the working class, and the capitalist utilizes the pool of surplus workers to increase surplus value by lowering, holding, or minimally increasing wages—even in the face of advancing worker productivity. Indeed, advancing productivity through the utilization of machines serves to throw additional workers into the industrial reserve army: "The great beauty of capitalist production consists in this—that it not only constantly reproduces the wage-worker as wage-worker, but produces always, in proportion to the accumulation of capital, a relative surplus population of wage-workers." [75]

Marx sums up the impact of the industrial reserve army in the following passage: "The industrial reserve army, during the periods of stagnation and average prosperity, weighs down the active labour-army; during the periods of over-production and paroxysm, it hold its [i.e., the active labor army's] pretensions in check." The manipulation of the labor supply by capitalists, and the existence of an industrial reserve army, is "a lever of capitalist accumulation, . . . a condition of existence of the capitalist mode of production" that is "convenient to the activity of exploitation and to the dominion of capital." [76] The cycles of prosperity,

---

[72] *Capital,* vol. 1, pp. 189–90.
[73] Ibid., p. 191.
[74] *Manifesto of the Communist Party,* in *Selected Works,* vol. 1, p. 115.
[75] *Capital,* vol. 1, p. 842.
[76] Ibid., p. 701.

stagnation, and depression, then, contribute to the variation in wage levels with the assistance of an industrial reserve army. Worker organization may serve to partially buffer the active proletariat from wage exploitation, but it is no panacea to the problem.

CAPITAL VS. LABOR AND THE IMPOVERISHMENT THESIS

Now that we have defined the value of labor and the subsistence level, let us next review Marx's propositions concerning the course of the working class's economic condition. Keeping in mind the distinction between necessary and surplus labor, we may see that there exists an inherent opposition of interests over the movement of the rate of surplus value: any increase in the rate is damaging to the worker, while any decrease in the rate is in opposition to the interests of capital accumulation. Even with a growth of constant capital and productivity, the interests of capital and labor cannot be fused. For surplus value and wages by definition are always inversely related; if wages increase relative to surplus value the worker gains, but if surplus value increases relative to wages the capitalist profits. Given the existence of the industrial reserve army (along with other resources of manipulation and power available to the capitalist), relative wages typically suffer at the hands of capital and surplus value. Marx phrases the whole idea in the following manner:

> Even the *most favourable situation* for the working class, *the most rapid possible growth of capital,* however much it may improve the material existence of the worker, does not remove the antagonism between his interests and the interests of the bourgeoisie, the interests of the capitalists. *Profit and wages* remain as before in *inverse proportion.*[77]

Both labor and capital may simultaneously realize *absolute* gains, though relatively this is, as we have noted, impossible. For example, under an eight-hour day workers may produce a hundred dollars' value and receive wages of fifty dollars for a rate of surplus value of 100 percent. Given machinery that for the moment increases their output to four hundred dollars per day, wages may be absolutely raised to one hundred dollars (either through good will or organized pressure); but the relative position of the worker deteriorates as the rate of surplus value climbs to 300 percent. So again from Marx, "If capital is growing rapidly, wages may rise; the profit of capital rises incomparably more rapidly. The material position of the worker has improved, but at the cost of his social position. The

---

[77] Marx, *Wage Labour and Capital,* in *Selected Works,* vol. 1, p. 167.

social gulf that divides him from the capitalist has widened." [78] The working class thus forges for itself "the golden chains by which the bourgeoisie drags it in its train." We should also recognize that the working class may realize an absolute gain in wages as in the illustration used above, while still suffering a decline in real wages insofar as the price of other commodities they must purchase for subsistence have increased to an even greater extent.

In further clarifying the relative decline of the worker's social position vis-à-vis the capitalist, Marx employs the following illustration:

> A house may be large or small; as long as the surrounding houses are equally small it satisfies all social demands for a dwelling. But let a palace arise beside the little house, and it shrinks from a little house to a hut. . . . The occupant of the relatively small house will feel more and more uncomfortable, dissatisfied and cramped within its four walls.

Thus:

> Although the enjoyments of the worker have risen, the social satisfaction that they give has fallen in comparison with the increased enjoyments of the capitalist, which are inaccessible to the worker, in comparison with the state of development of society in general. Our desires and pleasures spring from society; we measure them, therefore, by society and not by the objects which serve for their satisfaction. Because they are of a social nature, they are of a relative nature. [79]

Marx, then, held no illusions regarding the ability of capitalism to clothe, house, and feed the active members of the working class, or even to raise their standard of living.

What, then, is the status in Marxist theory of the idea of the increasing impoverishment of the proletariat? As Mandel has pointed out, certain of Marx's writings on economics have a tendency to portray a movement toward increasing absolute impoverishment of the working class. For example: "Along with the constantly diminishing number of the magnates of capital, who usurp and monopolise all advantages of this process of transformation, grows the mass of misery, oppression, slavery, degradation, exploitation." [80] But also we have: "In the course of time, the workers' wages decline in a twofold sense: first relatively, in comparison with the development of wealth generally; and second, in the absolute sense, the sense that the amount of goods the worker receives in exchange becomes

---

[78] Ibid., pp. 167–68.
[79] Ibid., p. 163.
[80] *Capital,* vol. 1, pp. 836–37.

smaller and smaller." [81] As Mandel further notes, Marx never expounded the thesis of absolute impoverishment in mature works. The key to understanding on this point is that the thesis of relative impoverishment applies in large measure to the active working class, whereas absolute impoverishment is relevant to the situation of the industrial reserve army, the unemployed, and those the system throws out of the production process together with their families.[82]

As the accumulation of productive capital increases, so does the industrial reserve army and its misery: *"This is the absolute general law of capitalist accumulation."* [83] Capitalism, according to Marx, "overworks a part of the labouring population and keeps the other part as a reserve army, half or entirely pauperised." [84] Inasmuch as this concept provides our key to the understanding of contemporary poverty, we shall meet with it again in Chapter 8. Suffice it to note here, in Nicolaus's words, that "in the advanced stages of capitalist development, the 'exploitation' of the working class appears as prosperity beside the poverty of this never-working sub-proletariat." [85] But we shall not limit poverty to the industrial castoffs alone; poverty in the Marxist sense applies to those working and nonworking, proletariat and subproletariat whose incomes are inadequate to allow them to live at or above what is for our society today considered the social subsistence minimum.[86]

This completes our overview of Marxist sociohistorical assumptions and economic foundations. We shall need the assistance of the foregoing analyses throughout the next chapter as we take up the larger issues and problems of capitalist economic and social class development.

---

[81] Ernest Mandel, *The Formation of the Economic Thought of Karl Marx* (New York: Monthly Review Press, 1971), pp. 58–59.

[82] Mandel, *Marxist Economic Theory,* vol. 1, pp. 150–51.

[83] Cited in Mandel, *The Formation of the Economic Thought of Karl Marx,* p. 151.

[84] Karl Marx, *Theories of Surplus Value: Elections,* edited by G. A. Bonner and E. Burns (London, 1951), p. 352.

[85] Nicolaus, "Proletariat and Middle Class in Marx," p. 37.

[86] See Paul A. Baran and Paul M. Sweezy, *Monopoly Capital* (New York: Monthly Review Press, 1968), p. 288.

two ——————————————————————————

MARXIST THEORY: DEVELOPMENTAL ECONOMICS

The roots of capitalism can be traced through such developments as the emergence of trade, the introduction of a money circulation, the expansion of the market, the uprooting of the peasantry, the primitive accumulation of wealth through plunder, the expropriation of Church and Crown lands, and the triumph of the bourgeoisie over the consumption extravagance and hoarding of wealth by the state and nobility. This is not our purpose in this section, however, for these events are not directly germane to our present concerns (Mandel has presented us with an extensive discussion of the foundations of industrial capitalism [1]). Suffice it to stress here that the key event of European economic evolution was the rise to social and eventually political power of the capitalist class over the unproductive and stagnating monarchies and nobilities left over from the feudal period. Our concern in this section will be with changes within the organization of capitalist production in its formative stages. By pointing out these changes, we may more clearly grasp the sources of alienation and the initial forces of class formation. It shall also point the way to the increasingly social nature of production in capitalist development.

As noted in Chapter 1, the main road to enlarged surplus value is the increased productivity of labor. To quote Marx: "The very mode of production must be revolutionised, before the productiveness of labour can

—————

[1] See Ernest Mandel, *Marxist Economic Theory,* vol. 1 (New York: Monthly Review Press, 1968).

be increased. By that means alone can the value of labour power be made to sink, and the portion of the working day necessary for the production of that value, be shortened." [2] The two critical methods of revolutionizing the productive capacity of labor-power are (1) rationalizing the *social* organization of the work process and (2) employing more advanced instruments of production in the mechanical sense. Both methods have been utilized during the accumulation of capital, the social organizational changes being the major breakthroughs in raising productivity during the early stages of growth and the deployment of machinery coming to dominate at the onset of the Industrial Revolution.

The first stage of capitalist development Marx termed *simple cooperation:* "A greater number of labourers working together, at the same time, in one place (or, if you will, in the same field of labour), in order to produce the same sort of commodity under the mastership of one capitalist, constitutes, both historically and logically, the starting point of capitalist production." [3] Thus, previously independent artisans of a given kind are assembled under the direction of a single entrepreneur, expropriated of their individual ownership of instruments of production, and hired as wage labor to produce surplus value for the capitalist. Their traditional skills as artisans are exercised, but they have been alienated from the means of production and alienated from the value they produce (with the exception of the necessary wage). They are told from above where to work, when to work, what to produce, and denied the right to decide upon the disposition of the product. The process of alienated labor is underway. Surplus value is increased through a simple enlargement of scale and by lengthening the working day (absolute surplus value).

But the limit to surplus value may soon be reached under a regime of simple cooperation, and it becomes necessary to organize the productive process along more revolutionary lines. These new lines of organization Marx termed *manufacture.* Manufacture introduces a *division of labor* into the production process. It is precisely a revolution within the division of labor that constitutes the essence of manufacture. Manufacture may take two forms: first, an article may be produced by laborers belonging to *various* independent handicrafts assembled as one unit under a single capitalist, and through each of whose hands the article must pass on its way to completion. [4] Skills of past craft production are maintained to a large extent, but combined and assembled for more efficient utilization. In the second, and progressively the prevailing, mode of manufacture, members of a given craft perform only some fraction of the total movements

---

[2] Karl Marx, *Capital,* vol. 1 (Chicago: Charles H. Kerr & Company, 1908), p. 345.

[3] Ibid., p. 353.

[4] Ibid., pp. 370–71.

required in the production of a commodity so that each task is repeated over and over again by a given individual for the sake of efficiency. By eliminating excess handling and complex movement, necessary labor time can be reduced. Further, the craftsman as such can be eliminated, since labor has been stripped of its special quality. As Marx observed, "While simple co-operation leaves the mode of working by the individual for the most part unchanged, manufacture thoroughly revolutionises it, and seizes labour-power by its very roots." "It converts the labourer into a crippled monstrosity, by forcing his detail dexterity at the expense of a world of productive capabilities and instincts; just as in the States of La Plata they butcher a whole beast for the sake of his hide or his tallow." [5]

The process of alienating the worker from himself as creator has begun; the craftsman adept at using a variety of tools in skilled ways is reduced to an unskilled, interchangeable component of the production process, using a single tool in a repetitive fashion. This does not mean, however, that *all* work is similarly unskilled and repetitive. Along with the greater division of labor comes a greater proliferation of work positions —truncated though they may be: "Manufacture, therefore, developes a hierarchy of labour-powers, to which there corresponds a scale of wages," depending upon the cost of training the worker, among other things.[6] This hierarchy, however, is increasingly leveled off during the next important stage of production, the *machine stage*.

Up through manufacture, revolutions in the means of production were largely social-organizational. With the machine stage the focus shifts from human organization of labor to the instruments of production: "In manufacture, the revolution in the mode of production begins with the labour-power, in modern industry it begins with the instruments of labour." [7] The laborer is transformed from a tool user to an appendage of a nonhuman power-driven machine. The process of alienation from self as creator is pushed to the extreme, as the worker becomes more and more remote from the article produced and from control over its production. From the standpoint of wages, the worker's position is eroded owing to the easy replaceability of his functions and the growing industrial reserve army thrown off by capital-intensive methods of production (Marx was well aware that replacement was possible and likely in a transitional stage of industrial production, but was pessimistic over the longer-run labor absorption process.) We may benefit from Marx's own summary here:

> Further, as the *division of labour* increases, labour *is simplified*. The special skill of the worker becomes worthless. He becomes transformed

---

[5] Ibid., p. 396.
[6] Ibid., p. 384.
[7] Ibid., p. 405.

into a simple, monotonous productive force that does not have to use intense bodily or intellectual faculties. His labour becomes a labour that anyone can perform. Hence, competitors crowd upon him on all sides, and besides we remind the reader that the more simple and easily learned the labour is, the lower the cost of production needed to master it, the lower do wages sink, for, like the price of every other commodity, they are determined by the cost of production. *Therefore, as labour becomes more unsatisfying, more repulsive, competition increases and wages decrease.*[8]

We should remember our previous discussion concerning Marx's views on relative and absolute wages, as well as the fluctuations of these wages within given economic contexts. We also note with Marx, that "the less the skill and exertion of strength implied in manual labour, in other words, the more modern industry becomes developed, the more is the labour of men superseded by that of women." [9] Women present lower levels of previous training and they are able to operate mechanical processes not requiring excessive muscular strength. This further means—and this is extremely important—that more members of a given family unit are thrown onto the labor market, spreading the value of a worker's labor-power over the whole family; thus, although the capitalist pays more to purchase two or three family workers than he did for one before, capital still gets more out of its money inasmuch as it is able to purchase each member for progressively less than the preceding member.[10] This may easily be seen as another approach to enlarging surplus value, and like other forms of relative surplus value derives initially from the accumulation and utilization of industrial capital.

What, then, are the limits to the capitalist's utilization of industrial machinery? Again, the answer lies within the rationale of surplus value: "As long as the labour spent on a machine, and consequently the portion of its value added to the product, remains smaller than the value added by the workman to the product with his tool, there is always a difference of labour saved in favour of the machine. The productiveness of a machine is therefore measured by the human labour-power it replaces. . . . The limit to his using a machine is fixed by the difference between the value of the machine and the value of the labour-power replaced by it." [11] The capitalist does not apply machinery out of sheer infatuation with mechanical power; he does so only if the machine will work more cheaply for him than

---

[8] Marx, *Wage Labour and Capital,* in Marx and Frederick Engels, *Selected Works,* vol. 1 (Moscow: Progress Publishers, 1969), p. 170.

[9] Marx and Engels, *Manifesto of the Communist Party,* in *Selected Works,* vol. 1, p. 115.

[10] *Capital,* vol. 1, p. 431.

[11] Ibid., pp. 427, 429.

will human labor-power. If labor-power can be hired for less than the cost of producing the machinery, the capitalist will always choose the former alternative. Marx points out that the decision will vary from country to country and from time to time, but it will always be made on behalf of maximizing surplus value. Far from saving profit for the capitalist, machinery may increase the cost of production "as when wretches and slaves do cheap or free work." And in pointing to a condition which we shall encounter in our discussion of the United States labor force today, Marx adds that frequently the more machinery a country has the larger is the pool of unemployed who will work for less than the cost of further machinery: "Hence nowhere do we find a more shameful squandering of human labour-power for the most despicable purposes than in England, the land of machinery." [12] A short extension of the above principle leads us directly to the exploitation of foreign labor by advanced capitalist economies, and hence to an underpinning of imperialism. But this is a problem of later concern. We turn our attention now to further ramifications of the machine stage.

MACHINES, AUTOMATION, AND VALUE

We now come to a critical point in the discussion of Marxist theory, for it is in the area of its relevance to advanced industrial production that it must stand or fall as a viable framework of contemporary understanding. Inasmuch as Marx formulated his theory in the middle of the last century, at a time when industrial development and the industrial sector—even in England—were comparatively young and undeveloped in both technique and size, it might be thought such a theory would have little to contribute today. But the construction of a theory does not rest on all the events of history; the construction and strength of a theory rest upon the capacity to take hold of a limited number of events and trends and through these build a logical structure of thought which can penetrate the events of the future as they are compressed or encapsulated in the relevant events of the moment.

Marxist theory succeeded in this and is very much a theory capable of dealing with advanced technological society; indeed, Marx himself directed attention to the future. He states: "As soon as a machine executes, without man's help, all the movements requisite to elaborate the raw material, needing only attendance from him, we have an automatic system of machinery, and one that is susceptible of constant improvement in its

---

[12] Ibid., p. 430.

details." [13] The question is *how much attendance* did Marx envisage would be required if such an automatic system of machinery were developed to the full extent? Quite clearly, Marx was thinking in terms of very advanced production techniques, if not even in terms of complete automatic processes. For example, in discussing "the historical vocation of capitalism" and its fulfillment, Marx argues that a final prerequisite to the completion of this vocation is the attainment of an industrial state in which "the sort of labour in which the activities of men can be replaced by those of machines will have ceased." [14] Such would indeed be a highly automated society, beyond that which we have before us today, meaning that the historical vocation of capitalism could still be defined as incomplete within the Marxist framework (we shall fully attend to this problem later in the chapter).

In a further passage from the recently translated (in small part) *Grundrisse* (considered by Marx to be an outline of future volumes, only a portion of which were ever completed as *Capital*), we again see the importance of automation as conceived by Marx:

> But once absorbed into the production process of capital, the means of labour undergoes various metamorphoses, of which the last is the *machine,* or rather, an *automatic system of machines* ("automatic" meaning that this is only the most perfected and most fitting form of the machine, and is what transforms the machinery into a system). This is set in motion by an automaton, a motive force that moves of its own accord. The automaton consists of a number of mechanical and intellectual organs, so that the workers themselves can be no more than conscious limbs of the automaton. [15]

And in a subsequent passage Marx lays the basis for what we shall later on in the book define as the new working class, the inclusion of many technicians and scientists in the productive proletariat: "The tendency of capital is thus to give a *scientific character to production,* reducing direct labour to a simple element in this process." [16] Moreover, Marx makes clear that the advanced sector of the labor force is not a new, independent class, but rather an integral component of the industrial proletariat when he says that "once the productive forces of the means of labour have reached the level of an automatic process, individual labour in its direct form is transformed into social labour." And: "Individual labour ceases altogether to be productive as such; or rather, it is productive only in collective labour, which subjects the forces of nature." [17]

---

[13] Ibid., p. 416.
[14] Marx, *The Grundrisse,* edited and translated by David McLellan (New York: Harper & Row, 1971), p. 85.
[15] Ibid., p. 132.
[16] Ibid., p. 135. Italics mine.
[17] Ibid., pp. 146, 136.

Hence, there are no sharp splits in the productive class, no new bourgeoisie of scientists and technicians. Also, the respective contributions of individual workers become increasingly merged and unidentifiable. The entire problem of accounting value assumes new perspectives under automation. Just how does the machine influence the labor theory of value?

First let us recall that labor is the source of value under the on-going mode of production. But also recall that not all use-value is the product of labor—natural air, water supply, soil, etc. being exceptions. These work for man gratuitously. Machinery, Marx observes, makes a similar contribution to human existence:

> After making allowance, both in the case of the machine and of the tool, for their average daily cost, that is for the value they transmit to the product by their average wear and tear, . . . they each do their work gratuitously, just like the forces furnished by nature without the help of man. The greater the productive power of the machinery compared with that of the tool, the greater is the extent of its gratuitous service compared with that of the tool. In Modern Industry man succeeded for the first time in making the product of his past labour work on a large scale gratuitously, like the forces of nature.[18]

Under average or moderate industrial development, where human labor is still a predominant aspect of production, the labor theory of value holds, since the machine transfers to its product only the amount of value it itself has received from the labor that produced it. The more expensive the machine the more expensive the product.

Under advanced and automatic production, however, Marx draws our attention to some profound shifts in the direction of gratuitous mechanical forces: "But as heavy industry develops, the creation of real wealth depends less on labour time and on the quantity of labor utilized than on the power of mechanical agents which are set in motion during labour time. *The powerful effectiveness of these agents, in its turn, bears no relation to the immediate labour time that their production costs.*"[19] And: "*Labour does not seem any more to be an essential part of the process of production. The human factor is restricted to watching and supervising the production process.*"[20] Under automation the worker "is no longer the principal agent of the production process: he exists alongside it."[21]

Automation yields use-values in such proportions that labor as the source of value is reduced in significance and becomes increasingly difficult to measure. In Marx's words, "As soon as labor, in its direct form, has ceased to be the main source of wealth, then labour time ceases, and

---

[18] *Capital,* vol. 1, pp. 423–24.
[19] *Grundrisse,* p. 141. Italics mine.
[20] Ibid., p. 142.
[21] Ibid.

must cease, to be its standard of measurement, and thus exchange value must cease to be the measurement of use value." [22] Both advanced machine production with its large measure of gratuitous use-value and the highly social and interdependent supporting system of labor render the labor theory of value together with its underlying rationale of wage distribution and surplus value difficult, if not logically impossible, to apply.

What, then, becomes the measure of wealth in the place of labor time? Time continues to be fundamental, but emphasis is reversed from labor time as the measure of wealth to *disposable* time, or as we would have it, leisure time: "It is no longer the labour time but the disposable time which is the measure of wealth. Labour time as the measurement of wealth implies that wealth is founded on poverty, and that disposable time exists in and through opposition to surplus labour time." [23] With the material abundance produced by advanced machine technology, wealth is not founded on poverty, and scarcity can no longer be the measure of value.

We shall further pursue the implications of this line of thinking when we take up alienation and liberation later in the chapter. For it would be inappropriate to continue as if the ideal were the reality, as if the historical vocation of capitalism had come to fruition, and as if automation had been carried to the point of ascendancy over labor as the source of use-value. *Although automated production has been advanced well beyond the point at which we currently justify our distribution of wealth and has significantly altered the relative balance of necessary labor versus disposable time, we have at work in our society powerful class interests which prevent the realization of the full social benefit of existing productive forces and are misusing and blocking the progressive social advance of science and technology.* The labor theory of value continues to be the operative one despite the twisted and distorted form it has had to assume in advanced industrial society. Capitalism and the capitalist class *cannot* live without the threat of poverty and scarcity hanging over wage labor. Unfortunately, millions of people cannot live like humans with these perquisites, and tens of millions live much below the level of comfort and dignity that is available from currently existing means of production. As should become clear as we spell out the needs and contradictions of capital, capitalism as a system is not interested in human liberation and the emancipation of labor; it is grounded in scarcity and inequality, and by its own internal logic must preserve both or fail as a system. It is irrational from the standpoint of society not to introduce machinery that costs the same as (or even more than) hired wage labor. But criteria of surplus value dictate decisions not according to their rationality or irrationality from society's perspective but only according to their profitability to the capitalist class.

---

[22] Ibid.
[23] Ibid., p. 145.

THE INDUSTRIAL RESERVE ARMY REVISITED

The most appropriate place to discuss the expansion of the industrial reserve army is in connection with the machine stage of production, the advanced machine stage in particular. As Engels points out to us, "machinery becomes the most powerful weapon in the war of capital against the working class; . . . the very product of the worker is turned into an instrument for his subjugation." [24] The increase of the rate of relative surplus value through increased productivity inevitably throws people out of work; the increase is achieved only by diminishing the number of workmen employed by a given amount of capital.

Marx notes that "bourgeois political economists insist that all machinery that displaces workmen, simultaneously and necessarily sets free an amount of capital adequate to employ the same identical workmen." [25] This is, of course, true. But it overlooks two problems: first, there is no guarantee that the capital in question will be invested so as to employ the displaced workers—or any workers for that matter (employment is not the goal of investment); anyway, it is not the capital of the industry that displaced the workers that might employ them later, but some "new and additional capital that is seeking investment." [26] Secondly, and more frequently the case, displaced workers are not typically flexible on the labor market after being stunted for years by a repetitive job, especially middle-aged and older workers. Marx captures the point well when he writes: "And even should they find employment, what a poor look-out is theirs! Crippled as they are by division of labour, these poor devils are worth so little outside their old trade, that they cannot find admission into any industries, except a few of inferior kind, that are over-supplied with underpaid workmen." [27]

The main locus of resistance and protection for the working class in capitalist society against the encroachments of capital, states Marx, are the trade unions or labor organizations.[28] Unions are also important centers or vehicles for the development of worker solidarity, class consciousness, and political opposition. However, Marx was under no illusions regarding the potential of the trade union movement to accomplish anything more than eliminating some of the more glaring injustices and inequities of the

---

[24] Engels, *Socialism: Utopian and Scientific,* in Marx and Engels, *Selected Works,* vol. 3, p. 140.

[25] *Capital,* vol. 1, p. 478.

[26] Ibid., p. 478.

[27] Ibid.

[28] Marx, *Wages, Price, and Profit,* in *Selected Works,* vol. 2, p. 75.

wage labor-capitalist system. In the critical words of Marx, unions "fail generally from limiting themselves to a guerilla war against the effects of the existing system, instead of simultaneously trying to change it, instead of using their organised forces as a lever for the final emancipation of the working class, that is to say, the ultimate abolition of the wages system." [29]

CENTRALIZATION AND FINANCE CAPITAL

Accompanying the advance of machine technology in the development of capitalism has been the joint-stock company or corporation. The growing size of industry necessitated a larger financial resource base than most individual capitalists could supply. It became almost mandatory for the individual captain of industry to go public, to open ownership to a broader reservoir of financial wealth than his own. The forward thrust of technology precipitated the conditions that would lead to a battle of size. The emergence of the joint-stock company or corporation as the dominant form of business enterprise (the phenomenon of the corporation far antedates its ascendancy) is explicable not only in terms of the financial requirements of heavy industry but also in administrative and market terms: the field of operation, in all of its diversity and complex technical and legal forms, called for something more than a mere capitalist entrepreneur, or at least a combination of skills that rarely could come or survive in a single person. Anyone attempting to fight the wave of the future, the large impersonal corporation, found the going too tough to go it alone very long.

The rise of the corporation introduced a new problem for political economy: if before it was a simple matter of ascertaining the location of power and control in business in the hands of the individual capitalist owner-entrepreneur, under the joint-stock corporation this became a difficult empirical problem. The money capitalist, the person holding the stocks or paper-claims on surplus value, may not and frequently is not in any way involved in the control and decision-making functions of the company. In a sense, the capitalist himself has been alienated in a formal way from the means of production even if he holds rather large amounts of stocks, not to mention the army of small shareholders. However, because ownership of business capital has been broken down from a single to a multiple source does not mean ownership has been so widely multiplied that there are no owners in positions of control, or that hired administrators have a free rein with the company's money.

But let us return to the idea of the joint-stock company as it was initially set forth by Marx. With regard to the emergence of the modern

---

[29] Ibid., pp. 75–76.

corporation, "Marx was one of the first," Avineri points out, "to predict this development as a necessary outcome of the internal needs of ever-growing capitalist expansion." [30] In *Capital,* Marx noted the "transformation of the actually functioning capitalist into a mere manager, administrator of other people's capital." He directed attention to the difference between the fictitious capital of the stockholder and the actual capital of industrial production and how gambling with such titles of ownership replaces labor as the chief method of acquiring capital and carries with them financial *power:*

> [Stocks] merely convey legal titles to a portion of the surplus-value to be produced by [actual capital]. But as duplicates serving themselves as commodities for sale and thus circulating as capital-values they are illusory, and their value may fall or rise independently of the value of the actual capital, upon which they represent a claim. Gain and loss through fluctuations in the price of these titles of ownership and their centralisation in the hands of railroad kings, etc., naturally becomes more and more a matter of gambling, which takes the place of labor as the original method of acquiring capital and also assumes the place of direct force.[31]

In tracing through the logical ramifications of the joint-stock company, Marx saw the rise of monopoly capital, state intervention or state capitalism, and a new financial aristocracy or finance capital:

> [The corporation represents] the abolition of the capitalist mode of production within capitalist production itself, a self-destructive contradiction which is prima facie only a phase of transition to a new form of production. It manifests its contradictory nature by its effects. It establishes a monopoly in certain spheres and thereby invites the intervention of the State. It reproduces a new aristocracy of finance, a new variety of parasites in the shape of promoters, speculators and merely nominal directors; a whole system of swindling and cheating by means of company promoting, stock jobbing, and speculation. It is private production without the control of private property.[32]

The expansion of capitalism through the corporation destroys the competitive market structure and monopoly takes over as "little fish are swallowed by the sharks and the lambs by the wolves." (Marx referred to mergers as centralization and growth of the individual firm as concentration.) In further spelling out the nature of monopoly capital, Engels writes that "the producers on a large scale in a particular branch of industry in

---

[30] Shlomo Avineri, *The Social and Political Thought of Karl Marx* (Cambridge: Cambridge University Press, 1970), p. 179.

[31] *Capital,* vol. 1, p. 561.

[32] *Capital,* vol. 3, pp. 478–80.

a particular country unite in a trust, a union for the purpose of regulating production. They determine the total amount to be produced, parcel it out among themselves, and thus enforce the selling price fixed beforehand." As business waxes and wanes, concentration continues until "the whole of the particular industry is turned into one gigantic joint-stock company; internal competition gives place to the internal monopoly of this one company." [33] When we examine in the next section the contradictions and crises of monopoly capital as portrayed by Marxist theory, we shall further pursue Engels's conclusion that "in any case, with trusts or without, the official representative of capitalist society—the state—will ultimately have to undertake the direction of production."

But first we must address ourselves further to the aforementioned problem of power or control within the joint-stock company or corporation. Marx and Engels seemed to have viewed the new form of business as largely separating ownership from control, seeing fictitious capital holders divorced functionally from the actual managers of industrial capital. Engels, for example, states:

> All the social functions of the capitalist are now performed by salaried employees. The capitalist has no further social function than that of pocketing dividends, tearing off coupons, and gambling on the Stock Exchange, where the different capitalists despoil one another of their capital. At first the capitalistic mode of production forces out the workers. Now it forces out the capitalists, and reduces them, just as it reduced the workers, to the ranks of surplus population, although not immediately into those of the industrial reserve army. [34]

Considering Marx's view of the lumpenproletariat (defined as an irrelevant and parasitical layer beneath the working class), we tend to get a similar impression from him of the new capitalist as redundant and removed from the industrial process: "The finance aristocracy, in its mode of acquisition as well as in its pleasures, is nothing but the *rebirth of the lumpenproletariat on the heights of bourgeois society.*" [35] Comparisons to the lumpenproletariat and the industrial reserve army invite the conclusion that the financial aristocracy has nothing to do with production—indeed, that it is not even interested in its further development, but only in creaming off what capital is already in existence.

In the capitalist economy of their period, Marx and Engels were no doubt correct about the position of "the wolves of finance" and their superfluity to production, and especially in the France from which the lumpen-

---

[33] Engels, *Socialism: Utopian and Scientific,* in *Selected Works,* vol. 3, pp. 143–44.

[34] Ibid., p. 145.

[35] Marx, *The Class Struggles in France,* in *Selected Works,* vol. 1, p. 208.

proletariat comparison derived. Yet the *merger and fusion* of industrial and financial interests into finance capital which later Marxist theorists such as Lenin viewed as the new center of industrial-financial power and control does, in fact, find expression in Marx, too.[36] It is this model of power, industrially grounded finance capital, which we shall later find useful and indispensable to an understanding of social and economic power in contemporary corporate capitalism. This model does not rule out—indeed, it allows for—a very large and significant sector of entirely superfluous and parasitical financial interests. What it does rule out is the separation and cleavage of industrial from financial power and control; it sees the two as inseparably linked and tied together in myriad ways, neither of which could last long without the other. In the most important instances, one cannot even speak of links but of the same people. But we are getting ahead of ourselves.

Next on the agenda is the Marxist analysis of contradictions and crises within the developed stage of capitalism. Once again, an understanding of the original theory is essential to our future discussions of the modern class system.

CONTRADICTIONS AND CRISES

As Giddens has pointed out, Marxist economic theory posits no single causative chain of capitalist crisis; there are multiple factors and multiple possible causal chains, and Marx never systematically traced them all out. Giddens also draws our attention to the fact that Marx never predicted a *final* ruinous crisis toward which the system was working.[37] Rather, crises are an integral part of the system that restores a reversal of the cycle, and not something that totally breaks it down. This aspect of Marxist theory is functionalist insofar as it views capitalism as a system periodically swinging into serious disequilibrium but restoring normalcy through self-adjusting mechanisms. Yet, in our application of economics to class relations we shall see that Marxism is preeminently a form of conflict theory. But this is not our concern here. Suffice it to note that periodic crises serve to galvanize the *social and political* conflict which generates the breaking forces of change.

But severe crises occur, albeit not necessarily totally disastrous in consequence to the system. (To millions of its members, of course, severe crises and the virtually permanent subcrises are completely disastrous.)

---

[36] *Capital,* vol. 1, p. 371.
[37] Anthony Giddens, *Capitalism and Modern Social Theory* (Cambridge: Cambridge University Press, 1971), p. 55.

What are the forces at work which precipitate crises? We shall deal here with only one causative line of crisis, the one which stands out as central both to the original Marx and to contemporary Marxist economic theory. If a single word can label this crisis, it is *overproduction,* overproduction not of use-values but of exchange-values. Recalling that labor is paid at value but produces surplus value, we may readily observe that the worker himself will not be in a financial position to demand all of the exchange-values he has created. (This fact may be multiplied if we include with surplus value the productive powers of automated machinery.) The worker and his machine produce overproduction.[38] Since the sole aim of capital is to accumulate wealth and not to meet social needs of consumption, an ineradicable contradiction exists: subsistence wages cannot command access to surplus value accumulating to the capitalist. In Marx's words:

> The real limitation upon capitalist production is *capital itself.* It is the fact that capital and its self-expansion are the beginning and end, the motive and aim of production; that production is regarded as production for *capital,* instead of the means of production being considered simply as means for extending the conditions of human life for the benefit of the *society* of producers.[39]

Hence:

> The ultimate cause of all real crises is always the poverty and restricted consumption of the masses, in contrast with the tendency of capitalist production to develop the productive forces in such a way that only the absolute power of consumption of society would be their limit.[40]

With the wage labor force unable to gain sufficient access to the productive forces of society, overproduction results, industrial cutbacks occur, and unemployment rises to new levels—still further exacerbating the condition of overproduction: "The life of modern industry becomes a series of periods of moderate activity, prosperity, over-production, crisis and stagnation." [41] Profits turn down and forces are activated toward centralization of capital into still larger concentrations which create, in turn, even greater threats to future overproduction and unemployment arising from the new economies of scale. We have, to quote Engels, "the absurd contradiction that the producers have nothing to consume, because con-

---

[38] See Raya Dunayevskaya, *Marxism and Freedom* (London: Pluto Press, 1971), pp. 141–43.
[39] Marx, *Capital,* vol. 3, pp. 278–89.
[40] Marx, *Capital,* vol. 3, p. 528.
[41] *Capital,* vol. 1, p. 495.

sumers are wanting." [42] Even more aptly phrased: *"The mode of produc- tion is in rebellion against the mode of exchange."* [43]

Despite the above quotations from Marx and Engels, Gottheil con- tends that "whatever the statements to the contrary, it appears that Marx carefully avoided attaching any significance to the underconsumption theory of the crises." [44] Gottheil cites Marx from *Capital*: "It is purely tautology to say that crises are caused by the scarcity of solvent consumers, or of paying consumption." However, the empirical point stressed by Marx and Engels regarding overproduction is that the crises stem from labor producing greater value than it is given rights to consume; as a *result* of this contradiction, capital encounters inadequacies in the market.

The devices by which capital seeks to overcome the crises of over- production shall occupy our attention in later chapters. Here we might take cognizance of a few developments suggested by Marx and Engels. As one factor in militating against stagnation Marx points to "the creation of a vast number of employments, at present indispensable, but in them- selves superfluous." [45] In a similar vein, systematic waste militates against stagnation through an "anarchical system of competition" and "the most outrageous squandering of labour-power and of the social means of produc- tion." Thus, redundant bureaucratic expansion and inflated forms of cir- culating goods attach themselves to the social surplus. The use of protective tariffs was also noted, but more importantly, Engels stressed the exporta- tion of capital as a means of disposing of surplus value: "Thus it comes about that the overwork of some becomes the preliminary condition for the idleness of others, and that modern industry . . . hunts after new consumers over the whole world." [46]

A further avenue of dealing with the juxtaposition of surplus and want noted by Marx and Engels is some form of welfare and reform whereby the state intervenes to attempt to restore the impoverished back into the economic system. The state, being an instrument of capital, is not, of course, going to obtain the funds from capital, but rather from the wages of those in the labor force. To quote from Marx: "Pauperism constitutes one of the incidental expenses of capitalist production; but capital knows how to shift this burden, for the most part, from its own shoulders to those of the working class and the lower middle class." [47] (These words are

---

[42] Engels, *Socialism: Utopian and Scientific,* in *Selected Works,* vol. 3, p. 148.
[43] Ibid., p. 142.
[44] Fred M. Gottheil, *Marx's Economic Predictions* (Evanston, Ill.: Northwest- ern University Press, 1966), p. 142.
[45] *Capital,* vol. 1, p. 581.
[46] Engels, *Socialism: Utopian and Scientific,* p. 141.
[47] Cited in Robert Pinker, *Social Theory and Social Policy* (London: Heine- mann Books, 1970), p. 36. (From *Capital.*)

finally being echoed by Democratic politicians today.) But even given the preference on tax issues (direct taxes and the abolishment of all indirect ones), Marx still contended that "no modification of the form of taxation can produce any important change in the relations of labour and capital." [48] This does not mean that Marx was opposed to reform; he was usually strongly in favor of reforms of all kinds; he just did not believe that reform was the ultimate answer or could be the answer to the crises and contradictions of capital. Hence, no reform legislation can hope to prevent such crises.

The intervention of the state in the economy is not limited to dealing with poverty; as contradictions worsen the state is called upon to play a more and more direct role in the economy, to the point of taking over aging and stagnant industries and assuming a major role in shoring up private companies through public funds. This development of state capitalism is not in itself socialism although it may represent a step in that direction. As Engels notes, "The modern state, no matter what its form, is essentially a capitalist machine, the state of the capitalists, the ideal personification of the total national capital." Yet even though "state ownership of the productive forces is not the solution of the conflict . . . , concealed within it are the technical conditions that form the elements of that solution." [49]

Before leaving the problem of economic crises, a word must be said regarding Marx's concept of the declining rate of profit. Like other hypotheses deriving from Marxist theory, that of the falling profit rate is deduced from the labor theory of value, but conditioned by a multiplicity of other variables. Insofar as labor is the source of value, the greater the ratio of machine capital to variable (labor) capital the lower will be the rate of profit: $s/(c + v)$. As noted in the previous chapter an advance in productivity from machine technology may momentarily allow a profit gain, but under competition the other producers must follow, forcing exchange-values back down to necessary labor time and lowering the rate of profit. Mitigating this downward movement on real prices, however, is the gradual erosion of competition and the establishment of national and international monopolies, firms which are able to circumvent the laws of competitive survival and reap large profits through monopoly pricing. Also working against a falling profit rate are such factors as the increasing availability of cheaper machinery, cheaper foreign materials and capital goods, increasing surplus value through relative wage reductions (supported by excess labor reserves), and increasing surplus value through such methods as the speed-up. However, the same factors which work against falling profit rates can, in turn, promote them—factors such as the role of unions

---

[48] Marx, *Wages, Price, and Profit,* in *Selected Works,* vol. 2, p. 83.
[49] Engels, *Socialism: Utopian and Scientific,* p. 145.

and the state in obtaining higher wages and limitation of labor exploitation. We might also take cognizance of the fact that, regardless of the powerful influence of monopoly pricing in hedging against a falling rate of profit, the capitalist in the twentieth century has witnessed an overall fall in profit rate—even as he experienced a huge *increase* in the total *mass* of profits (profits in the U.S. reached an all-time high in the third quarter of 1972).[50]

The introduction of the concept of automated heavy machinery and its gratuitous creation of use-value further necessarily alters the equation of falling profit rates. As Marx himself observed, automation reduces the importance of labor while increasingly placing machinery in the position of variable capital capable of yielding use-value beyond the original cost of its production. Such automation then would tend to increase both the rate and mass of profits. Under capital automation is thus used in a manner which works against the social and economic position of labor, when automation could be the road to emancipated labor.

ALIENATION AND LIBERATION

Emancipated labor and hence emancipated humanity is the goal toward which Marxist theory is oriented. Somewhere between Marx's philosophy of liberation and his laborious economic analyses the theory leaves its empirical foundations. It leaves the empirical world not because a science of liberation is impossible, but because there are no subjects upon which to empirically validate the hypothesis. However, in rooting out the sources of alienation, Marxist theory directs attention to very probable means of its elimination. What does Marx mean by alienation? Our discussion at the chapter's outset tracing the stages of development in capitalism goes a long way toward definition. The crux of alienation is to be found in the division of labor, and more specifically, within the context of labor activity and relations. Let us examine Marx's own statements in the *Economic and Philosophical Manuscripts of 1844*:

> What constitutes the alienation of labour? First, that the work is *external* to the worker, that it is not part of his nature; and that, consequently, he does not fulfill himself in his work but denies himself, has a feeling of misery rather than well-being, does not develop freely his mental and physical energies but is physically exhausted and mentally debased. The worker, therefore, feels himself at home only during his leisure time, whereas at work he feels homeless. It is not the satisfaction of a need, but only a *means* for satisfying other needs. Its alien character

---

[50] See Martin Nicolaus, "Proletariat and Middle Class in Marx," *Studies on the Left* 7 (January–February 1967): 22–49.

is clearly shown by the fact that as soon as there is no physical or other compulsion it is avoided like the plague. Finally, the external character of work for the worker is shown by the fact that it is not his own work but work for someone else, that in work he does not belong to himself but to another person.[51]

Remember that the human essence lies in the capacity of people to *produce*. The human capacity for creative labor is the first and foremost trait of the species. If the labor or productive propensity of man has been mutilated or in some manner perverted so as to undercut its expression, the species has lost its humanity:

> We arrive at the result that man (the worker) feels himself to be freely active only in his animal functions—eating, drinking and procreating, or at most also in his dwelling and in personal adornment—while in his human functions he is reduced to an animal. The animal becomes human and the human becomes animal.[52]

The alienation of labor, in the above sense, implies that in the act of labor itself the worker is fragmented and shredded, has been stripped of a sense of purpose, and has lost sight of even the product he labors on; his work leaves him emasculated, frustrated, and often desperate, meaning his leisure will take on many of the same traits. In economic terms: "By means of its conversion into an automaton, the instrument of labour confronts the labourer, during the labour-process, in the shape of capital, of dead labour, that dominates, and pumps dry, living labour-power." [53] Psychologically, physically, and economically, the working class is pumped dry.

The alienation of labor as defined above also implies that the product of labor also confronts the worker as an alien object which dominates him. Insofar as the worker is denied access to the control and use of the results of the labor process, his universe stands beyond his reach and assumes an independent reality in itself. And the more that is produced under these circumstances the greater will be the objective world of alien property. People then fetishize what they make. "The thing turns man into *its* thing," writes LeFebvre, "disguising its own origins and the secret of its birth, namely, that it is the product of specific human relations." [54] Not just material objects are forms of alienation and fetishism, but social institu-

---

[51] *Karl Marx: Early Writings,* translated and edited by T. B. Bottomore (New York: McGraw-Hill, 1964), pp. 124–25.

[52] Ibid., p. 125.

[53] *Capital,* vol. 1, p. 463.

[54] Henry LeFebvre, *The Sociology of Marx* (New York: Vintage Books, 1969), p. 47.

tions that dominate and control people as well.[55] To Marx, religion represents human alienation from self and society: "Religious suffering is at the same time an *expression* of real suffering and a *protest* against real suffering. Religion is the sigh of the oppressed creature, the sentiment of a heartless world, and the soul of soulless conditions. It is the opium of the people." [56]

At the heart of alienated property is money. Its accumulation comes at the price of pleasure and self-development, and only through its expenditure can one exist at all. A person's power is only as large as his pocket-book and the self no more important than the bank account. Money is the key to full participation in life: "And everything which you are unable to do, your money can do for you; it can eat, drink, go to the ball and to the theater. It can acquire art, learning, historical treasure, political power; and it can travel. It *can* appropriate all these things for you, can purchase everything; it is the true *opulence*." [57] Little wonder, then, that money is the most fetishized of all commodities.

Because man is alienated in practical labor activity, he is also alienated from his "species-life," that is, from all the potentialities that mark man off from the animal world. This includes the important dimension of relating cooperatively with other people, particularly in the labor process. Man is thus alienated from other men and from human life as such. And through all of this, people have alienated themselves from nature, and have reduced it as well to the status of a commodity to be exploited and standing externally to human life. On all fronts, capital has transformed the world into a selling process, a cash-nexus relationship.

Such, in brief outline, is the Marxist concept of alienation. Our next task in this section is to examine the path out of alienation to liberation as sketched in Marxist theory.

An avenue out of alienation that first must be crossed off from the standpoint of Marxist theory is the "consciousness" route; the entire body of Marxist thought is in reaction to the possibility of abolishing alienation through an internal transformation of individual consciousness. *Consciousness is the product of objective social and economic relations and not an autonomous power in itself.* Alienation is rooted in social and economic structure and no pronouncement by internal consciousness can alter this fact. At the rudimentary material level of separation from the objects of labor this fact is most evident: "People cannot be liberated as long as they are unable to obtain food and drink, housing and clothing in adequate

---

[55] See Bertell Ollman, *Alienation: Marx's Conception of Man in Capitalist Society* (Cambridge: Cambridge University Press, 1971).

[56] *Marx: Early Writings,* pp. 43–44.

[57] Ibid., p. 171.

quality and quantity." [58] If in Marxist theory "the realm of freedom begins where necessity ends," the elemental prerequisite to the end of alienation is material security—obviously no mere matter of consciousness. By material security here is meant something better than the subsistence wage level, carrying with it the perennial threat of the industrial reserve army. Beyond the prerequisite of material security an end to alienation demands an end to the psychologically and physically crippling nature of the existing division of labor, an end to the powerlessness of the worker in the production process, and an end to the system of property relations that deprives the producers of their products and sets man against man in exploitative relationships. In brief, the end of alienation demands an end to capitalism as an economic system.

Returning to the question of material security, we are led to inquire as to what level of material abundance is required to liberate people from the demands of necessity that govern their lives. On the one hand, Marx evidently did not have in mind a veritable cornucopia of goods and luxuries, since "the production of too many useful things results in too many *useless* people." [59] On the other hand, he was no Saint Francis of Assisi viewing poverty as holy; simplicity perhaps, yes, but cultivated material deprivation, no. Anyone with the strong orientation Marx had toward production could never make a virtue of material self-sacrifice. It is precisely through the enlarged forces of production that Marx foresaw the emancipation of labor, the reduction of necessary labor time so that all members of society "can develop their education in the arts, sciences, etc., thanks to the free time and means available to all." [60] No longer is it necessary for the surplus labor of the masses to be the condition for the accumulation of social wealth, or for the spare time of a single class to be based on the lifetime of wage labor by the masses: "Capital in this instance [automated production] has quite unintentionally reduced human labour, the expenditure of energy, to a minimum. This will be to the advantage of emancipated labour, and is the condition of its emancipation." [61]

But again, Marx is here stressing *time*—free time as opposed to necessary labor time—as the essence of liberation, and not gross consumption of all and any objects machine technology is capable of producing. Keenly aware of the contrived sources of a large number of human "needs," Marx contended that capitalism by its very nature drives people to excessive and needless consumption simply to maintain the viability of private accumulation of surplus value and the further expansion of capital

---

[58] Marx and Engels, *The German Ideology,* in *Selected Works,* vol. 1, p. 27.
[59] *Marx: Early Writings,* p. 172.
[60] *Grundrisse,* p. 142.
[61] Ibid., p. 138.

itself. In the *Grundrisse* Marx states that "capital, with its restless striving after the general form of wealth, drives labour out beyond the limits of its natural needs, and thus produces the material elements needed for the development of the rich individuality." [62] The problem is that the creation and stimulation of superfluous and artificial needs of consumption continue unabated as an extension of capitalism's own needs of expansion, at a time when it would be possible to direct society's productive powers to the goal of individual liberation and self-development.

By emancipated labor Marx is not referring to idleness or spectatorship. In the sphere of nonmaterial production, human activity in its emancipated form cannot be made "merely a joke, or amusement." To Marx, "really free labour, the composing of music for example, is at the same time damned serious and demands the greatest effort." [63] To the extent that industrial labor itself can be free, it must be socialized, socially planned, and under the guidance and direction of labor itself. As Marx points out, "The labour concerned with material production can only have this [free or emancipated] character if (1) it is of a social nature, [and] (2) it has a scientific character, . . . the activity of a subject controlling all the forces of nature in the production process." [64]

While alienation itself cannot be abolished within the capitalist mode of production, the forces of production may nevertheless be developed to the point of being able to eradicate material insecurity and to drastically reduce the amount of necessary labor time—*if* these forces were applied in a rational way to achieve these ends. Indeed, Engels envisaged the possibility of material freedom as long ago as 1880, before the efflorescence of mass production on an advanced automated basis: "The possibility of securing for every member of society, by means of socialised production, an existence not only fully sufficient materially, and becoming day by day more full, but an existence guaranteeing to all the free development and exercise of their physical and mental faculties—this possibility is now for the first time here, but *it is here*." [65] Today, as Baran and Sweezy point out, capitalism has clearly achieved this potential.[66] But as a class-oriented economic system capitalism is prevented from establishing material freedom for all.

Our discussion of the crucial philosophical and economic components of Marxist theory is now complete. We have laid the foundation for an understanding of its specific class aspects.

---

[62] Ibid., p. 86.
[63] Ibid., p. 124.
[64] Ibid.
[65] Engels, *Socialism: Utopian and Scientific,* p. 149.
[66] Paul A. Baran and Paul M. Sweezy, *Monopoly Capital* (New York: Monthly Review Press, 1968), p. 342.

three ───────────────────────────────

MARXIST THEORY:
CLASS AND REVOLUTION

───────────────────────────────────

The social class structure of capitalist society rests upon an economic foundation. More specifically, class structure rests upon what may be termed the mode of production, which itself consists of the forces of production and the relations of production. The forces of production include instrumental, technical, and organizational aspects of material production. Thus, machines, know-how, and work relations may be subsumed under the rubric of productive forces. Also subsumed within the forces of production is science. Marx writes: "*The development of science,* of this ideal and at the same time practical wealth, is . . . one aspect, or form, of the *development of human productive forces* (i.e. wealth).[1] In brief, the productive forces encompass all the means whereby human beings build their material wealth; they are the *means* of production.

The relations of production, beyond those work relations included in the productive forces, consist of the manner in which individuals are articulated with or tied into the productive forces.[2] One group or class, the capitalists or bourgeoisie, own and control the means of production, including both labor-power and the surplus value produced by it. A second class, the workers or proletariat, are devoid of ownership of the means of

───────────────

[1] Karl Marx, *The Grundrisse,* translated and edited by David McLellan (New York: Harper & Row, 1971), p. 120.

[2] See Irving M. Zeitlin, *Marxism: A Re-Examination* (Princeton, N.J.: Van Nostrand Company, 1967), pp. 64–66.

production and sell their labor-power to the capitalist for exploitation in the creation of surplus value. The relations of production, in this sense, are simply the formal property relations governing access to and utilization of society's wealth. We have a propertied capitalist class and a property-less working class—expropriators and expropriated. These are the two historically crucial classes in the capitalist mode of production, the bourgeois epoch. There are other classes, but as we shall discuss momentarily, capitalists and workers are the decisive class forces.

In the first chapter we examined the economic pivot of Marxist theory. Here we might again stress the fundamental nature of the mode of production to the rest of social structure—or superstructure, if you will. Class relations find expression not only within the economic relations of production, but also in various forms elsewhere in the society. For example, class relations may be examined via the legal statutes, especially those dealing with property relations; or through the state and political processes; or in the sphere of morality; or in interactional and social psychological forms.[3] Indeed, it is in these social and political domains where class relations assume their most concrete and significant manifestations, where much of the empirical research regarding social class development must be done. Nevertheless, as we shall soon discover, the events within the mode of production are the overall conditioning and determining ones.

In Chapter 2 we discussed the evolution of capitalist productive forces and the central crisis of overproduction, and noted finally that capitalism as a productive force developed internal contradictions as a form of economic relations and distribution. Within the Marxist framework we might say that the bourgeoisie represented a revolutionary productive force within the context of the new ruling property relations (new upon the dethronement of the feudal order). The relations of production were in cooperation or harmony with the development of the forces of production. Yet capitalist property relations cannot forever serve to advance the progression of human productive force, of human wealth and well-being. Capital ceases to be productive when it "meets a barrier in capital itself." [4] The barrier of overproduction, relative wage decline, unemployment, and stagnation prevents society from rationally applying and extending the forces of production for its own benefit and self-realization. Alienation is heightened and liberation is held in abeyance. In Marx's words: "In the development of the productive forces a stage is reached where productive forces and means of intercourse are called into being which, under the existing relations, can only work mischief, and which are, therefore, no

---

[3] A. S. Makhov and A. S. Frish, eds., *Society and Economic Relations* (Moscow: Progress Publishers, 1969), pp. 12–16.

[4] *Grundrisse*, p. 86.

longer productive, but destructive, forces (machinery and money)." [5] And:
"The more this contradiction develops, the clearer it becomes that the
growth of production forces can no longer be limited by the appropriation
of the surplus labour of others; the masses of workers must appropriate
their own surplus labour." [6] The material conditions are created for the
formation of a new revolutionary class, the working class, whose revolution
will eliminate the impediments to the emancipation of labor and the social
uses of social surplus.

Marx makes it clear that new relations of production have no chance
of success until all the productive potential of capital has been exhausted.
He states that "with this general prosperity, in which the productive forces
of bourgeois society develop as luxuriantly as is at all possible within
bourgeois relationships, there can be no talk of a real revolution. Such a
revolution is only possible in the periods when *both* these *factors,* the
modern productive *forces* and the *bourgeois productive forms* come in
collision with each other." [7] The exhaustion of potential within the old
order must also be accompanied by technical conditions for the implementation of the new one, such as the predominance of heavy, centralized
industry and substantial state capitalism.[8] A summary statement from
Marx is in order:

> No social order ever perishes before all the productive forces for which
> there is room in it have developed; and new, higher relations of pro-
> duction never appear before the material conditions of their existence
> have matured in the womb of the old society itself. Therefore mankind
> always sets itself only such tasks as it can solve; since, looking at the
> matter more closely, it will always be found that the task itself arises
> only when the material conditions for its solution already exist or are at
> least in the process of formation.[9]

An interesting and salient question arises in this connection: How
present were the conditions for social revolution in Marx's day as seen
by Marx? There are indications that Marx and Engels considered the
productive potential of capitalist relations to be nearing exhaustion or
already in a destructive phase in the last century. For example, Engels
wrote that "the ruling big bourgeoisie has fulfilled its historic mission,

---

[5] *Karl Marx: Selected Writings in Sociology and Social Philosophy,* translated
and edited by T. B. Bottomore and Maximilien Rubel (New York: McGraw-Hill,
1964), p. 64. (From *The German Ideology.*)

[6] *Grundrisse,* p. 145.

[7] Karl Marx, *The Class Struggles in France,* in Karl Marx and Frederick
Engels, *Selected Works,* vol. 1 (Moscow: Progress Publishers, 1969), p. 289.

[8] *The German Ideology,* in *Selected Works,* vol. 1, pp. 51–52.

[9] Preface to *The Critique of Political Economy,* in *Selected Works,* vol. 1,
p. 504.

that it is no longer capable of the leadership of society and has even become a hindrance to the development of production." [10] If such were the estimation in 1877, what might be said now? We shall have much to say on these matters in later chapters, including why capitalist relations of production have survived nearly a century beyond Engels's diagnosis.

ON CLASS

What constitutes a class under the Marxist schema? At the end of the third volume of *Capital* Marx had begun to spell out in precise terms the definition of class; but then the manuscript breaks off. We are left without a codified definition of social class from the "father" of social stratification. Marx was actually so occupied with the dynamics of the class system he evidently took for granted that his readers understood implicitly what for him constituted a class. Marx does, however, contribute some fragmentary statements on class definition. Let us try to piece together the essentials of a class in Marxist theory.

First, we are told directly and may see from the theory that the Marxist class model is in one important way dichotomous: bourgeoisie and proletariat, with an individual's membership in these classes being determined by his position in the organization and relations of production. According to Marx, in the objective sense of occupying a common position of being propertied or propertyless, individuals may be spoken of as constituting a category or aggregate, a "class-in-itself." Although a class-in-itself is fundamentally important to the Marxist theory of conflict and change, other developments and conditions must be present for a class-in-itself to become a class-for-itself, a more substantive and socially crystallized group. Chief among these conditions for an aggregate of people with a common position in the system of production to be transformed into a viable social class is the recognition of common interests and a common class opponent. In Marxist thinking, "the separate individuals form a class only insofar as they have to carry on a common battle against another class; otherwise they are on hostile terms with each other as competitors." [11] In the capitalist epoch, this means that unless the bourgeoisie and proletariat recognize their respective internal interests vis-à-vis each other, each will engage in internal competition and conflict among themselves. Such internal competition may happen during the process of class formation, and no doubt will occur; but interclass conflict must replace intraclass conflict as the dominant fact before class formation can come to fruition.

[10] Engels, *Karl Marx*, in *Selected Works*, vol. 3, p. 85.
[11] *The German Ideology*, in *Selected Works*, vol. 1, p. 65.

The recognition of common interests and opponents implies the emergence of a class consciousness. We shall probe into the matter of class consciousness in the next section, since it is an important subject in itself. Before turning to a key summary quotation from Marx, one further condition of a class-for-itself must be noted. The contradiction between the forces and relations of production in the economic base is paralleled in social structure by the conflict between capital and labor. The objective economic contradiction finds its subjective expression in the political struggle between capitalists and workers. The class struggle is a political struggle, and for the working class to wage an effective political struggle requires the existence of a political party. In brief, Marx explains that the organization of the proletariat as a class means its organization as a political party as well.[12] In what is probably the most succinct definitional statement on class in the original Marx, we have from *The Eighteenth Brumaire of Louis Bonaparte:*

> In so far as millions of families live under economic conditions of existence that separate their mode of life, their interests and their culture from those of the other classes, and put them in hostile opposition to the latter, they form a class. In so far as there is merely a local interconnection among these small-holding peasants, and the identity of their interests begets no community, no national bond, and no political organisation among them, they do not form a class.[13]

From this passage we may isolate the following definitional criteria of social class: (1) common position in the economic mode of production; (2) separate way of life and cultural existence; (3) conflicting and hostile interests vis-à-vis another class; (4) social relationships and social community extending across local and regional lines; (5) a societywide class consciousness; and (6) political organization. Needless to say, if all of these criteria are applied, we have extremely stringent conditions to meet before we have a social class-for-itself. Yet, each must be present to a degree, and for class revolution to a very substantial degree, before we have a class in the Marxist sense. Each of these conditions tends to follow in an empirical if not logical sequence, from objective position to common interests and culture, to social community, to class consciousness, and finally to political organization.

The above does not mean, however, that social class is an all-or-nothing entity. It is a matter of degree. It is a matter of degree as to how many of the criteria will be present in a given case, and also a matter of

---

12 See Ralf Dahrendorf, *Class and Class Conflict in Industrial Society* (Stanford, Calif.: Stanford University Press, 1959), p. 17.
13 *Selected Works,* vol. 1 (London: Lawrence & Wishart, 1962), p. 334.

degree with each separate criterion. The greater the number of criteria present and the greater the intensity of each, the greater is the class as revolutionary potential. We shall return to the question of class and revolution later in the chapter.

Marx recognized that within the two major classes there existed gradations; these gradations, however, do not overshadow the dichotomous relation to the means of production. Further, with the concentration of capital and the automation of production it should be expected that members of the two respective classes will become increasingly homogeneous, divided into "two hostile camps." Marx also took into consideration the fluid nature of the class structure throughout the capitalist epoch, though it becomes decreasingly fluid as the historic mission of capital is fulfilled. Referring to the United States' social classes, Marx wrote that "they have not yet become fixed, but continually change and interchange their elements in constant flux." [14] And although the dynamic aspect of the Marxist class model is dichotomous, Marx frequently discussed the activities of other strata in the population. Perhaps we might say that his cross-sectional or descriptive view of society was multilayered and his revolutionary theoretical view dichotomous.

We are able to decipher two major trends in the shape of the class structure through the application of the Marxist economic theory of capitalist development. First, the class structure tends toward polarization between an increasingly concentrated capitalist class and an expanding proletariat (and industrial reserve army). The proletariat expands at the expense of petty capitalists, independent artisans, peasantry, and any other strata that represent outmoded productive forces or property relations. Marx considers the lower-middle class of independent capitalists and producers as conservative or reactionary, "for they try to roll back the wheel of history." [15] A second trend in class structure which accompanies the first, and which as Nicolaus has stressed is a necessary aspect of the Marxist economic model, is the rise of a "surplus class" or new middle class.[16] This introduces a third major grouping and suggests that, depending upon one's purposes, a trichotomous class model may be utilized as well as a dichotomous one. For example, descriptively speaking, the trichotomous model may at times prove to be more useful whereas in terms of revolutionary theory the dichotomy of class structure may be more powerful. The essentials of Marxist theory, however, must be grasped from the dichotomous class framework.

---

[14] Ibid., p. 405.

[15] *Manifesto of the Communist Party,* in *Selected Works,* vol. 1, p. 118.

[16] See Martin Nicolaus, "Proletariat and Middle Class in Marx," *Studies on the Left* 7 (January–February 1967), 22–49.

PROLETARIAT AND MIDDLE CLASS

A very difficult question for Marxist class theory has to do with just where the proletariat begins and the new, surplus middle class ends, and precisely what role the latter plays in developed capitalist society. We have already spoken of the proletariat as being a propertyless class. However, being propertyless is not an exhaustive criterion of proletarian status. An individual may be propertyless and still not be counted among the proletariat—e.g., a domestic servant in the employ of a capitalist. We have also referred to the proletariat as that class which produces value and surplus value as a result of its labor in the means of production. The proletariat is the producing class; it produces the material means of existence—from survival to luxury. Viewed alternatively, Engels states that "The proletariat is that class of society which procures its means of livelihood entirely and solely from the sale of its labour and not from the profit derived from some capital." [17] A further mark of proletarian status, if the concept of alienation is to be of major importance here, is the performance of labor which is fragmented, which is purposeless from the individual's standpoint, over which the worker has no control, and which offers no or slight security from displacement or replacement by another worker owing to the repetitiveness of the work. In short, a proletarian is also a person who is at once both indispensable to the existence of the society and readily dispensable should another warm body be standing behind him.

Now, a pure proletarian would embody all of these traits: propertylessness, producer of means of existence, lives solely from the creation of value through labor and not at all from surplus value, and works at a fragmented and insecure job. A pure proletarian exploits no one, while he is himself exploited by others. Depending on how many of these traits or criteria we demand for inclusion in the proletariat, our proletariat will be larger or smaller, more or less solid in proletarian character.[18] Let us examine the several strata of capitalist economy on the basis of this definition of the proletariat.

At the core of the proletariat is the factory worker and all those laborers who play a direct role in construction and support of the production process. Transport, installation, and maintenance of the instruments of production and the necessary labor of distribution may also be included,

---

[17] Engels, *Principles of Communism,* in *Collected Works,* vol. 1, p. 81.
[18] See Stanislaw Ossowski, *Class Structure in the Social Consciousness* (New York: Free Press, 1963), pp. 74–79.

so long as it involves wage labor (a self-employed electrician running a small shop is petit bourgeois, despite his manual labor status and function). What is the class status of technicians and engineers, the highly educated and skilled members of the production process? Are they proletarians, working class? If, say, an engineer is in the employ of capital and works at the design of automated machinery, he is propertyless and directly tied to the production of value, and hence working class. If he is paid a salary or wage that is no more than the cost of his reproduction (even though this sum would run higher than that of an assembly-line worker), he lives solely from necessary labor, and hence is proletarian in this sense as well. However, if he is paid a salary or wage over and above the cost of subsistence, and out of the surplus value or profit of capital, he is so much the less a member of the working class in this important sense. Finally, with the increasing division and specialization of engineering labor, and with the rising number of such engineers, we can imagine the engineer as being proletarian in the sense of performing fragmented and meaningless work and suffering job insecurity as well. (We may also imagine an engineer being in quite the converse work and job situation, a large and secure property owner highly placed within a major corporation.)

Marx considered the technician and engineer as natural by-products of scientifically conditioned production techniques, a highly trained or *new* working class overlaid upon the traditional factory work force: "This is a superior class of workmen [referring to engineers, mechanics, joiners, etc.], some of them scientifically educated, others brought up to a trade; it is distinct from the factory operative class and merely aggregated to it." Marx adds that "this division of labor is purely technical" and that "it looks very like intentional misleading by statistics . . . when the English factory legislation excludes from its operation the class of laborer last mentioned in the text [i.e., engineers, etc.]." [19] To a very large extent, then, technicians and engineers are working class in the Marxist model of class —individuals very critical to the increase of productivity and surplus value. Scientists, like technicians and engineers, are new working class to the extent that their work is integral to the increase of productivity and the improvement of material support systems, and to the extent that they meet the other criteria of proletarian status. A scientist's value or cost of production is obviously much higher than the factory worker's, and thus, even if the scientist were paid a subsistence wage (as the majority are), we are able to see that the working class has within it a notable income differential. The new technological working class is not, then, in most instances a part of the surplus middle class.

We move next to a stratum that occupies a much more ambiguous

---

[19] *Capital,* vol. 1 (Chicago: Charles H. Kerr & Company, 1908), Chapter 15.

status vis-à-vis labor and capital than the technological stratum, which we have seen is much closer to proletarian status than anything else, and is becoming increasingly proletarianized. This ambiguous stratum is the commercial or white-collar worker, as we would have it today. The clerical or commercial worker is similar to the proletarian in that this person is hired at a wage or salary by property owners and works at a fragmented and insecure job. The commercial worker is not proletarian in the sense of producing material means of subsistence; like the capitalist, the white-collar worker lives off the surplus value created by the producing working class. Nevertheless, the commercial worker is exploited by the capitalist in much the same way as the factory worker: the commercial worker's wages are typically less than the savings in surplus value or profit which by his efforts he helps the capitalist realize. Marx puts it as follows:

> The commercial laborer does not produce any surplus value directly. But the value of his labor is determined by the value of his labour-power, that is, of its costs of production, while the application of this labour-power, its exertion, expression, and consumption, the same as in the case of every other wage laborer, is by no means limited by the value of his labour-power. His wages are therefore not necessarily in proportion to the mass of profits, which he helps the capitalist to realize. What he costs the capitalist and what he makes for him are two different things. He adds to the income of the capitalist not by creating any direct surplus-value, but by helping him to reduce the costs of the realization of surplus-value. In so doing, he performs partly unpaid labor.[20]

In the important sense of having to sell labor-power for the purpose of enhancing the surplus value and profit of the capitalist for exploition, the commercial or white-collar worker is very much a member of the working class. To be sure, insofar as the commercial worker contributes to the ultimate expansion of productive capital, he is a member of the producing proletariat. This is not to say that *all* white-collar clerical and sales workers are members of the producing class. In the private capitalist and financial sector there has arisen a tremendous overlay of purely superfluous white-collar workers who contribute in no way to the maximization of surplus value, are totally unproductive, and live entirely off the surplus value created by the working or producing classes. The functions which they perform make sense only within the limits of capitalism and are completely dispensable to the material and social well-being of the society from a non-capitalist perspective. Insurance, real estate, credit institutions, advertising, and much of the entire financial apparatus must so be classified.

Yet from a capitalist perspective and system, these surplus consumers

---

[20] *Capital,* vol. 3, p. 353.

and other partial surplus consumers are extremely important and indispensable precisely for the reason that they help consume the surplus (in addition to their functional importance in servicing and operating the capitalist structure). As Nicolaus has pointed out, a class that produces more than it consumes must be balanced off by classes that consume more than they produce or the system would immediately collapse rather than simply suffer periodic crises of overproduction.[21] Also as Nicolaus observes, Marx's theory of the surplus middle class remained embryonic, though he did refer to the constant increase of the middle classes standing between the workers and capitalists.

Also included in these unproductive, surplus-consuming, and capitalist-dependent intermediate strata are domestic and personal servants ("lackeys") and ideological employees in government, law, military, and religious functions.[22] For the most part, the functions performed here are in the service of the property-owning capitalist class. There are, however, *unproductive* workers who perform *socially necessary* functions quite separate and distinct from the prerequisites to the survival of capitalist production and organization. Most health workers belong to this unproductive but necessary class intermediate or apart from labor and capital. Educational workers, apart from those linked to the means of production, might also be included under the rubric of unproductive but socially necessary labor force. Both health and educational workers are indirectly important, even indispensable, to the continued and increased productivity of the working class per se. Their typically propertyless, employee status also links them to the proletariat, as well as does their alienating working conditions. Independent professionals, whether in medicine, education, or whatever, and professionals paid salaries beyond the cost of their labor-power are members of the bourgeoisie or middle classes either by virtue of their propertied status, predominantly surplus-derived income, or uniquely capitalist-dependent function.[23]

No hard and fast lines between proletariat and middle class can be drawn. There exists a distinctly proletarian core and an equally distinctive middle class, but the boundary lines of each are blurred and objectively uncertain. We shall attempt further clarifications in dealing with contemporary class structure. It is enough to note here that subjective factors

---

[21] Nicolaus, "Proletariat and Middle Class in Marx," 40.

[22] *Capital,* vol. 1, p. 487. Marx writes: "What a beautiful arrangement, where a factory girl sweats in the shop for 12 long hours so that the factory owner can use a part of her unpaid labor to take her sister as maid, her brother as groom, and her cousin as policeman or soldier into his personal service!" Cited in Nicolaus, "Proletariat and Middle Class in Marx," 41–42.

[23] See *Essential Writings of Karl Marx,* edited by David Caute (New York: Collier Books, 1967), pp. 67–68.

of culture, identification of interests, social relationships, class consciousness, and political ideology—all of those factors outlined as class criteria in the previous section—must necessarily enter into a person or group's class placement. The objective economic criterion as discussed here is not often sufficient. The relationship between the objective economic and the noneconomic cultural and social dimensions of class will be examined in a subsequent section. But first we have a few comments to make concerning other broad social strata within the Marxist perspective.

RULING CLASS, LUMPENPROLETARIAT, AND PEASANTRY

Just as the proletariat must become a class-for-itself before taking social power, so must have the bourgeoisie have formed a class-for-itself prior to the overturning of the feudal ruling classes. In Marx's words, "The bourgeoisie formed itself into a class under the feudal system and absolute monarchy . . . and, . . . already formed into a class, it overthrew feudalism and monarchy, in order to turn society into bourgeois society." This prerevolutionary class formation covered a considerable time period and "required the greatest efforts." [24] The capitalist epoch finds the bourgeoisie in a process of continual integration and crystallization until its boundaries are rather clearly defined, surely more clearly than those of any other class. The overturning of the old order opened up the class structure of society in a way that made it seem to all classes that the bourgeoisie was the representative of the interests of the entire society apart from the old ruling class. Individuals consigned to lowly life stations by birth were set free to climb into the ranks of the bourgeoisie or middle classes, a process which may continue throughout the capitalist period.

Ruling classes are by no means homogeneous, and the ruling class of the capitalist period is no exception. One division within the bourgeoisie noted by Marx is between the intelligentsia or ideological component and the active industrial bourgeoisie. The ideologists of the intelligentsia "make the perfecting of the illusion of the class about itself their chief source of livelihood." [25] They are the rationalizers, justifiers, and systematizers of the bourgeois political status quo. These conceptualizers of capitalism are not actually full-fledged members of the ruling class, but are hired servants who like other bourgeoisie live entirely off the value created by others. That the intelligentsia is not purely bourgeois is attested to by the fact that in the course of the development of the proletariat as a class-for-itself,

---

[24] *Karl Marx: Selected Writings in Sociology and Social Philosophy*, p. 187.
[25] *The German Ideology*, in *Selected Works*, vol. 1, p. 48.

members of this same intelligentsia "cuts itself adrift, and joins the revolutionary class" for they have "raised themselves to the level of comprehending theoretically the historical movement as a whole."[26] (This is a further confirmation that objective economic position does not exhaustively define proletarian status or membership.)

The most important cleavage within the ruling class, as Marx discusses in *The Class Struggles in France, 1848–1850,* is that between the financial aristocracy and the industrial bourgeoisie. In Marx's analyses, the financial aristocracy is not interested in producing wealth, but only in confiscating it. The financial aristocracy had the upper hand, since it "made the laws, was at the head of the administration of the state, had command of all the organised public authorities, [and] dominated public opinion through the actual state of affairs and through the press."[27] The momentum of the period, however, was on the side of industrial capital rather than what was the essentially unproductive and usurious methods of the financial aristocracy. Momentarily, the bourgeoisie of industry and the proletariat had common cause against the waste, parasitism, and extravagance of the idle rich. Yet the immense success of industrial capital itself called into being an alliance of financial and industrial interests which became increasingly two sides of the same ruling class. There remain, however, certain conflicts of interest which wax and wane through business cycles.

Another stratum—or actually mass—which Marx occasionally refers to is the lumpenproletariat. The lumpenproletariat is not to be confused with the industrial reserve army, though there would seem to be the distinct possibility of overlap between the two. The industrial reserve army consists of displaced and potential members of the proletariat as an active, producing work force, whereas the lumpenproletariat is primarily a socially deviant and occupationally marginal assemblage of people lacking any articulation whatsoever with the producing class other than a parasitical one. In his analysis of French counterrevolutionary activity of 1849, Marx describes the lumpenproletariat of Paris as follows:

Alongside decayed *roués* with dubious means of subsistence and dubious origin, alongside ruined and adventurous offshoots of the bourgeoisie, were vagabonds, discharged soldiers, discharged jailbirds, escaped galley slaves, swindlers, mountebanks, *lazzoroni,* pickpockets, tricksters, gamblers, procurers, brothel keepers, porters, *literati,* organ-grinders, ragpickers, knife grinders, tinkers, beggars—in short, the whole indefinite,

---

[26] *Manifesto of the Communist Party,* in *Selected Works,* vol. 1, p. 117.
[27] *The Class Struggles in France, 1848–1850,* in *Selected Works,* vol. 1, especially 205–17.

disintegrated mass, thrown hither and thither, which the French term
la bohéme.[28]

How many of these people were lumpenproletariat instead of proletariat
by choice rather than chance cannot be said. Certainly we can envisage a
route leading from the proletariat to the industrial reserve army to the
lumpenproletariat, as well as vice versa. We may also envisage a lumpenproletariat which is disinclined and/or unsuited for productive labor on
a permanent basis. This would represent the core of the lumpenproletariat,
while like other strata its boundaries would be permeable and blurred.

   We know that Marx and Engels considered the lumpenproletariat
to be a repository for failures from all classes, including the lumpenproletariat itself, and to be primarily situated in the larger cities. We also know
that Marx and Engels considered the lumpenproletariat to be more dangerous than helpful to the proletarian revolution. Engels writes: "The *lumpenproletariat,* this scum of depraved elements from all classes, with
headquarters in the big cities, is the worst of all the possible allies. This
rabble is absolutely venal and absolutely brazen." [29] Marx portrayed the
lumpenproletariat in hardly less caustic terms:

> The "dangerous class," the social scum, the passively rotting mass thrown
> off by the lowest layers of old society, may, here and there, be swept
> into the movement by a proletarian revolution; its conditions of life,
> however, prepare it far more for the part of a bribed tool of reactionary
> intrigue.[30]

These conceptions of the lumpenproletariat invite comparisons with the
contemporary class structure, but we shall resist entering into such at this
time. Almost needless to say, the lumpenproletariat can scarcely qualify
in any way for eventually becoming a class-for-itself, or for that matter,
even a class-in-itself—at least in the terms Marx originally ascribed to it.

   The last class to be examined here is the peasantry. The peasant is
a producer, naturally, of food; but as the owner of his own instruments of
production, the peasant produces on an outmoded basis of production,
i.e., that of the small, independent artisan or manufacturer. Like the
handicraftsman, the peasant is doomed, since "agriculture comes to be
more and more merely a branch of industry and is completely dominated
by capital." [31] The pressures of a money economy and the competitive

---

[28] *The Eighteenth Brumaire of Louis Bonaparte,* in *Selected Works,* vol. 1,
p. 442.
   [29] Engels, Preface to *The Peasant War in Germany,* in Marx and Engels,
Selected Works, vol. 2, p. 163.
   [30] *Manifesto of the Communist Party,* in *Selected Works,* vol. 1, p. 118.
   [31] *Grundrisse,* p. 41.

mechanization of agriculture force the peasant into indebtedness, and submit him to overburdening taxation and appropriation of his land. The
capitalization of agriculture drives him off the land and into the city: "He
is a future proletarian." [32] Marx is not, of course, sympathetic, for the
peasantry is chained "to the stupidity of rural life," not to mention their
backward political tendencies.

However, the peasantry may be revolutionary allies at times. For
example, the mass of small and landless peasants can improve their position in agriculture through the confiscation and redistribution of large
feudal holdings and become financially successful peasants (small rural
capitalists). "Hence," to quote from Marx. "the peasants find their natural
ally and leader in the *urban proletariat,* whose task is the overthrow of the
bourgeois order." [33] But the peasantry and proletariat seek to overturn
capital for different reasons, meaning that although they may be allies on
the question of revolution, they must inevitably enter into conflict over
postrevolutionary economy. The peasant, in effect, represents a feudal
mode of production, whereas the proletariat seeks to establish a socialist
one. Where agriculture has not been largely capitalized prior to proletarian-
led revolution, a peasant-proletariat conflict is to some degree inevitable.
This could happen only in a relatively immature industrial society (if it
were mature, agriculture would be heavily capitalized and centralized),
and as we shall learn presently, self-sustaining revolutions are not scheduled
by Marxist theory to transpire in such premature conditions.

RULING IDEAS AND CLASS CONSCIOUSNESS

In Chapter 1 we learned that Marxist theory holds the economic structure
to be primarily determinative of other cultural areas and institutions, while
at the same time recognizing the conditioning influences of noneconomic
ideas and beliefs. The term *ultimately* was applied to the causal status of
economic factors, implying that while the class struggle is being fought
out or controlled within the status quo at philosophical, ideological, and
political levels of consciousness, the movement of material forces and
relations of production will assert themselves with decisive force in the
end. Indeed, the economic variable is all along the crucial one.

Secondly, at the outset of this chapter we observed that in the growing contradiction between the forces and relations of production the proletariat suffers psychologically and materially from the retardation and

---

[32] Engels, *The Peasant Question in France and Germany,* in *Selected Works,*
vol. 3, pp. 459–60.
[33] *The Eighteenth Brumaire,* in *Selected Works,* vol. 1.

irrational use of the forces of production and represents the interests for revolutionizing the relations of production. The bourgeoisie, of course, desire the preservation of the status quo on all fronts. We have also pointed out that a new ruling class, such as were the bourgeoisie, depicts itself and believes itself to represent the real interests of all classes except the old ruling class. In this situation, then, the bourgeoisie generate and are at first largely successful in establishing the competitive individualist world view and ideology throughout all classes of the society. The feudal order could not prevail against the ultimately determinative economic relations of capitalism. The ideas justifying capital, as these ideas are found in every institutional area, became the ruling ideas. In a well-known passage from Marx:

> The ideas of the ruling class are in every epoch the ruling ideas: i.e., the class which is the ruling *material* force of society, is at the same time its ruling *intellectual* force. The class which has the means of material production at its disposal, has control at the same time over the means of mental production. . . . The ruling ideas are nothing more than the ideal expression of the dominant material relationships, the dominant material relationships grasped as ideas.[34]

Note that ruling ideas do not gain their ascendancy magically or automatically: they are consciously and subconsciously disseminated through the means of mental production, i.e., the press, the schools, the churches, the state, etc.

Thus, the argument merely states that ruling ideas hold sway *not* because they are self-evidently right or have a detached and independent existence in history, as the bourgeoisie and all of those they have convinced might believe; but rather ruling ideas hold sway because they are made to *appear* as naturally right and autonomous by those who wield institutional power.[35] Even historians (and other social analysts as well, we might add to Marx) "take every epoch at its word."[36] (This is done so today under the rubric of scientific neutrality.)

To take an epoch at its own word, to accept as given the ruling ideas, is to engage in reification and to fetishize the world. It is to be in a position of alienation. To persist in the bourgeois world view at a time when the contradictions between the forces and relations of production are growing is to have a distorted mental picture of reality, to have false consciousness. False consciousness is not an all-or-nothing phenomenon; it is a matter of degrees of reality and unreality. The opposite mental

---

[34] *The German Ideology,* in *Selected Works,* vol. 1, p. 47.
[35] See Frank Parkin, *Class Inequality and Political Order* (New York: Praeger Publishers, 1971), pp. 84–85.
[36] *The German Ideology,* in *Selected Works,* vol. 1, p. 50.

picture of the world under developed capital is class consciousness. Class consciousness is simultaneously revolutionary consciousness, for it under stands the source of alienation and material bondage to be in the capitalist mode of production, and that capitalist relations must be replaced by socially organized, controlled, and utilized production. Class consciousness in the bourgeoisie is an outmoded and false consciousness under developed capital. Class consciousness in the proletariat is a consciousness of material reality, and a rejection of the rationalizations and ideological creations of the old ruling class. It is the acceptance of the proletariat as the new ruling class and of proletarian ideas as the new ruling ideas. Hence working-class consciousness is not restricted to workers as such, but can arise in other classes from the observation of the situation of the proletariat.[37]

Insofar as the capitalist period contains within it cycles of prosperity, stagnation, and decline, class consciousness fluctuates within these cycles.[38] As objective material conditions deteriorate (as when there is a relative decline in wages or an expansion of the industrial reserve army), class consciousness comes to the fore; whereas when the objective conditions are favorable, subjective conceptions are more falsified—the working class being pulled along by golden chains. But under any circumstances subjective revolutionary ideas cannot catch hold without the objective conditions providing for a revolutionary class.[39] Yet the objective conditions by themselves cannot create the revolution until and unless working-class consciousness takes firm root. But insofar as the economic structure is ultimately the critical variable in determining human consciousness, there is a strong tendency working against the continued successful inculcation of bourgeois ideas in the proletariat and other classes as well, particularly at times when the economic contradictions assert themselves most blatantly and openly.

Wilhelm Reich draws a distinction between two kinds of class consciousness. One is "filled with knowledge of the contradictions of the capitalist economic system, the immense possibilities of a socialist planned economy, the need for social revolution to establish a balance between the form of appropriation and the form of production, the progressive and retrograde forces of history, etc." [40] The other "has no such far-reaching perspectives; it is concerned with the trivial problems of every-

---

[37] *Karl Marx: Selected Writings in Sociology and Social Philosophy*, p. 65. (From *The German Ideology*.)

[38] See Ernest Mandel, *The Formation of the Economic Thought of Karl Marx* (New York: Monthly Review Press, 1971), p. 26.

[39] *The German Ideology*, in *Selected Works*, vol. 1, p. 48.

[40] Wilhelm Reich, "What is Class Consciousness?" *Liberation*, October, 1971, pp. 22–24.

day life." The former is the class consciousness of the radicalized intelligentsia or revolutionary leadership, whereas the latter is the class
consciousness of the masses. Taken each by themselves the trivial concerns of everyday life for the masses, such as food, clothing, family relations, fashion, sexual satisfaction, and leisure activities do not constitute
class consciousness, but *"in conjunction with one another* [they] could
become class consciousness." The content of the revolutionary leader's
class consciousness is not of a personal kind, whereas that of the masses
is entirely personal. The great task is to bridge the gap between the two
forms of consciousness, to abolish the distance between the objective
sociological process and the subjective consciousness of the masses. The
most important step in achieving this goal is the rejection of the principle
of self-denial and the recognition of the potential for abundance and personal liberation. Reich summarizes as follows:

> Everything that contradicts the bourgeois order, everything that contains a
> germ of rebellion, can be regarded as an element of class-consciousness;
> everything that creates or maintains a bond with the bourgeois order,
> that supports and reinforces it, is an impediment to class-consciousness.[41]

Reich's interpretation concurs with Marx insofar as neither expects
class consciousness to present itself as an automatic, mechanical response
to objective conditions and both recognize that there exists considerable
individual discontents which provide important latent sources for a potentially unified class consciousness. However, Reich seems comfortable
with a looser definition than does Marx. Marx's conception includes a
greater measure of class organization and grasp of broader issues than
Reich's personal level and trivial concerns. (Reich does not list politics
and economic conditions among his trivial concerns, though he later
speaks of the politicization of the masses and of workers grasping the
meaning of surplus value and control of workplace.) Reich's version of
class consciousness at the end boils down almost to a knowledge of a
personal pleasure-pain principle and how to achieve a greater proportion
of pleasure than pain—under the understanding tutelage of more articulate leaders. The trivializing and individualizing of personal problems and
concerns is precisely the opposite of Marxist class consciousness. It is a
successful holding tactic of capitalism, of reducing all to psychology and
sex. Such a form of class consciousness is unlikely to produce the revolution that at least Marx himself had in mind and certainly will not prepare the working class for its role in the future society.

---

[41] Ibid.

CLASS AND REVOLUTION

Revolution is the capstone of Marxist theory. And an understanding of revolution in Marx requires a firm grasp of all that has gone before this point. As Tucker has stressed: "In a basic sense, . . . revolution was the master theme of Marx's thought, and an exposition of the Marxian revolutionary idea in complete form would be nothing other than an exposition of Marxism itself as a theoretical system." [42] In this sense, then, we need add relatively little regarding revolution as such. A number of points, however, require clarification.

First, of the two large driving forces behind the revolution—the restriction and limitation on material security and equality, and the inhibition of the production and creative potential of the human species—it is the inhibition of the productive and creative forces rather than the insecurity and inequality which is the most important. The two forces are, of course, interrelated, but the emphasis is on the production more than the consumption aspect. Marx never denied capitalism's ability to materially maintain the working class; what capitalism cannot accomplish is the liberation of the workers by turning over the control of the productive forces to them. Revolution is required to free the means of production from capitalist control and direct them toward human needs and freedom from economic necessity.

Second, the revolution presupposes that all of the productive forces of the old society have developed and that the old property relations are clearly a hindrance to the further development and rational use of material production. This does not mean that the polarization of a society must be complete and that all peasants, petite bourgeoisie, and artisans have been proletarianized before revolution may successfully be carried through.[43] What is assumed is that the internal contradictions are substantial and that a majority of the work force has sufficient class consciousness and organization to succeed politically.

Third, the revolution is preeminently political. To Marx, "the *political aspect* of a revolution consists in the movement of the politically uninfluential classes to end their *exclusion* from *political life and power.* Its standpoint is that of the State. . . . Every revolution breaks up the

---

[42] Robert C. Tucker, "The Marxian Revolutionary Idea," in Clifford T. Paynton and Robert Blackey, eds., *Why Revolution? Theories and Analysis* (Cambridge, Mass.: Schenkman Publishing Company, 1971), p. 215.

[43] Engels, *The Peasant Question in France and Germany,* in *Selected Works,* vol. 3, pp. 471–72.

old society; to this extent it is *social.* Every revolution overthrows *the existing ruling power;* to this extent it is *political."* [44] Such is necessarily the case, since all class struggle is also political struggle. Only in a society without classes can social change cease to involve political struggle and revolution. In this connection, Marx and Engels contend that it is within the *democratic* republic which the political struggle between capital and labor must be carried out.[45] Hence, universal suffrage and political freedoms are "new arms not to be disdained." (And also not to be abused, according to Engels: "The workers' movement is based on the sharpest criticism of existing society; criticism is its vital element; how then can it itself avoid criticism, try to forbid controversies? Is it possible for us to demand from others freedom of speech for ourselves only in order to eliminate it afresh in our own ranks?" [46])

However, Marx was extremely pessimistic concerning the prospects of nonviolent revolution once the bourgeois state had been thoroughly bureaucratized and militarized, since once it is clear that democratic processes are leading toward working-class power, the state as an instrument of the ruling class will abandon or repress such processes. Prior to this, though, the democratic form of government is essential to working-class organization and movement. In the same vein, Marx argued that recourse to terror tactics on the part of or on behalf of the working class is a certain indication that the revolutionary condition is unripe, and that such attempts are doomed to failure.

Fourth, the revolution leads to total *social* revolution, the reconstruction of society on an all-encompassing scale. Only through revolutionary action can the working class prepare itself to accomplish this rebuilding task. From Marx: "Revolution is necessary not only because the *ruling* class cannot be overthrown in any other way, but also because only in a revolution can *the class which overthrows it* rid itself of the accumulated rubbish of the past and become capable of reconstructing society." [47]

Fifth, and in a related vein, the revolution does not and cannot succeed by simply taking over the old forms of bureaucratic power. Although the proletariat is indeed the new ruling class it is in theory and will become in actuality a universal class, making the old forms of ruling-

---

[44] *Karl Marx: Selected Writings in Sociology and Social Philosophy,* pp. 238–41.
[45] *Critique of the Gotha Programme,* in *Selected Works,* vol. 3, p. 27.
[46] Cited in Monty Johnstone, "Marx and Engels and the Concept of the Party," *Socialist Register,* edited by R. Miliband and J. Saville (New York: Monthly Review Press, 1967), p. 143.
[47] *Karl Marx: Selected Writings in Sociology and Social Philosophy,* p. 65. (From *The German Ideology.*)

class dominance and control obsolete. A people's revolution does not seek "to transfer the bureaucratic-military machine from one hand to another, but to *smash* it, and this is the preliminary condition for every real people's revolution on the continent." [48] (In 1871 Marx evidently did not feel the United States had such a bureaucratic-military machine—which indeed it did not. So at the time he could envisage a nonviolent revolution in America.)

Sixth, Marx held that revolution is in essence a world event and not something that can uniquely happen in a single capitalist society—or at least be successful in long-run goals. Revolution is a universal because so is capital: "The need of a constantly expanding market for its products chases the bourgeoisie over the whole surface of the globe. It must nestle everywhere, settle everywhere, establish connexions everywhere." [49] More than that, capital "compels all nations, on pain of extinction, to adopt the bourgeois mode of production; it compels them to introduce what it calls civilisation into their midst, i.e., to become bourgeois themselves. In one word, it creates a world after its own image." [50] Thus, any instance of revolution in a single country is but a separate manifestation of world revolution. Although Marx's theory led him to locate the initial revolutions in the most advanced capitalist societies, he did not rule out the possibility of revolution in a less developed country, but only as a "signal for a proletarian revolution in the West." [51] As early as 1870 Marx wrote: "The English have all the *material* necessary for the social revolution. What they lack is *the spirit of generalisation and revolutionary fervour.*" [52]

Elsewhere, and at the same point in time, Marx alludes to a more important obstacle to the English revolution, and one which we may generalize to most other cases as well: ethnic hostility *within* the proletariat and the manipulation of the resultant cleavage by the ruling class:

> In all *the big industrial centres in England* there is profound antagonism between the Irish proletariat and the English proletariat. The average English worker hates the Irish worker as a competitor who lowers wages and the *standard of life.* He feels national and religious antipathies for him. He regards him somewhat like the *poor whites* of the Southern States regard their black slaves. This antagonism among the proletarians of England is artificially nourished and supported by the bourgeoisie. It knows that this scission is the true secret of maintaining its power. [53]

---

[48] Marx to L. Kugelmann, 1871, in *Selected Works,* vol. 2, p. 420.
[49] *Manifesto of the Communist Party,* in *Selected Works,* vol. 1, p. 112.
[50] Ibid.
[51] Preface to the Russian edition of 1882 to *Manifesto of the Communist Party,* in *Selected Works,* vol. 1, pp. 100–101.
[52] Marx, confidential communication, in *Selected Works,* vol. 2, pp. 174–75.
[53] Ibid., p. 176.

Finally, the revolution is not a single event but rather a *process*. We shall look into certain of Marx's ideas regarding the evolution of socialist society toward the end of the chapter, but we might take as an illustration of the processual aspect of the revolution in connection with nationalization ("the expropriation of a few usurpers by the mass of people" as opposed to "the expropriation of the mass of the people by a few usurpers." [54]) In answer to the question of whether it will be possible to abolish private property at one blow, Engels responds definitely no. He makes reference to the "gradual expropriation of landed proprietors, factory owners, railway and shipping magnates, partly through competition on the part of state industry and partly directly through the payment of compensation in currency notes." [55] In both industry and agriculture, then, we have a view of gradual socialization of the means of production. In the same context, nationalization is not simply a matter of violent seizure of the means of production but may involve state competition (mortally feared by the ruling class and, of course, not permitted before the triumph of working-class power) and indemnification.

Throughout our discussion of revolution we must remind ourselves of what we have said before about the role of human action in history. The revolution is not, then, an inexorable and inevitable event that will take place regardless of human will and action. The objective conditions may well be present, but still Marx can offer no guarantee of revolution without the subjective and human factor also being present at the same time.

DICTATORSHIP OF THE PROLETARIAT

The first step in the revolution is to raise the working class to the ruling class, "to win the battle of democracy." By winning the battle of democracy Marx is not referring primarily to the fact that the proletariat has simply outvoted the opposition party in parliamentary elections. We have seen that Marx held out little hope for revolution through this means, though he valued universal suffrage as an organizing instrument. But the voting franchise is rarely a free and universal one, and responds mainly to property ownership. Thus, the will of a proletarian majority can rarely be attained through the vote within capitalism. Marx held that a majority preference would ultimately abolish the distinction between state politics and society insofar as the proletariat constitutes the universal class. A classless society requires no political state, since the state is an instrument

---

[54] *Capital,* vol. 1, p. 837.
[55] Engels, *Principles of Communism,* in *Selected Works,* vol. 1, p. 90.

of the status quo and oppression of one class by another. Thus, by universal suffrage and winning the battle of democracy Marx goes beyond political life to the control and advance of industrial life as well.

But inasmuch as the revolution can never be a single-step action, there must necessarily be a transitional stage between the capitalist state and the more distant classless stateless society. This transitional society is socialist society and its ruling class is the proletariat. Under the rule of the proletariat, the transitional socialist society is moved toward real communism. In a rare reference to the "dictatorship of the proletariat," Marx wrote in his *Critique of the Gotha Programme:*

> Between capitalist and communist society lies the period of the revolutionary transformation of the one into the other. Corresponding to this is also a political transition period in which the state can be nothing but *the revolutionary dictatorship of the proletariat.*[56]

To the extent that the proletariat has attained a universal, majoritarian status (and it must necessarily have moved a considerable distance in this direction in order to have the revolution be successful in the first place), the dictatorship is a means whereby the vast majority are in control of production and political life at the expense of a small and reactionary minority.[57]

How are control and decision making exercised in the dictatorship of the proletariat? Is it a dictatorship in the sense of an individual or inner clique of self-appointed leaders of the proletariat ordering in a monolithic and unilateral manner the rest of society? Very clearly Marxism is a very embodiment of antiauthoritarianism and antibureaucracy. What is it to be, then? In point of fact, Marx and Engels said little regarding the details of actual organization of proletarian rule, for they were not monolithic planners. However, a broad indication comes in their discussion of the Paris Commune. These references suggest that Marx and Engels held an exceedingly egalitarian and representative notion regarding proletarian power. For example, subsumed under the dictatorship of the proletariat are the concepts of the working class itself running the affairs of politics and industry rather than distant officials at the top of a hierarchy; universal suffrage and the right of recall of representatives; binding mandates on delegates to representative bodies; and equal wages to representatives and workers alike.[58]

These conceptions do not imply, however, the elimination of all

---

[56] *Critique of the Gotha Programme,* in *Selected Works,* vol. 3, p. 26.
[57] See Erich Fromm, ed., *Socialist Humanism* (London: Penguin Press, 1967).
[58] Engels, Introduction to Karl Marx, *The Civil War in France,* in *Selected Works,* vol. 2, pp. 188–89.

authority and total autonomy to the individual. This extreme, too, is avoided. In attacking the anarchist Bakunin's ideal society, Engels writes:

> In [Bakunin's] society there will above all be no *authority,* for authority = state = an absolute evil. (Indeed, how these people propose to run a factory, operate a railway or steer a ship without having in last resort one deciding will, without single management, they of course do not tell us.) The authority of the majority over the minority also ceases. Every individual and every community is autonomous; but as to how a society, even of only two people, is possible unless each gives up some of his autonomy, Bakunin again maintains silence.[59]

And elsewhere Engels states that "wanting to abolish authority in large-scale industry is tantamount to wanting to abolish industry itself."[60] (A comparison of anarchism and Marxist socialism may be found in Chapter 13.)

But the presence of authority is not incompatible with the elimination of bureaucracy and bureaucrats with their prerogatives, privileges, distance, tenure, and immunities. Thus, Marx could write: "Nothing could be more foreign to the spirit of the Commune than to supersede universal suffrage by hierarchic investiture."[61] Marx was decidedly antibureaucratic and scorned—even ridiculed—bureaucracy as a form of organization: "When you play the fiddle at the top of the state, what else is to be expected but that those down below dance?"[62] (Not the least among his reasons for disliking bureaucracy is that he was convinced that the greater the bureaucratization of the state the more difficult and violent would be the proletarian revolution.) In an even more explicit rejection of bureaucracy, Marx states that "freedom consists in converting the state from an organ superimposed upon society [i.e., bureaucracy] into one completely subordinate to it [i.e., dictatorship of the proletariat]."[63] In the socialist state, then, there is authority but not authoritarianism, organization but not bureaucracy.

ECONOMIC RELATIONS AND SOCIALIST TRANSITION

The final goal of socialist economy is the production of abundant use-values, justice in distribution, elimination of commodity (money-exchange) production, and the emancipation of work from rigid division of labor. In

---

[59] Engels to T. Cuno, 1872, in *Selected Works,* vol. 2, pp. 425–26.
[60] Engels, *On Authority,* in *Selected Works,* vol. 2, p. 377.
[61] *The Civil War in France,* in *Selected Works,* vol. 2, p. 221.
[62] *The Eighteenth Brumaire,* in *Selected Works,* vol. 1, p. 436.
[63] *Critique of the Gotha Programme,* in *Selected Works,* vol. 3, p. 25.

the transitional stage to real communism, the elimination of bourgeois principles of organization is accomplished in a gradual fashion—the speed of which is determined both by the rate of material advance and the rate of change in individual psychology. Abundance, distributive justice, free goods, and voluntary labor depend upon revolutionary changes in both production and cultural spheres. The production changes come easier and more rapidly than the development of socialist mentality, and, as under other modes of production, the former significantly conditions the latter. The real availability of necessary use-values, for example, erodes the fetishism of commodity exchange and forces awareness of free exchange. This, in turn, raises the possibility of free and voluntary labor, full self-development, and the end of rigid specializations.

Commodity production, then, must survive capitalism at least for a certain transitional time period. But it is not commodity production geared to the profit of individuals and separate industries, or on behalf of state officials. If surplus value is appropriated and used for any other purpose than raising all at once the well-being of the entire society, and if labor-power is valued as a commodity for individual or state exploitation, we do not have transitional socialism but capitalism or state capitalism. The socialist economy has the purpose of withering away commodity production, not perpetuating it in the interests of a new ruling class.[64] Money and surplus value (and hence necessary labor time), though still used and present, is not capital in the sense defined in Chapter 1 when employed by the proletariat in production, but socially determined use-value. It serves administrative functions only. However, the money market must continue to function in consumer distribution as long as consumer goods must be treated as commodities, i.e. until they are produced, one by one, in sufficient quantity to meet social needs. As we shall point out presently, the foregoing does not apply to certain socially necessary goods and services which should and must be provided on a universal use-value basis.

Marx and Engels were convinced that capitalist production was growing increasingly irrational, wasteful, and inefficient and that a socially planned economy would immediately begin to introduce use-values on an extensive scale: "Once liberated from the yoke of private ownership, large-scale industry will develop on a scale that will make its present level of development seem as paltry as seems the manufacturing system compared with large-scale industry of our time." [65]

Among the measures valued both for purposes of enhancement of productivity and the elimination of alienated labor is the development

---

[64] See Mandel, *The Formation of the Economic Thought of Karl Marx,* pp. 98–99.

[65] Engels, *Principles of Communism,* in *Selected Works,* vol. 1, p. 92.

of educated labor. In contradistinction to the narrowness and debilitation of labor under supposedly efficient extreme specialization of tasks, work under the socialist transition is increasingly geared toward the generalization of workers' productive abilities and understanding.[66] Greater flexibility and a broader knowledge of the production process are required not only because of the advancing state of technology, but also on account of workers' control requiring that workers possess a grasp of the system wider than a single, narrow facet. The fragment of a man that performs repetitive motions for a lifetime cannot be expected to exercise generalized intelligence required under workers' control. The reduction of the division of labor and the increased popular participation in decision making are both necessary components in the achievement of the classless society.

In agriculture as in industry collective control and production of scale are the goals. The peasant, like the small handicraftsman, cannot survive on the principle of individual operation in large-scale capitalist production, and the latter is, of course, incompatible with a rationally planned agricultural economy. Agriculture is the original source of all wealth, and the soil is a use-value that belongs to society at large. To Marx, the importance of agriculture requires that it not be left to a few individuals "to regulate . . . according to their whims and private interests." Furthermore, "the scientific knowledge we possess, and the technical means of agriculture we command, such as machinery, etc., can never be successfully applied by cultivating the land on a large scale." [67] And while cooperatives are essential to *persuade* the peasant out of small-plot, individual production (Marx and Engels opposed forced collectivization as being politically and economically unfeasible), in the end "to give up the soil to the hands of associated rural labourers, would be to surrender society to one exclusive class of producers." [68] However, cooperatives are valuable in the transitional phase, for (in industry) "By deed, instead of by argument, they have shown that production on a large scale, and in accord with the behest of modern science, may be carried on without existence of a class of masters employing a class of hands." [69]

Other economic steps to be taken during the transitional stage include: progressive income taxes, high inheritance taxes, and abolition of inheritance outside direct generational lines; gradual expropriation of agricultural and industrial property through state competition and compensation; high wages paid to state workers and organization of labor to

---

[66] Ibid., p. 93.

[67] Marx, *The Nationalisation of the Land*, in *Selected Works*, vol. 2, pp. 288–89.

[68] Ibid., p. 290.

[69] Cited in Shlomo Avineri, *The Social and Political Thought of Karl Marx* (Cambridge: Cambridge University Press, 1970); see especially pp. 174–84.

achieve the same in remaining private industries; equal liability to work for all members of society; centralization of credit and banking systems by the state; the physical development of rural areas; demolition of all unsanitary and badly built houses and flats; and centralization of communication and transport.[70]

We have from Marx some statements concerning changes in *distribution* of wealth in addition to the foregoing which deal primarily with production. There is no doubt concerning Marx's intentions of major changes in both distribution and the criteria governing it: "An altered means of distribution will derive from a new, altered basis of production emerging from the historical process." [71] Before examining the individual bases of distribution, there are first the necessary expenditures which must be deducted from the total social product, and these are as follows: replacement of the means of production and for the expansion of production (including labor); reserve or insurance funds to provide against accidents and natural calamities, etc.; consumption for the costs of administration aside from production (considerably *restricted* in comparison to present-day society and constantly diminishing as the new society develops); the common satisfaction of needs such as schools, health services, etc. (considerably *enlarged* in comparison to existing society and progressively expanded); and for funds for those unable to work, etc.[72] Altogether, this obviously suggests a much expanded social-sector use of the economic surplus.

Now we come to the nature and criteria of individual distribution. We might first note that the reduction in the division of labor is in itself a powerful step in the direction of a classless and egalitarian economic distribution. But as in other spheres in the socialist transition, distribution of individual reward also bears marks of the old order. In the case of economic reward, the contribution through value-creating and value-sustaining labor remains as the decisive criterion. Marx discusses the issue in his *Critique of the Gotha Programme:*

> What we have to deal with here is a communist society, not as it has *developed* on its own foundations, but, on the contrary, just as it *emerges* from capitalist society; which is thus in every respect, economically, morally and intellectually, still stamped with the birth marks of the old society from whose womb it emerges. *Equal* right here is still in principle—*bourgeois right*. The right of the producers is *proportional* to the labour they supply; the equality consists in the fact that measurement is made with an *equal standard*, labour.[73]

---

[70] Engels, *Principles of Communism*, in *Selected Works*, vol. 1, p. 90.
[71] *Grundrisse*, p. 152.
[72] *Critique of the Gotha Programme*, in *Selected Works*, vol. 3, pp. 16–17.
[73] Ibid., pp. 17–18.

Unequal labor contributions thus render economic inequality, but the inequality differs from capitalist society inasmuch as it stems from productive labor rather than differential access to the appropriation of surplus value, usually founded upon property ownership. Moreover, even given equal labor contributions (and, of course, equal access to the social consumption fund as noted above), inequality would still be present, since "one worker is married, another not; one has more children than another, and so on and so forth." In brief, in this first phase of development, labor continues to be the major measure of value and of reward; but labor cannot be exploited through private appropriation of surplus value, the utilization of which is social and socially decided.

Marx did not uphold inequality as a social value or as a universal necessity. Rather: "Right can never be higher than the economic structure of society and its cultural development conditioned thereby." Only after men have been freed from enslavement by the division of labor and work becomes an enjoyment in itself, and after the productive forces have been advanced to the creation of abundance, "only then can the narrow horizon of bourgeois right be crossed in its entirety and society inscribe on its banners: From each according to his ability, to each according to his needs!" [74] And given the extent of abundance suggested here, not labor but automated machinery is the main source of value, or at least a very high degree of socially interdependent labor, rendering labor as a measure of value and reward obsolete (see Chapter 2). Disposable time replaces necessary labor as the yardstick of wealth, and the individually creative use of time rather than the consumption of commodities becomes the measure of the individual qua individual. In the process, the economic foundation of the social status system is smashed. Thus, the inequality of developed socialist society is the inequality of individuality.

Real communism as envisaged by Marx is clearly a utopia. It is a society which administers itself without a bureaucratic state, an industrial apparatus that produces without hierarchical authority and dehumanizing division of labor, an economy with voluntary and free labor, a social structure without social classes and rural-urban differences, a culture with pure

---

[74] Ibid., p. 19. There are other passages, however, which suggest that Marx would seek to achieve extensive equality before the realization of some distant real communist society. For example: "But one of the most vital principles of communism, a principle which distinguishes it from all reactionary socialism, is its empiric view, based on a knowledge of men, that differences of brain, of intellectual capacity, do not imply any difference whatsoever in the nature of the stomach and of physical needs; therefore the false tenet, based upon existing circumstance, 'to each according to his capacity,' must be changed, in so far as it relates to enjoyment in its narrower sense, into the tenet, 'to each according to his need'; in other words, a different form of activity, of labour, confers no privileges in respect of possession and enjoyment." *Essential Writings of Karl Marx*, p. 231. (From *The German Ideology*.)

ideas and without ideology, and a psychology that knows no alienation. "Like all other social formations, it should be conceived in a state of constant flux and change" [75]; but it is the last historical epoch. It is not the goal itself of human development, but a necessary condition and form to the realization of that end.[76] Thus, communism is really only the beginning of the development of full human self-realization. In reading this conclusion we have traveled far beyond the realm of social science to moral philosophy, the final and necessary end of any social science worthy of the name.

POSTSCRIPT: MARX AND THE THIRD WORLD

Marxist theory as written by Marx is intended to illuminate the events of an advanced capitalist society. This should be evident at every point, not the least of which holds that the progressive potential of capital must be exhausted and that the bourgeoisie must have structured a system of power to enhance their interests. Now, in Marx's day the Third World—the underdeveloped regions of Africa, Asia, and Latin America—was little more than a large plantation and mine for cheap raw materials and foods to funnel into the advanced capitalist economies. Even today the industrial core of most Third World countries is minimal and native industrial bourgeoisie equally scarce. What industrial capitalism and bourgeois power is present is typically derived from, owned by, or dependent upon a metropolitan nation. There is a subimperialism or exploitation by the national ruling classes of the masses, but again, this relation is not typically one of capital and labor in the industrial sense. Rather, national exploitation tends to be agricultural, commercial, fiscal, and domestic. The primary form of exploitation in the Third World is international, i.e., imperialistic. And only relatively recently has the exploitation of the Third World shifted significantly, proportionately speaking, from plantation and mine to factory. Mining has, in fact, been the locus of considerable agitation and militancy within the Latin American industrial labor force, and urban factory workers may develop politically along lines of the working class under the rule of capital. Although the Third World has not yet provided a society structurally adapted in full to the Marxist theory of revolution, there have been significant Third World revolutionary developments with theoretical foundations in Marxist socialism—as in China, Vietnam, and Cuba.

[75] Engels to Otto von Beonigk, in *Selected Works,* vol. 3, p. 485.
[76] *Karl Marx: Early Writings,* translated and edited by T. B. Bottomore (New York: McGraw-Hill, 1964), p. 167.

Although Marx never dealt with colonialism per se, he held that bourgeois power could not be secured without expansion and control in the world market. Capitalism is a world system: "National bounds are inadequate for its development." [77] He thus broached the question of imperialism and alluded to the fact that imperial power signals the rule and strength of the bourgeoisie—or the final stage of capitalism, as Lenin later put it. Marx also made reference to certain links between the industrial class system and that of less developed societies. For example, he presages Lenin's labor aristocracy thesis in discussing the English working class: "In relation to the Irish worker [the English worker] feels himself a member of the *ruling* nation and so turns himself into a tool of the aristocrats and capitalists of his country *against Ireland,* thus strengthening their domination *over* himself." [78] He also observed the debilitating impact of European technology on labor-intensive Third World economies: "Thus, it has come about that a machine invented in England today, within a year robs millions of workers in China of their daily bread. They bought the cheaper commodities of the English and allowed their own manufactory workers to perish." [79] (Something of the reverse is happening today.)

Finally, Marx directed attention to the contentious and militaristic foreign policy that must develop under the rule of expanding bourgeois economic needs, and its corollary of splitting the international working class and exhausting the national working class both financially and physically: "If the emancipation of the working classes requires their fraternal concurrence, how are they to fulfil that great mission with a foreign policy in pursuit of criminal designs, playing upon national prejudices, and squandering in piratical wars the people's blood and treasure?" [80] While Marx is in all likelihood referring here to intercapitalist strife—and there was plenty of disaster to follow in this area—we may easily extrapolate the same thesis to wars of national liberation such as those fought in China, Indochina, Algeria, and South Africa.

Marx both anticipated and welcomed change in the Third World. That he welcomed it is evident in his references to India: "We must not forget that these idyllic village communities, inoffensive though they may appear, had always been the solid foundation of Oriental despotism, that they restrained the human mind within the smallest possible compass, making it the unresisting tool of superstition, enslaving it beneath traditional rules, depriving it of all grandeur and historical energies. We must not for-

---

[77] *The Class Struggles in France, 1848–1850,* in *Selected Works,* vol. 1, p. 213.
[78] Marx to S. Meyer and A. Vogt, 1870, in *Essential Writings of Karl Marx,* p. 198.
[79] Engels, *Principles of Communism,* in *Selected Works,* vol. 1, p. 85.
[80] Marx, "Inaugural Address of the Working Men's International Association," in *Selected Works,* vol. 2, p. 18.

get that these little communities were contaminated by distinctions of caste and by slavery." [81] And that he anticipated change is suggested when he subsequently says: "The question is, can mankind fulfil its destiny without a fundamental revolution in the social state of Asia?" [82] Marx anticipates that the instability in these raw-material-supplying economies will be more violent than in the advanced economies once the capitalist mode of production is introduced. [83]

Did Marx feel that it was possible for the agrarian societies to make the leap over the capitalist stage of production directly into socialism? Can peasants with a proletarian ideology make a socialist revolution? The weight of Marx's entire theory says no. Revolutions yes, socialist revolution no, for the socialist revolution requires an advanced industrial base and an industrialized proletariat to take charge of creating the new order. However, with respect to agricultural forms that were communally organized, as in certain cases in nineteenth-century Russia, Marx and Engels wrote that they could serve as a *starting point* for communist development *if* the higher form of communism was already in existence in another country to serve as a model. [84] However, this says nothing concerning industrial production and organization. We must conclude that socialism in the orthodox Marxist sense must be built upon the social wreckage and industrial might of capitalism, and even only then on an international foundation. Marxist revolutionaries such as Lenin, Mao, and Castro have had to variously modify this aspect of Marxist thought and pursue a noncapitalist industrial base directly from a predominantly agrarian society, though all three had a degree of industrial capitalism (largely foreign-owned) in their countries and for a short time allowed some native capitalist activity.

---

[81] *The British Rule in India,* in *Selected Works,* vol. 1, p. 492.

[82] Ibid., p. 493.

[83] *Capital,* vol. 3, p. 140.

[84] Engels to N. F. Danielson, in *Selected Works,* vol. 3, p. 50; and Preface to the Russian edition of 1882 of *Manifesto of the Communist Party,* in *Selected Works,* vol. 1, pp. 100–101.

four ———————————————————————

INEQUALITY
AND
EGALITARIANISM

The study of social class must be based on an analysis of social inequality. For without social inequality in the Marxist sense there would be no social classes: social classes consist precisely of groups of persons occupying common positions of inequality. Although sociologists generally agree that without social inequality there can be no social classes, it is also generally held that social inequality may exist without there being social classes.[1] That is to say, a society may evince a range of stratified individuals on a ranked scale from high to low without in any way comprising a social class system. The validity of the latter assertion depends, of course, on how a social class is defined. If we take a Marxist definitional approach, as we do in this book, the study of social inequality in modern societies is by definition the study of social classes as well; inequality in capitalist society is always *class* inequality and inequality always finds expression in the existence of social classes. A preindustrial tribal society may consist solely of separately ranked individuals or family units, but a capitalist social order is always class-stratified.

That a capitalist society is always class-stratified does not necessarily imply the classes are social and political entities or realities, i.e., that they are classes-for-themselves. Quite the contrary, the ruling ideologies of the

---

[1] See, for example, Dennis H. Wrong, "Social Inequality Without Social Stratification," in Gerald W. Thielbar and Saul D. Feldman, eds., *Issues in Social Inequality* (Boston: Little, Brown and Company, 1972), pp. 91–104.

period may deny the existence of classes and assert that conflict and change involve only individuals or at least nonclass groupings. Or if the ruling ideology acknowledges the existence of classes, the class system is held to be primarily a cultural and social status system virtually devoid of real economic clashes of interest.[2] In keeping with the dictates of the ruling ideas of the period, social scientists tend to fulfill their superstructural status; for example, in an essay appropriately entitled "The Decline and Fall of Social Class," Robert A. Nisbet writes:

> The term social class is by now useful in historical sociology, in comparative or folk sociology, but . . . it is nearly valueless for the clarification of the data of wealth, power, and social status in contemporary United States and much of Western society in general. . . . So far as the bulk of Western society is concerned, and especially the United States, the concept of class is largely obsolete.[3]

Either way, whether they define class in primarily cultural and social terms or discount the idea of class divisions entirely, such approaches are similar in diverting attention away from the ineradicable difference of interests of groups of people occupying contrasting positions in the system of production and distribution, away from the Marxist insight into the nature of the dynamics of capitalist society.

But to divert attention away from an underlying social reality is not the same thing as eliminating that reality. The current social upheavals in the Western world attest to the dynamics of class under capitalism. Fundamentally, we are witnessing, not a random struggle among millions of individuals for higher positions on some continuum of incrementally ranked statuses, but the formation of social classes and class struggle. A fundamentally class-stratified society is slowly and painfully becoming increasingly aware of insurmountable class differences of interests, transforming its class structure from one in-itself to one for-itself. While social scientists go on writing and talking about the statistical validity of sophisticated measures of social status and the individual bases of inequality, the reality of the class nature of social inequality under capitalism is working itself out in daily practice and historical events.

The presence of class conflict, formation, and struggle does not signify the end of the ruling ideas of economic classlessness or individual economic conflict. Though it is an increasingly difficult appearance to sustain, the notion of the classless, individualized struggle persists. As Marx observed, ancient ideas weigh down like a nightmare on the brains of the living.

---

[2] See W. Lloyd Warner et al., *Yankee City* (New Haven: Yale University Press, 1963).

[3] In Edward O. Laumann et al., eds., *The Logic of Social Hierarchies* (Chicago: Markham Publishing Company, 1970), pp. 570, 574.

THE NATURE OF INEQUALITY

For the duration of this chapter our focus shall be on inequality rather than social class as such, a topic we deal with specifically in the following chapter. Even though the discussion of inequality must necessarily treat the individual, the individual so treated is considered to be primarily and fundamentally linked to a social class. The class linkage is very strong in some cases and very weak in others, and displays many degrees of strength in between.

The kind of inequality of critical concern in the present study of social class is first and foremost an inequality of economic power, an inequality of command over the means of production and the goods and services rendered thereby. Thus, inequality is far from limited to differential access to material consumption, though inequality of material condition is a prime ingredient of the class-stratified society and the one we shall focus upon in this chapter. Inequality also includes differential position in the *production* process, both in terms of the nature of the work performed and in relations to the instruments of production. Although we may have the case of equality in material consumption and inequality in the production process, such modified egalitarian paternalism and division of labor is not only uncommon from an individual standpoint but impossible under a system of capitalist class relations. The class with power over the production process is the same class that appropriates a massively disproportionate share of the social product; if the producing class appropriated the bulk of surplus value for social purposes, a capitalist system would no longer exist. In brief, a significant and consistent relationship exists between the two basic aspects of economic inequality, the inequalities of consumption and production.

Looking at the problem in another way, we might say that inequality is not a simple phenomenon, but rather encompasses subinequalities of a diverse nature. Purchasing power, possessions, property relationships, control over production, work requirements, work security, and alienation all go into the making of inequality of economic power. These various components of inequality are closely articulated with one another and together give rise to social class divisions. These class traits tend to cluster in one direction or another so that the propertied enjoy the positive manifestations of them and the propertyless the negative manifestations. But close articulation does not mean 100 percent correlation and the existence of sharply and clearly delineated social classes. Rather, close articulation gives rise to class cores, in between which is found a blurring and overlapping of social strata, making them more or less purely capitalist or proletarian in character. The major trend is toward a more clearly perceptible class structure, both objectively and subjectively speaking.

In addition to the composite variable of economic inequality, two further dimensions of inequality deserve mention, neither one of which is sufficiently independent of economic power to exert a clearly autonomous influence on the class system. First, there is social prestige or honor, sometimes referred to simply as social status. Social status finds its abiding source and support within the field of economic power. Periodically and circumstantially prestige is capable of asserting itself in its own right, but in capitalist society it cannot long stand by itself. Secondly, there is political power. Again we have what Marxist theory observes to be a dependent and derived phenomenon, dependent upon command of the means of production and derived from possession of propertied wealth. Under given circumstances political power may rise upon noneconomic forces; but without an economic foundation in the wealth of society no political power or party can long survive. Indeed, political power is in practice scarcely distinguishable from economic power, for politics and the state embody the class struggle and the class struggle is firmly constructed upon the material mode of production. In effect, economic and political power can be separated only for analytic purposes, for in practice the two are fused. Following Max Weber, American sociology has pursued the logic of independence between economic class, social status, and political power, but it has yet to produce through such an approach any meaningful clarification of the important and decisive events of capitalist society.[4]

So by inequality we mean inequality of economic power and all of its corollaries in the status and (especially) political spheres. In speaking of inequality we do not mean to focus attention on differences in personality development and personal character. We assume that such personalized, individualized manifestations of inequality have been restricted and truncated by the pecuniary values generated in capitalism as a way of life. Full self-realization and liberation could only mean *greater* individual differences or inequality in the personality sense.

Nor by inequality are we going to be referring solely to inequality of opportunity to better oneself individually. Inequality of economic power subsumes inequality of opportunity, and as long as economic inequality exists equality of opportunity cannot have any base in reality. Inequality of economic condition may be partially offset within the capitalist system by creating programs for greater equality of opportunity, but such programs cannot be carried very far within the limits of a system of private control

---

[4] Max Weber, "Class, Status, and Party," in Hans Gerth and C. Wright Mills, eds., *From Max Weber: Essays in Sociology* (New York: Oxford University Press, 1958).

and appropriation. Hence it should not be at all surprising that all of the rhetoric about equality of opportunity has issued into little substantive change. Inequality of opportunity persists from generation to generation in a consistent fashion. At best an individual may see himself or his children add a few more questionably useful possessions to the family hoard, and perhaps achieve real material gain; but these changes are likely to be of a very ephemeral and mechanical nature, adding little to opportunities for economic, political, social, and psychological security and development.

We thus come back to economic inequality as an irreducible and fundamental determinating factor of capitalist society. As we endeavored theoretically to document in our discussion of Marx, economic inequality is the critical support system of the capitalist mode of production. There can be no reconciliation, within such a system, of opposing interests in consumption or production; such conflict can only be redefined, reclassified, reinterpreted, and finally obfuscated through ideological deception and diversion. Bourgeois ideology may attempt to come to terms with inequality in a variety of ways—by justifying it, rationalizing it, or even promising change. Within social science the most predominant mode of dealing with inequality is simply to assert that it is *universally necessary* for *any* society to function effectively or even to survive. By giving inequality a universal and necessary status such social science exonerates all social and economic systems, not the least of which is capitalism, from any *responsibility* for inequality. If all social systems must have inequality to survive, the argument goes, so must our own capitalist system, and anyone who thinks otherwise must be against the survival of mankind. Actually, anyone who thinks social inequality unnecessary and destructive may only be opposed to the survival of the ruling class and his own powerlessness.

Before turning to a closer examination of the bourgeois rationalizations of inequality, a brief comment is in order regarding the importance of the psychological aspects of inequality. In evaluating the psychological role in inequality one may find it helpful to return to Marx's theses of absolute versus relative immiseration. In terms of consumption or material condition, inequality may be viewed absolutely or relatively. Persons or groups may be absolutely unequal—i.e., absolutely impoverished—or they may be unequal and impoverished only relative to others. Relative inequality has, of course, a psychological as well as a material base, and either aspect may be stressed. While we wouldn't deny the presence of an important psychological component to inequality, which Marx acknowledged, it would be gross hyperbole to assert as two contemporary students of stratification have done, that "the differential distribution of positive feelings about oneself is perhaps the essence of inequality." [5] Such a judgment

---

[5] S. M. Miller and Pamela Roby, *The Future of Inequality* (New York: Basic Books, 1970), p. 172.

renders both the material and the production aspects of inequality to the status of secondary phenomena. It turns the Marxist model of inequality on end, in the true tradition of American psychologically-oriented, subjective social analysis.

___

IS INEQUALITY NECESSARY?

The best-known sociological rationalization of inequality has been set forth by Kingsley Davis and Wilbert E. Moore. Their argument is couched in the language of "functionalism," meaning that, in the case of stratification, inequality serves a necessary purpose in the life survival of a society. Inequality preserves the degree of equilibrium required for the maintenance of the social system; without inequality the social organism would fall into disequilibrium and the effective functioning of the system would be endangered. Nonfunctionalists, too, may adhere to the necessity of inequality and, in effect, for the same reasons as those set forth by Davis and Moore. What is the logic of the functionalist rationalization?

Although the functionalist argument is similar to the kind the average person might present in defense of social inequality, Davis and Moore have stated the argument in more sophisticated and precise form.[6] It runs something like this: Every society must distribute its members into the various jobs within the division of labor and induce them to perform their work competently. If all positions were equally important and required equal skill, it would then make little difference as to which individuals performed which jobs; but such is not the case. Thus, a society must offer rewards, as incentives to acquire the skill level needed to perform important jobs. The greater the skill requirements and importance of the job, the greater must be the rewards "built into" that position. In the words of Davis and Moore: "Social inequality is thus an unconsciously evolved device by which societies insure that the most important positions are conscientiously filled by the more qualified persons." Although rewards of prestige and leisure are also cited, the argument clearly hinges on rewards of a material nature.

Economist Adolph A. Berle, Jr. argues for the necessity of inequality in similar terms when he writes that "the system is not equalitarian . . . nor probably, should it be. Superior character, high ability, greater capacity to render those services which society needs not only can but should be rewarded more highly." [7] Berle argues that those with scarce talents and

___

[6] For functionalist statements on inequality and a critical appraisal, see the collection in Reinhard Bendix and Seymour Martin Lipset, eds., *Class, Status, and Power* (New York: Free Press, 1966), pp. 47–72.

[7] *Power Without Property* (New York: Harcourt, Brace and World, 1959), p. 145.

those performing functionally important services not only can but *should* be unequally rewarded, thus adding to his plea for privilege an explicit *moral* imperative, something which the functionalists at least leave implicit. Even the much more liberal economist Robert Heilbroner is able to discern no other alternative to making a society run than by unequal rewards distributed through the market mechanism in which scarce and important commodities receive higher rewards.[8]

More recently, the psychologists have gotten into the "necessity of inequality" act, expectedly enough using the highly questionable criterion of IQ. (Whether it is to the credit or discredit of sociologists that they formalized a bourgeois theory of inequality a quarter of a century before the psychologists did is a moot point, but quite clearly sociologists should be applauded for not overtly basing their rationale on such a fetish as the IQ test.) Carrying the brunt of the load for psychology has been Richard Herrnstein and Arthur Jensen. The Herrnstein thesis is similar to the Davis-Moore scheme in asserting that unequal material rewards are required to place talented and skillful people in society's important positions so that the system will function effectively. Herrnstein adds the psychologist's touch by contending that intelligent people (empirically speaking, those with higher IQs) rise to the top of the system and then transmit their mental abilities to their children, who intermarry and begin forming an intergenerational meritocratic elite. The case is sealed with evidence such as that of accountants having significantly higher IQs than truckdrivers or lumberjacks. The racial factor is stressed in the work of Jensen, who resurrects the dead horse of genetic bases of racial stratification.

There are so many flaws in the rationalization of inequality that it is difficult to know where to begin a critique. A few of the more glaring inconsistencies might be mentioned. First, in view of the inestimable amount of blundering and ineptitude in highly remunerated positions, it is painfully obvious that the most important positions are, in fact, not always filled by the more qualified persons. (The semihumorous Peter Principle, asserting that people are promoted to the highest level of their *in*competence, seems to hold about as much validity as the functionalist principle.) In fact, to *fulfill* the imputations of the functionalist "most important–most qualified" dictum requires upsetting the foundations of the entire stratification system itself, i.e., the social, political, and economic transmission of power and privilege from one generation to the next. T. B. Bottomore points out, in opposition to the functionalists, that "it would be a more accurate description of the social class system to say that it operates, largely through the inheritance of property, to ensure that each individual maintains a cer-

---

[8] *Between Capitalism and Socialism* (New York: Random House, 1970), pp. 94–102.

tain social position, determined by his birth and irrespective of his particular abilities." [9] Note the phrase "irrespective of his particular abilities"— meaning that the transmission of inequality has little if anything directly to do with intelligence, let alone such a bourgeois contraption as IQ scores. Since when does one have to score high on an IQ test to inherit the family's social privilege, wealth, and power? But class and hence educational privilege does in itself contribute in a large way to IQ differentials within the population. IQ then "justifies" the original class inequality.

Secondly, assuming that somehow *despite* the stratification system the "most qualified" persons entered the "most important" positions, we must ask: What are the objective criteria that are used to evaluate importance? Is the $20,000-a-year accountant working on corporate tax deductions more important than the $8,000-a-year lumberjack? Are the twenty-one people on the American Revolution Bicentennial Commission staff who receive more than $30,000 a year more important than the $10,000-a-year truckdriver? The Marxist theory of value would say that precisely the reverse is true. In the general field of occupations, the picture of importance becomes genuinely confusing; self-justifying evaluations predominate. As Frank Parkin has pointed out: "To suggest, for example, that managers are more highly rewarded than factory workers because they make a greater contribution to the productive system is to offer more of a value judgment than an explanation." [10]

Thirdly, even further assuming that somehow a hierarchy of importance could be objectively established, where is the hard evidence confirming the assertion that unequal rewards must be built into the more important positions in order to get them filled? Nor are we given any guidelines as to *how* unequal the rewards must be in order for society to remain healthy. Must there be billionaires and paupers? Idle rentiers and poverty-line workers? Or only six-figure vs. four-figure income spreads? Or something even less unequal? Put another way, how much of a reward is necessary for society to bribe its members into becoming high-ranking administrators and executives, physicians, scientists and professors, generals and admirals, large stock- and bondholders, presidents, consultants, corporate lawyers, university deans, movie stars, and so on? (Why assume we need such career specialists in the first place?) At what level of material reward would such positions go wanting for lack of able candidates? And for

---

[9] *Classes in Modern Society* (New York: Vintage Books, 1968), p. 11. As Frank Parkin has remarked: "Given the cultural, educational, and environmental cosseting which children of the upper or professional middle class generally receive, we should expect even the dullest of them to acquire a sufficient gloss of learning, as well as all-important social skill, to fit them for some kind of respectable white-collar job, however routine and humble." *Class Inequality and Political Order* (New York: Praeger Publishers, 1971), p. 58.

[10] *Class Inequality and Political Order*, p. 19.

positions of relative "insignificance," what is the size of the shrunken pittance society dangles before the eyes of the unqualified? Subsistence wages? Welfare? Nothing? Where do the millions of unemployed fit into this scheme? Dependent mothers and children? The incapacitated? The elderly? Quite clearly, these types don't "fit" anyplace; most are, in fact, counted out.

Here we see the real reason why the laboring mass of people do, in fact, work in a wage-oriented society, and it has very little to do with built-in rewards: they work because they *have* to work to survive. The higher-paid strata tend also to have to work, but the incentive that brought them into their careers is hardly a solid cash deal; as Chomsky surmises: "I doubt very much that Herrnstein would become a baker or lumberjack if he could earn more money that way." [11] Among the rewards of high-paying positions are very strong intrinsic satisfaction or psychological incentives, whereas low-paying jobs tend to be the dullest and most psychologically alienating.

No one could at present realistically expect that in a large, impersonal industrial society people would acquire certain skills and work in certain positions solely as an altruistic expression for the well-being of society. Yet social altruism in conjunction with the self-satisfaction that comes with knowing one's labor has been done effectively and makes a contribution to the social group one identifies with and belongs to cannot be overestimated as a source of motivation and incentive. For example, China has gone a long way toward developing this potential. That nonmaterial rewards and incentives play an extremely important role in occupational placement is evident from the fact that the majority of people choose an occupation on grounds other than what they ultimately expect to earn or gain from it materially. Even within a given job category, performance to a large extent does not depend on the materialistic carrot-and-stick principle. If the functionalist argument for inequality were valid, the kibbutzim of Israel could not survive on their voluntary labor principle and egalitarian reward system, let alone *prosper* economically as they have. To be sure, the question is how long our own society can survive *with* the reward-and-inequality system we now have. We are witnessing severe "disequilibrium" *because* of inequality.

Finally, there are difficulties with the notion that whoever acquires skills and talents required to perform a job must be unequally compensated. To the extent that a person spends money or loses pay in the process of training for a career or job, nothing in the ideology of egalitarianism would invalidate subsequent compensatory rewards. But in the case of

---

11 Noam Chomsky, "The Fallacy of Richard Herrnstein's IQ," *Social Policy,* May–June 1972, p. 20.

contemporary inequality in the United States, the compensatory rewards for those with training is frequently far in excess of the costs to the individual. Take, for example, the physician whose education has been financed mostly by taxpayers and only a small proportion of the total overhead by himself or his family. Relatively speaking, his own costs have been slight. Adding these personal costs to the earnings forfeited by continuing on in school rather than entering the job market early, we could hypothetically enter a generous figure of compensation at $100,000. (A manual laborer might question the fairness of granting $10,000 a year for eight years of higher education as he sweats in a mentally and physically crippling job for an average wage less than that, and counting $20,000 of personal expense when parents may have picked up that tab.) At the average physician's $45,000 (reported) annual earnings it would be only a matter of a very few years before the overall costs of skill acquisition and training (most of which is actually gained *after* formal schooling and while on salary or earnings) are compensated for. Yet the physician's earnings continue to increase significantly, while the worker's paycheck is losing ground to inflation. Most inequality has a relatively small basis in compensatory rewards for previously incurred personal costs.

But within *market-contested* occupational earnings, there is no question that scarcity of supply decisively influences their amounts. Thus, in the case of physicians, the fewer there are relative to the number of prospective patients the higher will be their material reward. The ability to market a scarce and inelastically demanded skill or service is unquestionably the most decisive factor in determining competitive occupational reward.[12] The flaw or omission in the necessary-inequality argument is the fact that in any population or society there is an abundance of human potential which if socially tapped would be more than sufficient to eliminate the inequality-creating scarcity in most occupational fields. For example, physicians are not in possession of some rare and difficult talent that is socially available in such small quantities that the country has a severe shortage of doctors. It is simply that the mechanical process of becoming a doctor of medicine is so restrictive that even gaining entrance to a college of medicine is virtually impossible except for a privileged few. When the publicly controlled engineering and scientific professions were opened widely for all capable students in the late fifties and throughout the sixties, who have now glutted *market-supported* jobs (but certainly not finished all the work society *needs* to be done), the privately controlled medical profession was "expanding" medical school enrollments by a few openings per entire college. By contrast, the state controlled medical system in Sweden has been producing doctors and dentists at a much

---

[12] *Class Inequality and Political Order,* p. 21.

more accelerated rate, so much so in the case of the latter that an employment problem has made an appearance. As a result the Swedish taxpayers see their medical professionals paid less than American medics, while at the same time receiving more extensive medical benefits.

Robert Theobald has succinctly stated the problem of scarcity as a source of inequality: "In effect, . . . it is precisely those groups who are most successful in restricting supply which are entitled to the largest quantity of resources. . . . It is those who are willing and able to preserve scarcity who will increase their claims on available abundance." [13] Or from C. Wright Mills: "Like other privileged groups, the professional entrepreneurs and the entrepreneurial professionals seek to monopolize their positions by closing up their ranks; they seek to do so by law and by stringent rules of education and entrance." [14] The credential system serves as an important weapon against abundance and for the artificial preservation of scarcity and inequality. Scarcity lies at the foundation of the market-oriented capitalist system, and capitalists everywhere will have as their chief goal the preservation of the excess of human demand over supply, even at a time when the resources of society are great and potententially great enough to rid us of the humiliation and degradation of the twin forces of exploitation and want.

But the most profound and massive inequalities of reward are not even found in the occupational market of supply and demand, artificially designed or otherwise. The gigantic and society-rupturing inequalities stem from the private ownership of the means of production, from absentee ownership, which is not an occupation at all but a *mechanism* of exploitation. Inequality stemming from excess compensatory earnings or artificial scarcity of skills pales in comparison to the massive inequities of reward arising from absentee ownership. It is in the category of unearned income rather than earned, however inequitably earned it might be, that the real critical gap is opened up. We shall statistically document this later on in the chapter. Suffice it to note here that it is less serious that a small class of large property owners are in *possession* of so much wealth than it is that their wealth gives them the power to control the *production* side of inequality. The inequality of power in the production process is ultimately more important than inequality of material condition. And it is this power over production and rewards which gives the capitalist class the ability to dangle material rewards before the masses, sucking into their orbit those who can best render service, not to society, but to their own class. It is not intelligence which accumulates material rewards. Rather as Chomsky points out: "Wealth and power tend to accrue to those who are ruthless,

---

[13] *Free Men and Free Markets* (New York: Doubleday, 1965), pp. 62–63.
[14] *White Collar* (New York: Oxford University Press, 1951), p. 140.

cunning, avaricious, self-seeking, lacking in sympathy and compassion, subservient to authority, willing to abandon principle for material gain.[15] Creative intelligence applied in a socially innovative and critical fashion tends not to be rewarded but rejected and repressed (not that creative intelligence ought to be more highly rewarded materially or requires material reward to be exercised). And as Aronowitz suggests, the IQ test is little more than a selective device for maintaining mechanical bureaucratic discipline and a rationalization for the division of labor.[16] Even taking the IQ test uncritically for what it is, Deutsch and Edsall have drawn our attention to the fact that, in the case of alleged racial differences, the average difference between white and black children is less than that which is attributable to social (read class) environment according to Herrnstein's own argument.[17] Class equality would erase interracial IQ differences.

Even certain critics of the capitalist system contend, to quote Weisskopf's view, that "a high degree of income equality could be attained in a capitalist society only at a very high cost in productive efficiency." [18] Weisskopf assumes with the functionalists and IQ psychologists that persons making the greater contributions to production, or occupying the more important positions, receive commensurately greater material reward. (All of the inequality theorists are correct in asserting that under bourgeois or capitalist economic principles material rewards leading to personal consumption weigh heavily in the incentive system, though it may also be argued—as above—that even under capitalism few so-called important positions would go wanting for incumbents given only the median income.) As suggested above, there is no clear relationship between productive labor power and material reward, indeed, as far as the main capitalist class and working class is concerned, Marxist theory tells us explicitly that under capitalism an inverse relationship exists between material wealth and material contribution. Capitalism itself could no doubt function *more* efficiently with *more* equality. Of course, if labor power was rewarded according to what it produced as under the Marxist concept of socialist transition, or if inequality of wealth were largely abolished as under the Marxist concept of pure communism, capitalism would cease to be capitalism and would by definition be "inefficient" unto itself. The

---

15 Chomsky, "The Fallacy of Richard Herrnstein's IQ," p. 21.

16 Stanley Aronowitz, "The Trap of Environmentalism," *Social Policy,* September–October 1972, pp. 34–38.

17 Karl W. Deutsch and Thomas Edsall, "The Meritocracy Scare," *Society,* October 1972, pp. 71–79.

18 Thomas E. Weisskopf, "Capitalism and Equality," in Richard C. Edwards, Michael Reich, and Thomas E. Weisskopf, eds., *The Capitalist System* (Englewood Cliffs, N.J.: Prentice-Hall, 1972), p. 128.

capitalist class requires general inequality, insecurity, and scarcity for the working class, for if abundance and security pushed the value of wage labor under that of leisure and free time, the capitalist class would lose control over the working class and could not pursue its ends of power, profit, and growth.

From functionalism down to the present, apologists of inequality such as Herrnstein, Jensen, Nathan Glazer, Daniel P. Moynihan, Edward Banfield, Daniel Bell, and others have repeated the same monotonous theme: those who have plenty deserve to have plenty for they are superior human beings indispensable to the well-being of society, while those who have less or little deserve to have less or little for they are inferior human beings dispensable or even dangerous to the well-being of society. If social science makes any future progress at all, these modern-day bourgeois ethnocentrists will look as silly as the social evolutionists of the nineteenth century sitting in their London and Paris drawing rooms pontificating on the superiority of English and French civilization. S. M. Miller and Ronnie Steinberg perceive reality differently:

> The disturbing truth is that we live in a *pseudomeritocracy,* whose ideology is that "success" springs solely from merit but whose reality is that some with ability get substantial rewards, while many with equal ability are left in the dust, and others with less ability may on numerous occasions attain even higher rewards.[19]

A final word regarding reward is required in response to the contemporary conservative position (eighteenth-century liberalism) as espoused by economist Milton Friedman, erstwhile advisor to Eisenhower and Goldwater (Nixon has purportedly been converted to Keynesian economics—nothing like being contemporary). Friedman's axiom, in contrast to the Marxist ideal of "From each according to his ability, to each according to his needs," runs "To each according to what he and the instruments he owns produces."[20] Considering that most people in a corporate capitalist society own no instruments of production, an outside observer might find it difficult to conceive how most people would make a living. Like all minds still living in the eighteenth century, Friedman's has neglected to perceive that advanced production is social, yet appropriation is still private. His principle makes any sense at all only in a society of small farmers and tradesmen, not in the age of Tenneco and ITT. Not to be outdone by the moral defense of inequality offered by the more liberal Berle, Friedman adds to the above explanation of inequality that once a person

---

[19] "The New Assault on Equality," *Social Policy,* May–June 1972, p. 13.

[20] *Capitalism and Freedom* (Chicago: University of Chicago Press, 1962), p. 162.

has accumulated great wealth it is no more unethical for his son to inherit the fortune than for a son to inherit a good voice! [21] In this, Friedman parts company with even the most devout sociological functionalist. The IQ people would, however, explicitly outdo Friedman, since they would add that good voices, good brains, and similar inheritances handily go right along with good wealth.

POPULAR EGALITARIANISM

To what extent has the rationalization of inequality penetrated the masses of people in the larger population? Are they accepting the existing distribution of rewards and material benefits? As a whole would they desire a more equitable reward system? Do they feel that some inequality is necessary or is there a broadly based movement for substantive equality? There is no single empirical study, or even a group of studies, that can provide us with any sort of definitive answer to these questions on popular egalitarianism. Fragments of data may be stated on both sides of the issue. For example, Robert Lane argues on the basis of interviews with workers that we cannot look to "the People" or the working class for a consistent and relatively unqualified defense of equality. He cites blue-collar people as rejecting white-collar careers and income levels, acknowledging the relationship between income and ability, believing that education and "more important" jobs should yield higher income, and sympathizing with millionaires who must pay high taxes.[22] Lane found that the workmen he studied believed that material equality would deprive men of their incentive to work and develop skills. Generally, according to Lane, the men preferred the existence of an unequal society with a few men of great wealth to look after things.

In summing up his results, Lane adheres to the view that "society, by using income as a reward technique, can often insure that the individuals will put forth their best efforts." For Lane, equality would pose too many problems of moral, interpersonal, and motivational adjustment in the sample of workers he studied: "Their life goals are structured around achievement and success in monetary terms. Take these away and life would be a desert." [23]

---

[21] Ibid., p. 164.
[22] Robert E. Lane, "The Fear of Equality," in Kenneth M. Dolbeare, ed., *Power and Change in the United States* (New York: John Wiley & Sons, 1969), p. 131.
[23] Ibid., p. 136.

Lane's study apparently confirms the functionalist argument for the necessity of inequality. But a moment's reflection tells us that such information really confirms nothing but the efficacy of the self-fulfilling prophecy and the potential force of rationalizations. How could a manual worker's life be structured around anything but "achievement and success in monetary terms"? If his subsistence wages were taken away—and indeed this is a constant threat—his life would be a material as well as a psychological desert. It is nothing but a play on words to say that the proletariat works from a motivation to achieve and succeed in the unequal society. "Achievement and success" in the working class means little more than staying alive and well, of participating in a very modest way in whatever goods and services the system makes available. Furthermore, recent labor and political trends give indication that there is mounting dissatisfaction among the broad stratum of working people with the distribution of income, the equity of the tax structure, and the balance of power. In brief, the ideological rationalizations of the lazy poor, the benevolent rich, the ability-income equation, and political paternalism are under fire. The working class is returning the self-fulfilling prophecies and self-justifying rationalizations to the ruling class and its established figures in somewhat damaged form.

Aside from the drift of large-scale political forces, there is ample statistical evidence that a large proportion of the American population are more egalitarian than inegalitarian. Very possibly the only reason empirical research sometimes turns up an inegalitarian bent in the "masses" is that they are presented with a social structure that offers them slight alternative of response. It may be compared to asking a Los Angeles motorist idling his car in a traffic jam and breathing exhaust fumes if he believes his automobile is a necessary phenomenon. What other way of life can a man and wife choose for themselves and their children other than "achievement and success" in monetary terms, of involuntary climbing on the backs of other people in a near-desperate attempt to attain decency and security? But despite the staged and framed system of material reward presented to them as necessary and inevitable by the apologists of inequality, growing numbers of people are becoming profoundly and deeply dissatisfied with the arrangement of things. This dissatisfaction is evident in numerous studies revealing popular support for a guaranteed income, socialized medical and dental care, federally organized and guaranteed employment, public housing for those in need, free higher education for those in need, a more progressive tax structure, more public ownership of natural resources, increased federal retirement benefits, greater public regulation of monopolies and utilities, greater government support in housing and education, and a more equitable distribution of material wealth all round.[24] The minority civil rights dimensions of such egalitarianism increased during the sixties, despite the "white backlash" in reaction to ghetto riots.[25] On some questions greater egalitarianism has the support of a substantial minority and on others of a slight-to-decisive majority. The desire for greater egalitarianism cuts across age, race, and class lines, though it tends to drop off noticeably among the affluent. Our stress on the material reward aspect of economic power should not distract one from recognizing the parallel thrust toward workers' control and popular decision making. The demands and accomplishments in the area of industrial and political democracy have been on the upswing in recent years, though devastating setbacks continue to occur with clocklike regularity. In spheres of both reward and control, it is possible to perceive general indifference and active opposition to progressive change, even among those persons and groups who were most supportive of progress only a few years ago.

Although support for the authoritarian-inegalitarian argument is not lacking, we might well agree with Lee Rainwater's contention that "there is no evidence that working-class people will not support equalitarian goals. Working-class people repeatedly say that they believe in a society in which no one has to be below the mainstream level." [26]

We have thus far dealt with some theoretical issues surrounding inequality. Our second major task in this chapter is to delineate from a statistical standpoint the extent of economic inequality in the United States. Specifically, our concern will be with the distribution of income and wealth.

INCOME DISTRIBUTION

In a treatment of the inequality of material rewards, the most meaningful dimension for the large majority of people is direct personal or family

---

[24] See, for example, Angus Campbell, *White Attitudes Toward Black People* (Ann Arbor: University of Michigan Institute for Social Research, 1971), pp. 23, 26, 57, et passim; Richard F. Hamilton, "Black Demands, White Reactions, and Liberal Alarms," in Sar A. Levitan, ed., *Blue-Collar Workers* (New York: McGraw-Hill Book Company, 1971), pp. 130–53; Milton Rokeach, "Religious Values and Social Compassion," *Review of Religious Research* 11 (Fall, 1969), p. 34; and Herbert Mc-Closky, et al., "Issue Conflict and Consensus Among Party Leaders and Followers," in Dolbeare, op. cit., pp. 48–52, and McClosky, "Consensus and Ideology in American Politics," in Dolbeare, op. cit., p. 107.

[25] Richard F. Hamilton, "Liberal Intelligentsia and White Backlash," in *Dissent*, Winter 1972, p. 226.

[26] "Making the Good Life: Working-Class Family and Life-Styles," in Levitan, op. cit., p. 227.

income. In fact, this statement could be amended to read: direct personal or family income *from salaries or wages*. However, salaries or wages are not always directly the most meaningful aspect of material reward for two categories in the population: the very poor and the very rich. The poor often depend extensively or exclusively on social transfer payments, including welfare, while the rich "depend" extensively or exclusively on the appropriation of surplus value, e.g., dividends, capital gains (income from the sale of stocks or other property), and interest. These two strata, the superrich and the destitute existing side by side on a large scale, are the inevitable products of corporate capitalism and this system's abiding and cardinal characteristic. The very rich and the very poor are abiding and cardinal in the identification of private capitalism owing to the nature of the system itself: the unchallenged and overriding drive for the maximization and appropriation of surplus value through the exploitation of labor power. As technology advances within the corporate capitalist system, the welfare-dependent poor and the class of surplus appropriators will increase numerically if not also proportionately to the rest of the population, as fewer people produce more, and more people become jobless poor or jobless rich.

That two categories in the population depend heavily on sources of income other than salary and wages does not mean, of course, that the remainder depend *entirely* on salary and wages. The vast majority of the population, including many of the poor, rely almost entirely on job income, even while supplementing this to various degrees from other sources. Indeed, poor people may draw small investment dividends, and more frequently rich people receive government subsidies—sometimes large enough to create moderate richness in themselves.

Overall income inequality may be viewed from a variety of statistical perspectives. Table 1 presents the percentage distribution of white and non-white families and unrelated individuals by total money income levels for 1960 and 1970. This table in itself does not tell us the full extent of income inequality nor the degree of change. It does tell us that the population is distributed along a wide range of income levels and at least a part of the structure has adjusted itself upward over the ten-year period from 1960 to 1970. It also reveals that whites are as a group distributed more highly than nonwhites, and families higher than unrelated individuals. We begin to get a better grasp of inequality when we learn elsewhere that the 20 percent of family units receiving $15,000 and over take over 40 percent of the total, and conversely, the over 30 percent of family units receiving $7,000 and under end up with less than 15 percent of that income total.[27] These figures suggest that at least half of United States family

---

[27] *The Statistical Abstract of the United States, 1972* (New York: Grosset & Dunlap, 1972), p. 317.

TABLE 1

Families and Unrelated Individuals by Total Money Income in 1960 and 1970, in Constant Dollars (1970), by Race of Head

	1970		1960	
	White	*Nonwhite*	*White*	*Nonwhite*
Families				
Total	100.0% (46.5m)	100.0% (5.4m)	100.0% (41.1m)	100.0% (4.3m)
Under $3,000	7.5	20.1	13.4	36.4
$3,000–$4,999	9.5	17.0	13.3	21.8
$5,000–$6,999	11.3	16.4	16.8	15.8
$7,000–$9,999	20.1	18.2	25.7	15.3
$10,000–$14,999	27.9	17.3	20.7	8.0
$15,000 and over	23.7	10.9	10.2	2.8
Median income— dollars	$10,236	$6,516	$7,664	$4,236
Unrelated Individuals				
Total	100.0% (13.4m)	100.0% (1.9m)	100.0% (9.5m)	100.0% (1.5m)
Under $1,500	21.4	35.1	35.1	51.9
$1,500–$2,999	25.5	24.0	21.2	19.1
$3,000–$4,999	17.7	17.7	17.3	14.9
$5,000–$6,999	12.4	11.0	13.8	9.1
$7,000–$9,999	12.7	9.6	9.1	3.9
$10,000 and over	10.2	2.7	3.7	1.0
Median income— dollars	$3,283	$2,243	$2,439	$1,145

Source: U.S. Bureau of the Census, *Current Population Reports,* Series P-60, No. 80, "Income in 1970 of Families and Persons in the United States" (Washington, D.C.: U.S. Government Printing Office, 1971), Table 9, p. 23.

units are involved in substantial inequality in one way or another, with the majority of these being on the deprived end of the scale.

Focusing on the more revealing and direct measure of income inequality we may observe the *proportionate* distribution of income among white and nonwhite families and unrelated individuals for 1947 and 1970 in Table 2. The clear facts here are that the bottom fifth of family income units receives only about one-twentieth of total personal income whereas the top fifth receives over two-fifths of total income. The median income of the bottom fifth in 1970 was $3,054 compared to $23,100 for the top fifth. Furthermore, among unrelated individuals, an often unconsidered category of over 15 million persons, the bottom fifth receives a bare 3 percent of that category's income compared to over 50 percent received by the top fifth. Interestingly enough, nonwhite family income is more unequally distributed than white. Most significantly, the proportionate

TABLE 2

Percentage Share of Aggregate Income in 1947 and 1970
Received by Each Fifth of Families and Unrelated Individuals,
Ranked by Income, By Race of Head

	White		Nonwhite	
	1947	*1970*	*1947*	*1970*
Families				
Total	100.0%	100.0%	100.0%	100.0%
Lowest Fifth	5.4	5.8	4.3	4.5
Second Fifth	12.1	12.3	10.3	10.4
Third Fifth	16.9	17.4	16.0	16.5
Fourth Fifth	22.7	23.4	23.7	24.5
Highest Fifth	42.8	41.1	45.7	44.0
Top 5 percent	17.7	14.2	17.1	15.4
Unrelated Individuals				
Total	100.0%	100.0%	100.0%	100.0%
Lowest Fifth	1.8	3.5	2.6	3.0
Second Fifth	5.7	8.0	7.9	7.9
Third Fifth	11.8	13.9	15.2	13.5
Fourth Fifth	21.3	24.5	25.4	24.5
Highest Fifth	59.4	50.2	48.9	51.0
Top 5 percent	34.2	20.3		19.6

Source: "Income in 1970," Table 14, p. 28. (Capital gains not included.)

income distribution has remained substantially unaltered over an entire generation. At least *two* generations have seen virtually no improvement in the proportionate distribution of income in the United States.[28]

At the closer focus of income *tenths* the extremes of inequality are even more visible in the sense that the bottom tenth of family units receives only 1 percent of money income compared to the almost 30 percent taken by the top tenth.[29] Whether looking at it by fifths or tenths, fully 80 percent of the population are either approximately at or below an equal proportion income level. Only 10 percent would really stand to lose substantially from a major redistribution of income toward greater equality, though all of the top 20 percent would have to give ground. In dollar terms, those with incomes of over $15,000 would have to yield income in progressively greater amounts proportionate to their incomes to the

---

[28] Gabriel Kolko, *Wealth and Power in America* (New York: Frederick A. Praeger, 1962), p. 14.

[29] *The Statistical Abstract of the United States,* p. 317.

underlying majority of the population, though the shift would not be sharply marked until at least the $25,000 level. The validity of these figures is implied by the fact that if total personal income were divided equally, a family of four would receive over $15,000, or about 50 percent more than the actual median income for a family of that size.

The significance of the extent of income inequality (matched repeatedly in other advanced capitalist countries [30]) is exceeded only by its persistence through time. Through all phases of the capitalist economic cycle, and through "conservative" and "liberal" presidential administrations, the various income strata of the population continue in their places. The economic model delineated by Marx tells us in advance that there can be little noticeable change in the relative distribution of income by classes. Under a privately incorporated and controlled economy the absolute best that the underlying population can hope for is to hold their own unequal status through whatever political or organizational device they can employ so as to coerce the maximum culturally determined subsistence wages out of the ruling class. The politically powerless and occupationally marginal cannot even hope for this much, and can only expect to lose ground relative to the ruling class and even to the rest of the underlying population or proletariat. Such has been the actual case.

Any departure from the past norms, such as the expanded social consumption of surplus value or an expanded proportion of income to the underlying population at the expense of and relative to the vested interests, could only occur at the cost of the integrity of capitalism as a system and the advance of the social control and ownership of the means of production. Any income redistribution or equalization schemes that fail to include proposals for progressive socialization of the means of production can at most expect to achieve extremely modest results if any at all. As we shall observe in Chapter 10, the existing tax structure has little or no redistributive impact; and to achieve equality through taxation within capitalism is politically and economically illogical and impossible, though a reduction of inequality is not. If the underlying population were indeed powerful enough to institute and impose such a system of equalizing taxation, it would also be powerful enough to socialize the means of production, a much more efficient and workable path to equality. Equality through taxation is illogical for this reason, and impossible for the reason that to rely solely on taxation of income is not to achieve real equality at all but to redistribute inequality. More importantly, taxation leaves untouched the power side of economic inequality, since decision making and control may remain in narrow class hands. But again, if the working class could suc-

---

[30] For example, on Australia see S. Encel, *Equality and Authority* (Melbourne, Australia: Cheshire Publishing, 1970), p. 110.

ceed in equalizing material reward through taxation, it could also succeed in controlling the forces of production.

___

We have already alluded to race and family status as factors affecting the amount of income received. In this section we shall look further at these and other important influences on income position. We shall rely primarily on *median* income (the figure that half the population makes more than and half less than) as the statistical indicator, keeping in mind that, although a more balanced comparative device, the median does not reflect income extremes as well as does average or mean income. More will be said of the extremes in the subsequent section.

Inasmuch as race is an important determining factor in many of the subsequent analyses of income, it might be well to begin with a general comparison of racial categories. From a median income of $3,445 (in 1970 dollars) in 1950, white family heads increased the figure by 1970 to $10,236.[31] During the same period, nonwhite family heads were increasing their incomes from $1,869 to $6,516. In relative terms, the ratio of nonwhite to white income was .54 in 1950, .55 in 1960, and .64 in 1970. Comparatively speaking, then, the sixties (at least until 1968) were "good" years for nonwhites. But the pace of change over the past twenty years has seen nonwhites gain on the average one point every two years on whites, meaning that at this rate it would require until the middle of the next century to equalize median *racial* income (the inequality *within* racial groups could at the same time persist). Regionally, white male income earners in the North and West are less than 25 ratio points above nonwhites, but in the South the imbalance approaches 50.[32] Yet, as Marx once observed, the result of extreme exploitation of blacks in the South does not accrue as a benefit to white workers. Rather, the ruling class plays on racial conflict to hold down income of *all* workers, white and black, with the result that, despite their relatively superior material position with regard to southern blacks, southern whites receive considerably less (well over $1,000 in many occupational categories) than their northern counterparts. As a final note in this connection, it makes little difference for males whether the white-black comparisons involve full-time

___

[31] U.S. Bureau of the Census, *Current Population Reports,* Series P-60, No. 80, "Income in 1970 of Families and Persons in the United States" (Washington, D.C.: U.S. Government Printing Office, 1971), Table 10, p. 24. All income data cited in this and the subsequent section may be found in this source, unless otherwise specified.

[32] Table 48, p. 100.

year-round workers or some part-time working period.[33] The blacks' two-thirds of white income tends to hold for all working periods. Among females, however, blacks fare considerably better relative to whites, with full-time black female workers having incomes of over four-fifths of the white female income. And for females working less than full-time year-round, the black-white difference is progressively erased. There is little justice to be found in this, though, for female workers putting in 14 to 26 weeks a year have total money incomes of less than $1,900, which amounts to only about half of comparative white male income.

Related to the income inequality between racial categories is the income differential between central cities and suburbs. In metropolitan areas of a million or more inhabitants, median family income in the suburbs is almost $2,000 higher than in the central cities.[34] The difference between central-city and suburban blacks is also substantial, suggesting that color is not a sufficient explanation in itself for the central city–suburb differential. Black or white, families that can afford it prefer to escape from congested areas. But the impact of race on income is evidenced by the fact that central-city whites in metropolitan areas of a million people or more have median family incomes of $1,700 more than suburban blacks. In metropolitan areas of less than a million persons, central city–suburban income differentials are rather small in both racial categories, with blacks throughout such areas evincing a median income of less than two-thirds that of white families.

White families in metropolitan areas earn on the average about $2,000 more than white families in smaller communities, who earn, in turn, $2,000 more than white farm families. Black residential differences along the rural-urban continuum are similar to white differentials, with a $4,605 median for nonmetropolitan-nonfarm black families and $3,106 for black farm families.

Among other status categories reflected in income are age and sex, the latter being much more significant than the former. Both the young and the elderly are on the low end of the spectrum in terms of individual income, a relationship which holds true in both white and black categories and regardless of whether workers are full-time or part-time, year-round or seasonal.[35] Male teenagers working full-time year-round have incomes only two-fifths the size of persons in the 35-to-54 age range, and male workers 20 to 24 years old only two-thirds of this middle-age group. In part at least, these gaps reflect the needs of middle-age workers to support families, and also in part skills or seniority they have acquired on the job.

---

[33] Table 34, p. 74; Table 51, p. 111.
[34] Table 16, p. 30.
[35] Table 45, p. 95.

But to some unknown extent, age differentials reflect traditional values regarding the worth of age itself. To some other unknown extent, age inequality is the result of the greater power of middle-age people over that of youth—organizational, political, prestige, and prior economic status included among power leverages. Yet age begins to work against the average person beyond about 55, as power and work potential tend to fade. Full-time workers 65 and over are at only two-thirds the income level of the middle-age worker. While the above facts hold for blacks and women as separate groups, the impact of age is sharply reduced in both cases. Blacks and women are relatively powerless groups *as such*. Unlike many white males, their command over resources does not greatly alter with age.

For many older persons, though, income levels are maintained and even enhanced—*if* they happen to be significant property owners. As we noted in the previous section, unrelated individuals—many of whom are older persons—have a more unequal distribution of income than the general family-unit population. In point of fact, the top income fifth of persons over age 64 hold over half of the income of this elderly group. Furthermore, a significant portion of the nation's wealthiest persons are over 64 years old. Perhaps it is among the elderly that the capitalist system's capacity to produce inequality is best observed: consider the image of two men, neither lifting a finger of productive labor, one an indigent castoff from the industrial labor force and the other a centimillionaire rentier.

We shall more fully treat the impact of sex on income inequality in the next section when we discuss educational and occupational influences. Suffice it to point out here that the $9,223 median earnings of white males in the full-time year-round labor force in 1970 was about $3,800 greater than earnings of fully employed females, rendering a ratio unfavorable to females by over 40 points (.59).[36] A black female-to-male ratio of .70 is slightly more favorable. These ratios hold for those working fewer than fifty weeks a year as well.

Two further considerations regarding income distribution among family units are the number of earners per family and sizes and types of family. First, as to number of earners, additional earners increase a family's median income from $8,352 for a family with a fully employed head and no other earners to $11,190 for two earners, to $14,438 for three, and $16,688 for four or more.[37] Thus, it requires at least three additional earners to match the income of the head or chief breadwinner, attesting to what Marx observed regarding the subsistence criterion being applied

---

[36] Table 52, p. 113.
[37] Table 29, p. 69.

to the *family unit* rather than the individual worker as such. Wives and other working family members are not paid as individuals, but as depen dents and subsidiaries to the chief or central breadwinner. Yet it is precisely the additional income, however small, which keeps a large percentage of blue- and white-collar families at or above the subsistence level. And many of the so-called affluent working families, actually about half of those over $15,000, would be reduced to nonaffluence should additional family earners stop working.

Family type—that is, husband-wife or female-headed—has a great influence on income. With both the sex and additional-earner factors working against the female-headed family, a three-child female-headed family median for whites of $3,715 is greatly exceeded by the $11,271 of the three-child husband-wife counterpart.[38] The black female-headed family expectedly fares no better. Also, family *size* significantly conditions the share of income reward realized by *individual* family members. Given total family income, individuals in one-child families have greater income resources than two-child units, two-child more than three-child, and so on. Family size itself is insignificantly related to family income, so that every additional child reduces by an important fraction the income resources available to individual members, an extremely persuasive fact in itself for family-size limitation.

EDUCATION, OCCUPATION, AND INCOME

Continuing our analyses of income-influencing variables, we turn now to the two most important "achieved" statuses: education and occupation. But caution is needed in referring to education and occupation as achievement variables, inasmuch as parental economic status or class position is in itself the prime determinant of educational and occupational "achievement." In other words, what we are witnessing in the following data is largely the "feedback" effect of educational and occupational placement upon a person's inherited class status, leaving as a factor of varying importance the completely independent influence of personal educational and occupational attainment.

That education is a critical factor in income determination, or at least serves as an important class instrument in the preservation of inequality, may be observed in the average lifetime earnings of persons at given educational levels. For example, as of 1968 a college graduate 25 years old or more could expect a lifetime income of $586,000 compared

---

[38] Table 19, p. 43.

to $350,000 for a high school graduate and $196,000 for someone with less than an eighth-grade education.[39] The full and direct impact of education may be more clearly observed in Table 3, where the median annual income for families with full-time year-round working heads 25 years old or over is given. The marked increase in income with the climb through the ranks of education is impressive. Also very significant is the striking correlation between age and income as mediated by education: for example, from an income of $15,211 in the age cohort 25–34, a person with an advanced degree peaks at $22,534 in the 45–54 age cohort—some $7,323 higher—whereas the high school graduate advances only $2,876 from the age cohort 25–34 to 45–54. Such is the monetary difference between a "job" and a "career."

The link between education and income inequality may be further illustrated by the fact that, whereas 58 percent of persons with advanced degrees are in $25,000 or above median family bracket, 48 percent of college graduates, 34 percent of those with some college, 23 percent of high school graduates, 17 percent of those with some high school, 12 percent of those with eight years of schooling, and only 7 percent of those with

TABLE 3

All Families With Head 25 Years Old and Over
by Total Median Income in 1970 for Year-Round Full-Time,
by Years of School Completed and Age

	Total	25–34	35–44	45–54	55–64	65 or over
College						
5 years or more	$19,083	$15,211	$19,044	$22,534	$21,640	$ —
4 years	16,356	13,538	17,340	19,179	17,213	14,169
1 to 3 years	13,566	11,834	13,843	15,638	14,804	11,394
High School						
4 years	11,807	10,478	11,953	13,363	12,496	10,166
1 to 3 years	10,832	9,142	10,713	12,041	11,602	8,425
Elementary School						
8 years	9,772	8,047	9,740	10,366	10,240	8,266
less than 8 years	8,424	6,994	8,087	9,023	8,761	6,902

Source: "Income in 1970," Table 28, pp. 61–63.

---

[39] *The Statistical Abstract of the United States,* p. 111.

less than eight years are in this higher-income category.[40] Conversely, the proportion of those with college or graduate degrees having family incomes of less than $7,000 is only about 6 percent, compared to 25 percent for those with eight years or less.

Given the consistently strong correlation between education and income we might expect that the top income fifth would have an over-representation of better-educated persons and the bottom fifth an over-representation of lesser-educated ones. Table 4 reveals the relative income placement of families with heads at given levels of educational attainment. Although the several income strata clearly mirror the educational back-grounds of their occupants, it is not impossible for the undereducated to make an appearance in the top income fifth or even top 5 percent, nor for the more highly educated to count among the bottom fifth. However, the probabilities are clearly low.

The ever-present racial influence is not erased through education. The persistence of race as an unequalizing variable may be well illustrated by the fact that black families with college graduates at their heads have a median annual income a bare $500 higher than white families headed by

TABLE 4

*Fifths of Families Ranked by Size of Money Income in 1970,
by Years of School Completed by Head*

	Total	Lowest Fifth	Second Fifth	Third Fifth	Fourth Fifth	Highest Fifth	Top 5 Percent
College	100.0%	100.0%	100.0%	100.0%	100.0%	100.0%	100.0%
4 years or more	13.9	3.7	6.1	10.3	17.7	31.7	49.2
1 to 3 years	11.2	5.5	8.7	11.6	14.3	16.0	15.2
High School							
4 years	32.0	19.8	32.9	38.4	38.1	30.7	22.5
1 to 3 years	16.7	18.7	19.9	18.3	15.0	11.7	6.9
Elementary School							
8 years	12.7	20.6	16.1	12.0	8.7	6.2	3.8
less than 8 years	13.5	31.7	16.2	9.4	6.2	3.7	2.3

Source: "Income in 1970," Table 12, p. 26.

---

[40] Table 28, p. 61.

high school graduates,[41] while black high school graduates lag behind white high school graduates by over $3,000.

Neither is the ever-present sexual influence on income erased through education. Indeed, inequalities of income for given levels of education are greater between the sexes than between blacks and whites. To duplicate the above racial illustration, all females working full-time year-round and having completed college reported median annual incomes of $8,156 in 1970, $1,411 less than for male high school graduates.[42] But for a female to enter the full-time job market upon completion of high school, her deficit to the male high school counterpart can be expected to be almost $4,000 ($5,580 vs. $9,567). The *job* aspect of female work, including that done by college graduates, is evident in data disclosing that female income doesn't vary much according to age; for example, women college graduates in the age cohort 25–34 have a median income of $8,116, which increases by a mere $1,000 in the 45–54 age group, while men graduates in the younger age grade see an $11,887 median income rise almost $5,000 in the 45–54 age cohort.

So far we have considered a number of rather powerful influences on income inequality—or at least variables that display a significant correlation with income. (Correlation is by no means proof of causation even if the direction of influence is known, as in the sex-income tie, since an apparently causative variable may itself be the intermediary of some other determining factor.) But none of these variables are as persistent and important as occupation. Increasingly over the past century a product of education, occupation fixes a person into the system of income inequality more powerfully than any of the previously discussed predictive variables. Occupation is the factor most closely linked to the Marxist definition of class position—position in the system of production. The linkage between occupation and social class placement is extremely complex, and we shall reserve a detailed discussion of it until the next chapter. Suffice it to point out here that there is considerable overlap and even inconsistency between occupational categories and social classes, and the social class divisions are not perceptible in occupational income statistics save in the most obvious categories such as the "self-employed" and "laborer." Of importance is the fact that membership in the ruling class is not at all visible in occupational statistics. The United States Census Bureau has no occupational category called "capitalist" or "financier." Such people are either excluded entirely or are buried in the "professional" or "managerial" or "sales" categories. None of the broad occupational categories have median incomes which clearly place them as being predominantly or characteristi-

---

[41] Ibid.
[42] Table 49, p. 102.

cally ruling class. Indeed, with the exception of self-employed professionals and perhaps salaried professionals and managers, the median incomes of all other major occupational categories place them as a whole among the middle masses or even lower (see Table 5).

The white-collar–blue-collar division is not particularly helpful in determining class position, though this division is still overall quite important. The division is salient in the sense that the "affluent" occupational categories are all white-collar—e.g., professional, managerial, and non-retail sales—while the submedian-income categories are all blue-collar—e.g., service workers, laborers, and the blue-collar unemployed. However, much income blurring is found at the blue-collar–white-collar cross-over occupations of retail sales, clerical workers, self-employed businessmen, lower-level professionals, craftsmen, and operatives.

As in the case of education, and related to it, the higher-income white-collar occupations evince marked income increases from entrance to mid-career, whereas blue-collar workers can expect much less noteworthy increases. Thus, even though starting as young men with incomes similar to those of their upper-blue-collar counterparts, white-collar career workers can anticipate a doubling of income during career development compared to an increase of about one-third for the blue-collarite.[43] Herman Miller has analyzed census data so as to provide information on occupa-

TABLE 5

Occupation of Heads by Total Median Family Income in 1970

Professional	$14,482
Self-employed	21,096
Salaried	14,135
Managerial	14,014
Self-employed	10,015
Salaried	15,114
Sales	12,325
Clerical	10,471
Craftsmen & Foremen	11,294
Operatives	9,602
Service workers	8,562
Laborers	8,118
Farmers & Farm managers	6,138
Farm laborers	4,672
Private household workers	3,177

Source: "Income in 1970," Table 33, p. 73.

---

[43] Herman P. Miller, "A Profile of the Blue-Collar American," in Levitan, op. cit., p. 59.

tional income change for specific age cohorts through time. Miller's data disclose that during the 1960-to-1970 period, the biggest income gains were realized by the professional and managerial categories, especially the age cohort born from 1926 to 1935 (aged 25–34 in 1960 and 35–44 in 1970), which increased its average earnings (in constant dollars) for married white males by 57 percent.[44] This compares to an increase of 41 percent for clerical and sales workers of the same age cohort, 33 percent for skilled workers and operatives, and 28 percent for service workers and laborers. Starting from markedly lower levels in 1960, nonwhite workers made an overall 75 percent gain in this particular age cohort, 50 percent for nonwhite blue-collar workers. Already at higher levels in 1960, older white and nonwhite age cohorts realized more modest increases during the decade. Worst off in the comparative sense were unskilled white workers in the 45–54 age cohort in 1960, who attained average yearly increase of less than 1 percent.

Education, it might be noted, exerts only a slight positive effect on blue-collar income within specific manual occupations such as craftsmen and operatives, though it exerts a very palpable effect on initial skilled-vs.-unskilled placement. Within white-collar occupations, however, additional years of education add significantly to annual earnings.[45] For example, for an operative or craftsman to drop out of high school rather than to go to college means a modest $700 annual earning loss, compared to a $2,400 difference for a professional or managerial worker. There is little income incentive, then, for a future blue-collar worker to continue in school as he looks at the relationship between education and income of the blue-collar work force.

As with education, occupational placement tends to tie one into affluence, modest comfort, or hard-pressed living conditions. Thirty percent of male full-time year-round professionals and managers earned $15,000 or more in 1970, and nearly 20 percent of sales personnel, but only 5 percent of clerical workers, 6 percent of craftsmen, 2 percent of operatives, 3 percent of service workers (household servants excluded), 1 percent of laborers, 6 percent of farmers, and 2 percent of farm laborers.[46] Conversely, the percentages of those earning under $7,000 in 1970 were in the order of the above listed groupings, 12, 18, 24, 26, 23, 40, 50, 58, 73, and 89. The most affluent of the broad occupational categories is the self-employed professional with nearly three-fifths having reported earnings ("reported" is an important modifier in this case)[47]—of $15,000

[44] Ibid.

[45] Ibid., p. 66.

[46] Table 55, p. 117.

[47] Many may find it difficult to believe that in 1970 less than half of the physicians and surgeons in the U.S. had total money incomes of over $25,000 and that over one-fourth had less than $15,000.

or more in 1970, and the poorest is the farm laborer with over three-fifths
of the full-time year-round male workers in this category earning under
$4,000.

Table 6 contains data informing us of the occupational representation
in the various income fifths of the population. Professionals and salaried
managers are proportionately overrepresented in the top fifth (and grossly
overrepresented in the upper 5 percent), while self-employed businessmen
and clerical and sales workers are almost evenly represented and blue-
collar and farm workers are underrepresented. When approaching the
bottom fifth, almost the precise opposite holds true. The lower-white-collar
and skilled blue-collar are the occupational strata most evenly distributed
across income fifths. (It should be noted that in both Tables 4 and 6
the distributions would in all likelihood be more lopsided if the data were
based solely on individual earnings rather than family income, since
second and additional earners are more often found in lower-white-collar
and blue-collar families than in the upper-white-collar levels.) Upper-
white-collarites consistently improve their showing by income fifths, while
other semi- and unskilled blue-collarites are declining.

TABLE 6

Fifths of Families Ranked by Size of Money Income in 1970,
by Occupation of Heads of Families

	Total	Lowest Fifth	Second Fifth	Third Fifth	Fourth Fifth	Highest Fifth	Top 5 Percent
	100.0%	100.0%	100.0%	100.0%	100.0%	100.0%	100.0%
Professional	14.2	5.2	8.3	13.2	18.7	25.8	36.2
Self-Employed	1.6	0.8	0.6	0.6	1.4	4.7	11.6
Salaried	12.6	4.4	7.7	12.6	17.3	21.1	24.6
Managerial	16.7	9.9	11.5	13.4	20.0	28.8	39.8
Self-Employed	4.1	5.5	4.3	3.3	3.3	4.1	5.6
Salaried	12.6	4.4	7.2	10.1	16.6	24.7	34.3
Sales	6.0	4.2	4.9	6.4	6.8	7.7	7.9
Clerical	7.8	7.8	9.2	8.4	7.4	6.0	3.5
Craftsmen & Foremen	20.1	13.9	22.0	24.3	23.1	16.6	6.3
Operatives	17.5	20.2	24.4	20.8	14.2	8.1	2.7
Service workers	7.8	14.3	8.7	6.9	5.6	3.8	2.0
Laborers	4.9	8.9	6.9	4.1	2.9	1.7	0.3
Farmers & Farm managers	3.4	9.6	3.0	2.0	1.3	1.3	1.5
Farm laborers	1.0	3.5	0.7	0.3	0.1	0.1	0.1
Private household workers	0.6	2.5	0.3	0.1	0.1	—	—

Source: "Income in 1970," Table 12, p. 26.

The perennial unequalizer of race displays only modest signs of weakening among full-time male workers within the several occupational categories. In this area, it is of significant note that the ratio of black to white earnings among fully employed males is lowest among professionals (.70) and highest among clerical workers (.88).[48] The greater equality in clerical occupations reflects in part the more formalized pay grades of government jobs in which blacks made gains in the 1960s. The overall tendency is for ratios to be lower the higher the skill and status of the occupation, as among professionals, managers, and craftsmen. However, among fully employed females the black-to-white earnings ratio begins to approach 1.0, even slightly exceeding it among clerical workers and among schoolteachers within the salaried professional category. Yet black women are largely underrepresented compared to white women to begin with in such important categories as managerial, sales, and skilled blue-collar. But the differences between black and white females absolutely pale compared with female-male differences *within* racial groups. There can be little solace for a black female professional earning the median $7,705 in comparison to her white female counterpart's $7,861, when across the sex gap the white male professional is earning $12,421. Indeed, despite the inequity of the black male's $8,675 compared to his white professional counterpart, it is *higher* than the *white female's*. In short, black and white sisterhood makes economic sense.

Women may work for a variety of reasons, but in view of their over-representation in lower-status and lower-income jobs, we might expect that a prime motivation for married women to enter the labor force is family need. That such is the case is suggested by the fact that at every broad occupational level, men whose wives are in the paid labor force earn less than those men whose wives are not in the labor force. For example, among professionals and managers whose wives are not employed, the median annual earnings are $12,504 compared to $10,446 for those who have working wives.[49] In general, then, the higher the husband's income the less likely it is that the wife will be employed outside the home. And whatever occupation she might enter, her income expectations range from at best two-thirds of male income if a salaried professional to at worst a mere two-fifths of male income if a sales worker (women are concentrated in the over-the-counter and cash-register—"dirty" white-collar—sales jobs).[50] Only 2 percent of fully employed female professionals have incomes over $15,000 compared to 28 percent of males; among salaried managers the figure is 5 percent compared to 33 percent of males, and

---

[48] Table 56, p. 120.
[49] Table 32, p. 72.
[50] Table 50, p. 110.

among sales workers less than 1 percent compared to 16 percent of males. Since women work under such discriminatory burdens, one can only conclude that it is largely pressing economic need which induces many married women into the labor force.

Our main concern in this section is with the lower segment of the income population, and as in the above discussion, U.S. census data serve as the chief source of information. The census provides much illumination on the nature and extent of the low-income population, but it is not very valuable when it comes to the superrich. Indeed, the full details of the incomes of the superrich are only partly known to the Internal Revenue Service. It would take this information, plus the candid disclosures of tax lawyers, trust executives, and the superrich themselves to even begin to approach a valid income specification for this upper 0.2 to 0.3 percent of income receivers. We know, for example, that a bare 3.6 percent of the 1969 income of those taking in a million dollars or more is in the form of salaries, and the figure is only 9 percent for those with annual incomes between a half and one million (compared to 91 percent for the $5,000-to-$15,000 category).[51] Dividends, capital gains, and interest account for the bulk of the income of the superrich, all sources that are minor factors in the ordinary person's dollar count.

Although only a small part of the top income group, dozens of the chief executive officers of the nation's top corporations receive annual salaries exceeding two and three hundred thousand dollars, topped in 1971 by W. M. Batten's $397,000 at J. C. Penney, W. Hicklin's $387,000 at Avon Products, L. K. Eilers's $385,000 at Eastman Kodak, and H. S. Geneen's $382,000 at ITT.[52] With the annual bonus, Geneen's total remuneration of $812,000 leads the pack. But even counting deferred compensation, stock options, expense accounts, and dividend income from his $8.8 million worth of ITT common stock, Geneen, as most other leading executives, cannot come near matching the annual incomes of those whose fortunes yield capital far outstripping the few hundred thousand received by the corporate elite in executive remuneration. Many of the big property names are themselves active officers such as Ford, Busch, Kaiser, Firestone, Houghton, Land, Hewlett, Hilton, Stone, Hughes, Rockefeller, and numerous other greater and lesser names famous and unknown to the public at large. Many of the big-income rich are not directly involved in

---

[51] *The Statistical Abstract of the United States,* p. 383.
[52] *Forbes,* May 15, 1972, p. 205.

corporate work either as executives or directors. But whatever their activity or position, the capital generated by their family fortunes greatly
exceeds the salaries of top hired executives. To be sure, through the exercise of stock options, top executives may eventually acquire the wealth to
place them among the income millionaires and multimillionaires. Yet only
a minority of the income superrich are *not* inheritors; only a minority have
accumulated their million-dollar annual yields through their own firms or
while in the employ of one of the giants. We shall take a closer look at
wealth in the next section.

First, however, we are going to take a closer look at the opposite
and more crowded end of the income spectrum, the poor. We shall not
enter into a theoretical analysis of poverty here, reserving this for Chapter
8, but rather simply describe from a formal statistical standpoint the distribution of poverty as defined by the federal government. "Poverty thresholds" are established by the Social Security Administration and adjusted
annually—usually upward—according to family size, age, sex, and residence. Thus, in 1970 the official poverty threshold for a nonfarm family
of four was $3,968, for a couple with the head under sixty-five years of
age $2,604, for a single male under sixty-five $2,092, and for an elderly
female $1,855, and so on for various categories. Presumably, food costs
and calorie demands are important criteria, since farm thresholds are 85
percent of nonfarm, and the female lower than the male. But whatever
the adjusted threshold, it is obvious that the definition is minimal to unrealistic, and draws attention only to the most destitute segment of the
population. Furthermore, the annually adjusted increase in the poverty
threshold is so inadequate in the face of inflation and tax increases (since
1959 the poverty level for a family of four has been increased by only
about $1,000) that to say—as government statistics do—the percentage
of poor declined from 22 percent in 1959 to 13 percent in 1970 is wholly
unrealistic. But the state prefers to convey the impression that the system
is progressive and improving. That such is not the case is suggested by the
statistics themselves, which show that under the Nixon administration the
number of officially defined poor increased by 1.2 million in 1970 alone,
a year in which the profits of many large corporations attained all-time
highs.

Defining who are the poor—pinpointing those categories and sectors
of society that suffer the heaviest material deprivation—can tell us much
about the manner in which the capitalist system grinds out its extremes of
inequality. Knowing who the poor are guides us to potential reservoirs of
discontent and class radicalism, as well as to the kinds of structural changes
required to increase equality. In 1970, according to the federal government,
some 5.1 million families and another 5 million unrelated individuals
made up a combined poverty-stricken total of 25.5 million persons. To

this figure the government adds another 10.2 million "near-poor" persons whose incomes are between 100 and 125 percent of their respective poverty thresholds and for whom "a slight reduction in their incomes, unemployment, illness, change in family size, or some other factor, could drop these households below the low-income level." [53] It is an inescapable fact that about one in five inhabitants of the United States live under extremely hard-pressed material conditions, and that one in three find their condition inadequate by even the most modest middle-class standards.

The poor are disproportionately young and old: 34 percent of the poor (8.5 million) are under 14, 15 percent (3.7 million) between 14 and 21, and 19 percent (4.7 million) 65 years old or above. Almost seven in ten, then, are within the dependent school-age or retired limits. Adding to this the 1.7 million females under 65 heading families and 1.5 million under 65 unrelated females, we see that another 13 percent go into the female and young and old total. Thus, the destitute poor are more likely than not to be those whom our society defines as dependents, or at least not hired and paid as chief breadwinners. Yet a significant minority *are* working males. The elderly have the highest *probability* of being poor, with one in every four falling below the poverty threshold.

Ethnically speaking, seven in ten poor persons are white (one of whom is Spanish-speaking) and three in ten black. However, the probabilities of being poor are almost three-and-a-half times greater for blacks than whites, and over two-and-a-half times greater for Spanish-speaking people than for Anglos. Thirty-four percent of blacks are poor, 28 percent of Mexican Americans, and 10 percent of the Anglos. But as a group, by far the worst off materially and economically are American Indians.

Owing to their weakened earning power, females are impoverished more often than males. Despite the fact that overall about two in ten persons are in families with female heads, over four out of ten persons in *poor* families have female heads. And with there being two-thirds women in the general single population, we find that nearly three-fourths of the individual poor are females. In terms of probabilities, members of female-headed families are likely to be poor about 40 percent of the time compared to less than 10 percent for members of male-headed families, and unrelated females also about 40 percent compared to 25 percent for unrelated males. If a person is under 18 years old in a female-headed family, his chances of being poor are about 50-50. Combining several of the most negative poverty-influencing variables, we are able to isolate the fact that out of the nearly 1 million black children living in female-headed families

---

[53] U.S. Bureau of the Census, *Current Population Reports,* Series P-60, No. 81, "Characteristics of the Low-Income Population, 1970" (Washington, D.C.: U.S. Government Printing Office, 1971), p. 14. All statistics cited in this section on the low-income population are found in this source.

in the nonmetropolitan South, fully 87 percent of them are beneath the poverty threshold. White children are "better off," with only 45 percent of 600,000 in a similar situation falling below the poverty line.

In terms of residence, almost half of the poor family units are located in metropolitan areas, three-fifths of these being in central cities and two-fifths in suburbs. Two-thirds of all poor unrelated individuals reside in metropolitan areas, more in the central cities than in suburbs. Despite the greater *numbers* of poor in metropolitan areas, the *chances* of being poor are greater in rural nonfarm and farm residences, where 14 and 19 percent of all families are poor, respectively.

Full-time work offers no guarantee that a person will not be counted among the poor, even if that person is a male family head. Of the 3.2 million male family heads under the poverty threshold in 1970, one-third worked 50–52 weeks of the year, most full-time. Almost another one-third worked, but less than 50 weeks, while over one-third did not work in the paid labor force at all. Of the latter group, the majority were elderly and most of the rest were either ill or disabled. A small percentage was unemployed. This suggests that poverty has little to do with laziness or unwillingness to work.

Of all full-time year-round white male family heads in the labor force in 1970, almost 4 percent were poor compared to 12 percent of their black counterparts. Among full-time working female family heads, 13 percent of the whites and fully 32 percent of the blacks were poor. The racial factor is so strong that, among male family heads, whites working full time only 27–39 weeks are less likely to be poor than blacks working full time 50–52 weeks. Indeed, whites working less than half the year are only 5 percentage points more likely to be poor than blacks working year-round. The same bias against black females is not as strong as against males, but is still present and very significant.

The fact that there are so many working poor accounts for the further fact that 49 percent of the income of poverty families comes from *job earnings,* much to the contrary of much popular thinking. Only 19 percent is derived from Social Security (most, of course, accounted for by persons over 65), 22 percent from public assistance and welfare (the majority accounted for by female-headed families), and the remainder from other sources. Among nonelderly male family heads in poverty, the large majority of income is derived from earnings, as few qualify for any other type of income transfer. Annual public assistance and welfare payments to all families find a median at $1,300, with the majority of families in poverty drawing no such payments at all. Unrelated individuals are graced with a median annual welfare payment of $857, with at least three-fourths of the single poor not on the welfare rolls. In brief, the bulk of the income received by those in poverty is either earned or derived from previous wage withholdings of financial investments; a relatively small part comes from direct public assistance and welfare, and nearly all of this goes to female-headed families and, to a lesser extent, the elderly. Any reduction in welfare spending thus primarily takes extremely critical dollars out of the hands of mothers, their young children, and the elderly.

How poor are the poor? The data indicate that the poverty population is not crowded just below the threshold, but is distributed across a wider range. For the poor, the average difference between annual income and the threshold line in 1970 for families was $1,420 and for unrelated individuals $810, amounting to an overall deficit of $11.4 billion. While one-quarter of poor families were within $500 of the poverty line, another one-quarter were over $2,000 away from it and a majority over $1,000 away. Female-headed families and single females suffer larger deficits than male-headed families and single males, blacks larger deficits than whites, and unrelated individuals larger deficits than families.

Income is a fundamental part of economic inequality, but it does not tell the whole story. It is conceivable that a person could be materially rather wealthy and yet have a very modest income, insofar as the wealth represents assets such as a house, cars, personal valuables, insurance policies, cash savings, etc., all of which represent money spent but may yield little or nothing or even be an expense at present. Thus, it is necessary to examine the distribution of wealth beyond the income variable, and so we turn next to a brief view of marketable assets.

INEQUALITY OF WEALTH

By *wealth* we shall here mean tangible assets and equities of the personal sector of the economy, excluding such items of personal possession as cars, clothes, television sets, and other household consumer durables. Suffice it to note about this category of nonfinancial personal estate that it largely mirrors the inequality in the distribution of purchasing power or income. *Gross total estate,* much of which is home equity, attained a mere $6,721 median in 1967; liquid assets (savings and checking accounts and government savings bonds) counted for only 13 percent of that sum, producing a median of $660. Clearly, a large segment of the population has relatively little wealth of any kind, financial or nonfinancial, liquid or illiquid. A sizable minority are in net terms worth very little, nothing, or are in debt.

Jefferson's comment that "the property of this country is absolutely concentrated in a very few hands" only need be revised today by shifting the emphasis from land to capital.[54] Nor need we alter Jefferson's view

---

[54] *Jefferson Himself,* edited by Bernard Mayo (Boston: Houghton-Mifflin, 1942), p. 144.

that the consequences of this enormous inequality produce so much misery for the bulk of the population. Nor has the validity of his assertion that, whenever there is in any country numbers of unemployed poor, the laws of property have been so far extended as to violate personal rights, if again we shift the emphasis from an agricultural to an industrial economy.

The best estimates on the concentration of wealth today indicate that one-half of 1 percent of adults possess at least one-third of the nation's private wealth.[55] Since in the mid-sixties the number of millionaires passed 100,000 and those with fifty millions exceeded 1,000, the tabulators of great American fortunes concentrate now only on centimillionaires, of which there are well over 150 known to the public. The wealthiest 1 to 2 percent of the adult population completely dominates the most crucial area of the economy—corporate stock—as well as corporate and state and local bonds, while holding the decisive proportion of federal bonds, mortgages and notes, and cash. By far the chief repository of the tiny economic elite's wealth, however, is corporate stock, which accounts for the large majority of the holdings of the nation's richest families and individuals. As one moves down the hierarchy of wealth to include, say, the top tenth, corporate stock is still the single most important locus of wealth, but life insurance, bonds, mortgages and notes, and cash and savings increase in relative importance. But these are forms of wealth which, however useful in attaining personal ends, cannot render the social and economic power found in the ownership and control of corporate stock.

Beyond the top one-half of 1 percent with their one-third of the wealth, the Federal Reserve Board reported in the 1960s that the top 5 percent had 53 percent of the wealth and the top 20 percent had 77 percent. *This leaves the "bottom" 80 percent of the population with 23 percent to divide up, with the actual division leaving the lowest fifth of the population with a mere 0.5 percent share.* But even this leaves much unsaid at the depths of society, for the lowest tenth had a *deficit* net worth in the sixties. The *liquid* cash assets are so little for a sizable segment of the population of affluent society as to be a joke—if it were at all a humorous matter. In 1970, 16 percent of families had no or minus liquidity, another 14 percent had less than $200, and still another 12 percent between $200 and $499.[56] Twenty-two percent could muster a cash hoard of from $500 to $1,999. Plainly, the majority of the population cannot meet an emergency

---

[55] Research by Robert Lampman, Gabriel Kolko, the University of Michigan, and the federal government have been helpfully summarized and evaluated by Ferdinand Lundberg, *The Rich and the Super Rich* (New York: Bantam Books, 1969), Chapter 1.

[56] *The Statistical Abstract of the United States,* p. 315.

without "pawning" something and/or going into debt. Minor surgery could wipe out the total liquid "wealth" of many people—not to mention the possibility of a serious medical experience, which relatively few people can cover unless they are insured to the hilt and pay hundreds in annual premiums. Nor can the majority really afford to take a two-week vacation without skimping elsewhere or borrowing (Bank Americard generously offers $500 at 18 percent interest for vacation needs, at least for those respectable enough to hold the card).

Yet we know that private individuals and families held over $50 billion in savings in 1970, a real challenge for the big corporations to shake loose. The reason why the majority of the population has such meager liquid assets in the face of a $50 billion private savings account is the same reason why the big corporations are having difficulty in shaking loose this $50 billion: the top income tenth of the population is holding, and has held since at least the 1920s, fully three-fourths of *net* savings, with the bottom half of the population either having no net savings or, as is the lowest tenth, deep in the hole. When a few have most of the hard cash, arithmetic tells us the many will have only a few dollars. And while the rich and affluent find it difficult to spend their billions in amounts sufficient to keep the wheels of industry turning full speed, the masses with their meager cash holdings find it impossible to exercise the purchasing power and consumptive behavior they would like to. Hence, the savings accounts of some pile up interest at the same time that many others are piling up debts. But such is the essence and nature of capitalism as an economic system.

We could go on to detail how income-in-kind and billions worth of expense accounts further extend inequality, but it is rather well known that analyses that focus on income as such greatly underestimate the true extent of economic inequality in the United States. (Inequality of wealth in Great Britain is evidently even greater than in the United States; in Great Britain 1 percent of the adult population held 42 percent of personal wealth in 1960 and less than 5 percent 75 percent of the wealth.[57]) It is necessary, however, to comment further on the important matter of stock ownership, for this is the pivot of economic power in corporate capitalism.

The "people's capitalism" myth was accurately exploded by C. Wright Mills when he wrote that "the idea of a really wide distribution of economic ownership is a cultivated illusion: at the very most, 0.2 or 0.3 percent of the adult population own the bulk, the pay-off shares, of the corporate world." [58] Mills's own careful research on the question of stock

---

[57] Ralph Miliband, *The State in Capitalist Society* (New York: Basic Books, 1969), p. 25.

[58] *The Power Elite* (New York: Oxford University Press, 1956), p. 122.

ownership, together with other university and government assessments, indicate that around 1 percent of the adult population hold 80 percent of corporate stock and the top 5 percent *of this 1 percent* has half of this or 40 percent of the total.[59] The shares, and to a lesser extent the dividends, of corporate capitalism belong almost exclusively to a few hundred thousand households. But the decisive power belongs to far, far fewer persons than this. In connection with our discussion of control of the corporations in Chapter 8, we shall probe this matter further. It is enough to note here that controlling ownership belongs in the hands of several hundreds to a few thousand persons who hold or control anywhere from a few percent to an outright majority of the stock of the nation's leading businesses. With a host of concealment devices, used to avoid both mere detection and taxes, the nation's larger wealth holders may make the size and extent of their fortunes less conspicuous behind impersonal institutional names and fronts. But as any beginning sociology student should know, institutions are made up of and stand for real, live people.

The large majority of real, live people in the United States couldn't even recognize a stock certificate, let alone claim ownership of one. Less than one-fourth have any stock at all, and only 6 percent have more than $10,000 worth. Moreover, relatively few people are ever likely to see much more than that, unless pure luck or blood is on their side, for the majority of big stockholders have their fortunes dumped on their laps through inheritance—if they already haven't been cut in so as to assist the chief holder to "distribute" his wealth and avoid taxes and enumeration. The closest most people will ever come to their part of people's capitalism is having their employer arbitrarily deduct money from their salaries or wages to invest in pension funds, money by the growing scores of billions which goes into the coffers of big business to be used as the tiny fraction of economic rulers dictate to the rest of the population. Ultimately, the most important aspect of economic dictatorship, and the aspect of greatest concern to equalitarians, is not the tremendous concentration of wealth as such, but the fact that through such concentration the nation's vast economic resources are controlled and used. As individual persons or families the controllers are no doubt becoming smaller stockholders in overall relative and percentage terms, even while their fortunes are increasing absolutely. Yet they retain control by virtue of their joint ownership of the financial institutions into which the wealth of the growing masses is funneled for use and reinvestment. From what we know of capitalism as a system, it takes no ingenuity to conclude that all of these controlled monies will be invested so as to produce more of the same, and without much regard—save for averting a mass uprising—for social and personal need.

---

[59] Lundberg, *The Rich and the Superrich,* Chapter 1.

And this is the essence of economic inequality. It is the essence of capitalism and is found, to a greater or lesser extent in all advanced capitalist states.

This concludes our review and analysis of inequality as an aspect of social class. Our next task is to move beyond this narrower focus on inequality to an examination and definition of the larger concept of social class.

five

SOCIAL CLASS
AS
PROPERTY CLASS

Although many social scientists acknowledge Marx to be the father of social class analysis, to the large majority of students of stratification the chief inspiration is Max Weber. The literature of American social class analysis has been completely dominated by the Weberian orientation, at least whenever there has been any attempt at theoretical construction. Weber has traditionally been considered more valid and more relevant than Marx. In the light of the Weberian sweep of sociological class theorizing in the United States, it is mandatory that we examine the central concepts of this approach and seek to find out why Weber has been dominant over Marx.

Whereas the Marxist model of social class is an essentially dichotomous one, based on the fundamental single factor of economics, Weber's framework is by contrast "multidimensional." However, it is no argument in favor of Weber's approach to social stratification to simply assert that it is multidimensional (and therefore correct) and that Marx's approach is single-factor (and therefore wrong). In the first place, this would be to underestimate the actual complexity of Marx's "single-factor" analysis; Marx's economic variable, as we have seen, is itself composed of sub-dimensions. Furthermore, Weber himself finds the foundation of the class system in the relationship to property, and thus in the final analysis his is also a "single-factor" theory. In any event, it would erroneous to claim validity for a multidimensional approach simply by virtue of its complexity and to find error in a single factor approach simply by virtue of its simplicity. A simple approach may be as scientific as a complex one, even more so insofar as simplicity is the ultimate goal of scientific explanation.

Weber, then, underscores three social stratification variables: class, status, and power. Class is the broadest of the three concepts and requires the most exposition. Weber here moves from the individual toward the group, from class situation to social class. One's *class situation,* to Weber, is the typical probability of one's procuring goods, gaining a position in life, and finding inner satisfactions—a probability which derives from one's relative control over goods and skills and their income-producing uses within a given economic order.[1] Weber's stress, then, in class situation is on *material condition.* Class situation is set by "specific life chances," in the material sense to the extent that these opportunities provide for both physical and psychological well-being within a given historical situation. A class is any group of persons occupying the same class status or situation, or a number of people with common life chances and similar economic interests in goods, income, and labor markets.[2]

Now we come to the Weber typically ignored by the detractors of Marxism: " 'Property' and 'lack of property' are, therefore, the basic categories of all class situations." [3] Weber was primarily concerned with the monopoly and privilege which stem from property ownership, and the hegemony over life chances engendered by such ownership. Thus, Weber's conception of class is identical with market situation and people's ability to take command over material resources produced by a society: "According to our terminology, the factor that creates 'class' is unambiguously economic interest, and indeed, only those interests involved in the existence of the market." [4]

Weber goes on to specify three types of classes: property class (the determinative one), acquisition or commercial class, and social class. A property class is primarily determined by property differences or differentiation of property holdings of its members. Weber then introduces a pair of euphemisms for bourgeoisie and proletariat: "positively privileged" and "negatively privileged" property classes (this sort of neutralized language is one of the reasons for Weber's appeal to many contemporary social scientists—though rarely is this particular aspect of his class theory discussed, perhaps owing to its obvious Marxist implications). The key word to the understanding of the positively privileged property class is *monopoly* —monopoly over high-priced consumer goods, over their sale, over savings

---

[1] Max Weber, *Economy and Society,* Vol. 1, edited by Guenther Roth and Claus Wittich (New York: Bedminster Press, 1968), p. 302.

[2] Ibid., p. 927.

[3] Ibid.

[4] Ibid., p. 928.

and investment, over elite education, over executive positions, and most importantly over appropriation and accumulation of unconsumed surpluses.[5] Thus, this class lives typically from property income, "income from securities." They are the capitalist class, pure and simple. The negatively privileged property class are themselves the objects of ownership, "that is they are unfree." Like Marx, Weber must take recourse to a third, intermediate, or "middle" class standing in between the two major property classes to accommodate many additional people who are neither entirely positively or negatively privileged. These people live off both property and labor.

Weber observes that property classes are aggregates of similarly situated persons who do not in themselves constitute a social group, and may or may not develop into such a group (or class-for-itself). Nor are property classes "dynamic," necessarily resulting in class struggles or class revolutions.[6] Weber also adds that the transitions from one class status to another vary greatly in the fluidity and ease with which an individual can enter a class, making the unity of classes highly relative and variable. By implication, then, the positively privileged property class is more closed, while lines into the other classes are more fluid. Yet Weber contends that only persons who are completely unskilled, without property, and irregularly employed are in a strictly identical class status, suggesting that major property owners are not. Weber also makes reference to "outcasts," the "debtor class," and "the poor" as being among the negatively privileged property class, and in light of the foregoing, occupying identical class statuses. Since factory workers or the Marxist proletariat are not as such "outcasts" and debtors, yet still without property and the objects of ownership, Weber seems to recognize two variously situated underclasses, one worse off than the other. This is in fact the case and its basis is in occupation or employment position which brings us to the second type of class categorization: acquisition or commercial.

By *acquisition classes* Weber refers to occupational gateways to life chances as opposed to property ownership. Again we have positively and negatively privileged classes and "middle classes." There is no necessary connection between property and acquisition classes, though through the illustrations of bankers and financiers, industrial entrepreneurs, shipowners, etc. Weber indicates that the positively privileged acquisition class significantly overlaps with the positively privileged property class. Furthermore, the privileged acquisition class may attain a monopoly on executive posi-

[5] Max Weber, *The Theory of Social and Economic Organization,* translated by A. M. Henderson and Talcott Parsons (New York: Oxford University Press, 1947), p. 425.
[6] Ibid.

tions and insure the security of its position by influencing or controlling the economic policy of the state and other organizations. At the top levels, Weber's distinction between property and acquisition classes borders on the purely analytical, as it also does at the bottom. The negatively privileged acquisition class consists of workers lacking a monopoly on skills or training and hence with low access to income, whereas the middle classes are comprised of professionals (not sufficiently monopolistic or enriched to be included in the privileged class), many government officials, craftsmen, and workers with exceptional monopolistic assets.

Finally, a *social* class is composed of a plurality of class statuses between which an interchange of individuals on a personal basis or in the course of generations is readily possible and typically observable.[7] A social class based on class interests may or may not develop. The emphasis here shifts from economic interests and position to association based on these material conditions. It is a step in the direction of a class-for-itself. Rather vaguely, Weber identifies four broad social classes: the "working" class, the "lower middle" classes, the "intelligentsia," and the privileged classes, a breakdown based largely on the combination of occupational and property classes.[8]

The second major stratification variable discussed by Weber is "social status." Status of the social variety rests upon a typically effective claim to positive or negative privilege with respect to social prestige derived from "mode of living" or "style of life" and family hereditary prestige or of an occupation. A *social stratum,* then, is a plurality of individuals who enjoy the same level of prestige. Weber points out that "the type of class most closely related to a stratum is the 'social' class, while the 'acquisition' class is the farthest removed. Property classes often constitute the nucleus of a stratum."[9] By way of further clarification, Weber observes that "with some over-simplification, one might thus say that classes are stratified according to their relations to the production and acquisition of goods; whereas status groups are stratified according to the principles of their *consumption* of goods as represented by special styles of life."[10] Of special importance to social status is formal education, insofar as education shapes cultural behavior. And as previously noted, occupational position is a significant conditioner of social prestige, honor, or status.

Weber takes pains to make clear that, even if social status or status group is wholly determined by class situation—and to Weber this need not necessarily be the case—this does not make the two dimensions iden-

---

[7] Ibid., p. 424.
[8] Ibid., p. 427.
[9] Ibid., p. 429.
[10] *Economy and Society,* p. 937.

tical. Weber points out that propertied and propertyless people can and do belong to the same status group. The status group sets restrictions for membership on such things as association and marriage, not on property, occupation, or income per se. Indeed, status groups in their operation may and frequently do monopolize and restrict economic or educational opportunities, thus playing an independent role. Status also stands in opposition to the "pretensions of sheer property." Nevertheless, as Weber himself understood and made clear, class situation as defined by property ownership and secondarily by acquisitional (occupational) position is much more fundamental to social status than social status is to class status. Styles of life require material resources, and so does education as a determinant of life styles; and occupational prestige cannot by itself support status group membership, nor can claims to aristocratic or hereditary status. At least in a capitalist society, the entire complex of status groups would collapse in the wake of economic or property revolution—a fact keenly perceived by Weber.

The third concept within the Weberian framework is power: "In general, we understand by 'power' the chance of a man or a number of men to realize their own will in a social action even against the resistance of others who are participating in the action." [11] While power is usually desired for its practical utility, it may be valued for its own sake. Power may be manifest in any institutional framework, including the economic, and the latter kind of power may be the consequence of power existing on other grounds. Power also operates independently of social status, and may or may not render prestige. Power may take the form of party power in the organized political sense. Here, too, party power may represent classes or status groups, or a combination of these, or neither. But again, it is necessary for Weber to affirm that property classes represent the most dominant underpinnings of political parties, together with the influences of acquisition classes where the latter are not in complete harmony with property classes. In other words, the most single important seat of power is class, i.e., economic power. The very definition of power as the ability of a person or group to realize their aims even against opposition must necessarily contain a weighty economic component, and some would argue that power in capitalist society is always primarily (if not exclusively) economic ownership and control.

Like Marx, Weber was deeply involved in political life, though as a liberal and not a socialist. (Weber offered his personal support and involvement as a German nationalist in the First World War, even though he recognized the hopelessness of the German effort against eventual American power on the side of the Allies.) Although Weber made statements

---

[11] Ibid., p. 926.

such as "the appropriation of the means of production and personal control, however formal, over the process of work constitute among the strongest incentives to unlimited willingness to work," [12] and felt it possible for workers to play an effective part in industrial management, he consistently opposed socialism in practice if not in principle. He was skeptical of the possibility of worker rationality in industry, of any motive to economic action other than selfish gain, and of democratic socialism. While seeing Western capitalism as expropriating freedom not just in economic life but throughout all dominant institutions, it was not capitalism as such which Weber seemed to fear but *bureaucratism* as it flourished under capitalism, and as he feared it would flourish even more under the rubric of socialism.

STRATIFICATION VARIABLES TODAY

The most systematic latter-day effort at theoretically constructing a Weberian multidimensional framework for the analysis of social class is Milton M. Gordon's in his book *Social Class in American Sociology*.[13] We are able to agree with Gordon, and with Runciman in his more recent analysis,[14] that Weber has conceptualized in a distinct and exhaustive manner the dimensions of stratification, but seriously question the real theoretical and research utility, practicality, and relevance of the Weberian approach to the central issues of social class (as Runciman does also). It has not proven to be particularly fruitful as thus far applied, and has been the theoretical rationale for some highly dubious kinds of class research.[15] While in all likelihood not Weber's intentions, his elevation of social status to an "equal" of class and power has provided an excuse for approximately forty years of increasingly sophisticated and arid methodological exercises in "discovering" the status structure of communities and sample populations.[16]

Yet no one could question the need for more than one simple variable in a viable model of social class; a theory is by definition composed of several elements. The position held to here is that one must look *first* and *always* at property classes or ownership, as Marx and as Weber himself did, if the operation of a society's structure of inequality is to be understood. From property we can explore more fruitfully the other dimensions of stratification such as occupation, status, and power, and examine the

---

[12] *The Theory of Social and Economic Organization*, p. 263.

[13] Durham, N.C.: Duke University Press, 1958.

[14] W. G. Runciman, "Class, Status, and Power?" in J. A. Jackson, ed., *Social Stratification* (Cambridge: Cambridge University Press, 1968), pp. 25–61.

[15] See, for example, Richard P. Coleman and Bernice L. Neugarten *Social Status in the City* (San Francisco: Jossey-Bass, 1971).

[16] See, for example, *Sociological Inquiry* 40 (Spring 1970).

manner in which these latter influence property classes. We agree with Mills that "prestige is the shadow of money and power," [17] and with Parkin that a reification of the multidimensional approach "tends to obscure the systematic nature of inequality and the fact that it is grounded in the material order in a fairly identifiable fashion." [18] To hold or control large blocks of property is to have economic and political power directly or indirectly, but to hold and exercise power independently of property is possible only if such power is in support of or irrelevant to the interests of property—a not very sizeable area of operation in industrial society. To exercise independent power in opposition to established property is to engage in revolutionary activity, itself even impossible without the material wealth and resources of a class.

While we concur with Mills and Parkin in their criticisms of the multi-dimensional approach, we cannot agree with Mills's judgment that for the broad middle strata of modern society there has been "a shift from property to a new axis of stratification, occupation," [19] or with Parkin's view that "the backbone of the class structure, and indeed of the entire reward system of modern Western society, is the occupational order." [20] Certainly their emphasis upon the salaried and wage nature of reward for growing masses of people as opposed to independent employment is well-placed and significant in consequence. But occupation as such has always been important to daily sustenance for the masses, and the shift from self-employment to salaried and wage work is the *result of the increasing preponderance of property in shaping industrial society, not its demise. And far from being the backbone of the reward structure, occupational remuneration is largely shaped by the power of organized property over salaries and wages and over the very composition and makeup of the occupational structure itself.* The chief axis of stratification within capitalist society has been and always will be property and the power accruing to its holders, and the chief cleavage of inequality is between the free income derived from property by absentee owners and the wages earned by the masses of workers.

In short, we agree with Ralph Miliband's statement that "the economic and political life of capitalist societies is *primarily* determined by the relationship, born of the capitalist mode of production between two classes—the class which on the one hand owns and controls and the working class

[17] C. Wright Mills, *The Power Elite* (New York: Oxford University Press, 1956), p. 83.

[18] Frank Parkin, *Class Inequality and Political Order* (New York: Praeger Publishers, 1971), p. 17.

[19] C. Wright Mills, *White Collar* (New York: Oxford University Press, 1951), p. 65.

[20] Parkin, *Class Inequality and Political Order*, p. 18.

on the other." [21] Mills, too, is able to see the dependent status of the occupational variable in class society when he says: "Not so much free labor markets as the powers of pressure groups now shape the class positions and privileges of various strata in the United States." [22]

Occupation is not even in itself the primary arbiter of prestige, although performance may be esteemed or celebrated. Occupational prestige is largely the reflection of the monetary reward associated with an occupation. Money is both power and prestige, and as noted previously, money for the masses is mediated through occupation but quantitatively decided by the powers of organized property.

But those who dwell on occupation as the pivotal point of the class system are infinitely closer to meaningful accounting than those *still* dissecting the status system. In the 1970s much of the sociological establishment continues to slumber on the chimera of status stratification. At the risk of engaging in straw-man destruction, we cannot resist quoting Talcott Parsons's recent "updating" of hard-core social class analysis:

> We may suggest the usefulness of divorcing the concept of social class from its historic relation to both kinship and property as such; to define *class status,* for the unit of social structure, as position on the hierarchical dimension of the differentiation of the societal system; and to consider *social class* as an aggregate of such units, individual and/or collective, that in their own estimation and those of others in the society occupy positions of approximately equal status in this respect.[23]

In concert, Daniel Bell adds that "as the traditional class structure dissolves, more and more individuals want to be identified, not by their occupational base (in the Marxist sense), but by their cultural tastes and lifestyles." [24]

What sort of social science methodological make-believe is it that can find space in learned journals to dispense with kinship, property, and the class structure of capitalist society itself in an analysis of stratification and inequality, and put in their place such meaty substances as "position on the hierarchical dimension of the differentiation of the societal system" and "cultural tastes"? For those who have not yet understood the meaning of the Marxist phrase "bourgeois social science," the foregoing suffices as an illustration.

---

[21] Ralph Miliband, *The State in Capitalist Society* (New York: Basic Books, 1969), p. 16.

[22] *White Collar,* p. 299.

[23] "Equality and Inequality in Modern Society, or Social Stratification Revisited," *Sociological Inquiry* 40 (Spring 1970): 24.

[24] "The Cultural Contradictions of Capitalism," *The Public Interest* 21 (Fall 1970): 22.

A MARXIST MODEL OF CLASS

In this section we shall develop a classification system with which to perceive and analyze the contemporary class structure. We take the family as the basic unit of stratification, and the chief lifelong earner as the primary entity in setting a family's social placement, though in some instances a two-earner husband-wife pair could raise classification difficulties as far as the family unit is concerned. Where no other dependents are involved, such cases of dual dominance rendering divergent class placement could be treated as any other unrelated individual case. Where dependents are involved, it would be necessary to identify or make a decision as to which parent is in the most important aspects the operational head. Fortunately for research purposes, the chief economic figure in the biparental family is almost always the husband, or when dual leadership exists both parents belong to the same class. In cases where the wife is the economic dominant, she, of course, would set the family's class position. For later purposes in this section, we shall be obliged to follow the census's procedure of counting as head of a family the male if present in the home, or, if he is not present or there is none in the first place, the person acknowledged as head by other household and kinship members.

A Marxist class model must begin with property as central to class definition. Thus we have two major classes, the propertied capitalist class which owns and controls the means of production and the propertyless working class which sells its labor power. The capitalist class lives entirely or chiefly off of surplus value, while the working class lives entirely or chiefly off of income paid them for value-creating labor. Thus, the *source* of income, whether it be from capital or from labor, is a pivotal criterion of class placement. And the source of income is, in turn, determined by its relationship to property: one is entirely or chiefly dependent on property ownership for income or one is entirely or chiefly dependent on the sale of his or her own labor power.

In brief, class position is broadly determined by a person's property placement and relationship to the means of production. Our contention is that, with the modifications of this broad generalization to be discussed below, all members of the society can be classified as either capitalist or working class, or at the least noncapitalist—as belonging in objective interest primarily to one or the other of these historically decisive classes. In terms of objective interest, that interest can only be defined as profit for the capitalist class and as material and social well-being for the working class. These two objective interests are today totally and unqualifiedly incompatible. The actual extent to which members of the respective classes are aware of this incompatibility matters in terms of change, but not in the least in terms of the clash of objective interests. However, to the extent that the conflict of interests goes unrecognized and unchallenged, to the same extent will the material and social well-being of the working class relatively and in many instances and cases absolutely deteriorate. And the proof of this does not and increasingly will not require much sophisticated scientific research, for its validation is ubiquitous in almost every field of physical and psychological sensation.

Beyond this initial broad classification scheme it becomes immediately necessary to specify further refinements. The first and most important additional criterion of class placement, not really a separate and independent criterion at all but rather an operational aid in deciphering class position, is *functional status* or *position*—i.e., a person's main role as being either directly necessary to the material and social well-being of the working class or as being primarily exploitative of and/or parasitical upon the necessary labor of others. While not always essential in determining class placement, functional status is indispensable in defining the basic subclasses within the dichotomous class model.

The major subclass within the working or noncapitalist class is the goods- or commodity-producing class or working class proper. Quite clearly, this class composes the core of the socially necessary labor force without which society as a whole could not long survive in the material and physical sense. We include in the working class proper even those workers who, because of little or no alternative employment, impersonally labor and produce commodities which are not conducive to social well-being (are not social use-values) as such but only serve to protect the interests of or enrich the propertied class. A plethora of gadgets and material waste for profit might be used to illustrate, ranging from the manufacture of diamond necklaces to napalm bombs. Workers in an industry or job category which is essentially wasteful or destructive could find ample constructive use for their abilities under a *socially* rational mode of production.

The traditional proletariat or working class is the largest single stratum. Counting craftsmen, operatives, and laborers, including those in agriculture, in 1970 this working group comprised between 40 and 45 percent of family heads in the labor force. This category includes only blue-collar workers, and shall be referred to as the traditional working class. *But added to the traditional working class must be the "new working class," or the white-collar personnel who work in production-related scientific and technical jobs.* The chief distinction between the traditional and the new working class is level of formal education and skill requirements in job performance. In automated industrial production, however, the manual-mental distinction in labor is progressively erased.

The traditional and the new working class occupy the same property position insofar as both depend entirely or extensively on earned income from salary or wages. An engineer who has built up a corporation on the strength of defense contracts and pays himself a salary as chief executive officer while taking millions of dollars of wealth and income from capital is obviously not new working class. Nor is the physicist who runs a consulting firm at a huge profit or receives $100,000 a year in personal fees, for *size* of income is itself a guideline to class position inasmuch as a large income must almost necessarily be derived to a great extent from surplus created by other's labor. What labor could conceivably have an exchange value worth $100,000 a year, or even $50,000? Certainly exploitation or parasitism must enter at some point if not in the entire sum. The earned income of the new working class could be and more typically is higher than that of the traditional working class, and there is nothing within the Marxist frame of reference which would disallow this, at least to the extent that the technician's labor is the more productive for the time rendered, and assuming that individual productivity can even be measured in social production.

The size of the goods-related new working class would be difficult to specify precisely, but the more than 2 million scientific, engineering, and technical personnel in the U.S. labor force are, with a small percentage of significant exceptions, privately or publicly hired employees earning incomes all or most of which could be assigned to their own labor value rather than to surplus value created by others. Moreover, although many of the skills of new-working-class people are being wastefully or destructively applied, as in the case of the huge drain on scientific and technical manpower by the military and quasi-military agencies and interests, most possess the fundamental knowledge and capabilities to greatly advance the real social well-being of the population—as the new working class has already done in the past, albeit in a constricted and frequently distorted way.

One of the reasons it is difficult to assay size of the commodity-producing new working class is that within the scientific and technical category is included a sizeable group of *service*-producing personnel, particularly in the fields of health and education (in Marxist language, nonproducing but socially useful workers). In fact, the entire salaried professional and technical segment of the labor force is at question here, some 13 percent in all. To illustrate the distinction between goods-producing and service-producing personnel (we shall avoid the term *nonproducing* as it is misleading when discussing the socially necessary labor force), we might cite the manual laborer involved in the production of microscopes (or the engineer who designs them) as an example of the former and the laboratory technician who uses one in the analysis of blood samples (or the salaried general hospital physician who acts upon the results) as an example of the latter. In some instances, the goods-related or services-related status of the work is unclear, as could often be the case in scientific education. Moreover, health and education and other human welfare activities are so basic to the overall productive capacities of a society that to distinguish between goods-producing and service-producing categories within the hired professional and technical stratum is not particularly useful if not operationally impossible. While recognizing the existence of a small percentage of exceptions, we shall include in the new working class virtually all of the hired professional and technical workers. It may be granted that many of these workers would perform other kinds of work within a noncapitalist economic order, but as in the case of the traditional working class, their fundamental abilities could be directly applied to the enhancement of social or material well-being without any padding or waste for profit or system purposes. For example, a social worker would confine working time to personal adjustment problems as such or enter a related field of recreation, education, or medicine, rather than play detective, accountant, bureaucrat, or some other system-created make-work.

There is also a blue-collar element to the service-producing class, typically with less education than the white-collar group, though no less important in the overall capacity of the service sector to render itself socially useful. Maintenance and custodial personnel in hospitals, schools, universities, and other public institutions may be used as examples, as might public safety or communications workers not counted within the traditional working class. In an age of automation, and with the possibility of creative leisure-time use, many service workers in recreation and entertainment could conceivably (and desirably) qualify as rendering socially or culturally necessary services. By virtue of their predominantly propertyless and low-income status, if not also by virtue of their functional status, the bulk of the roughly 10 percent of blue-collar service workers who are family heads can be included within the noncapitalist working class. Again, significant exceptions may be pointed out, such as a variety of personal servants who cater to the "needs" of the propertied *and* protect and identify with their masters' interests.

A further important element within the service-producing class whose property and income position is similar or identical to the new working class is the white-collar salaried workers, including the majority of managerial, sales, and clerical occupational categories. In terms of both source and size of income, a significant minority of higher and top managerial personnel could in no manner be counted as working class; however, the large majority of managers are relatively humble both in property and income. More importantly, it is the management rank and file who are closest to the production process and who perform most of the necessary tasks as defined even by strictly capitalist terms. Their functional status is typically germane to the efficient organization and distribution of both goods and services. Frequently, however, managers are involved in the direct exploitation of other workers and/or are largely superfluous to the problem of efficiently channeling goods and services to the consuming population. But more frequently and to a much greater extent, the majority of managerial personnel are themselves the objects of exploitation inasmuch as they save for the capitalist amounts of surplus value markedly greater than what they are paid in salary or wages. And as to functional status, managers and administrators (in much reduced numbers and personal power than we witness today) are for the foreseeable future as necessary for a socially planned society as for one run by and for a single exploiting class.

We count, then, the large majority of salaried managers, many of them transfers from the scientific, technical, and professional strata, as being among the service-producing working class and ultimately the new working class. We may thus add perhaps as many as another 8 percent to the latter major class grouping, including all industrial, agricultural, and governmental sectors. But we must exclude, in addition to substantially propertied and highly salaried managers, a category of managerial personnel who are entirely or largely in the service of money per se, i.e., financial managers performing purely capitalist accounting services obviously beyond the requisites of socially necessary currency or exchange needs and geared mainly toward financial aggrandizement at the expense of the laboring population. The functionally necessary status, from the standpoint of a socially planned economy, of most banking, insurance, finance, savings-and-loan, brokerage, and real estate managers is tenuous to say the least, and no less so is that of advertising and promotional staff. Perhaps the appropriate label for ordinary financial management might be subcapitalist, insofar as they are not themselves major owners or highly salaried but yet perform strictly system-dependent tasks. Many lawyers and accountants, as salaried professionals, would be equally vulnerable outside the logic of capitalism.

The some 15 percent of the labor force who are family heads and work as sales and clerical workers tend as a group to be very close to the traditional working class in terms of dependence on earned income, size of income, and, we might add, precariousness of job security and repetitiveness and alienation. Yet these lower-white-collar workers occupy an ambiguous class position insofar as they, like managers and other service-producing strata, find their ultimate source of income in the labor of others, even while conserving and distributing the surplus value of a society through their own exploited labor. Functionally, in an administrative and distributive sense, a moderately large proportion of sales and especially clerical workers are required for any industrial society. But an even larger proportion in both government and private sectors, and especially in private sales, serve a mainly subcapitalist purpose and could be entirely dispensed with in a socialist economy. Very frequently, clerical and retail sales jobs are not filled by family heads but by wives and other secondary earners related to manual laborers or other white-collar workers. In general terms of property, income size and source, and functional status, we might for accounting purposes add 10 percent for lower-white-collar workers to the working class, while recognizing that much of the remainder are objectively more closely associated and situated with the working class than with the capitalist class.

There remain two nonpropertied and noncapitalist categories to be identified: the humanistic intellectuals and the lumpenproletariat. Humanistic intellectuals and artists of all sorts pose a special probem for any system of class analysis, a problem frequently solved by placing them in a neutral or distinct class unto themselves, a tempting alternative here. But we shall avoid this alternative and locate humanistic intellectuals within either the capitalist or the working class, and do so on the basis of their functional status as well as the other class criteria (most are propertyless and of modest economic means). In the case of intellectuals, their functional purpose is *ideological,* either capitalist or socialist. The majority of American intellectuals are ideologically capitalist, though very frequently tempered by a strong welfare-statist viewpoint. In view of the strong reformist strain in the ideology of the majority of intellectuals, a degree of reformism sometimes abreast or even in advance of the laboring masses, it would be a mistake categorically to place nonsocialist intellectuals in the capitalist class or to characterize them as apologists for the interests of this class. Indeed, the majority of humanistic intellectuals are employed in work settings in universities and colleges having many structural similarities with those of other workers; the term "knowledge factory" is typically no exaggeration. The large majority of humanistic intellectuals, we would argue, are most closely linked to and overlapped with service-producing professionals and belong to that component of the new working class. As with other white-collar strata discussed above, a significant minority may be found in the dedicated full-time employ of capitalist and imperialist interests. Frequently—and decidedly the case among the highly educated who reach top advisory positions to capitalist elite—they are not truly intellectuals at all but intellectual technicians.

Finally within the underlying population, we come to the lumpenproletariat, an assemblage of people not only propertyless and powerless, but with no recognized and legitimate position in the system at all or at least with only sporadic and uncertain positions. Their tangential position means that the size of their income is below the subsistence level, and the source is a combination of the most degrading types of labor and equally degrading types of support payments. (Note that even the earned Social Security check in the United States has long carried a stigma with it, as do most other forms of social transfer or welfare payment except military ones.) In part, the lumpenproletariat consists of the most unskilled portions of the industrial reserve army or unemployed. But it also includes a host of illegitimate occupations, creating affluence and even riches for some, which feed off the underbelly of capitalism—e.g., those linked to drug traffic, prostitution, gambling, and any and all sorts of black market activities and crime. For many, these pursuits are a way out of the industrial reserve army and the only means of survival; for some they are chosen careers. The lumpenproletariat also embraces hundreds of thousands, indeed millions, of nameless, faceless human derelicts who for psychological, physical, economic, or age reasons have simply given up on living and dropped out to the level of mere breathing survival. There are also a growing number of younger cultural dropouts, some striving for a new communal existence and others who could only be classed among the lumpenproletariat.

In its propertylessness, poverty, and alienation, the lumpenproletariat is akin to the working class. Even more than the proletariat, the lumpenproletariat has been victimized by the power of capital; it lacks even such a modest instrument of defense as the labor union. Its chief defenses are total apathy and religious sectarianism, drugged oblivion and personal violence, psychoses and death. Of the numerous hallmarks of pure capitalism, a disoriented, demoralized, and socially estranged lumpenproletariat is one of the most distinctive, tragic, and dangerous. In the present context we are "neo-Marxist" regarding the lumpenproletariat, for we disagree with Marx's categorical labeling of this stratum as contemptible "scum." For all of his structural and historical thinking, Marx was evidently unwilling to see the sociological causes of lumpenproletariat status or to acknowledge the very small gap between proletarian and lumpenproletarian positions. Admittedly, a portion of the lumpenproletariat would have things no other way, and are loyal and devout capitalists, which brings to mind Engels's comment regarding the blurred line between crime and capitalism. This portion of self-defined criminals and thugs compose the lumpenproletariat Marx defined as untrustworthy allies of the working class and dangerous tools of the reaction; they are the "rogues" whom Lenin would treat "fiercely," perhaps shooting one in ten on the spot. Yet this is a small minority of the total lumpenproletariat, itself the most frequent victims of this "financial aristocracy" at the bottom of capitalist society.

So again keeping in mind the significant exceptions, we shall count the lumpenproletariat not only as noncapitalist in position and objective

interests, but as the most dispossessed sector of the proletariat or traditional working class. Its size is difficult to estimate, for it shows up only
minimally in occupational and income data; many are so far outside of
the system that they are not even enumerated by the census of population.
But if we can assign one in five inhabitants of the U.S. to the poor, we
can surely assign one in twenty to the lumpenproletariat.

We have already drawn attention to two subcategories which are not,
in the balance of class criteria, part of the broad working classes, one
being the stratum of subcapitalist financial personnel (the smaller vested
interests) who would be entirely superfluous to an economy geared to
use-values, and the other, equally specious stratum of servants to capitalists. By servants to capitalists we do not refer to the babysitter or
housecleaning lady who assists a working-class housewife attempting to
supplement her husband's subsistence income; both parties are here the
objects of exploitation. We refer to the chauffeur in the Cadillac or Rolls
Royce, the butler and maid in the mansion, the private tutor to the heir
or heiress, the groundskeeper on the estate, the chef in the family kitchen,
the bartender at the exclusive private men's club, the pilot of personal jets,
bodyguards and call girls, etc. Servants to capitalists live entirely off the
surplus value of the working class and meet exclusively the personal needs
of the ruling class. Typically, though certainly not always, their loyalty and
identification are with the master and not the working class.

Included within the subcapitalist or capitalist servant classes is an
important segment of government officials and employees who either depend upon capitalism as such for the continuance and expansion of certain
government bureaucracies (subcapitalists) or are directly and explicitly
serving the interests of large property holders (servants of capitalists).
How much of, for example, the Department of Health, Education, and
Welfare could be eliminated or completely transformed under an economy
of use-values is uncertain, but the change would be drastically large. Or,
without a foreign policy guided by imperialists, the Department of Defense
would surely contract in size rather than continue to dominate the entire
governmental process. The military itself would be sharply reduced and
not scattered across the face of the globe, and would cease engaging in
wars against the Third World either directly or by proxy. Not all of government belongs to these two capitalist-related subclasses, of course; the
majority are members of one segment or another of the working class,
though a very few come directly from the legitimate capitalist class, its
core, and even its ruling element.

Also excluded from the propertyless is the "old middle class" of independent professionals, small businessmen, and family farmers, all of
whom "own and control" their own means of production. This diminishing vestige of nineteenth-century liberal economy comprises at most 10

percent of the working family heads in the labor force. Despite their ownership and independent status, we would not count them among the capitalist class and obviously not the ruling class. Their ownership is frequently nothing more than indebtedness to large financial interests and their control is typically little more than what time they are going to open and close their doors, if that. In effect, the majority of these petty capitalists are no less owned nor more free than the factory worker with whom they often trade places or become workmates of. And rarely are they able to hire and exploit labor to any significant degree, at least by comparison to the capitalist class. Themselves exploited through taxes, markets, interests, pricing, and supplies, petty capitalists face the power of corporate capital in a manner sometimes more crushing than the hired wage worker. The small farmer is particularly close to the hired laborer inasmuch as both create value through work and receive meager compensation for their efforts. And while small businessmen live off labor, their economic situation is frequently similar to the workers' and their hours of work considerably longer. The small businessman, like the farmer, often ends up tired or bankrupt and entering a salaried or wage position. Surely less than half of these small entrepreneurs could be counted as prosperous, successful petty capitalists.

The consistent exception to the economic precariousness of petty capitalism in business and agriculture is the petty capitalism within certain professions, medicine in particular and law to a lesser extent. In the case of the majority of practicing private physicians and among the higher circles of law, wealth and income mount to heights far above the real exchange-value of skilled labor of any kind, let alone activity of a non–value-creating kind as in medicine or law. Thus, in terms of property and size and source of income, much of the medical profession and part of the legal profession are adjuncts to the capitalist class. Functionally, law is to a large extent subcapitalist; that is, capitalism as a system is responsible for the incredible proliferation of property laws and lawyers. The success of the capitalist class would be unthinkable without the constant presence of hired legal skills, both to devise the most hospitable and enhancing economic statutes and to maximize surplus value within and frequently outside of the existing legal framework. Lawyers abound in corporate higher circles. Still, the rank-and-file lawyer is typically no closer to the capitalist class in an objective sense than many other service-producing professionals and managers, and a small but growing minority are applying their skills on behalf of the powerless against the overwhelming power of capital. This trend is of enormous import, placing the participants functionally and ideologically within the working class.

Functionally, medicine is or should be humanistic rather than petty-capitalist. Indeed, much medicine is more than petty-capitalist; it is corporate-capitalist when it comes to the superprofits of the drug companies, hospital supply industries, and insurance firms. A portion of the medical profession itself are strictly subcapitalist or servants of capitalists insofar as they cater to and treat exclusively or primarily the rich, who pay the subcapitalist physicians out of the profits of labor. Good health is not a luxury but a necessity and a right. As with all such other essentials, health services should be equally and universally available. Health services exist on the social surpluses created by labor, and should be dispensed, in turn, on a strictly socially owned and controlled basis, rather than being opened up to profiteers exploiting a life-and-death market for personal gain. The only comparable form of such base exploitation lies at the death-making end of the human spectrum, the profits of war industries. But in medicine as in law, a small and dedicated minority are striving toward making theirs a genuinely social service rather than a means of self-aggrandizement or pillar of capitalism. In a society based on the production of use-values, law would greatly diminish in both size and importance but medicine would increase in both quantity and quality. Under a system of social medicine physicians employed by society cease to be petty capitalists and become members of the service-producing segment of the new working class. Their property, income, and functional statuses (and, we might add, conditions of work) could render them as nothing other.

We have left until last the capitalist class per se, and shall leave a full discussion of it for later. Suffice it to note here that the legitimate capitalist class is in relative terms infinitesimally small—2 percent of the population at most with a core of less than 1 percent and a ruling element of a mere few thousand family fortunes. These are the propertied and often powerful rich, whose size and source of income is pure capitalist, and whose functional status is the unabashed, large-scale exploitation of hundreds of millions of persons both domestically and internationally (this latter point also sets them off from the petty capitalist and subcapitalist). Their conditions of work—if they happen to work—differ beyond description from those of the rest of the population, and if they are alienated it is of their own doing and of a very different sort than found in the working class.

In numerical terms, then, the large majority of the population is either working-class or closely related to it in terms of Marxist criteria. A minority, perhaps no more than one-fifth, are viable petty-capitalist, subcapitalist, and servants to capitalists; and a miniscule but decisive fragment of the population are fully legitimate capitalists. Little wonder, then, that Marx defined capitalism as the expropriation of the many by the few and socialism as the expropriation of the few by the many.

As a shortcut to the above class analysis we may use a method which yields about the same proportionate balance of classes (though probably mixing up some membership), by simply taking stock ownership as the criterion of class placement. The similarity in results to more complex analyses using other Marxist class criteria implies that property—and corporate property in particular—is strongly related or practically identical to other dimensions of social class analysis, so much so that class research having limited resources could take extent of corporate property holdings as the determinant of class placement with considerable accuracy. In broad class terms (and nothing would prevent more refined breakdowns), four-fifths or more of the population would be proletarian or quasi-proletarian (with no direct corporate property holdings), the large majority of the rest being quasi-capitalists (with moderate or low stakes in corporate property). Two percent or less would be capitalists with decisive or total stakes in corporate property. Cutting in the underlying population through involuntary or even voluntary pension and retirement plans in no way creates capitalists out of proletarians, though it may serve to exert a procapitalist influence on their economic thinking. It simply magnifies the power of legitimate capitalists who are thus enabled to control larger blocks of property with relatively less stock.

What we are arguing for is the reintroduction of property as the central variable in social class analysis, assisted mainly by income analysis and secondarily by occupational analysis. By the same token, we are led to an understanding of what should be the practical goal of stratification research: the exercise and consequences of economic and political power. Conversely, our argument suggests a temporary moratorium on research in areas of lesser import to the understanding of social class and inequality, such as social status and prestige hierarchies, noneconomic cultural attributes and life styles, and purely social patterns of interaction. *Or if prestige, life styles, and interaction are the objects of research, the intent should be the clarification of their significance for economic and power inequalities.*

CLASS CONSCIOUSNESS

The class framework developed in the preceding section is essentially an objective one—i.e., it does not directly include the psychological (subjective) dimension, namely, class consciousness. By "subjective" we do not mean to imply that class consciousness is some vague inner psychological state shared by individual class members or some mass psychological consciousness. Rather, by "class consciousness" we refer, with Lukács, to *"the sense, become conscious, of the historical role of the class."* [25] It in-

---

[25] Georg Lukács, *History and Class Consciousness* (Cambridge: M.I.T. Press, 1971; originally published 1922), p. 73.

cludes not only a psychological awareness of common and conflicting class interests, but also an understanding and comprehension of the changes required to alter the course of society in the direction of objective class interests. The subjective dimension of class consciousness must be present to a decisive extent before it is possible to pursue successfully a rationally organized system of production and distribution and a working-class state. In James Weinstein's words: "If the producers are to participate in determining social priorities—if they are to govern themselves and make history—they must understand and want socialism and must join together in a popular movement to attain it." [26] Or from Gilbert Merkx: "Revolutionary practice must be informed by the theoretical understanding of the society in which the practice takes place." [27] This is not an academic or sophisticated understanding, but a clear perception of concrete economic and political events in one's immediate milieu.

The subjective aspect of class consciousness forms a reciprocal tie with objective economic and political actions, each influencing and reinforcing the other.[28] Simply performing an objectively political or revolutionary act does not create class consciousness or understanding, just as understanding is insufficient, as Marx argued, to change the world. Furthermore, attaining consciousness and understanding is not a spontaneous development, but a gradual process of learning and mutual education. As to the class-conscious segment or vanguard of the society, their role, in Paul Le Blanc's words, is to "articulate a convincing revolutionary perspective which links the issue or set of issues around which people are struggling to a broader set of issues, to an understanding of the crisis of our society, to an emphasis on the common interests of the entire working class, and to an understanding of the need for socialism." [29]

The most articulate spokesman on the subject of class consciousness in American sociology has been C. Wright Mills. Mills specifies three components of class consciousness: (1) a rational awareness and identification with one's own class interests; (2) an awareness of and rejection of other class interests as legitimate; and (3) an awareness of and readiness to use collective political means to the collective political end of realizing one's interests.[30] Mills agrees with the Marxist interpretation of the importance of class consciousness to social change and revolution: "The first lesson of modern sociology is that the individual cannot understand

---

[26] "The Left, Old and the New," *Socialist Revolution* 10 (July–August 1972): 9.

[27] *Monthly Review* 24 (September 1972): 59.

[28] See David Shapiro, "On Psychological Liberation," *Social Policy* (July–August 1972): 9–15.

[29] "Socialists and Labor in the United States," *Monthly Review* 24 (September 1972): 38.

[30] *White Collar*, p. 325.

his own experience or gauge his own fate without locating himself within the trends of his epoch and the life chances of all the individuals of his social layer." [31] Yet Mills's chief precaution regarding class consciousness is that objective position and interest may be a poor indicator of subjective orientation and understanding of social class—there is no necessary connection between the two. In fact, such a connection may never develop.

However, Mills is quick to add that "because men are not 'class conscious' at all times and in all places does not mean that 'there are no classes.' " [32] Or, if people do not grasp the class causes of their conduct, "this does not mean that the social analyst must ignore or deny them." Mills continues: "If political mentalities are not in line with objectively defined strata, that lack of correspondence is a problem to be explained; in fact, it is the grand problem of the psychology of social strata." Such research would involve us in an analysis of, among other things, socialization, political propaganda, education, and mass communications, of the ideas of the ruling class as compared to the events of daily life. Mandel phrases it this way: "In the last analysis the question boils down to this: Which force will turn out to be stronger in determining the workers' attitude to the society he lives in, the mystifying ideas he receives, yesterday in the church and today through TV, or the social reality he confronts and assimilates day after day through practical experience?" [33] Mills in the 1950s felt the answer lay more in the area of mystification than reality. The 1960s have set the stage for class awakening, and the 1970s may witness the beginning of that awakening. The objective material conditions for the emergence of class consciousness have been progressively ripening. But, as did Veblen, it is easy also to express many doubts, and at moments even grave pessimism, over a growing awareness of class interests and their achievement.

The standard format of class research in which respondents are asked to indicate their class identification or position (often from among stated alternatives), is typically of little value. "Middle-class" and "working-class," the two labels the large majority of people respond to, tend to be little more than options for nonmanual and manual work or white-collar and blue-collar jobs. The linkage is not complete, though, since many manual workers identify themselves as middle-class and many nonmanual workers as working-class. Regardless, the terms *middle-class* and *working-class* carry little meaning and command less loyalty, and are used inconsistently or loosely by many persons. On occasion these "class" identifica-

---

[31] Ibid., p. xx.

[32] Ibid., pp. 294–95.

[33] Ernest Mandel, "Workers and the Permanent Revolution," in George Fischer, ed., *The Revival of American Socialism* (New York: Oxford University Press, 1971), p. 184.

tions will find correlation with other behavioral and attitudinal variables, but usually by way of their own relationship with occupation and especially education. In any event, the correlations so turned up are typically small and greatly overshadowed by differences between the propertied and the propertyless.

The fact that the large majority of Americans think of themselves as vaguely middle-class—or middle of the working class or whatever "centrist" label is chosen—should not be interpreted as signifying a failure on the part of the population to recognize objective social classes. Quite to the contrary, this middling, working identity *is* objectively rather accurate. For despite the common income range of two or three thousand dollars to fifteen thousand, the fact is that this income inequality is of secondary importance (though surely important) compared to the *similarity* of interests of the underlying masses concerning job security, inflationary squeezes, peace, rising personal tax burdens, public school quality, food and housing costs, medicine, consumer rights, clean air and water, street safety, and dozens of other matters which concern the ruling class only insofar as they threaten to disrupt their system of power and wealth. The ruling class in their personal lives are either profiting by these large-scale problems and/ or remain largely unaffected by their existence—typically both. The ruling class have no job worries, they profit from inflation and global militarism, they shift the tax burden to the masses, their children attend exclusive private schools, they eat and live in kingly fashion, they call on (or are called upon by) personal physicians, they have no consumer problems, and they can largely escape whenever they want the environmental and social destruction they have wreaked upon society.

While a vague "common man" class identification does not fit, for example, Mills's definition of class consciousness, and while the rejection of ruling-class interests has not yet crystallized on a very large scale, the class interests of the working classes are gradually becoming more sharply focused, and a movement toward polarization may be taking place. Furthermore, events indicate a trend toward collective political action on behalf of working-class interests and against ruling-class interests.

Merkx has argued that a main source of contemporary group consciousness has been "structural alienation," that is, a militant consciousness based upon being relatively *divorced* from the means of production and the organization of work.[34] Blacks, women, and youth, for example, have emerged as more or less self-conscious groups based upon their marginal economic and social status. Whether these manifestations of consciousness can surmount their original "ethnic" orientations and coalesce as a mutual propertyless and alienated class-conscious force is an important question

---

[34] "Revolution in America," *The Monthly Review* 23 (January 1972): 28–42.

of the hour. If the alienation of these groups is turned inward against themselves and each other—or one might add, against the majority white working classes and vice versa—social revolution would suffer a serious setback and open the way for repression and fascism. The critical task for the class-conscious left, writes Merkx, "is to promote the consciousness of a common class situation and interests among structurally alienated groups, and develop the recognition of common interest between these groups and the working class." [35]

While statistical evidence concerning the extent of popular perception of a Marxist dichotomous class model is scarce—and although we feel that broad, nonstatistical trends in political behavior are more illuminating anyway—three pieces of survey evidence might be mentioned. The first is a study by John Leggett. Leggett's research to some extent relates to the Marxist definition of class consciousness and quite completely to that of Mills.[36] His sample of Detroit auto workers in 1960 (*before* the prime awakener of Vietnam and even the crest of the civil rights movement) disclosed that a majority of blacks (three-fifths) and almost one-quarter of whites were class conscious. An additional group of about 30 percent in both black and white samples fell in between those with and without class consciousness. Among white *unemployed,* one-third were class-conscious and another one-third marginally so. Certainly these figures would be greater today.

A second suggestive item involves an English sample of industrial workers, the majority of whom held to a dichotomous "money model" of the class system—that is, a class structure with one large central class plus one or more classes based on wealth.[37] Most of the remainder had no or vague class imagery, and only 8 percent a prestige image of classes as life style strata. Ironically, after the authors of this study asserted in their text that these workers viewed the class system as a natural datum of social existence that individuals had to accept and adapt to, auto workers in one plant that was studied struck their firm, calling for a more equitable distribution of excess profits and hanging a top company official in effigy—a good lesson as to why we place greater confidence in collective political actions and trends than in social science research as indicators of class consciousness. This is entirely true of the capitalist class which is virtually unavailable and inaccessible for survey research and could certainly not be taken at their word regarding class interests, conflicts, and collective action. Such are secret and confidential data among the ruling class, and

---

[35] *Monthly Review* 24 (September 1972): 63–64.
[36] John C. Leggett, *Race, Class, and Labor* (New York: Oxford University Press, 1968).
[37] John Goldthorpe et al., *The Affluent Worker in the Class Structure* (Cambridge: Cambridge University Press, 1969), p. 150.

to some extent as objectively unrecognized as in the working classes—
though obviously to a far more limited degree.

A final study of class consciousness, more recent than the two other
investigations cited and disclosing considerably more class consciousness
than either of the other two, was conducted by Martin Scheffer on two
samples of white workers, one mainly skilled and stable and the other
mainly unskilled and unstable.[38] (The measures were almost identical to
those used by Leggett.) Over one-third of the stable-income workers
registered significant class consciousness, while only about one-fifth of the
low-income workers did so. The large majority of both samples were in
some manner sensitive to class differences, and spoke of them in predominantly material and financial terms. Class-conscious workers made
the following kinds of observations on the class structure:

> [There are] definitely social classes, the investors and the working man.
> Big business has this state controlled. [The profits] don't go to the low
> income or to my class of people, the working class.
>
> The owners of industry get the profits—they should raise the wages and
> share the profits.
>
> The business class gets the profits; there's no profit to be had for the
> workin' man. I sure don't favor it—workin' man goes broke trying to
> keep his family in what it needs while they is puttin' away all the profits.
>
> The classes are clear to me—money makes the difference. The big
> organizations and the money people are gettin' the profits, not the work-
> ing people. I agree that we ought to divide the wealth equally.
>
> Big business class has more power than the worker—just look at the
> way they carry on. Things are getting worse—big business has their
> own way and they're trying to eliminate the unions.
>
> The working man's lot is getting worse in most places. When they begin
> to realize this they will get together and demand their share.

Employing a research framework similar to Leggett's Detroit research conducted over a decade earlier, Scheffer's respondents from a western city of
70,000 suggest that class consciousness has sharpened during the decade
of the sixties.

That such is the case might be further suggested by the case of a
steel plant where instances of disciplinarian action against workers breaking rules climbed from a few hundred in 1965 to 3,400 in 1970. Andrew
Levinson stresses especiallly a changing world view among young blue-
collar workers, a large proportion of whom are seeking new life styles and
rejecting security and possessions as the only life goals. Vietnam veterans
count heavily in this group. Levinson argues that "this is the first gen-

---

[38] Martin W. Scheffer, "The Poor, Separate Class or Working Class: A Comparative Study," Ph.D. dissertation, University of Utah, 1971.

eration since the Thirties to view itself realistically as workers, without a deep sense of personal guilt or a belief that by some magic they or their children will be elevated to the middle class." [39]

A NOTE ON SOCIAL MOBILITY

Social mobility is a major preoccupation in stratification research. The empirical study of social mobility mainly involves examinations of inter-generational occupational movement, the literature concerning which is abundant. The results are unequivocal regarding the transmission of privilege through education and occupation. What movement there is amounts largely to minor adjustments upward or downward on a relatively narrow range of positions within the underlying population. Numerous in-fluences have been suggested, such as ethnic and religious background, childhood training schedules, parental value systems, peer group affili-ations, etc. Formal education is the mechanical avenue to occupational mobility, and educational background of parents is vitally important to mobility in children. But behind such educational privileges and other "life chances" lies primarily wealth. For example, fully 80 percent of 1965 high school seniors who graduated did not attend college in 1967 if their family income was under $3,000, as compared to only 13 percent of those with family incomes of $15,000 and over.[40] Or to take another example: the probability of low-socioeconomic-level high school students in the second-from-the-top ability quartile of going to college is *less* than that of high-socioeconomic students in the lowest ability quartile.

The importance of mobility within the income and occupational ranges of the working classes is not to be questioned. Few if any would disagree that $25,000 a year is preferable to $5,000, or that it is more promising to finish college than to drop out of high school, or that it is safer to work as a scientist or manager than as a construction worker. While we would not deny the salience of such very prominent and critical differences, the greater issue is not with the operation of the mobility system but why such a stepladder society exists in the first place and how and why it is perpetuated. Why is the working class as a whole set up as so many rungs on a ladder on which a person is pushed and pulled up and down? In whose interest is this system of interfamily competition? Who really benefits by it? What are the consequences for collective action? Why are certain abilities rewarded and others not rewarded or even

---

[39] "The Rebellion of Blue Collar Youth," *Progressive* (October 1972): 38–42.
[40] Samuel Bowles, "Getting Nowhere: Programmed Class Stagnation," *Society* 9 (June 1972): 47.

punished? Why are certain members of the working classes recruited or coopted into the ruling class or hired as servants?

The reason Marxist theory does not have time for refined studies of occupational or social mobility is that there are larger questions which must be answered first. It focuses upon questions such as the above. And most of the answers may be found in the rationale for ruling-class manipulation of the labor force and of the means of production as a whole. The pivotal answer to such larger questions concerns the interests of the ruling class in maintaining the underlying population as a self-contained, introspective society unto itself, concentrating on intraclass differences and relative standings and avoiding the larger and fundamental class division. Intraclass emphases focus attention on keeping up with Joneses and their late model car while the Fords rake in two-thirds of a billion dollars in net profits in a single year. The attention is held to getting the next job up the line or a white collar for children, rather than what really might be in a society that places human needs and contentment above the narrow economic machinations of a small but powerful class. It holds the working-man's eyes on the next pay raise so he can pay some insurance premium intended to pay for his children's college education, instead of asking why there is no open and free system of higher education right through graduate and professional schools not only for his children but for himself if he wanted it.

The stepladder trap, with all of its missing rungs and blocked accesses, is a custom-built net of confusion, hostility, and mutual recrimination within the underlying population. It is a subterfuge, and a very effective one at that, to divert concern away from the construction of a secure, satisfying, and humane economic and social order. Equality within the broad working classes would put an end to the internecine strife and warfare between black and white, male and female, young and old, educated and uneducated, affluent and poor. The focus would be put where it belongs: between the ruling class and the working class, between the vested interests and the underlying population. It would pull the working class toward thinking in terms of change *of* the system rather than the killing and hopeless struggle of reaching the top rungs *within* the existing system. But equality and change of the system are dependent upon one another, and to understand this is to be on the road to class consciousness.

six

THE WORKING CLASS:
PERSPECTIVES
ON EMPLOYMENT

The propertyless worker occupies the center stage in this chapter and the next. Our concern is with what Thorstein Veblen called the underlying population, within which we have placed the large majority of the population. This is a working class in the loose sense, though a major portion of it is Marxian proletariat. It is a working class not only in the manner analyzed in the previous chapter, but in the sense that those in it are under a physical compulsion to sell their time to an employer so as to persist as family heads or individuals. They cannot live off property, but must work on its behalf and for its aggrandizement. We shall, at least for the purposes of this chapter, loosen up the definition of *working class* even to the point of including the propertyless subsisters previously considered as sub-capitalist or servant classes, who in a theoretical sense are closely tied to the system of private property but in a physical sense have an equally difficult time of "making ends meet." In other words, the working class as viewed in this chapter consists of all those persons who would gain from a redistribution of property and wealth and power and, beyond that, from a progressive socialization of the means of production.

As we are largely dependent on all-inclusive government labor force statistics, by necessity we must inadvertently include in our discussions many members of the propertied and voluntarily property-dependent classes. So in reviewing the data presented in this chapter, we are fully aware of their "contaminated" nature.

The civilian labor force consists of all those persons employed at the time of survey or, if unemployed, had within the previous four weeks engaged in some job-seeking activity. This definition is very important, for it means that the unemployed segment of the labor force includes only those actively and recently seeking work and excludes those who for whatever reason have dropped out of the job market for a month or longer. By definition, then, official unemployment statistics seriously underestimate both the true extent of joblessness and the actual size of the available work force.

The more than 83 million civilian labor force participants in the United States in 1971 consisted of more than 4.7 million unemployed (5.7 percent) and the rest currently employed; more than 51 million males and almost 32 million females (37 percent); and more than 9 million nonwhites (11 percent). Participation rates for males 16 years old and over approach 80 percent (96 percent for males 25–44) and 43 percent for females (53 percent for females 35–54). At 75 percent, nonwhite males are under the 80 percent white participation rate for males, while the nonwhite female rate of 49 percent is 7 points above the white female rate.[1] Overall, this puts about 60 percent of those 16 years old and over in the labor force, but only 3 percent of 20 million elderly are involved, meaning only a modest majority of all 16- to 65-year-olds are in the labor force. Including the under-16 population, we may note that a minority of approximately 40 percent of all Americans are labor force participants. The fact that the majority of the population are not in the paid labor force raises important questions regarding the equity of weighting the material reward and consumption system so heavily toward work role. It suggests that a social democracy must at least socialize all consumption considered as necessary and normal for the times.

Of the more than 56 million persons 16 years old and over not in the paid labor force, more than 35 million report they are "keeping house." How many of these unpaid work hours are actually necessary no one knows, but it is certain that females do the bulk of this unpaid labor, and that in paying the head of a family, an employer and the system as a whole are getting in return the labor of two people—one in the wage laborer and the other in the home "servicing and repairing" this variable capital. An additional 9 million are in school, and again a large proportion are undergoing an apprenticeship in learning for necessary work participation without pay and thus constitute a subsidy to the system. Both housekeepers and students are making free and substantial social contributions to the economic viability of the system, but yet are largely dependent for such necessities as medical care on the breadwinning fortunes

---

[1] *The Statistical Abstract of the United States, 1972* (New York: Grosset & Dunlap, 1972), p. 210.

of the family head. Among the remaining 12 million non–labor force adults are an unknown but significant number of persons who have simply dropped out of the labor force, even the "housekeeping" labor force, from frustration in job-seeking, injury and illness, and crushing humiliation in working.

Owing to the increased number of female workers, the proportion of the adult population in the labor force has been on the rise during this century from slightly over half at its beginning to the three-fifths of today. The increase would be even greater were it not for the counterbalancing factors of lesser teenage and elderly labor force involvement. School continuation and earlier retirement have significantly contributed to holding back the rate of labor force expansion and, by the same token, the number of unemployed as well. And to say that working women are in any way responsible for male unemployment is to beg the question of why unemployment persists on a large scale. Indeed, by the very fact of their working, women with low wages further subsidize the profits of the ruling class. And women are often hired over men for precisely that reason. The number of working women is lower than it might be if adequate day-care centers for children were available and especially if many women had *any hope of finding a job*. The relationship between working women and full employment should receive greater attention, and must deal with both the problems of productive employment in the home and women out of the labor force who desire rewarding and remunerative work. As Carolyn Shaw Bell remarks, "Any full employment policy should involve some very searching questions about the nature of employment and the role of women in our society." [2] Perhaps as many as 20 percent, or even more, of working-age women not in the labor force are absent from it owing to the lack of suitable employment and would like to work if given the chance. This figure will surely increase with the annually increasing volume of young women prepared to teach but unable to find placement in the money-starved public schools, and the same holds true for other social service trainees. The discouraging job and career markets will lead growing numbers of both young men and women to withdraw from the labor force, perhaps helping the government hold down unemployment statistics but hurting the society through the loss of energy and skills.

We should note further in this connection that women are heavily dependent for paid labor on the social services and government sectors, where they constitute 54 and 43 percent of workers, respectively. Another major employer of women is the subcapitalist sectors of finance, insurance, and real estate, where 52 percent of employees are women. Women form the working backbone of this sector, doing the bulk of the tedious paper-

---

[2] "Implications for Women," *Social Policy*, September–October 1972, p. 12.

work and being receptionists, with men holding down the decision-making
and often high-paying positions. The other major female employer is retail
trade, where 46 percent are women; here, too, women are on the floor
almost exclusively, and rarely in the office in any other than secretarial
capacities. But for expansion, women must ultimately look toward the social
sector of the economy in search of greater employment opportunities, the
most vulnerable sector under the guidelines of capitalism.

The largest single employment sector of the labor force is manufacturing, with over 14 million production workers in this area and about
20 million employees all told. In addition, production workers total almost
one-half million in mining, 2.8 million in construction, and 3.9 million in
transportation and utilities. Counting all employees in manufacturing and
material production, we have 29 million workers, to which could be added
the 3.9 million farm workers. In short, goods production remains the center
of the employment market.

Next in size comes the distribution sector's 15.0 million employees,
and the functionally related finance–insurance–real estate category's some
3.7 million. This trade and finance sector is grossly inflated not only from
the standpoint of what constitutes a socially necessary labor force, but even
unto capitalism as such. Hacker's comments that "most white-collar jobs
come into being not so much because they are needed (that can never be
proved) but as and when the cash can be found to underwrite them" and
that "the inflation of white-collar occupations is now necessary for the
prosperity of the economy"[3] apply here as well as to most other sectors,
including manufacturing's nonproduction workers. Hacker is reiterating
Marx's analysis of the stabilizing consumption role of the surplus class in
capitalist society (see Chapter 3).

In third place is government, with 12.6 million on the payroll in
1970; together with the services sector, government is the society's fastest
growing employer. *The* fastest growing employer sector is state and local
government, exploding from 6.1 million in 1960 to nearly 10.0 million
in 1970. Federal employment expanded a very modest 2.3 to 2.7 million
over the same decade. The large portion of government employment is
nonmanual labor; at the federal level, for example, only one-third of
employees are manual workers and most of these are linked to the military.
To a significant extent, government employment is a function of the needs
of the private sector and not geared toward the accommodation of social
needs as such. Therefore, government employment and government-cre-
ated employment fluctuates to serve the private corporate economy, taking
in and letting out slack when deemed necessary by the ruling class. Need-

---

[3] Andrew Hacker, *The End of the American Era* (New York: Atheneum,
1970), pp. 17, 21.

less to say, the bourgeois state is padded with excess manpower in many areas (not, of course, where it might be detrimental to the interests of the ruling class, such as in the Justice Department's Anti-Trust Division). This is not to say that too many people are employed by government; the problem is that the use of manpower by government has been restricted to areas supportive of or noncompetitive with the corporate economy, and not fully utilized for the promotion of public and social well-being. More, not fewer, collectively assigned workers would be the result of a rationally, socially planned economy, especially in medicine, education, social welfare, and other service areas, but also in goods production.

Lastly, the private service sector employed 11.6 million persons in 1970. This sector has seen marked expansion during the past decade, and has played a major role in absorbing the slackening growth or shrinkage in other areas. Aside from a minority consisting of physicians, successful hotel and restaurant entrepreneurs, entertainment stars and employees, and the like, the private service sector includes a large portion of the underemployed (working but poor or near-poor). It does much to subsidize through low wages "the good life" of the affluent and the profits of employers. The private service work force is for the most part an old-fashioned servant class in modern trappings—many of which are exceedingly thinly veiled. Like employees in retail trade, another low-income sector, the service labor force employs a disproportionate number of the powerless—i.e., females, nonwhites, and youth. Even more poorly paid, however, are workers in the agricultural sector, whose median income is $8.50 per day—and even this reflects a marked improvement over 1965 preunion wage rates. How ironic that the workers most directly responsible for putting food on the tables of America are her most poorly paid citizens. But the irony fades when one notes the hundreds of millions in net profit taken each year by the big food corporations such as Tenneco, General Foods, and Monsanto.

Table 7 presents the occupational breakdown of the labor force by race and sex in 1970 and 1960. During this decade the largest proportionate increases were in professional, technical, and clerical categories, while the greatest decline was in farm work. Unskilled labor was the other area of noteworthy decline. The proportions of other blue- and white-collar categories, while showing numerical increases, were relatively stable during these years. Whites were twice as well represented in nonmanual occupations in 1970 as nonwhites. Females were more heavily in white-collar occupations than males, due mainly to their high clerical concentration. One-third of the overall female labor force occupy clerical jobs and over one-fifth are blue-collar service workers. Szymanski has drawn our attention to the fact that during the past century, and especially during the past thirty years, it has been the shifting occupational roles of women that have accounted for some of the major shifts in the occupational

TABLE 7

Current Occupation of Employed Persons by Race and Sex,
1970 and 1960: Percent

	White		Black	
	1970	*1960*	*1970*	*1960*
Male				
Professional and technical	14.8	11.6	5.8	3.3
Managerial	15.4	12.2	4.1	1.4
Clerical	7.4	7.7	8.6	6.1
Sales	6.1	7.5	1.6	1.6
Craftsmen	20.6	21.3	14.2	10.0
Operatives	18.9	20.5	30.6	27.0
Nonfarm laborers	5.7	5.6	18.9	24.3
Service workers	6.0	5.5	11.7	15.6
Farm	5.2	8.1	4.5	10.6
Total Employed	100.0	100.0	100.0	100.0
Female				
Professional and technical	15.5	14.6	10.0	7.0
Managerial	14.7	4.4	1.4	0.7
Clerical	36.1	34.9	18.9	8.1
Sales	7.3	8.8	2.5	1.3
Craftsmen	1.1	1.4	0.8	0.9
Operatives	14.5	16.7	16.8	14.0
Nonfarm laborers	0.4	0.5	0.9	0.8
Service	18.8	17.2	48.1	63.7
Farm	1.5	1.5	0.5	3.6
Total Employed	100.0	100.0	100.0	100.0

Source: U.S. Bureau of the Census, *Current Population Reports,* Series P-23, No. 37, "Social and Economic Characteristics of the Population in Metropolitan and Non-metropolitan Areas: 1970 and 1960," U.S. Government Printing Office, Washington, D.C., 1971, Table 14, pp. 60–62.

structure. For example, since 1940 female workers have proportionately shifted heavily into lower-white-collar employment; moreover, overall growth of female labor has been disproportionately lower-white-collar. Thus, the widely noted growth of the white-collar segment of the labor force over the past thirty years has not been at the cost of a declining proportion of male manual workers, but is rather due largely to the influx into lower-white-collar positions, in greater proportions and numbers, of females, two-fifths of whom are wives of blue-collar males. Even though the new working class of professionals and technicians has greatly expanded, the proportionate loss has been made up for largely by the self-employed (petit bourgeois) and agricultural occupations.[4]

---

[4] Albert Szymanski, "Trends in the American Class Structure," *Socialist Revolution* 10 (July–August 1972): 107–9.

Mass unemployment is an essential ingredient of monopoly profits. Idle manpower is not something the capitalist class weeps about or wishes to take serious measures to eliminate, for a reserve army of workers is a potent strategy for keeping the regulars busy and uncomplaining—busy producing and uncomplaining about wages. As Lekachman observes: "Assured jobs and incomes will fatally disrupt the coercive management of labor." [5] This holds true whether one has in mind the old or new working class. The higher the productivity and the lower wage costs the higher will be the profits realized. Unemployment even on a recession scale does not disturb monopoly capitalists, who can go on profiting owing to their monopoly powers, while lesser creatures suffer and perish. The ruling class needs only as many active workers as is necessary to produce enough goods sold at monopoly prices to realize profit for expansion and growth. That men and women are unemployed and wanting couldn't mean less to corporate planners. Indeed, millions are consciously driven from their jobs —as was done by the business-owned Nixon administration early in its tenure—for the purpose of manipulating the economy (successfully, as it has turned out) in the direction of real corporate profits. Millions of the powerless are ruthlessly cut off from work for the political and economic interests of the powerful.

Although a wage-depressing army of unemployed is a useful tool to big property interests, much unemployment is an uncontrolled artifact of monopoly capitalism. Daniel Mason has remarked that "unemployment is a basic element of the capitalist system. U.S. monopolists won't, of their own volition, abolish unemployment, and—what is more to the point— can't abolish unemployment." [6] Even if it wanted to, the ruling class could not eliminate unemployment in the United States without violating the sacred tenets of capitalism; and by the same token, the massive unemployment that does exist is no less an inescapable by-product of the practice of these same tenets. There are many subtenets which we shall discuss, but most derive from the chief one: profit maximization overall and expansive growth. The pursuit of profit and growth by the ruling class leads to unemployment in several diverse ways, some intentional and controllable and others unintentional and uncontrollable.

Let us look first at the extent of unemployment at midterm of a

---

[5] Robert Lekachman, "Toward a Reordered Economy," *Dissent*, Fall 1972, p. 584.

[6] Daniel Mason, "The Problem of Unemployment," *Political Affairs* 50 (November 1971): 26.

typical ruling-class–oriented presidential administration. In early 1971 the official rate of unemployment was approximately 6 percent of the labor force. But this is only the beginning of the unemployment story. As Gross and Moses state: "Labor force definitions have been constructed so as to exclude millions of people in order to understate the dimensions of unemployment and the extent to which the economic system has failed to generate adequate and suitable job opportunities." Pursuing their definition of unemployment as "all those who are not working and are able and willing to work for pay," Gross and Moses calculate the real rate of unemployment (1971) to be 24.6 percent. Their figures include an officially unemployed category of 4.7 million, 7.1 million government-counted underemployed and part-time workers seeking full-time work plus job-wanters not counted, 5 million housewives (only one-seventh of women at home), 3 million students who would prefer to work (one-third of working-age students), 4 million persons aged 55–64 not working, 1.5 million uncounted unemployed and unemployables who could work given opportunities and/or training, and 300,000 persons in manpower programs—for a total of 25.6 million out of a real labor force of 104 million.[7]

This is the most realistic estimation of unemployment to date. The U.S. Labor Department, counting only officially unemployed, labor force dropouts, and part-time workers seeking full-time work, has itself estimated the real rate of unemployment to be well above 30 percent in many major cities. By including just this more limited group of categories we arrive at a national rate almost twice the figure usually given. To be strictly realistic, the full-time working poor should also be added to the above calculations, since this employment is not earning them a living wage.

An additional fundamental point regarding unemployment in the United States has been made by Sweezy: by adding to the 8.1 million officially and dropped-out unemployed in December 1970 the 2.9 million active military personnel, 1.2 million Department of Defense civilian employees, 3 million direct defense industry employees, and 7.1 million jobs created by the military multiplier effect, a grand total of unemployed and military employed reaches 22.3 million persons, over 25 percent of the official labor force.[8] Without the military-industrial complex and its global activities the corporate capitalism of today would be doing no better in employing the population than it did in the 1930s. Combining the Gross-Moses and Sweezy calculations, we may total some 14.2 million military-

---

[7] Bertram Gross and Stanley Moses, "Measuring the Real Work Force: 25 Million Unemployed," *Social Policy,* September–October 1972, pp. 5–10.

[8] Sweezy, "Economic Stagnation and Stagnation of Economics," *Monthly Review* 22 (April 1971): 9.

dependent employed with the 25.6 million real civilian unemployed to obtain nearly 40 million persons out of a real labor force of 104 million who are either military-dependent or out of work. Thus any serious assessment of the application of human resources under capitalism seems predetermined to discover wholesale irrationality and waste.

Like poverty, unemployment does not fall randomly over the population, but strikes more heavily on certain groups and areas than others. Appalachia has suffered the loss of hundreds of thousands of coal-mining jobs (a blessing in certain respects) due to automation and decline in coal consumption relative to other fuels. The decaying central cities have particularly high rates of unemployment as the numbers of unskilled jobs decline and service and industrial operations move to the suburbs or even further out. Many New England cities have been hit hard due to movement of textile and other manufacturing industries to low-wage and less unionized states of the South. Volatile defense spending has created boom and bust unemployment in aerospace cities such as Seattle, Wichita, and Los Angeles. Unemployment rates among teenagers are three to four times higher than the national average, and they are much higher than that for ghetto populations. Blacks face an unemployment rate almost twice that of whites, and blue-collar workers over twice the rate of white-collar. Females are slightly more likely to be job-hunting than males.

The average duration of unemployment is almost thirteen weeks, and 40 percent of the unemployed are without work for over ten weeks. If those who have dropped out of the labor force could be averaged in, the length of unemployment would be markedly longer. And as we shall observe in connection with the discussion of welfare, unemployment compensation is spotty and thin.

What happens to a person or family, aside from the material deprivation and loss, when in the throes of unemployment? Aiken and his associates discovered that among a group of laid-off automobile workers, aside from the loss of affective support and functional aid from social relationships in the work setting and the loss of contact with the union and its integrating influences, the depletion of financial resources and the lack of a job led to a reduced contact with kin and friends, an erosion of sense of social identity and usefulness derived from the work role, and a drastic readjustment of role expectations within the family.[9] Here are some typical comments from study respondents:

> I travel hundreds of miles a day to get a job. A lot of places they want young guys. I've borrowed until I don't borrow any more. I lost my car, too. I guess I'll have to go on welfare.

---

[9] Michael Aiken, Louis A. Ferman, and Harold L. Sheppard, *Economic Failure, Alienation, and Extremism* (Ann Arbor: University of Michigan Press, 1968), p. 2.

My boy won't be able to go to college. He's 17 years old, but he don't take an interest in high school anymore because he thinks he won't be able to go to college.

It's hard for me now. I'm unskilled, 52 years old, and a woman. Nobody wants to hire me. I've got no income, and you ask me if I got a hard break. It's hard to feel useless. I feel sick. . . . There's no hope and no future. . . . I'm 52 and there is nothing for me to do. . . . I might as well be dead.[10]

About the time this study was done, Adolf A. Berle, Jr. was rationalizing that unemployment in the United States is not as bad as concentration camps in the Soviet Union, with the clear implication that America's unemployed should not only be uncomplaining but actually be happy they aren't Russians.[11]

Established social science naturally has its own explanations of unemployment. Typical is that offered by Tiffany and his associates, who offer a probing analysis into the psychological traits of unemployment.[12] A sample of unemployed are labeled as the experimental, "work inhibited" ("lazy"?) group and are found to have weak self-images and poor interaction skills, and to be lacking in consideration of others, less sociable and helping, etc. Purportedly these personality traits are the *cause* of the "work inhibited" group's inability to maintain a job. Unfortunately, the time factor is not controlled, leaving the reader with the author's assertion that their analysis gives the correct cause-and-effect relationship. It is much more likely, given the exceedingly important place work occupies in social and psychological interaction, that sustained unemployment destroys self-image and undermines social relationships than the other way around. Aiken's research (above) confirms this interpretation. Few would deny that a certain amount of unemployment may be attributed to voluntary idleness or work inhibition, but it is surely erroneous to argue that the millions of officially unemployed are psychologically incapable of working. We will find serious clues to large-scale unemployment not in the structure of the unemployeds' minds but rather in the structure of monopoly capitalism.

We have already mentioned one factor which influences unemployment, and that is the preference of capital for a labor surplus. Almost uniformly, a labor surplus is at once trapped and unorganized, wide open for the most vicious sort of wage exploitation by capital. Beginning with

---

[10] Ibid., pp. 63–65.
[11] Adolf A. Berle, Jr., *Power Without Property* (New York: Harcourt, Brace and World, 1959), p. 146.
[12] Donald W. Tiffany, James R. Cowan, and Phyllis M. Tiffany, *The Unemployed: A Social Psychological Portrait* (Englewood Cliffs, N.J.: Prentice-Hall, 1970), Chapter 6.

children and immigrants in the nineteenth century and on through black migrants, rural whites, females, and Mexican Americans, corporate capital has taken pains to maintain a labor force in excess of immediate demands, one that is pliable and defenseless in character. (A labor surplus cannot always be attained, especially in sparsely populated industrializing societies such as the United States in the nineteenth century; the response may include the use of child and female labor, the importation of labor, and a high investment of capital which later creates its own labor surplus.) The unskilled and powerless surplus, often desperate to the point of starvation, has been brutally utilized as an instrument to undercut organized labor and create rifts within the working class. The surplus work force and organized labor have up to now largely reacted precisely as capital has intended—with mutual recrimination and hostility, narrowmindedness, and selfishness of purpose. A meeting and understanding of unorganized surplus and organized labor would be a serious blow to capital.

In our discussion of Marx we noted the tendency of capitalism toward overproduction of exchange values, and the response of cutting back on production. Veblen, too, was especially emphatic on the latter point. Returning to the midpoint in the first Nixon administration, we may observe the classic case in point, for then almost 30 percent of *existing* production facilities lay idle, and with it the workers. Consciously, corporate capital threw hundreds of thousands of men and women out of work in order to preserve the sacred ascendancy of money demand over supply of goods, of artificially created scarcity, and of profits. Even more than the need for an industrial reserve army, this is the root of unemployment under the regime of capital: the inability to keep the wheels of industry rolling and growing because of internally created imbalances of individual purchasing power and the production of goods and services not in the best interest of social well-being. Robert Theobald has phrased the issue rather lucidly in saying that "there should be no difficulty in finding useful work. Our scarcity is one of market-supported jobs, not of work that needs to be done." [13]

Closely linked to the overproduction impetus to unemployment is the advance of machine technology or automation. This link is not a necessary or causal one, however, as it is not high productivity or advanced technology per se which at this time leads to unemployment, but rather only as these factors operate within a market economy unable to engage the advancing forces of production in a rational and progressive fashion. We shall devote specific space to this subject in the next section, and so simply note here its impact on job loss or stagnation. The area of primary production has been the most notably affected by advancing mechaniza-

---

[13] Robert Theobald, *Free Men and Free Markets* (Garden City, N.Y.: Doubleday, 1965), p. 139.

tion. With the labor force expanding by 8.2 million workers from 1965 to 1970, the number of miners, basic lumber and wood product workers, primary metal workers, leather-product workers, and farm workers declined.[14] Stagnating or only slightly increasing were the numbers of jobs in construction, manufacturing, stone, clay, and glass products, fabricated metal, machinery, electrical equipment, transportation equipment, precision instruments, food products, textiles, wearing apparel, paper and printing, rubber, petroleum, and public utilities. The decrease in railroad jobs is well known. Among the primary and secondary industrial sectors only ordnance (guns, napalm, fragmentation bombs, etc.), plastics, drugs, trucking, and communications jobs made significant percentage increases during that "active" economic period. Sporting goods, toys, and tobacco products all witnessed job losses partially linked to automation. For specific illustrations, we might observe that a single Du Pont Company plant manufactures 70 percent of U.S. nylon consumption in three eight-hour shifts of 9 men each, and that Raytheon Manufacturing Company equipped its radio assembly plant with automatic equipment which reduced the number of workers from 200 to 2, and that by introducing automation a petroleum refinery can reduce its labor force from 800 to 12.[15]

In short, despite what we shall observe in the next section regarding rising output in manufacturing, agriculture, and related utilities, advanced capitalism cannot rely on these sectors to provide employment to a growing labor force. Preventing more serious unemployment during 1965 to 1970 (remembering all along that military spending gave a tremendous lift to maintaining manufacturing employment, and of course still does) were growth rates in the subcapitalist and service job classifications: trade, finance, personal services, and government. Out of the 8.2 million increase in job seekers and holders from 1965 to 1970, these subcapitalist and service occupational strata provided for over 85 percent. Government has become the single most important generator of employment, directly or indirectly accounting for one-quarter of existing jobs (upholding the Marxist label of state capitalism). Adding together the unemployed, the military-employed or -dependent, and the government-employed, we are talking about 34 million people, 40 percent of the officially defined labor force. Take these jobs away and the Depression of the 1930s would perhaps seem like a mere recession. Take away, further, the subcapitalist money-handling and paper shuffling jobs, and the servants catering to the personal whims of the bourgeoisie and the economy wouldn't even exist. If the majority or even a significant minority of all of these superstructure jobs

---

14 *The Statistical Abstract of the United States,* pp. 219–21.
15 Sidney Willhelm, *Who Needs the Negro?* (Cambridge, Mass.: Schenkman Publishing Company, 1970), pp. 146–47.

were really necessary as such and/or contributed to the overall well-being of society, there would be more limited room for criticism. But more often than not their design and creation are not out of social necessity or constructiveness, but for the sole purpose of preserving the capitalist system as an on-going enterprise of inequality and privilege.

How much proliferation in the service and administrative sectors is possible is unknown, but it is probably quite great. Yet automation places limitations here, too. Computers are rapidly becoming more economical to build and use, and are making major inroads into white-collar employment. Twenty years ago thousands of people were needed to perform clerical and accounting work that can now be handled by a few. We also know of the possibilities of automated servicing, buying, catering, and teaching. Automation is capable of spreading unemployment throughout almost the entire occupational structure. The extent to which it does so hinges on the profit calculations of the capitalist class, a particularly dubious and dangerous criterion when applied to such a potent social force as automation.

A final source of unemployment in the United States, but a minor source of employment elsewhere, is imperialism. General Instruments, for example, employs 12,000 workers in Taiwan, more than in the United States itself. Why do corporations go multinational in employment? Because Taiwanese women, for example, work for $20 a month, rendering profits ten times cost. Little wonder, then, that from 1966 to 1969 the value of finished products from foreign-assembled American-made parts increased by fifteen times.[16] The rank-and-file worker-consumer fails to benefit from this activity, for monopoly pricing goes up and not down, and the difference in unit cost to the corporation goes into the profit ledgers. The worker-consumer continues to pay monopoly prices while facing unemployment or threats of it. One must distinguish between multinational corporate imperialism and trade, though trade, too, may be conducted under the umbrella of imperialism. Trade with Japanese-owned firms, for example, is a different thing than activity between American-owned foreign subsidiaries and the metropolitan office. When terms of trade are equal, such exchange has been demonstrated to *create* employment in both economies—as has been the case with Japan and the United States. When terms of trade are imperialistically unequal, as between Latin America and the United States, everybody loses but the corporations—Latin America in the form of foreign exchange and the American working class in the form of possible jobs (Latin America's lesser foreign exchange means fewer demands for U.S. products, and hence also fewer jobs). Even the consumer fails to gain, because even if comparable foreign imports *could*

---

[16] Daniel Mason, "U.S. Imperialism and Latin America," *Political Affairs* 49 (July 1970): 13.

be sold very cheaply they are not, either due to protective tariffs or monopoly prices. As with automation, the guidelines for international corporate economic activity have little to do with employment and social
well-being, but are structured to meet the demands of profit and growth.
If inflation, war, unemployment, and misery are the outcomes, then this
is simply too bad for those affected.

There are other sources of unemployment, such as mismatches between skills and jobs. How seriously the government takes this problem is
illustrated by the scope of the federal Manpower Development and Training
Program, which maintains some 200,000 trainee positions while more than
4.5 million persons, according to official figures, go jobless. The overpro-
tected workers in the building and skilled trades have also been a reactionary
force obstructing an open and progressive employment market, in much
the same manner as the caste system in medicine. Certainly *not* among the
causes of unemployment is a demand and need for work to be done, and
this means genuine physical building and social service work and not redundant, parasitical, and destructive make-work. Many persons consider
full socially relevant employment to be possible without radical change,
but this is to completely overlook the nature of capitalism as a system.[17]

PRODUCTIVITY, EMPLOYMENT, AND WAGES

Marxist theory is very much concerned with productivity, since how much
a worker or work group can produce within a given time period holds the
key to the real value of the product and ultimately to the replacement of
the labor theory of value by the measurement of value by free time in a
fully advanced socialized society. Freedom from economic necessity can
only be achieved by progressive increase in production and decrease in
human effort. Freedom from economic necessity, we might recall, does
not imply idleness, but a freedom of time to engage oneself in individual
and social development and fulfillment, while not having to slave daily at
alienating and exhausting menial wage labor. Automation we understand
to mean any technological innovations, including mechanization and rationalization as well as automatic process control with feedback, which
serve to increase productivity with decreasing human effort.[18]

---

17 For an example of a liberal reform advocacy position on social problems,
see Jack Newfield and Jeff Greenfield, *A Populist Manifesto* (New York: Frederick
A. Praeger, 1972).

18 Dennis Gabor, *Innovations: Scientific, Technological, and Social* (London:
Oxford University Press, 1970), p. 48.

In his trenchant critique of the harmful impact of uncontrolled technology on the environment, Eugene Schwartz has written that "by accepting the forces of production as autonomous forces, and seeking to alter only the relations of production, Marxism has nurtured commodity fetishism and subordinated socialist man to the technological machine."[19] This statement is valid insofar as Marxism is equated with Soviet-style communism, but invalid when taken to refer to orthodox Marxist socialist principles. The stated goal of Marxist theory is to liberate the individual from the chains of economic determinism and from the fetishization of the material world. An orthodox Marxist would agree with Schwartz that machines should be used for human purposes and that wasteful consumption is a most destructive form of human behavior. In his attack on technology, Schwartz also errs in attributing bureaucratization and centralization to advanced technology. Technology is clearly not the chief root of the monolithic organization; rather, technology has provided the conditions and means for the natural tendencies of capital toward concentration and large bureaucracies are as much a stabilizing sop for surplus wealth, as a tool for dealing with this concentration. The more advanced the technology the *fewer* the people needed to operate production, not more.

Another common error in the analysis of technology which must be dealt with is the view that technology is *the* cause, or at least the most important cause, of the major phenomena popularly associated with it. For example, Slater tells us that "technology makes core policy in every industrialized nation, and the humans adjust as best they can."[20] This sounds good but is wrong, and is frankly dangerous if people are looking for the key to change, for it leads them to look at technology when they should be looking at the ruling class. The ruling class, not technology, makes core policy, and humans (and the environment we should add) are forced to adjust to *them* according to how they have decided to put technology into their service. It is one of the ironies of bourgeois social science to have long promulgated the view that Marxism is single-factor technological determinism when technology has turned out to be bourgeois social science's own favorite predictive variable. Marxist theory employs a class model of society, not a technological one. It knows that technology is a tool of the ruling class, to be used in the interests of profitability.[21] The use of technology in capitalist society is linked to economic necessity and

---

[19] Eugene S. Schwartz, *Overskill: The Decline of Technology in Modern Civilization* (Chicago: Quadrangle Books, 1971), p. 301.

[20] Philip Slater, *The Pursuit of Loneliness* (Boston: Beacon Press, 1970), p. 46.

[21] J. H. Westergaard, "The Withering Away of Class," in Jerry Anderson and Robin Blackburn, eds., *Towards Socialism* (Ithaca, N.Y.: Cornell University Press, 1966), p. 93.

to calculations of surplus value, and is deployed only when it can lead directly or indirectly to the increase of such surplus value. "The monopolies," Mandel points out, "do not want any increase in production to take place unless its absorption is *guaranteed*." [22] And given monopoly conditions, competition cannot force the introduction of new machinery until the undepreciated value of the old equipment is assured to be covered by the new.[23] Monopolists are not interested in using technology for raising productivity for human ends and purposes, but only insofar as it promises to raise profits. Technology is *at* the core of policy, but is only the *instrument* of policy made by the ruling class.

A closer look at this problem is in order, for it lies at the center of differences between private and social planning in the economy. Let us first take a hypothetical example and then a real one. Let us assume that with a given set of machines a manufacturer is earning $150,000 by selling 100,000 units at $1.50 per unit, but that by introducing a technological advance which would reduce the number of workers or number of hours each worker worked, the sale price of each unit could be lowered to $1.00, enabling more individuals to afford its purchase. Would the manufacturing company's directors reduce the work day and hold wages steady, and sell their product to more people at a lower price? Only if by so doing a larger profit could be realized, an outcome which is infrequent given typical monopoly capitalist circumstances. Clearly, instead of himself earning less and the worker working and consumer paying less, the corporate capitalist will always force the opposite situation if at all possible. Given free trade and a competitive economy, an original premise of Marxist economic theory, the manufacturer would be forced to install the advanced system or fall by the wayside to more efficient competitors. Such was traditionally the path to centralization of capital. But monopoly capital does not operate in such open circumstances; it creates its own economic environment. It can choose *not* to install automated equipment to save labor and increase freedom and consumption of necessities, for its monopoly status in the market enables it to produce inefficiently (or beneath what is technologically possible) and still price commodities at superprofit rates.

Now to look at an actual case of ruling-class policy: the automobile industry strikes an almost perfect parallel to the hypothetical case given above. Despite its popular image of automation advance, Detroit production has in principle not moved far beyond Henry Ford. With the number of production workers from 1947 to 1966 varying around 650,000, the

---

[22] Ernest Mandel, *Marxist Economic Theory,* vol. 2 (New York: Monthly Review Press, 1968), pp. 429–31.
[23] See Paul A. Baran, *The Political Economy of Growth* (New York: Monthly Review Press, 1968), p. 79.

production of automobiles more than doubled during that time. Yet this increase in productivity was obtained largely through an intensification of the work process. The main principle of "advanced automotive technology" in production is the Ford-invented speed-up. At the "modern" Lordstown, Ohio, Vega factories, for example, a car body rolls by a worker every 36 seconds, 800 every 8 hours.[24] What automation is stressed in these nightmarish plants is that of simply rationalizing part placement to the most homogeneous and unskilled movements. Strikes, absenteeism, and "psychological" problems have been rife at Lordstown, impelling General Motors to send in their toughest taskmasters to raise the level of surplus value. "It's not feasible or profitable for the Man to automate the plants," goes an essay in the *Liberator,* "the capitalist just thinks in terms of profits." [25] (The same piece refers to Detroit-style automation as "niggermation," with 40 percent of today's auto workers being nonwhite.) Automation could be used to reduce labor and lower prices, not to mention improve safety and even shift away from the internal-combustion engine; but ruling-class monopoly and profit interests disallow these possibilities. The $2.6 billion in net profit taken by General Motors and Ford in 1971 is not likely to be used to lighten the workloads of the men in the plants or lower the purchase price of automobiles. Rather, sustained speed-ups and inflated prices are the normal expectation.

Though technically not involved in the creation of surplus value, the personal service sector is also adept at maximizing its own gain through raising the absolute amount of labor put forth by the individual at a given wage. A black man working at a St. Louis drive-in diner for $70 a week reported: "When I go to work I'm supposed to mop the floors four hours and then cook four hours, but I never get out of there with just working eight hours because they always have something they want me to do when I get ready to leave." Within the eight-hour pay period, he observed: "These people try to work you to death." [26] The watchful eye of the foreman and the ten-minute work breaks are certain reminders that productivity through the forced intensity of labor effort was not limited to English factories in the nineteenth century.

Yet no one would dispute the fact that the predominant route to increased surplus value is through raising productivity by technological advance, though there are exceptions and we have noted one. Productivity increases stemming from advancing technology have completely transformed the agricultural sector and have doubled since 1950 in many manu-

---

[24] See Emma Rothschild, "GM in More Trouble," *New York Review of Books,* March 23, 1972, pp. 18–25.

[25] "Auto Unions and Niggermation," *Liberator* 10 (December 1970): 4–8.

[26] Lee Rainwater, *Behind Ghetto Walls* (Chicago: Aldine Publishing Company, 1970), p. 23.

facturing areas. Under monopoly capital, productivity gains have not been translated into lower consumer prices nor, as the Marxist framework suggests, has labor experienced wage gains relative to profits. Unorganized labor has slipped markedly in wages relative to corporate profits, while organized labor has barely held its own. Since 1965, gains in productivity of 5 to 15 percentage points were frequent in manufacturing, but real spendable wages *declined* for a worker with three dependents from $102.41 per week in 1965 to $101.49 in 1969 and to $99.66 in 1970.[27] With corporate profits rising during the same period, the insoluble conflict of interests between labor and capital may be clearly seen. Perlo points out that from 1957 to 1969 capital received 26 percent more goods for every dollar of real wages and salaries paid out.[28] The exploitation of unorganized female and minority labor in repetitive mechanical jobs has alone netted the capitalist class billions of profits annually.

James O'Connor has pointed out that the monopoly sector (large corporations) of the economy tends to encompass organized labor, with prices and wages. To the extent that organized labor can force wage increases with productivity gains (and as we have already pointed out, this has not been typical, at least in the sense of equitable wage increases), unorganized or competitive labor suffers as their own wages decline relatively and the prices of commodities are increased. Cheap labor in the competitive sector (small businesses) discourages automation there, and hence retards productivity and again wages. (This, in turn, lowers the demand for machinery from the monopoly sector.) The government, which has initially spent billions for raising productivity in the economy with expenditures for education and research, finds itself in a financial squeeze as political pressures mount to raise government workers' wages and salaries to remain abreast with union pay and corporate prices. With corporations and the rich systematically evading full tax contributions to government, profits are protected and government faces fiscal crises.[29] The logical trend is for government workers to organize and strike.

The worst victims of these events are workers in the competitive sector, particularly retail trade, personal services, unskilled labor, and agricultural labor. Unions typically find themselves siding with capital over the uses of increased productivity, i.e., for profits and wages rather than broad social investment through government—though there is clear evidence that the rank-and-file member is moving away from the narrowness of vision of union bosses and toward the recognition of the need for social and

---

27 *The Statistical Abstract of the United States,* pp. 224–25.
28 Victor Perlo, "U.S. Imperialism Today," *Political Affairs* 45 (June 1970): 23.
29 James O'Connor, "Inflation, Fiscal Crisis, and the American Working Class," *Socialist Revolution,* no. 8, March–April 1972, pp. 9–46.

environmental investments. Exacerbating the problem is the fact that a major portion of the competitive sector consists of minority-group members, for the economic difference of interest between the skilled monopoly worker and the unskilled competitive worker is reinforced by racial differences. Yet, there is much racial overlap, and even more overlap in broad material interests between the various sectors of the working class, such as in health, education, housing, transportation, product quality and safety, prices, environment, etc. Recognizing and acting upon these mutual social interests would spell trouble for monopoly capital and reactionary union elites. This is precisely why large capital and many labor bureaucrats fear politicians who seek to integrate the unorganized and minorities into the system. Both prefer to be powerful in a polarized, unequal society rather than common men in a cooperating system of social equality.

The unification of the underlying population—organized and unorganized, employed and unemployed, workers and social dependents—is, of course, the major challenge of progressive forces and the major threat to the status quo and reaction. The road to unification is littered with obstacles, the most imposing being the divisive manipulation of income, jobs, and taxes by the ruling interests, and sharpened by racial fears and prejudices. We might recall that Marx long ago pointed out the ruling-class strategy of shifting the welfare burden onto the petite bourgeoisie and working class. Black worker James Boggs has put it as follows: "This antagonism in the population between those who have to be supported and those who have to support them is one of the inevitable antagonisms of capitalism. And it is this antagonism, brought to a climax by automation, which will create one of the deepest crises for capitalism in our age." [30] Either way it will be a crisis for capitalism: unification would pose a crisis for monopoly capital, while disunity and conflict within the working class could severely disrupt the system.

Automation has beyond doubt undermined the sacred tie between work and income, production and consumption. Theobald is correct in saying that "cybernation . . . increases the ability to produce out of all proportion to any rise in rights to consume." [31] Marx foresaw this contingency and for just this reason envisioned the future measurement of value as being free time rather than labor time. The "social wage" paid out of the public fund for the normal needs of life must be increased, and a discretionary guaranteed income implemented. But as Theobald has also said, there is no shortage of work that needs to be done, only a shortage of market-supported jobs. As Robert Heilbroner has observed: "The

---

[30] James Boggs, *The American Revolution* (New York: Monthly Review Press, 1968), p. 37.
[31] Theobald, *Free Men and Free Markets*, p. 131.

systematic reconstruction of our cities, a task that is becoming an increasingly pressing necessity, could by itself provide millions of jobs for decades." [32] Numerous other realms of life could be mentioned, such as transportation, communications, and especially health, housing, and education. The salvaging of the earth itself will require monumental labor efforts and require a major transformation of human material life and production.

The ruling class and its political representatives can tinker endlessly with Keynesian and neo-Keynesian economic manuevers in attempts to deal with automation and employment, profits and wages, and social unrest. But to really put all willing and able people constructively to work, and to provide all with the resources and time to engage in satisfying leisure, the guidelines of corporate capitalism would have to be largely abandoned. Until this is done, we may continue to expect a divided and unequal society, brutalizing itself as well as innocent people elsewhere in the world.

UNIONS

The role of trade unions in the relations between capital and labor has been alluded to on a number of previous occasions. From the perspective of Marxist theory, the trade union or the organization of labor serves to reduce competition among workers and prevent capital from maximizing wage exploitation, as well as serving as a medium for consciousness raising and politicizing. The bitter opposition which capital has always evinced toward unionization in the United States attests to ruling-class fears of a strong and unified working class. While the chief battle for organization has shifted to the agricultural sector,[33] it wasn't until as late as the mid-1930s that the balance of law and government began to swing toward the recognition of the legitimacy of labor organization and its rights to strike and bargain collectively with capital. The half-century preceding this change was scarred with rancorous and violent repression of labor interests. In most instances, the capitalist class has pursued a successful policy of seeking to divide and conquer in the working class, pitting skilled

---

[32] Robert Heilbroner, *The Economic Problem* (Englewood Cliffs, N.J.: Prentice-Hall, 1970), p. 374.

[33] See Jerry J. Berman and Jim Hightower, "Battle for Lettuce: Chavez and the Teamsters," *The Nation*, November 2, 1970, pp. 427–31. On the labor battles during the Depression, see *Radical America*'s November–December 1972 issue on "Workers' Struggles in the 1930's."

against unskilled, natives against immigrants, Protestants against Catholics, and whites against blacks.[34]

The degree of union success in gaining advances in real wages, or of preventing declines, is significantly related to the relative size of the industrial reserve army of unemployed. If unemployment is high or rising, any advance in real wages is seriously impaired, while a low, stable, or declining rate of unemployment creates favorable conditions for the assertion of labor strength. Accordingly, we have already noted the stagnating and declining real wages of the late 1960s and early 1970s as a corollary of rising unemployment. This is another by-product of capitalism's inherent contradictions, and is a basic ingredient of the economic cycles. In a period of prosperity and labor demand, the ruling class begins to realize an expansion of surplus value but is soon faced with the prospect of having to cut a strengthened organized labor in on the profits. Conversely, with slowdowns in economic activity, capital sees a shrinking mass of profit but at the same time is able to take much of the loss out of a weakened labor force in the form of declining real wages. The option that capital—or at least the more enlightened segments of the ruling class since the first quarter of the century—has taken has been to recognize the need for stability or prosperity even at the cost of having an important sector of the industrial labor force unionized. Indeed, organization of the monopoly sector could even be made to work favorably for corporate capital, given the cooptation of labor leaders into the system. In Domhoff's words: "By making certain concessions and institutionalizing their conflict with labor, they [i.e., the ruling class] avoided the possibility of serious political opposition to the structure of the corporate system." [35]

The opinion is widespread that union leadership, at least, has become part and parcel of the corporate capitalist system. In 1945, when in proportionate terms unions were nearing a membership crest with about one-third of the industrial work force organized, Mills wrote: "As procapitalist, hardheaded, pressure-group captains and as members or would-be members of the national elite, in so far as labor men talk seriously of programs, they will invariably conceive of them [programs] as realizable alongside present corporations and within the present state framework." [36] More recently, Aronowitz evaluated union leadership in the following terms: "With few exceptions, particularly in textile and electrical corporations, employers regard labor leaders as their allies against the ignorant and

---

34 Bruce C. Johnson, "The Democratic Mirage: Notes Toward a Theory of American Politics," *Berkeley Journal of Sociology* 13 (1968): 104–43.

35 G. William Domhoff, *The Higher Circles: The Governing Class in America* (New York: Random House, 1971), p. 249.

36 C. Wright Mills, *Power, Politics, and People* (New York: Oxford University Press, 1963), p. 108.

undisciplined rank-and-file workers." [37] He adds that the unions' role as an organ of struggle has virtually disappeared. Booth argues that "the particular feature of American business unionism is the laxity with which it approaches the day-to-day class struggle, due to the identification of union interests with particular interests of the bosses." [38]

This last point is crucial. That union bosses (and in view of the pathetic state of democracy in most unions, there is merit in the label) have grown soft on fat salaries and retirement benefits—some in the vicinity of those of the corporate elite themselves—does not at all mean that union membership has followed a similar path. (Symbolically, George Meany raised his salary from $70,000 to $90,000 during the wage freeze.) Union elites have not been particularly authoritative of late, on occasion seeing their own membership striking before ordered—and even *against* their orders not to strike. Strike activity (with or without formal approval) attained unprecedented heights in 1970, as 3.3 million workers were involved in 5,717 work stoppages, resulting in over 66.4 million idle mandays during that year. That workers are becoming increasingly concerned with broader issues than wages per se is suggested by the fact that a large and increasing proportion of strike activity concerns aspects of work other than wages, though wage disputes still account for the majority of mandays lost. A further indication of difference between union hierarchy and rank and file—beyond wildcat strikes, slowdowns, and minority caucuses—is the increasing inability of union bosses to deliver working-class and even membership votes to their chosen political candidates. Union votes for McGovern and Wallace in the 1972 Democratic primaries were in opposition to the hierarchy's backing of Humphrey. Official AFL-CIO "neutrality" in the election hurt McGovern, although it is uncertain how much or whether an endorsement for him would have greatly narrowed the margin of loss. Aging union bosses must also confront an increasingly youthful membership; furthermore, in the primary industries such as steel, autos, and rubber, a white hierarchy confronts a large and increasingly non-white membership. Aronowitz sums up prevalent worker attitudes toward unions by saying: "At best the union is seen as little more than an insurance company. At worst it is seen as one of the evil institutions standing in the way of substantial gains, particularly for young and minority-group workers." [39] The union could hardly be called a truly reliable and effective insurance company considering the large gaps in security and protection the

---

[37] Stanley Aronowitz, "Which Side Are You On? Trade Unions in America," *Liberation* 16 (December 1971): 24.

[38] Paul Booth, "Theses on Contemporary U.S. Labor Unionism," *Radical America* 5 (January–February 1971): 1.

[39] Stanley Aronowitz, "Arthritic Unionism: Corporate Labor in America," *Social Policy,* May–June 1972, p. 43.

majority of members face—e.g., seeing their pensions vanish when their plant shuts down, or watching the Supreme Court undercut the position of unions vis-à-vis management.

The extent to which union leadership has washed its hands of the class struggle was in no way better illustrated than by their reactions to Nixon's New Economic Policy, a bonanza for big business and an attack on the integrity of labor. Yet, aside from some grumbling and a wage-price commission walkout, the response to the Nixon administration by labor was typically quite sheepish. Indeed, since his release from prison, ex–labor chief James Hoffa announced his confidence in and support of Mr. Nixon, as has the leadership of the longshoremen, maritime, teamsters, and building trades unions. The latter organizations, whose social vision William Gould argues "does not extend further than the next wage increases for their white memberships," has seen its links to the Nixon administration tightened with the appointment as secretary of labor of New York hard-hat boss Peter Brennan.[40] Teamsters boss and Nixon enthusiast Frank Fitzsimmons has seen the administration back away from compulsory arbitration in transportation, while the Teamsters have taken their $100,000-a-year legal business *to* a firm with which a top ex–Nixon aide has joined and *away* from its previous attorney, who investigated the Watergate scandal for the Democrats. The concept of the labor aristocracy has never been more tragically realized than in this case of vigorous official union support for and encouragement of the Vietnam intervention. And as is often the case, it has not been the labor aristocracy who has had, at least immediately, to pay the price of such barbarism, but the union membership through higher taxes, inflation, housing shortages, a divided society, and loss of life and limb. As in other institutions, union leadership support of Vietnam policy for a decade has undermined its own credibility to many and perhaps a majority of workers. A new breed of worker may yet build a new breed of union; the trend is already visible.

The first major step in building a new breed of union is to organize *all* members of the working class. As a percentage of the total labor force, union membership has risen almost imperceptibly from its 22 percent in 1950. During the period 1950–1970 the labor force increased by some 20 million persons, but unions enrolled barely one-quarter of that number. Since 1960, what gains have taken place have largely been attributable to independents and white-collar unionization rather than the AFL-CIO. From a 1955 peak of 33 percent of the nonagricultural work force in unions, the end of the 1960s saw this figure decline to 27 percent. Es-

---

[40] "Labor and Nixon: Moving the Hard Hats In," *The Nation,* January 8, 1973, pp. 41–43..

pecially vast and relatively untapped potential for organization lies within the white-collar and service sectors of the labor force.[41] Only about one sixth of the more than 38 million white-collar persons are in unions, and even this represents a 50 percent gain in absolute numbers over 1960. Mills has drawn our attention to a number of factors such as income, unemployment, education, work place, downgrading, and routinization of work which place much of the white-collar work force in a position similar to the factory worker, and which, in turn, encourages collective thinking rather than individual mobility aspirations. "Not job dissatisfaction in general, but a specific kind of job dissatisfaction—the feeling that as an individual he cannot get ahead in his work—is the job factor that predisposes the white-collar employee to go pro-union.[42] White-collar and service workers may engage and have engaged in strike activity, even though defined as illegal, without having organized labor unions. Government employees and public school teachers have been involved in both large-scale organizing and conflict activities in recent years, and should perhaps lead the way for further unionization outside the traditional blue-collar manufacturing and industrial sectors. But the competitive sector of the labor force is frequently and even typically involved in widely scattered small establishments, local production, and an elastic supply of labor, all making white-collar, service, and unskilled labor difficult to organize effectively.

A final note might be made regarding the worker and the union. A frequent assertion made is that union membership is taken lightly by the worker and that indifference and apathy regarding union activities and decisions is widespread. This may be enlarged by the further contention that the union member has a very narrow vision of the function of the union—as a veritable money liaison between management and the worker.[43] To the extent that the union is oligarchical and antidemocratic and the individual worker has been industrially disenfranchised, how is it possible for the typically tired and often frustrated worker to be enthusiastic and participatory regarding the union's acitvities, either within the plant or in the broader social arena? And with the union elite defining the relationship between worker and management in narrow wage terms, how is it possible for union membership to act politically within the union?

The evidence does, indeed, indicate that the working class in most capitalist societies, though significant exceptions may be cited such as in

---

[41] See Albert A. Blum et al., *White-Collar Workers* (New York: Random House, 1971).

[42] C. Wright Mills, *White Collar* (New York: Oxford University Press, 1951), p. 307.

[43] John Goldthorpe et al., *The Affluent Worker in the Class Structure* (Cambridge: Cambridge University Press, 1969), pp. 167–70.

France,[44] Italy, and Quebec,[45] are not making major demands through or outside of the union for a revaluation of the work process and for self-management or workers' control. Aronowitz argues that in the United States there does not exist a conscious workers' movement directed toward autonomy in the work place and in society.[46] The distance and frequent cynicism of many workers with regard to unions and government Aronowitz interprets as a possible rejection of established channels of change and an openness to new strategies, perhaps socialist ones. Whatever the case is and the outcome might be in this country, charges of indifference, apathy, and narrowness should for now, at least, be held in abatement regarding the rank and file; evidence may be cited to the contrary. The question is whether activism and discontent can be articulated in an effective social understanding and class consciousness.

The task of pulling working-class interests together is imposing, and must be conducted against not only the capitalist class but an important segment of the labor elite as well. With more trade unionists sitting as delegates to the Democratic national convention in 1972 than in 1968, AFL-CIO leadership nevertheless implicitly and at times openly rejected a liberal Democratic candidate with a near-perfect voting record on labor, while entering the embraces of a conservative who at the time had a quarter-century history of antilabor activity. These same labor elites rejected and at times ridiculed the wider political participation of other working-class elements such as blacks, Chicanos, women, young people, and the poor. Philip Shabecoff has remarked that labor rejection of "this exhilarating wider participation in a major political party is one of the tragedies of the 1972 campaign." [47] Obviously, a working-class movement that is to bring change to America cannot be led by friends, intended or unintended, of the likes of Richard Nixon. Labor has many leaders who understand the basic antagonism between capitalists and the industrial working class, and the McGovern candidacy was not without important endorsements—eight major unions including the auto workers, machinists, and state, county, and municipal employees unions. As one president of a state labor federation asserted: "Why in God's name are we playing Russian roulette with the labor movement by handing power over to the conservatives?" [48] This is the kind of question which labor, both leadership and membership, must answer if the working class as a whole is ever to even get a taste of welfare-state security, hardly to mention socialism.

---

[44] See Henri Lefebvre, *The Explosion: Marxism and the French Upheaval* (New York: Monthly Review Press, 1969).

[45] See *Quebec,* special issue of *Radical America* 6 (September–October 1972).

[46] "Arthritic Unionism," p. 41.

[47] "Did Meany Win? Labor's Credibility Gap," *The Nation,* January 1, 1973, pp. 9–13.

[48] Ibid., p. 12.

seven

THE WORKING CLASS: SOCIOPOLITICAL ISSUES

A thesis which has received considerable attention from class sociologists over the past decade concerns the extent to which the factory or blue-collar worker is in modern society "middle class" or bourgeois in material, cultural, and social aspects of life. For example, Zweig has written that, "working-class life finds itself on the move towards new middle-class values and middle-class existence. . . . The change can only be described as a deep transformation of values, as the development of new ways of thinking and feeling, a new ethos, new aspirations and cravings." [1] Zweig contends that the worker is concerned with home ownership, mobility for himself and for his children, savings and insurance, family equality and sociability, prestige and respect, and other aspects of so-called middle-class existence. Other writers and researchers take the opposing view that the manual worker has not become "middle class" or part of the bourgeoisie in cultural interests and behavior, social ties, and material life.[2] John Goldthorpe and David Lockwood, a pair of British sociologists, have done extensive work in evaluating this thesis. On a broad spectrum of psychological, cul-

---

[1] Ferdynand Zweig, *The Worker in an Affluent Society* (London: Heinemann, 1961), p. ix.

[2] See Goldthorpe et al., *The Affluent Worker in the Class Structure* (Cambridge: Cambridge University Press, 1969); Richard H. Hamilton, *Affluence and the French Worker in the Fourth Republic* (Princeton: Princeton University Press, 1967); and James W. Rinehart, "Affluence and the Embourgeoisement of the Working Class: A Critical Look," *Social Problems* 19 (Fall 1971): 150–62.

tural, political, social, and material variables, Goldthorpe and Lockwood find consistent differences between the factory work force and the "middle class."

Our previous analysis of occupational income confirms that, on the whole, white-collar workers are higher on the income ladder than blue-collar workers. The white-collar worker is also the greater beneficiary of more paid holidays and more frequent and longer paid vacations, medical insurance and sick leave with full pay, retirement pensions, and other bonuses and supplements.[3] A sizeable minority of blue-collar workers have no medical insurance, no protection against employment disruptions, and no retirement programs. That in overall terms white-collar workers are better off materially than blue-collar workers is beyond question, though there is ample amount of overlap as well. And evidence is consistent, though not particularly impressive, regarding sociocultural differences between white- and blue-collar workers.

However, the large part of the noneconomic differences in occupational comparisons is due to differences in the amount of formal education, and is not in any important way linked to some fundamental class differences. Nor are the economic differences themselves sufficiently different to warrant drawing distinctions of significance between manual and nonmanual workers. We have previously delineated a class model, and whatever the differences between so-called working- and middle-class occupational groups may be, they are neither of the extent nor of a nature to override the class boundaries set forth in Marxist theory. White-collar and blue-collar, nonmanual and manual workers may, and frequently are, members of the same class, and are typically members of the same broad underlying population or working class at large. This is not to disparage or dismiss as irrelevant the empirical research and arguments surrounding occupational groups. The point of contention is that occupation is not the decisive class variable, and must be placed within the larger perspective of property classes. To dwell on the specifics of differences between blue- and white-collar workers may be interesting to many researchers and students of stratification, but it is not the crucial domain of social class analysis and social change. The danger in occupational analysis is that it distracts from politically decisive struggles between social classes, and sets up as primary what are decidedly secondary and derivative phenomena. The proletarianization of white-collar workers, including the professional strata, is the dominant fact of contemporary occupational sociology rather than the embourgeoisement of the blue-collar worker.

Of related note is the thesis that manual workers possess a distinctive

---

[3] *The Statistical Abstract of the United States, 1972* (New York: Grosset & Dunlap, 1972), p. 230.

social psychology, in particular an authoritarian, narrow, and visionless character structure. Political sociologist S. M. Lipset has partially carried a reputation for his views on "working-class authoritarianism." Yet the most insistent on this score may be people who actually are in sympathy with the manual worker. On one occasion, Sexton and Sexton do a rather persuasive job of portraying the worker as bigoted, capitalist chauvinists, promilitary and fervently anti-Communist, superpatriotic, anti-intellectual, antistudent, anticounterculture, antiprivilege, repressive, and so forth.[4] Elsewhere the same authors specifically deny this image of workers, recognizing that "their labors support an enormous superstructure of people who make little or no social contributions."[5] (It would be most unfortunate for the future of the working class if the one-half or more of union members who voted for Nixon thought that hippies, blacks, students, and other Nixon scapegoats compose this superstructure when it is really Nixon and the ruling class he represents which is doing the real massive "free-loading.") The worker-as-bigot comes through as a strong theme in Lasson,[6] who quotes a worker as saying: "But I'd say a good 50 percent of the colored people just don't want to work. . . . Take the civil rights movement. There's money coming from somewhere for this. I don't know who's financing it but most of it is communist inspired. . . . They're nuts, and if we don't stop the reds in Vietnam we're going to be forced to stop them on Cape Cod. . . It gripes me to see these people on welfare who could get jobs if they wanted to." Another disconcerting "real-life" depiction of the blue-collar worker is that given by prounderdog psychiatrist Robert Coles.[7] Coles's manual workers appear in right-wing terms, and come through largely as racial bigots, emotional and flag-waving chauvinistic fundamentalists, irrationally antistudent and anti-intellectual, envious and hostile toward the more affluent and educated, etc.

With the number of Wallace supporters as large as it is, there is no denying the existence of considerable "social conservatism" in segments of the working class. But the extent of such reactionism may be easily exaggerated. And the reactionism itself may be the product of confusing and disorienting circumstances which the worker must face, and not at all ideologically motivated. Blue-collar social conservatism may be very easily misconstructed if taken only at face value. A part of the problem with

---

[4] Patricia Cayo Sexton and Brendan Sexton, *Blue Collars and Hard Hats* (New York: Random House, 1971), pp. 51–59.

[5] Patricia Cayo Sexton and Brendan Sexton, "Taking Workers Seriously," *Social Policy,* September–October 1972, pp. 48–54.

[6] Kenneth Lasson, *The Workers* (New York: Grossman Publishers, 1971), pp. 13–34.

[7] Robert Coles, *The Middle Americans* (Boston: Little, Brown & Company, 1971).

some of the worker-as-bigot, worker-as-narrowminded commentary is based upon the authors' personal selection of data, and not upon systematic research sampling or broad analysis of events. On the point of general or widespread working-class chauvinism and bigotry, the systematic evidence simply does not support it. As a prime example, manual workers have from the beginning been more opposed to the Vietnam War than those above them in the occupational hierarchy.[8] After empirical research on a large sample of southern California white workers, Ransford and Jeffries concluded that "there has probably been a tendency in the mass media to overstereotype the white working man as a narrow-minded intolerant bigot." [9] This is an understatement in view of their findings regarding the attitudes of workers toward student demonstrations and black demands, which on balance were far more moderate than bigoted and repressive. After a review of statistical survey evidence, Hamilton concludes that "the major lesson indicated by this review of the evidence is that the hypothesis of 'working-class authoritarianism' has very little support." [10]

Furthermore, empirical research conducted by Laumann produced findings that firmly indicated manual workers' *identification with* and *psychological affinity with* the more educated and successful white-collar occupational groups, presumably harboring the strong desire for their own children to move in precisely this direction.[11] The portrayal of manual workers as "anti–middle class" and "antistudent" is a minority portrait, and does not accurately reflect the position and social psychology of the majority of workers, white or black. The fact of the matter is that a very large segment of the blue-collar population would themselves have preferred to enter a white-collar career and the vast majority seek college educations and careers for their children. And no convincing evidence exists that, on the whole, manual workers deny the legitimacy and right of upper-middle-income groups to be where they are in the class structure nor are they the objects of blue-collar animosity or class hatred. In short, we may clearly recognize a broad spectrum of differences in class ideologies among workers, ranging from complete acceptance of the ruling-class defi-

---

[8] See, for example, Martin Patcher, "Social Class and Dimensions of Foreign Policy Attitudes," *Social Science Quarterly* 51 (December 1970): 649–74; Harlan Hahn, "Dove Sentiments Among Blue-Collar Workers," *Dissent,* May–June 1970, pp. 202–5; and James D. Wright, "The Working Class, Authoritarianism and the War in Vietnam," *Social Problems* 20 (Fall 1972): 133–49.

[9] H. Edward Ransford and Vincent Jeffries, "Blue-Collar Anger: Reactions to Student and Black Protest Movements," paper delivered at American Sociological Association meetings, Denver, Colorado, 1971.

[10] Richard F. Hamilton, "Class and Race in the United States," in George Fischer, ed., *The Revival of American Socialism* (New York: Oxford University Press, 1971), p. 106.

[11] Edward O. Laumann, *Prestige and Association in an Urban Community* (Indianapolis: Bobbs-Merrill, 1966), Chapter 3.

nition of reality to Marxist analysis. This divergence of ideologies is, to be sure, the primary obstacle to constructive change from within the masses.

THE NEW WORKING CLASS

In terms of our own class framework, the preceding section might be summarized by saying that there are social and cultural differences within the working classes, particularly between the formally educated or new working class and the traditional factory work force. However, with rising educational and skill levels in the traditional working class, and the routinization of much professional and technical work, these two broad working strata are drawing closer together on many class and cultural dimensions of stratification. Although economic inequalities within the larger working class have been and may increasingly become a point of conflict and political contention, these differences do not have the character of class struggle or class animosity, nor should they have. The objective locus of struggle is, and to be effective must be, between propertied bourgeoisie and propertyless proletariat—including both old and new working classes.

In the present section, our task is further to probe the question of the new working class, seeking a greater clarity of understanding regarding its nature and location within the larger class structure.

The essential thesis of new-working-class theory is that technological advance has transformed the nature of production so as bring into the traditional proletariat a considerably increasing amount of educated, technical, and scientific work requirements and workers. New-working-class theory is Marxist inasmuch as it defines much of the large and growing technical and professional strata not as a new bourgeoisie or new middle class replacing the free professional and small businessman, but as a specific growth of the working class, and as having typically proletarian class interests vis-à-vis the ruling class and traditional bourgeoisie. The professional, technician, engineer, or scientist is, in effect, a more highly educated member of the working class. He is a knowledge worker, though very frequently manual skills are also required (just as degrees of knowledge are required of primarily manual workers). Gorz stresses that the new working class specializes in the ability to do creative and independent work, to synthesize and analyze, to innovate and direct complex productive activities.[12] Their formal educational backgrounds incline them to think in terms of problem solving, designing, and efficiency.

We have detailed in Chapter 5 the class criteria which lead Marxist

---

[12] André Gorz, *Strategy for Labor* (Boston: Beacon Press, 1967), pp. 105–6.

theory to consider much of the professional and technological stratum as a component of the working class rather than as new "middle class" or an entirely independent class. Mills was among the first to stress the common property situation of technical-knowledge workers and manual laborers. He also laid early emphasis upon common working conditions: "Mechanized and standardized work, the decline of any chance for employees to see and understand the whole operation, the loss of any chance, save for a very few, for private contact with those in authority—these form the model of the future." With specific reference to the new white-collar strata, Mills writes: "No longer free to plan his work, much less to modify the plan to which he is subordinated, the individual is to a great extent managed and manipulated in his work." [13]

The routinization and powerlessness of much technological work activity observed by Mills is noted by Denitch as well: "The shift in the real and role authority of engineers and skilled scientists in industry reduces them as well to the role of a new highly trained working class." [14] Taagepera disputes the new working-class argument, contending that knowledge workers form an entirely new and separate class, but concedes that *as a class the thinking people have little to say. They are not even masters in their own house.* [15] A number of other writers have persuasively argued that the nature of work and degree of control in work place much of the salaried professional and technical work force within the proletariat, and predict that proletarianization is the dominant trend of the future.[16] They would conclude, with Mills, that "in historical reality, the 'new middle class' [Mills also used the term "new working class"] is merely a peculiar sort of new proletariat, having the same basic interests," [17] and with Hacker's suggestion that "those who were once known as the working class have simply put on white collars." [18] Mills takes cognizance of the fact that a thin upper layer may go over to the bourgeoisie, but believes that the shift would not count significantly in terms of either numbers or degree of power.

---

[13] C. Wright Mills, *White Collar* (New York: Oxford University Press, 1951), pp. 212, 226.

[14] Bogdan Denitch, "The New Left and the New Working Class," in J. David Colfax and Jack L. Roach, eds., *Radical Sociology* (New York: Basic Books, 1971), p. 343.

[15] Rein Taagepera, "The Revolt of the Thinking Class," *Queen's Quarterly* 78 (Spring 1971): 25.

[16] See, for example, David Laibman, "Technologists—Part of Working Class," *Political Affairs* 48 (April 1969): 52–59; Stanley Aronowitz, "Does the United States Have a New Working Class?" in Fischer, ed., *The Revival of American Socialism,* pp. 188–216; and Ernest Mandel, "Workers and Permanent Revolution," ibid., pp. 169–87.

[17] *White Collar,* p. 291.

[18] Andrew Hacker, *The End of the American Era* (New York: Atheneum, 1970), p. 37.

Yet Mills exercised due caution in moving from objective historical reality to the subjective aspects of class behavior: "Only by keeping objective position and ideological consciousness separate In analysis can the problem be stated with precision and without unjustifiable assumptions about wage-workers, white collar workers, and the general psychology of social classes."[19] With Veblen, Mills can see no historical inevitability in the ideological unification of the objective proletariat. As Veblen did, Mills laid heavy emphasis on the importance of prestige and status influences which are capable of pulling economic interests apart. But again with Veblen, Mills saw these prestige and status claims as illusory, and as becoming increasingly more so with changes in the nature and condition of work. Status cycles "do not modify the long-run reality of more fixed positions."[20] The status claims for self cannot consistently override objective realities of class.

The most potent force militating against this bourgeois-oriented holiday image of self within the new working class is what Gorz, Aronowitz, Denitch, Mandel, and others have pointed out as the contradiction between (a) the level of educational preparedness and innovative ability possessed by knowledge workers and (b) the restricted scope of daily work activity and decision-making authority that is actually theirs. In Marxist language, we have a clash between the forces and relations of production, with the forces of production capable of and increasingly desirous of moving technology and resources toward a greater social rationality and application, but choked off by paralyzing inequality within the relations of production.

It is within this context that Galbraith, as did Mills and Veblen before him, envisions what we are calling the new working class, including intellectuals, as being the most promising force for progressive change, having taken affront at the irrationality and destructive waste of unmitigated corporate power.[21] Again Mills invokes precautions concerning the possibility of the new working class accomplishing progressive ends even given its determination to do so: "The assumption that political supremacy follows from functional, economic indispensability underlies all those theories that see the new [working] class or any of its sections slated to be the next ruling class."[22] Such an assumption is wrong, argues Mills, for it confuses technical indispensability with the facts of power struggle. Marx and Veblen, to whom Mills is seemingly addressing his qualifying remarks, were well aware of the necessity for ideological and political struggle on the part of the economically essential class.

---

[19] *White Collar*, p. 296.

[20] Ibid., p. 258.

[21] John Kenneth Galbraith, *The New Industrial State* (New York: Signet Books, 1968), pp. 291–304; and C. Wright Mills, *The Causes of World War Three* (New York: Ballantine Books, 1960), pp. 141–87.

[22] *White Collar*, p. 298.

The new working class by itself can no more successfully transform power and privilege in society than it can lay claim to being a separate and new class apart from the traditional working class. Just as it is a component of the larger working class, so must the new working class form a common ideological and political force with the rest of the proletariat. As Denitch has put it: "The new working class must transform the labor movement and can become a significant social force only in alliance with sections of the old working class." [23] Denitch points to recent militance in France and Italy as illustrating the ability of new and old working classes to coalesce around the issue of industrial democracy.

At the core of common working-class concern are not just wage and salary issues, but also the larger and more central issues of decision making and control. These issues go to the very heart of the system, and challenge the right of elites to make decisions regarding the use and direction of technology and the investment and consumption of all that is produced by it. The issues are revolutionary.[24] The achievement of industrial and social democracy and the correlative social rationality in the application of the forces of production are, in the words of Richard Flacks, "in *fundamental* conflict with established institutions and political practices and cannot be implemented simply by having 'groovier' men and women running the Establishment." [25]

The latter point needs special emphasis in the age of "greening." Social equality and rational application of technology and human resources for the material and spiritual well-being of society can in no manner be attained by way of a so-called "middle-class revolution" in which morality and fashions are loosened up and "modern living" (be that what it may) holds sway. This "liberated" image of self, where it exists, cannot even produce any radical changes in individual personality let alone in the determining economic and political structure of a society. This structure affords the luxury of an illusory "holiday image of self" (to apply a Mills phrase) to the few, while depriving the many of substantive improvements in the quantity and quality of their lives.

ALIENATION

As a concept central to Marxist theory, alienation was given theoretical consideration in Chapter 2. Our intention in the present section is to

---

[23] Denitch, "The New Left and the New Working Class," p. 345.
[24] See John Case, "Workers' Control: Vision of a New Social Order," *The Nation,* February 14, 1972, pp. 200–206.
[25] Richard Flacks, *Youth and Social Change* (Chicago: Markham Publishing Company, 1971), p. 116.

examine the status of alienation in the contemporary working class. By definition we would not expect the past century to have witnessed any substantive decline in alienation, for capitalism as the source of alienation persists as before. The working class is still bereft of ownership of the means of production, control over the process and objects of production, a sense of purpose and understanding of the production process, and the constructive development of personal capacity for work. It is difficult to conceive how the sources of alienation could in any way dissolve under the rule of corporate capital and its mode of operation. Yet the nature and organization of work *have* changed over the past century, and greater changes are portended for the future. Thus, we would do well to examine the literature of social science on the question of alienation in advanced capitalist society.

Such a call for review does not mean that there is much to learn from alienation research that conceives of alienation as a purely subjective phenomenon, a psychological state rooted in the individual's mind rather than in the objective material order, or from research which loses sight of the simple and direct facts of alienated existence by laborious conceptualizing and statistical manipulation. Our concern is with the direct impact of propertyless and powerless work situations upon the individual and society.

The same school of thought that conceives of the working class as having been transformed into apprentice bourgeoisie also propounds a disalienation thesis. For example, Zweig states that "the new working man is a self-disciplined man, is much more thoroughly industrialized, more smoothly adjusted, and is part of the smoothly-working industrial machinery."[26] Zweig further contends that there is a growing measure of satisfaction with work in the factory, limited alienation of workman from work, and diminishing bases for class conflict. Barbash writes that "in the long run the development of industrialism has probably brought about a lessening of the tensions incident to work. The sources of these alleviating influences are technology, trade unionism, the welfare state, management philosophy, and full employment."[27] G. Rose observes: "Even in the extremely repetitive type of factory work, it is easy for the middle-class observer to overemphasize the tedium faction."[28] Such views suggest that modern work has contributed to the disalienation of the working class and, in projection, will progressively further modify alienating forces.

Other writers, both Marxist and non-Marxist, sharply disagree. Mandel sees more alienation today than in Marx's time.[29] Gorz asserts

---

[26] Zweig, *The Worker in an Affluent Society*, pp. 69–79, 210.

[27] Jack Barbash, "The Tensions of Work," *Dissent*, Winter 1972, p. 244.

[28] Gordon Rose, *The Working Class* (London: Longmans, Green and Co., 1968), p. 25.

[29] Ernest Mandel, "Workers and Permanent Revolution," pp. 169–87.

that "industry maintains a despotic and authoritarian society, under a hierarchy and discipline of military character, which demands of its workers both unconditional obedience and active participation in their own oppression. . . . Industry always demands for its repetitive jobs . . . a passive and ignorant labour force." [30] Mills writes that "as for wage earners generally, work seems to serve neither God nor whatever they may experience as divine in themselves. In them there is no taut will-to-work, and few positive gratifications from their daily round." [31] These perspectives affirm the continuation of alienation, even its intensification.

Although there is an occasional piece of empirical evidence indicating that job satisfaction among blue-collar workers is high,[32] the bulk of available data is overwhelmingly in the opposite direction—i.e., that work as such has neutral to negative import and impact on the typical worker.[33] Few factory workers report satisfaction with their choice or fate in their life's work.[34] Hamilton reports that among French workers 81 percent considered their jobs fatiguing, 64 percent had little or no like for their work, 46 percent saw relations with employers as hostile, 49 percent considered the product of their work as only fair to poor in quality, and 59 percent perceived too much waste in the production process.[35] White-collar workers were only slightly less negative in their evaluations. Upon analysis of research on factory workers, Goldthorpe and his associates concluded that "among our affluent workers generally, the experience of monotony, unabsorbing work and of an excessive pace of work were all apparent sources of deprivation and of job dissatisfaction." [36] These workers desired changes in work organization, physical conditions, hours and pace of work, routine requirements and supervisory methods. One worker remarked, "I'd like to change the ways they have of doing things. Their methods are outdated —and so are the tools. . . . But if you make a suggestion to the management of the shop—who've been here and nowhere else—it's a joke."

---

30 André Gorz, "Work and Consumption," in Anderson and Blackburn, eds., *Towards Socialism*, p. 317.

31 *White Collar*, p. 219.

32 For example, William H. Form et al., "The Accommodation of Rural and Urban Workers to Industrial Discipline and Urban Living: A Four Nation Study," paper read at the Seventh World Congress of Sociology, Varna, Bulgaria, 1970.

33 For instance, Robert Dubin, "Industrial Workers' Worlds: A Study of the 'Central Life Interests' of Industrial Workers," in Erwin O. Smigel, ed., *Work and Leisure* (New Haven: College and University Press, 1963), p. 54; and R. Parsler, "Some Social Aspects of Embourgeoisement in Australia," *Sociology* 5 (January 1971): 95–112.

34 S. M. Miller and Pamela Roby, *The Future of Inequality* (New York: Basic Books, 1970), p. 171.

35 Hamilton, *Affluence and the French Worker*, p. 77.

36 John Goldthorpe et al., *The Affluent Worker: Industrial Attitudes and Behavior* (Cambridge: Cambridge University Press, 1970), pp. 19–20.

And from another: "I'd like to have more to the job—as there used to be before the time for it was put down." [37]

The progressive intensification of alienation in work-worker relationships through rationalization of job specifications is well illustrated in the following comment from an auto worker:

> When the plant was running only a few cars through an hour I used to install the whole front and back seat assemblies. But when the cars speeded up, I was put on the job of installing the rack that the front seat slides back and forth on and my job was broken up and simplified. I'd like to do a whole fender myself from raw material to the finished job. It would be more interesting.[38]

This also serves to illustrate "Detroit-style" automation referred to in the previous section.

The words of industrial sociologist Arthur Shostak sum up what has been said thus far: "The typical worker appears lightly committed to his work, and his work appears to grow ever lighter in meaning for him." [39] Clearly, the high rates of absenteeism and turnover found throughout the factory work force, despite the loss of precious hourly wages, attest to the onerous nature of work and the strong need for frequent escape.

But what of the trends inherent in technological advance and automation? Do they promise relief from the pains of demeaning industrial labor? In the larger sense of heightening and highlighting the contradictions between the forces and relations of production, technological advance moves in the direction of disalienation. But the question still remains as to the impact of technological change on work within the existing system of property relations. Have greater automation and new-working-class growth altered the degree of alienation within the bounds of capitalism and economic exploitation of labor?

In an early analysis of this question, James Bright argued that, for production workers, a shift from machine operation to automated equipment requires progressively less dexterity, less knowledge of art and theory, less experience, less judgment, less decision making, and less control of the work place.[40] Furthermore, Bright's studies indicated that automated jobs offer fewer classifications and a flattening of job hierarchies, producing a more homogeneous work force. Social isolation on

---

[37] Ibid., pp. 21–23.

[38] Charles Walker, *Toward the Automated Factory* (New Haven: Yale University Press, 1957), p. 200.

[39] Arthur Shostak, *Blue-Collar Life* (New York: Random House, 1969), p. 59.

[40] James R. Bright, *Automation and Management* (Cambridge, Mass.: Plimpton Press, 1958), pp. 45–50.

the job is also increased. While agreeing with the above point of view regarding personal job skills, Gorz notes that, despite less direct individual involvement in work tasks, the automated-production-line worker may gain greater overall knowledge of a larger segment of the production process as he supervises and monitors work flow.[41] Blauner's position is that automation fully decreases alienation and gives the worker a sense of power, control, integration, and self-expression in production.[42]

The evidence regarding automation and alienation is mixed. Fullan's research on three samples of Canadian workers representing various stages of automation indicated that automation oil workers were less alienated in work and work relationships than mass-production auto workers, with craftsmen falling in between.[43] Furstenberg turned up similar results on samples of German workers.[44] Goldthorpe's data also disclosed that automation and crafts workers were less alienated than assembly-line workers, though the automation workers were less socially integrated on the job and held more hostile attitudes toward management.[45] Virtually all research agrees, however, that social ties on the job are relatively insignificant for all types of production workers. U.S. assembly-line workers studied by Shepard similarly followed the pattern of being the most estranged from work, while full automation (continuous-flow) workers were the least alienated in the blue-collar sample.[46] On these cross-sectional comparisons, then, automation workers do, in fact, evince fewer symptoms of alienation than nonautomation workers, though the results are not due so much to the fact that continuous-flow process workers are disalienated as it is to the high degree of alienation of mechanical and assembly-line workers. And on some aspects of work, the evidence is uneven and inconsistent.

Of perhaps greater significance than any other above pieces of research evidence is that offered by Chadwick-Jones in the form of a panel study of English workers who shifted from mechanical-operative work to continuous-flow process in tinning.[47] The results of this study support the

---

[41] André Gorz, "Capitalist Relations of Production and the Socially Necessary Labour Force," *International Socialist Journal* 2 (1964): 426.

[42] Robert Blauner, *Alienation and Freedom* (Chicago: University of Chicago Press, 1964).

[43] Michael Fullan, "Industrial Technology and Worker Integration in the Organization," *American Sociological Review* 35 (December 1970): 1028–39.

[44] Friedrich Furstenburg, "Structural Changes in the Working Class," in J. A. Jackson, ed., *Social Stratification* (Cambridge: Cambridge University Press, 1968), pp. 145–74.

[45] Goldthorpe et al., *The Affluent Worker in the Class Structure*, pp. 59–67.

[46] Jon S. Shepard, *Automation and Alienation* (Cambridge, Mass.: M.I.T. Press, 1971), pp. 98–99.

[47] J. K. Chadwick-Jones, *Automation and Behaviour* (London: Wiley-Interscience, 1969).

idea that automation *diminishes* the demand for individual dexterity and skills, while at the same time *increases* the worker's insight into a larger component of the production process. Far less physical effort was required, and workers initially expressed interest in the new technology. Wages were higher as well, and marked improvement was seen in safety and conditions. Yet the new technology had its negative impact as a counterbalance. The most frequent complaints concerned the inconvenience of having to work new shifts to accommodate the twenty-four-hour production process and the consequent disruption of social and family ties. After the initial interest in the new plant wore off, boredom became a common problem, with about half the sample reporting greater boredom on the new job than the old, and another quarter seeing no difference. There was less diversity, less change, less control, and less interest in the work itself compared to the operative tinning process. As one worker put it: "The job is more boring. I haven't got any responsibilities, you see, so I am not taxed in any way then. As a rollerman I used to carry responsibility. I've lost that now." [48]

Especially revealing, and in the same vein as the boredom experienced on the new job, was the common complaint of feeling "tired"—but tired in a sense tangibly different from physical exhaustion as from the operative job. One worker expressed it as follows: "I am more tired than I ever felt in the old works. I have no inclination at all, as if your mind seems to be dulled somehow. I don't seem to have any inclination and it isn't physical tiredness, it isn't exhaustion." [49] This condition suggests work that is much less demanding on a variety of fronts than operative labor, and is perhaps similar to the feeling one would have after watching eight hours of bad television. There were also complaints about a loss of social relations on the job, isolation, and, for many, a status drop. Furthermore, a flattening of the job hierarchy led the majority of respondents to foresee little or no promotional opportunities. And the new work situation failed to promote a feeling of economic integration with the production unit: "You are not part and parcel of the company, you are not adding anything. . . . The plant and the process is interesting but you are not part of it." [50]

While we have examined some findings regarding blue-collar technicians and operatives, nothing has yet been said about the formally educated new working class, the white-collar professionals and technicians. The data here are quite consistent in their indication of relatively lower levels of alienation in the new working class. An in-depth study by Car-

---

[48] Ibid., p. 91.
[49] Ibid., p. 100.
[50] Ibid., p. 102.

liner of eleven former blue-collarites who had moved into computer software disclosed that, despite a number of specific criticisms about work situation, these new technicians were decidedly improved in their disposition toward work.[51] They reported greater work interest and sense of challenge and more favorable remuneration and working conditions. In a similar vein, Kirsch and Lengermann found that computer personnel reported much greater variation, pace control, freedom of movement, innovation opportunities, and overall production knowledge than did machine operators.[52] Clerical workers fell in between. Finally, Shepard discovered that computer software personnel were the least alienated of six various white- and blue-collar industrial job position holders, though blue-collar automation workers were less alienated than white-collar office-machine operators and clerical workers.[53]

As the focus moves to the higher levels of educational training and experience in the new working class, the problem of alienation in work seems to be progressively relieved. Work is often the major focus of interest in life, and forms the context for the pursuit of self-realization.[54] This holds true for both the production and service segments of the new working class—that is, for the scientists and the social service professionals. Yet, for the bulk of the new working class, improvements in control, decision making, purpose, and integration are a matter of degree and certainly do not represent leaps into disalienation. Clearly the new-working-class worker has material and physical advantages over the factory worker, though exploitation continues to be the rule rather than the exception. And with the steady increase of educated manpower this exploitation should increase—even given breakthroughs in unionization. But with the heavy pressure off income and working condition issues, the new working class more keenly perceives its alienation in terms of control and self-management at the work place. And it is workers' control, not just of the immediate work place, but of the forces of production at large, which constitutes the full and only means of disalienation. For alienation is not in its most important aspects a matter of wages and consumption, but of creative production, an unattainable goal without social ownership and control of the means of that production. And note here that the emphasis is on *social* control, not just workers' control, since

---

[51] Lewis Carliner, "The White Collar on the Ex-Blue Collar is a Cool Collar," *Dissent,* Winter 1972, pp. 260–63.

[52] Barbara A. Kirsch and Joseph L. Lengermann, "Alienation in Work as Applied to Different Type Jobs in a White-Collar Setting," *Sociology and Social Research* 56 (January 1972): 180–94.

[53] Shepard, *Automation and Alienation,* pp. 98–99.

[54] For example, see Charles H. Anderson and John D. Murray, eds., *The Professors* (Cambridge, Mass.: Schenkman Publishing Company, 1971).

automation—indeed mechanization—renders more and more people superfluous to the task of production itself.

Nor is alienation entirely a work place problem. The worker brings an alienated self to the job just as much as he goes home with it. Political alienation and cynicism may have attained an all-time high in the United States. Survey research data indicate that from 1964 to 1970 the proportion of Americans who have abandoned faith in the present political process increased from 20 to 39 percent, while in the 1972 presidential election a bare majority of potential voters actually cast ballots—three-fifths for a man who symbolizes the alienation of the underlying population from political processes and power and who openly manipulates the political process in accordance with his aspirations. "There is something very strange in this country," according to Anthony Lewis, "a deadened quality, an end to caring." [55]

Yet we have argued that many persons, especially certain individuals in the new working class, catch *partial* glimpses of freedom. But they and the rest of the working class remain captives of the relations of production that render them accessories rather than the substance of the productive process. This fact remains unaltered, as much unaltered as the promise of greater individual and social freedom from the rational application of advanced technology and automation.

THE SUBSISTENCE WAGE

The Marxist proposition on working-class income, as discussed in Chapter 1, tells us that the working class as a whole is paid wages in the amount required to reproduce its labor power; i.e., they are given the purchasing power necessary to buy only the goods and services at a quality and quantity considered to be the culturally defined minimum level for existence. How does this proposition stand up today? Have the vaunted welfare state and labor union relegated this hypothesis to the realm of economic history? Yes, says Herman P. Miller, top economic statistician in the U.S. Census Bureau: "When the pieces are put together, it hardly seems appropriate to label blue-collar workers as economically 'squeezed.' " [56] Yes, say university sociologists Bensman and Vidich: "For skilled and semiskilled white union members, life in America has not been

---

[55] Quoted in *The Progressive,* November 1972, p. 3.

[56] Herman P. Miller, "A Profile of the Blue-Collar American," in Sar A. Levitan, ed., *Blue-Collar Workers* (New York: McGraw-Hill Book Company, 1971), p. 54.

at all bad." [57] The notion of the "affluent worker" itself suggests that the Marxist subsistence-wage hypothesis is invalid under the modern state and corporation.

Miller's pieces are not the same ones, evidently, that Jerome Rosow has put together: "After years of dependable job performance, many workers . . . find themselves worse off economically than when they started their working lives. This is a sad situation—in stark contrast to the American dream and our world of rising expectations." [58] Sexton and Sexton point out that to reach the federally defined income comfort level of about $10,000 a year, a person would have to work 40 hours a week, 52 weeks a year at $4.80 an hour—meaning that few production workers reach it.[59] What are the pieces these people are putting together that make them draw conclusions opposite to the affluent-worker idea?

Taking the Bureau of Labor Statistics definitions of lower, inter-mediate, and higher budgets for a four-person urban family (husband and wife plus 8- and 13-year-old children), we are able to draw estimates of the degree of economic squeeze or subsistence within the population. The "lower" budget for 1970 was $6,960; 32 percent of all families were *below* that level (having 16 percent of total personal income).[60] The "intermediate" budget was $10,664; an additional 22 percent of all families were *below* that level (having 13 percent of total personal income). Thus, 54 percent of all families were below the intermediate level of living. Further, median earnings of lower-white-collar and blue-collar occupational categories were below the intermediate level—that for un-skilled laborers approximately $3,000 below. To round out the distribu-tion of families on budget levels, we note that 27 percent fall between the intermediate and higher levels (having 29 percent of personal income), while 19 percent (having 42 percent of personal income) go over the $15,511 "higher" budget level.

Of greater relevance to the thesis of relative wage decline is the fact that the wage position of the working class, with the exception of highly educated members of the new working class, was worse with regard to budget requirement levels in 1970 than in 1960, a time when the median earnings of the broad occupational categories were near or slightly above the intermediate budget level.[61] Even the higher levels of the new working class, despite marked income gains, found their relative

---

[57] Joseph Bensman and Arthur J. Vidich, *The New American Society* (Chi-cago: Quadrangle Books, 1971), p. 152.

[58] Jerome M. Rosow, "The Problems of Lower-Middle-Income Workers," in Levitan, *Blue-Collar Workers,* p. 81.

[59] Sexton and Sexton, *Blue-Collars and Hard Hats,* p. 60.

[60] *The Statistical Abstract of the United States, 1972,* p. 341.

[61] Rosow, "The Problems of Lower-Middle-Income Workers," p. 80.

purchasing power slightly decline by 1970 from the 1960 baseline. This could be carried back at least thirty or forty years with the same conclusion: the working class has not achieved relative gains in the level of culturally defined subsistence living standards.

In more direct dollar terms, the average weekly take-home earnings of a manufacturing worker with three dependents did not improve—in constant dollar terms—from 1965 through 1971; at both times take-home pay was $102 (1967 dollars).[62] (In current dollar terms, the worker earned $97 a week in 1965 and $124 a week in 1971, but—thanks largely to sharply increased military spending—saw the purchasing power of the dollar shrink by 24 cents.) If the worker were on the job a full 52 weeks, yearly take-home constant dollar income would come to $5,304; for six years he has been on a treadmill going nowhere. Meanwhile, the major shareholders in his firm have been reaping ever larger profit harvests importantly due to a 10–25 point increase in worker productivity during the period. With the "lower" budget level for a family of four (1970) set at $6,960, the manufacturing worker with three dependents found that 1970 take-home pay of $116 a week added up to $6,032 a year—almost $1,000 less than the subsistence budget level. And the manufacturing worker is not an exception. All full-time wage and salary workers had weekly *gross* earnings of $130 in 1970, or a 52 week income of $6,760. If items such as air, water, physical safety, freedom of movement, privacy, quiet, etc., could be figured in, the argument that the working class is moving ahead in life would be exceedingly difficult to uphold. With the absolute number of unemployed at record levels and prices and taxes at all-time highs, any sanguine interpretation of working-class economic life must be considered totally suspect.

To keep up levels of aggregate demand in view of subsistence-wage levels for the large majority, corporate capitalism has had to invent means of extending purchasing power to the working class, tying them to the system in order to pay off the money extended to them. The ultimate success of such credit capitalism is to get people to borrow more money to pay off old debts. As of June 1970, an incredible $14 billion was owed on 300 million credit cards.[63] Total consumer debt was at $127 billion. In 1968, three-fifths of families with incomes between $5,000 and $7,500 were in debt—aside from home mortgages.[64] Andrew Levison uses the following illustrations to portray contemporary U.S. working-class subsistence:

---

[62] *The Statistical Abstract of the United States, 1973* (New York: Grosset and Dunlap, 1973), pp. 231–33, 350.

[63] John Rothchild, "The Screwing of the Average Man," *The Washington Monthly* 3 (October 1971): 39.

[64] Rosow, "The Problems of Lower-Middle-Income Workers," pp. 82–83.

Two-thirds of American families could not, without going into debt, pay for their child's tuition and required fees at a public university; 83 per cent could not handle the total expenses; 67 per cent could not pay for major medical expenses of $2,000 without insurance; a majority of 55 per cent could not afford even $1,000. Lastly, 42 per cent of the American people could not take a two-week vacation (at $30 a day for the entire family) without borrowing the money.[65]

Harrington has stressed that personal income frequently is not the prime immediate subsistence concern of the working class, for much of what the working class needs is not reasonably within the bounds of individual purchasing power.[66] Depth interviews with workers conducted by the University of Michigan Research Center in 1971 found that medical insurance, sick leave, retirement programs, health and safety hazards (25 million job injuries per year), and transportation problems ranked above wages as immediate concerns. Harrington writes: "What is revealing about these attitudes is that the first five complaints can be dealt with only through collective, and in most cases governmental, action. The classically 'private' drive for more income was subordinated to these other, much more social, values."

In view of the above data and discussion, we may conclude that the Marxist subsistence-wage hypothesis is as valid today as it was in the nineteenth century; certainly an ex-secretary of Health, Education, and Welfare is on solid ground when writing on the subject of "The Alienation of the American Worker." [67]

BENEATH SUBSISTENCE

In the previous section we noted that approximately one-third of U.S. families have incomes below the "lower budget" specified by the Bureau of Labor Statistics. In Chapter 4 an analysis of personal income led us to conclude that one in three persons occupies a seriously inadequate financial position relative to the norm and that one in five confronts definite physical and material deprivation. Whether one chooses to take as the subsistence level the "lower budget" or the "poverty line" is not critically important for our purposes in this section. Most of the authors cited here take at most the lower one-fifth of the population as their

---

[65] Andrew Levison, "The Working-Class Majority," *The Nation,* December 13, 1971, p. 628.

[66] Michael Harrington, *Socialism* (New York: Saturday Review Press, 1972), p. 357.

[67] Abraham Ribicoff, "The Alienation of the American Worker," *Saturday Review,* April 22, 1972, pp. 29–33.

point of reference. For reasons to be discussed, many authors distinguish between a poverty population and a working-poor population, attributing specific cultural traits to the former and viewing the latter in more purely economic terms. Our class model makes no such distinction, treating both groups as working class, albeit better- and worse-off segments of such.

We have observed that Marx did not define poverty or immiseration in purely physical terms, but included within the notion of subsistence a culturally relative and historically conditioned dimension. Yet the Marxist view of poverty in the material sense cannot simply be defined away. Material and physical deprivation is present to various degrees, and it is necessary to include in a Marxist model of class the assumption that capitalism generates not only serious and marked relative inequality but also absolute destitution. We previously have argued that for the bottom fifth of U.S. society the idea of relative immiseration is keenly felt and is progressively transformed into absolute deprivation as one moves, in Mill's terms, toward "the battered human beings living at the bottom of society." [68]

Despite differing views as to the causes and solutions of poverty, many social scientists are firm in their conviction that the material-physical element of immiseration is insignificant in the United States and that the psychological-relative element is the real issue. Starting with the softest comments, we have from Lee Rainwater the view that "poverty in American society is a phenomenon of relative rather than absolute deprivation. It is not so much that these families do not have the resources for a minimum standard of subsistance. . . . Men can exist happily and healthily on much less than the American poor have available, but only if their level of living does not mark them as different from and socially inferior to the great majority of their society." [69] Lewis Coser argues that "poverty in America is by and large no longer a problem of sheer physical survival, of utter immiseration and pauperism. Poverty in America concerns, in the main, not absolute but relative deprivation." [70] Rainwater and Coser couch their views in an economic-political framework of poverty analysis, seeing both causes and solutions within the structural realm.

A much more emphatic statement on the psychological basis of poverty comes from Walter B. Miller, who assures us that "poverty in the absolute sense is virtually nonexistent in the United States or, at best,

---

[68] C. Wright Mills, *The Sociological Imagination* (New York: Oxford University Press, 1959), p. 95.

[69] Lee Rainwater, *Behind Ghetto Walls* (Chicago: Aldine Publishing Company, 1970), p. 371.

[70] Lewis A. Coser, "What Do the Poor Need?" *Dissent* 17 (October 1971): 485.

sufficiently rare as to provide scant justification for the allocation of billions to its eradication." [71] Indeed, Miller doesn't even believe in poverty as relative, and objects to the use of the words *money* and *poor* to analyze poverty (naturally, since poverty doesn't exist to Miller): "The concept of Relative Deprivation is the logical keystone of the Poverty Ideology and serves to justify the entire Movement." [72] Underneath most such extremist evaluations of the good society lies an antiminority mentality, and here Miller doesn't let us down: housewives in suburbia, Miller informs us, have relative status deprivations yet they don't break up their families or demonstrate or riot; furthermore, in our golden past "the lowly immigrant, farm boy, or city urchin, consumed with envy and discontent upon beholding the spectacle of wealth and power around him, was fired with an iron resolve to emulate the objects of his envy, and embarked on a life of dedicated and energetic productivity." [73] In brief, the idea of poverty is merely a cruel hoax foisted upon the good society by ideologists. Whether to laugh or cry at such drivel is a problem. The facts and literature attesting to the reality of poverty are voluminous,[74] if these were ultimately necessary as proof.

There are other equally misleading projections of the subsistence population in the United States which in one way or another attempt to define away any current real economically produced poverty within corporate capitalism. Among the more intriguing is that offered by Bensman and Vidich. With a new twist on class terminology, Bensman and Vidich write: "Subworking classes are committed to almost nothing except immediate pleasure. . . . The original members of this class (hoboes, tramps, and bums) have been joined by cats, hippies, copouts, opouts, dropouts, surf bums, communards, and other economically marginal groups. Narcotics, alcohol, sex, or some other inarticulate activity short of suicide is used to absorb time, attention, and energy." [75] We may well recognize the existence of a lumpenproletariat without confusing it with structurally produced poverty and social dislocation.

---

[71] Walter B. Miller, "The Elimination of the American Lower Class as National Policy," in Daniel P. Moynihan, ed., *On Understanding Poverty* (New York: Basic Books, 1968), p. 266.

[72] Ibid., p. 273.

[73] Ibid., p. 276.

[74] See the following descriptive studies: Arthur Simon, *Faces of Poverty* (New York: Macmillan Company, 1968); Ben H. Bagdikian, *In the Midst of Plenty* (New York: Signet Books, 1964); Robert Coles, *Uprooted Children* (New York: Harper & Row, 1970); David Gottlieb and Anne L. Heinsohn, eds., *America's Other Youth* (Englewood Cliffs, N.J.: Prentice-Hall, 1971); and especially Todd Gitlin and Nanci Hollander, *Uptown: Poor Whites in Chicago* (New York: Harper and Row, Publishers, 1970).

[75] Bensman and Vidich, *The New American Society,* p. 153.

Let us return to the theories of those who recognize poverty as a reality, either relatively or absolutely speaking. With the implication that poverty is both real and material, Oscar Lewis would first appear to explain it in cultural terms. His phrase "the culture of poverty" is itself suggestive.[76] For a sizeable portion of the poor, argues Lewis, immiseration is due to a set of values and norms, a subculture, which inhibits and precludes them from successful participation in the economic and social life of the larger society. This poverty life style, like all subcultural phenomena, is largely transmitted through family and other primary groups from one generation to the next. It is a culture, writes Lewis, which undermines aspiration, work achievement, orientation toward the future, confidence in self, social participation, family organization, and other mainstream norms and values. Under attack from structurally oriented critics, Lewis has taken steps to shift his emphasis somewhat from cultural to economic influences. He virtually reverses his emphasis with the following statement: "Indeed, the subculture of poverty is part of the larger culture of capitalism, whose social and economic system channels wealth into the hands of a relatively small group and thereby makes for the growth of sharp class distinction." [77] He adds that the main reason for the perpetuation of the poverty subculture is to be found in the structure of the larger society itself. Yet he clings to the idea of the poverty subculture and its intergenerational transmission, even given a socialist revolution.

The balance of evidence contradicts Lewis's intergenerational subculture account of poverty. Rainwater's extensive research on the question leads him to conclude that whatever distinctive traits the poor may have that block their movement into higher levels of the working class, these traits are not faithfully transmitted from one generation to the next, but are acquired in the process of working out adaptations to demands of survival with the limited resources at hand.[78] With reference to blacks, Rainwater observes that they have created, particularly within the lower-class slums, "a range of institutions [such as female-centered families] to give structure to the tasks of living a victimized life and to minimize the pain it inevitably produces." [79] Furthermore, these situational adaptations to material disinheritance are not subcultural in the sense of carrying intergenerational commitment and loyalty; rather, each generation

---

[76] See Oscar Lewis, *La Vida* (New York: Random House, 1966), pp. xlii–lii.

[77] Lewis, "The Culture of Poverty," in Moynihan, *On Understanding Poverty*, pp. 198–99.

[78] Rainwater, "The Problem of Lower-Class Culture and Poverty-War Strategy," in Moynihan, *On Understanding Poverty*, p. 248.

[79] Rainwater, *Behind Ghetto Walls*, p. 6.

"has had a strong desire to perform successfully in terms of the norms of the larger society and has made efforts in this direction." [80] So long as the economic and political structure of the society remains unchanged, however, so do the circumstances and life chances of the poor.

The conclusion to be drawn from Rainwater's analysis is that changes in the structure of economic opportunities would produce fundamental changes in the way of life of the poor, including those who have created temporary alternative responses to deprivation. Another researcher into this question agrees with regard to black low-income groups: Ulf Hannerz concludes that "in most cases when opportunities for change appear . . . it would seem doubtful that internalized ghetto-specific culture would prevent changes from taking place." [81]

Another piece of research evidence which contradicts the cultural account of poverty is that presented by Scheffer in a study which compared white low-income with white blue-collar workers above them on the occupational and income scales.[82] Comparing the two samples, Scheffer probed an entire spectrum of cultural and social psychological variables in an attempt to isolate traces of a self-sustaining lower-income or poverty culture distinctive from that of the stable working class. The results consistently contradicted the idea of a poverty subculture. Where sample differences were significant, it was evident that the differences stemmed directly from greater or lesser income resources. The poor were especially aware of the gap between their values and aspirations and what, in fact, they could realistically have or expect to achieve. Scheffer concludes: It would seem highly probable that even a small upward change in income might produce a big change in behavior and general life style." [83]

Evidence is available which confirms Scheffer's hypothesis regarding the immediate impact of greater resources on life styles and social behavior. A 1966 experiment which increased Aid to Families with Dependent Children grants to a sample of young white Baltimore mothers from the regular $1,900 to $3,400 yielded significant and positive results. In a six-month period, the experimental group had better diets, worried less, felt better able to control things, spent more time on home improvement, were more involved with friends and relatives, and reported greater

---

[80] Ibid., p. 393.

[81] Ulf Hannerz, *Soulside: Inquiries Into Ghetto Culture and Community* (New York: Columbia University Press, 1969), p. 194; see also empirical data in Joseph A. Kahl and John M. Goering, "Stable Workers: Black and White," *Social Problems* 18 (Winter 1971): 306–18; and in-depth analysis by Mac. D. Gift, "Self-Concept and Social Change among Black Youth," Ph.D. dissertation, University of Utah, 1969.

[82] Martin W. Scheffer, "The Poor: Separate Class or Working Class? A Comparative Study," Ph.D. dissertation, University of Utah, 1971.

[83] Ibid., p. 131.

contentment.[84] There can be little doubt that in poverty we are confronting an economic and not a cultural phenomenon.

What are the changes required for the eradication of poverty? White or black, old or young, male or female, the changes required are changes in the relations of production governing the utilization of resources in the society. In employment, income, health, education, housing, environment, transportation, recreation, and other areas of economic and political life, the full participation of the poor and of all members of society can only be achieved by the progressive socialization of both available and potential material and human resources for total application to the elimination of inequality and powerlessness that beset so much of the working class under capitalism.

The prospects and forces for such change shall be examined in Chapter 12. Suffice it to remark here that, for now at least, Kolko remains essentially correct in saying that "no socially significant movement in American society today seeks to end poverty by attacking the basic, essential inequality upon which the economy rests, much less has a broad vision of a new society." [85] While the attack on inequality may be steadily mounting, the directions of the attack seem wide of the necessary target in order to succeed.

Meanwhile, as Piven and Cloward have persuasively demonstrated, a welfare strategy to suit the economic needs of the ruling class continues in force, a strategy manipulating the dependent and the industrial reserve army to meet requirements of the status quo.[86] We shall take up the issue of welfare within the context of our discussion of state capitalism in Chapter 10.

---

[84] *Trans-Action* 8 (September 1970): 8; originally published in *Child Welfare,* February 1970.

[85] Gabriel Kolko, *Wealth and Power in America* (New York: Frederick A. Praeger, 1964), p. xi.

[86] Frances Fox Piven and Richard A. Cloward, *Regulating the Poor: The Functions of Public Welfare* (New York: Pantheon Books, 1971).

eight

THE RULING CLASS
AND CORPORATE POWER

POWER

The next four chapters directly or indirectly concern the ruling class—its bases, organization, and method of operation. These chapters are concerned with power as it is exercised in the corporate economy and by the state, both nationally and internationally. The present chapter and the next focus upon the corporations and the ruling class, Chapter 10 on the state, and Chapter 11 on the imperialism as practiced by the corporations and the state. The ties between corporation and state and between national and international political economy are so pervasive that it is impossible to maintain any consistent separation in analysis.

The interpretation of power employed in our analysis will be Marxist, and unless other approaches have direct relevance for critical or comparative purposes, we shall not enter into them. Succinct summaries of various classical and contemporary theories of power are readily available.[1] To say our interpretation of power is Marxist implies that the capacity and ability to dominate and control the means of production, and all the political, military, and cultural spheres which may be subsumed under such material domination and control, are lodged in the ruling class, which is itself headed by a relatively small group of finance capitalists who direct vast amounts of national and international wealth. "Power" is not con-

---

[1] See, for example, T. B. Bottomore, *Elites and Society* (Baltimore: Penguin Books, 1966), and Geraint Parry, *Political Elites* (New York: Frederick A. Praeger, 1969).

ceived of as an independent dimension of stratification, but as another way of describing the control over the production and flow of material and social rewards and resources available to a society at any given time.[2] It assumes that such domination and control can be largely accomplished even in the face of opposition by others—and quite naturally so, for others are relatively powerless within the system of corporate capitalism.

H. L. Nieburg has laid the groundwork for a realistic understanding of the operation of power in contemporary society in his book *Political Violence*.[3] (However, we shall sharply dispute what seems to be his own acceptance of the legitimacy of the existing power system.) As the title of the book suggests, Nieburg considers the threat of force, force itself, and violence as essential ingredients to fully developed power. He also denies the existence and dismisses the ideal of the one-man–one-vote version of democracy. Nieburg argues both from fact and preference that power stems from the degree of strength inherent in the organization of special-interest groups, resulting in "a balance that is often quite different from the statistical fiction that all men and all groups are equally involved in any particular public interest."[4] Furthermore, Nieburg conceives of power as *legitimate* when the "bargaining strength and position of its holder is in close congruence with amount of power possessed. Power position and the demands of power, to be legitimate, must be continually tested through bargaining—i.e., through the employment of all measures available to a group for controlling and modifying the behavior of others, such as deterrence, compulsion, measured and appropriate reprisal, and violence up to warfare aimed at extermination or unconditional surrender. In a key phrase, Nieburg writes: "Beneath all forms of polite society lies a stratum of potential violence which constitutes the ultimate test of the viability of social groups and institutions."[5]

Thus, what Nieburg is saying is no more than that might makes one mighty, and that might shows no relationship to majorities or numbers. Kolko puts it directly: "In American society power responds to power, rather than to the powerless, and . . . competing factions, interests, and elites, none of whom have or depend upon a mass base, define the larger political strategy of the nation."[6] But what Nieburg is also saying is that might makes right—or, in his terminology, bargaining power provides for legitimacy and a test of viability. Thus, with regard to the state: "The

---

[2] Frank Parkin, *Class Inequality and Political Order* (New York: Praeger Publishers, 1971), pp. 44–46.

[3] (New York: St. Martin's Press, 1969).

[4] Ibid., p. 63.

[5] Ibid., p. 16.

[6] Gabriel Kolko, "Power and Capitalism in Twentieth-Century America," in J. David Colfax and Jack L. Roach, eds., *Radical Sociology* (New York: Basic Books, 1971), p. 226.

legitimacy of the state is strong when its norms have high congruence with those maintained by the prevailing coalitions of active power groups, and when state authority is responsive to their changing demands, personnel, and values." [7] Strength of bargaining position is the arbiter of every relevant value and institution: "General principles, ideologies, and ethical doctrines are meaningless except as they are reinforced by the bargaining outcomes of the behavior which they prescribe." [8] That Nieburg is not speaking only about facts but also about the way he prefers things to be is suggested by his evaluation of the legitimacy of student protest movements of the sixties (recalling that the sources of such protests were rooted in an opposition to war, racism, authoritarianism, sexism, poverty, etc.): "The often pseudo-rebellion on the college campuses has been treated much too generously and has not yet been tested for real viability." [9] Perhaps Professor Nieburg was subsequently satisfied by the Kent State, Jackson State, and other "tests" of the viability and legitimacy of interest and power groups in the United States. The state demonstrated, did it not, just whose interests were "legitimate" regarding peace vs. Vietnam?

Nieburg's theory of power is Marxist in implication insofar as it explains the operation of the material reward system and the control of social resources, though he refrains from drawing the obvious conclusion that the ruling class and their corporations and institutions hold nearly all of the heavy bargaining cards. For if he did draw this conclusion, he would also have to conclude that the ruling class and corporate capital are a legitimate power in America and around the world. In this, of course, Nieburg would stand diametrically opposed to Marxist theory, the central tenet of which is that the power position of the ruling class is *il*legitimate, for its role is destructive of the material and social well-being of society and the forward progress of history. Rather than assume, with Nieburg, that the powerful are legitimate, we would agree with Alvin Gouldner that, owing to their ability to enforce their moral claims, "the powerful can thus conventionalize their moral defaults." [10] Poverty is the result of Nieburg's bargaining theory; but poverty *is* illegitimate. Vietnam is the result of Nieburg's bargaining theory; but Vietnam *is* illegitimate. Nieburg himself catches a glimpse of the truth when, in complete contradiction to his entire thesis of legitimacy and viability as tested by power and violence, he writes that "physical sanctions and violence may be the least important methods of social control and leadership; they are certainly the least effec-

---

[7] Nieburg, *Political Violence*, p. 126.
[8] Ibid., p. 59.
[9] Ibid., p. 130.
[10] *The Coming Crises of Western Sociology* (New York: Basic Books, 1970), p. 297.

tive." [11] Could not by the same token a leadership based on social responsibility and human decency be the most effective?

A much less successful attempt to deal with the concept of power is that undertaken by Adolf A. Berle, Jr. in his book *Power*.[12] Berle's "pluralist" position on the structure of power is useful to examine, however, since it illustrates the central premises of this decaying theory and practice. Berle begins with the wholly unprovable (and thus untenable) assumption that "the instinct for power exists to some degree in everyone." A second and fully tenable assumption is that power invariably fills any vacuum in human organization. He then contends that power is invariably personal and that there is no such thing as independent class or group power, that groups can only assist the exercise of individual power through the process of organization. Berle is vague here, but if he means that it is individuals who act in powerful ways and not classes or groups as such, and that individuals as such are powerless without the institutional support of classes or groups, the main body of social science, including Marxist, is in accord. That this is, in fact, the intended meaning is suggested by Berle's next "law of power," which says that power is exercised through, and depends on, institutions: "Power is invariably organized and transmitted through institutions." Few if any contemporary power theorists would dispute this statement, which occupies the center of any valid theory of power. Also unchallenged is that power is invariably based on a system of ideas, since institutions are themselves composed of ideas—i.e., norms, values, beliefs, etc.

So far Berle's conception of power offers nothing new and little to object to; for the most part these "laws" are common assumptions in social science. But then comes the classic assumption of pluralism, an assumption which suddenly divides the readership: "Power is invariably confronted with, and acts in the presence of, a field of responsibility." Here the theory of pluralism breaks down in the presence of the ruling-class hegemony of irresponsibility. The bulk of the remainder of Berle's argument is dedicated to convincing the reader of the self-balancing nature of the field of responsibility, though tempered from classical liberalism by the recognition that large organizations balance off one another rather than smaller groups of individuals. Despite performing the obligatory act of denouncing the power theory of C. Wright Mills, who laid to rest the myth of pluralism, Berle at one point rises to the occasion in his study of power by acknowledging that "the immediate result [of the growth of heavily capitalized institutions] was the rise of the government bureau and

---

[11] Nieburg, *Political Violence*, p. 118.
[12] (New York: Harcourt, Brace, and World, 1969).

the corporate manageriat. They became and now are the primary holders of economic power." [13] Berle fails to add, as he must under his pluralist delusion, that the primary holders of economic power are the primary holders of power.

Max Weber was among the first to struggle theoretically with the meaning of the rise of the large organization. Whereas Marx concentrated his energies on the economics of centralization, Weber probed its sociological aspects. Weber observed that the means of administration of large economic organizations were not unique to them alone, but were becoming the dominant fact of all facets of modern social organization. The type of organization becoming predominant was bureaucracy. Chief among the identifying characteristics of bureaucratic organization are appointment to office, expertise and technical qualification, career structure, graduated salary, offices hierarchically arranged, official tasks organized by rules and functionally divided, and institutional resources distinct from the individual.[14] Like Marx, Weber was attuned to the fact that the accumulation of material wealth provided the mainspring of bureaucratic growth, and that material wealth and power today shore up bureaucracy in government, in the military, and in corporations. The emphasis here is not, however, on the growth of *technology* as a force *necessitating* bureaucracy. Although technological resources are invaluable in organizing and perpetuating the bureaucratic form of control, technology per se does not underlie bureaucracy. Imperial bureaucracies existed in the preindustrial era—witness ancient Egypt, classical China, and the medieval Church. In discussing the alienated nature of bureaucratic task division and specialization, Gintis has captured the truth of the matter by saying that "bureaucratized and routinized tasks do not flow from the nature of 'technology' but from the needs of centralized control." [15] And far from being the most efficient form of social organization (something Weber failed to recognize), the denial of full participation of labor in the control and organization of production actually sacrifices efficiency to the needs of bureaucratic control.

Marx was early aware of the power which bureaucratic organization

---

13 Ibid., p. 194.
14 Hans Gerth and C. Wright Mills, eds., *From Max Weber* (New York: Oxford University Press, 1958), pp. 196–244.
15 Herbert Gintis, "Alienation in Capitalist Society," in *The Capitalist System*, edited by Richard C. Edwards et al. (Englewood Cliffs, N.J.: Prentice-Hall, 1972), p. 280.

and control afforded its users. It was this awareness that led to his conviction that violent revolution would be required to effectively challenge bureaucratized ruling-class power, but that nonviolent revolution could be achieved in nonbureaucratized states. Weber made explicit the fact that bureaucracy is fundamentally a *form of power.* To Weber, bureaucracy was a "power instrument of the first order": "Where bureaucratization of administration has been completely carried through, a form of power relation is established that is practically unshatterable. . . . The ruled, for their part, cannot dispense with or replace the bureaucratic apparatus of authority once it exists," and "the idea of eliminating these organizations becomes more and more utopian." [16] Even those on the inside are trapped in "a fixed route of march."

The critical question then becomes: Who determines the route of march? Liberals and radicals alike generally agree that bureaucracy is not an autonomous power unto itself, but is a tool or instrument *of* power, mighty though it may at times be. For example, Dahrendorf writes that "as a medium and instrument of domination, bureaucracy stands at the disposal of anybody who is called upon to control it. As a constant in political conflict it accompanies and supports whatever group is in power by administering its interests and directives dutifully and loyally." [17] In Kolko's words: "The function of bureaucracy is to serve constituted power, not itself." [18] Weber provides the logical conclusion: "The consequences of bureaucracy depend therefore upon the direction which the powers using the apparatus give to it," this determination coming "only from the very top." [19] And who rules at the very top? The ruling class—the large vested interests—rules directly or through hired employees the decisive bureaucratic structures of corporate capitalism.

Weber also followed Marx in defining an antiauthoritarian form of organization: elected officials, short terms of office, liability to recall at any time, a principle of rotation, strictly defined mandate for conduct of office by the assembly of members, strict obligation to render an accounting to the assembly, obligation to submit every unusual question not foreseen to the assembly, a distribution of power among a large number of offices, and treatment of office as avocation and not a full-time occupation.[20] Marx would add that salaries should be no higher than those of non-

---

[16] *From Max Weber,* pp. 226–29.
[17] Ralf Dahrendorf, *Class and Class Conflict in Industrial Society* (Stanford, Calif.: Stanford University Press, 1958), p. 300.
[18] Gabriel Kolko, *The Roots of American Foreign Policy* (Boston: Beacon Press, 1969), p. 13.
[19] *From Max Weber,* pp. 228–30.
[20] *The Theory of Social and Economic Organization* (New York: Oxford University Press, 1947), p. 412.

officers and no higher than the value of their contributions to the material and social well-being of the society. We might also add that there should be the fullest possible diffusion of information and equally open access to group resources.[21] While Weber argued that democracy and bureaucracy were not two different political forms and that democracy could accommodate bureaucracy, as the founder of the ideal-type Weber could see the inherent opposition of democracy and bureaucracy and struggled unsuccessfully with the problem of a reconciliation of the two.

In attempting to satisfy the reality of bureaucratic organization within the context of ideological democracy, pluralists shifted the Weberian and Marxian definition of democracy aside in favor of a democracy of organizations; democracy was redefined as a competition among organized large-scale groups, rather than as a form of government of, by, and for the people. S. M. Lipset's definition will suffice here: "In essence, democracy in modern society may be viewed as involving the conflict of organized groups competing for support. . . . Democracy in large measure rests on the fact that no one group is able to secure a basis of power and command over the majority so that it can effectively suppress or deny the claims of the groups it opposes." [22] In the vision of pluralists, this is precisely the way power moves in modern society.

Some would agree with this version of big-league democracy, and add that it is not only necessary but a good thing, since democracy of, by, and for the people wouldn't work anyway, for the people are really too uninformed and stupid to make democracy work. In the words of Herbert McClosky:

> Even in a highly developed democratic nation like the United States, millions of people continue to possess only the most rudimentary understanding of democratic ideology. Democratic viability is . . . saved by the fact that those who are most confused about democratic ideas are also likely to be politically apathetic and without significant influence. Their role in the nation's decision process is so small that their "misguided" opinions or non-opinions have little practical consequence for stability.[23]

Even such a normally understanding critic of pluralism as Andrew Hacker has little faith in the democratic potential of the people: "Most people are ordinary. Moreover, ordinary people are relatively unintelligent, incapable

---

[21] See Jo Freeman, "The Tyranny of Structurelessness," *Berkeley Journal of Sociology* 17 (1972–73): 151–64.

[22] *Revolution and Counterrevolution* (New York: Basic Books, 1968), p. 433.

[23] Herbert McClosky, "Consensus and Ideology in American Politics," in Kenneth M. Dolbeare, ed., *Power and Change in the United States* (New York: John Wiley & Sons, 1969), p. 115.

of abstraction or imagination, lacking any special qualities of talent or creativity. They are for the most part without drive or perseverance; easily discouraged, they prefer the paths of security." [24]

Marxist theory has other explanations regarding why democracy isn't working—not even democracy of large organizations, the self balancing system of bureaucracies. Native intelligence and democratic sophistication are not the problems. Indeed, people are often cynical, and cynicism leads to apathy and ignorance. But to the extent that such apathy and ignorance is present, it is present not as a result of human failure but of reality of assessment and keenness of perception—the reality and perception of immovable and unreachable power. But active and informed opposition has been more typical of many people recently, people so active and informed that they have begun to make inroads into the centers of power. But to return to our basic question: Why are democracy and change so difficult to achieve today? Baran and Sweezy have the answer. "Votes are the nominal source of power, and money is the real source: the system, in other words, is democratic in form and plutocratic in content." [25] Democracy of the people, and even democracy of organizations, does not work because democracy as a political system requires material equality. Given the gross inequalities of wealth and resources in contemporary society, democracy has virtually no chance of working out its potential. Political rights are not enough, even when fully present—something that the ruling class tries hard to prevent. For beyond political rights there must be economic rights that enable the contestants to engage in the competition equally. As Frank Parkin observes: "Only if the main political contestants were to enjoy a roughly similar economic and social status could we say that pluralist democracy was a system of genuine political equality." [26] Democracy as a system of political equality *presupposes* social and material equality to enable contending groups to utilize political rights to the same degree.

Marxist theory holds that genuine political equality can never be attained under the existing system of property relations; we can only have bourgeois democracy—better than the total repressiveness of feudal regimes, but incapable of building a representative and equal system of social and economic relations. The material resources of the owners of the means of production are too great, too overwhelming, to "bargain" with. The ruling class only bargain among themselves. As Mintz and Cohen point out: "The concept of countervailing power is but another mirage. Power does not countervail. It attracts. Among the powerful, mutual assistance

[24] *The End of the American Era* (New York: Atheneum, 1970), pp. 161, 166.
[25] Paul A. Baran and Paul M. Sweezy, *Monopoly Capital* (New York: Monthly Review Press, 1968), p. 155.
[26] *Class Inequality and Political Order,* p. 182.

pacts are less painful than prolonged strife." [27] Even more to the point, Kolko writes that "should high status, rich men ever seek to make decisions dysfunctional to the more permanent interest of dominant power interests, even more powerful leaders would immediately purge them from decision-making roles." [28] What of the nonmonied elites who head up nonbusiness bureaucracies? As we shall learn presently, most nonbusiness bureaucracies of significance, including state and military ones, are under the direct or indirect control of the ruling class. In any regard, Heilbroner speaks the truth in saying that "a general acquiescence to the business system, when it does not descend to outright sycophancy, describes the general attitudes of nonbusiness leaders." [29]

All but the most unwavering believers would have to agree with C. Wright Mills that "liberalism [or pluralism] has been stretched beyond any usefulness as a way of defining issues and stating policies." [30] The rhetoric of liberalism has been given a tragically hypocritical ring in an era when a small handful of men can lead a society into a distant war that has cost it 55,000 lives (after 95,000 French dead), between $110 billion and $150 billion in immediate costs, and an estimated additional $352 billion in ultimate costs.[31] By far the biggest price has been and will be paid by Vietnamese themselves. Vietnam-style liberalism is, of course, not liberalism at all, but the product of bureaucratic authoritarianism of the worst and most brutal, callous kind. What court should try the immoral squandering of resources and lives of the Johnsons, Bundys, Rostows, McNamaras, Rusks, Nixons, Kissingers, and the ruling-class interests who stand behind such vain men and imperialistic foreign policies?

Though not so easily read as foreign policy, domestic events, too, cannot be understood within the never-never world of pluralism. We shall deal with both sides of this same corporate capitalist coin in greater detail as we progress through this chapter and the following two chapters. Suffice it to point out here that there are plenty of lesser minor issues which do not threaten the power of the ruling class directly concerning which the public can play make-believe democracy, at least those who want to continue to play. As William Connolly notes, the power centers are willing to let the public blow off steam on certain questions, to squabble about issues such as fluoridation, progressivism in the schools, and, we might add at

---

[27] Morton Mintz and Jerry S. Cohen, *America, Inc.* (New York: Dial Press, 1971), p. 75.

[28] *The Roots of American Foreign Policy*, p. 15.

[29] Robert Heilbroner, *The Limits of American Capitalism* (New York: Harper and Row, 1966), p. 57.

[30] *The Power Elite* (New York: Oxford University Press, 1956), p. 335.

[31] *The Statistical Abstract of the United States, 1972* (New York: Grosset and Dunlap, 1972), p. 243.

the moment, school busing, gun control, and abortion.[32] The property relations that have set the stage for such secondary issues as these, however, are beyond access and challenge.

Is bureaucracy inevitable even under the rule of a progressive, democratic majority? (For presented with the truth and a rational system of production and distribution, we assume the majority will be both democratic and progressive.) Marxist theory argues that it is not, though Marxist theory does see the need for authority and leadership. But this authority and leadership must meet the requirements of genuine democracy as outlined by both Marx and Weber.

Before moving on to an examination of the property relations that guarantee such a model democracy is not about to emerge under capitalism, a further caution is in order regarding the democratic potential within the population. Clearly, doubt and skepticism are at unprecedented heights regarding the democratic functioning of the state and society. Distrust and feelings of powerlessness are deep and widespread. But we cannot take this as indicative of popular incompetence, as McClosky has done after discovering what he interprets as "antidemocratic" postures among the people:

> The findings furnish little comfort for those who wish to believe that a passion for freedom, tolerance, justice and other democratic values springs spontaneously from the lower depths of the society, and that the plain, homespun, uninitiated yeoman, worker and farmer are the natural hosts of democratic ideology.[33]

McClosky feels that the educated liberals are the true bearers and sustainers of democracy—such as, we may assume, the parade of Rand wizards and Harvard professors who trek to Washington and around the globe upholding the sacred tenets of political equality and open democracy. Brimming with secrecy, deceit, and opportunism of the classic political sort, these "educated liberals" and the men who hire them have done more to discredit, undercut, and numb the democratic sensibilities of yeoman, worker, and farmer than can ever be measured or judged for consequences.

But "the lower depths of society" may yet assert their democratic spontaneity and throw out at least the accessible glaring fronts and figureheads of ruling-class dictatorship. Gains have already been made, however minor, toward attaining a system of power in which, in Mills's definition of democracy, "those vitally affected by any decision men make have an effective voice in that decision." [34] For example, the Democratic party's

---

[32] *The Bias of Pluralism* (New York: Atherton Press, 1969), p. 69.
[33] "Consensus and Ideology in American Politics," p. 115.
[34] C. Wright Mills, *The Sociological Imagination* (New York: Oxford University Press, 1959), p. 188.

1972 reforms opened the door to "the lower depths of society," and the response was impressive as women, youth, blacks, white workers, and welfare recipients helped write a relatively progressive platform, though it was certainly far from radical. Nevertheless, conservative intellectuals are already busily scheming to reinstate their own "majority" of reactionary bureaucrats in *full* power (they never were, of course, really unseated).[35]

POWER IN THE CORPORATIONS

The modern private business corporation is a paragon of bureaucratic organization, and enjoys the maximum of power which this form of organization offers. As the chief repository and employer of wealth and resources, the corporation is the most powerful bureaucracy in the capitalist system; it *is* the capitalist system. This is not to overlook or underestimate the power of the state, particularly as embodied in the executive branch. The latter has continually enlarged the scope of its power, not at the expense of corporate bureaucracies but in conjunction with them. The outcome is state capitalism. In this section we confine ourselves to an analysis of power *within* the corporate world, an essential prerequisite to the understanding of corporate power in the context of the larger society. The intentions here are to examine the relationship between the corporations and the ruling class and to explain the manner in which the ruling class bases its power and wealth in the corporate system. In the remainder of the chapter, then, we shall be examining the *economic basis of ruling-class power*.

Together with understanding the linkage between the corporations and the state, understanding the mechanics of corporate power represents at once the most difficult and the most important task of critical social science. With a number of outstanding exceptions, social scientists have largely turned their backs on these decisive issues, and when they have entered into them, they have accepted the formal blueprints and platitudes of the day. For example, federal and state regulatory agencies are often seen as protectors of the public interest instead of what they are—tools of corporate capital aiding in the smooth and profitable functioning of the large private concerns. And since the blueprints say that holders of corporate wealth are not the same official person as the managers of the corporation, economists write on the "soulful" corporation, comparing its

---

[35] See the discussion and analysis of this conservative move for Democratic party leadership in Irving Louis Horowitz, "Coalition for a Democratic Majority: The Operators Make Their Play," *The Nation*, January 15, 1973, pp. 72–75.

leaders to hard-working and responsible public servants.[36] It is this last illusion which we must dispel if the Marxist idea of a ruling class is to stand. Actually, the burden of proof should rest with those who claim that the holders of vast wealth and fortune sit at the mercy of the managers, and not with those who contend that the fabulously wealthy form a ruling class.

Victor Perlo has characterized the illusion of the separation of ownership from control—i.e., that stock or wealth holders have been divorced from positions of power—quite succinctly: "Various professors and writers, from outright apologists for big business to well-meaning liberals, accepted at face value the facade of hired managers, concealing the true character of control. They developed the theory that the managers now controlled the large corporations, and that these managers were a new and distinct class in society." [37] Liberals and pluralists would naturally wish to see a new managerial interest group, or competing managerial groups, add to a balance of interests, rather than witnessing an unprecedented growth of concentrated economic power in the hands of the property-holding capitalist class. The replacement of capitalists by experts in public finance and business management in positions of power would relegate the whole idea of class struggle and conflict to a historical museum. Indeed, with millions holding corporate stock, one could conceive of a new "people's capitalism" and capitalist socialization of the means of production, with conscientious and expert civil servant types efficiently running the forces of production for the commonweal! Obviously, if the liberal image of corporate power were correct, we should now be living in an economic and material utopia, for no nation has ever had such enormous wealth and resources at its disposal than the United States. But rather than even just a good society, not to mention a utopia, we have economic, political, and social disarray on a large scale. So let us look inside the corporate world for more realistic answers to questions of power.

The chief actors on the corporate stage are major shareholders, directors, and managers of the largest industrial and financial corporations. The answer to the question of corporate power lies within the relationships among these categories. In Chapter 4 we pointed to the tremendous degree of concentration of corporate stock, so we know from the start that the circle of major shareholders is relatively small; by definition, then, these huge fortunes must be articulated directly or indirectly with the largest corporations. From Treasury Department data we also know that, while

---

[36] See Adolf A. Berle, Jr., *Power Without Property* (New York: Harcourt, Brace and World, 1959), p. 143.

[37] *The Empire of High Finance* (New York: International Publishers, 1957), p. 48.

1 percent of the population holds almost four-fifths of corporate stock, a mere 0.1 percent holds two-fifths and an infinitesimal 0.003 percent well over one-quarter.[38] Even on the average, each of these individuals is a millionaire; but the *major* shareholders dwarf the "ordinary" millionaire. At this point we must interject a precautionary item: we are dealing with one of the most secretive areas of American society. It is exceedingly difficult to obtain the full extent of stock concentration, for there are numerous devices with which individuals and families—and families, not individuals, occupy center stage here—can disguise or conceal their actual holdings and influence. Thus, any estimate of a wealthy individual's stock holdings may almost uniformly be considered conservative.

Continuing from the above data, we further know that, with the proliferation of shares to growing numbers of *small* shareholders, the percentage of stock required for control continually is on the decline—meaning that far less than one-quarter of a firm's outstanding stock is needed to control it. Given the fact that, on the outside, no more than five hundred (two hundred is the common figure) corporations exert decisive economic leverage under the system of monopoly capital, and given the accompanying fact that the several thousands of major shareholders have virtually all of their big holdings in and around these several hundred firms, it is veritably self-evident that these shareholders have among them enough economic power to hold sway over the decision-making and control processes of the heart of corporate capitalism. To ask whether, in fact, these major owners actually do exercise decision-making control is to ask entirely the wrong question. The correct question to be asked is *how* do these propertied interests control the system in which their wealth is lodged? In answering this question, we can add further evidence to the decision-making centrality of the capitalist class.

There are many doors through which we might enter in order to answer the question of how the capitalist class dominates the corporate economy, but we shall go first to that of the relationship between stockholding and directing. Inasmuch as we have been variously critical of A. A. Berle, Jr., we owe him the favor of citing something he has written that is at least halfway correct: "Nominal power still resides in the stockholders; actual power in the board of directors." [39] This statement is only halfway correct inasmuch as major stockholders are directly or by proxy represented on the board of directors; thus, the major shareholders, unlike the legions of small and intermediate holders, hold actual power, not

---

[38] See Dick Roberts, "The Financial Empires of America's Ruling Class," *International Socialist Review* 30 (May–June 1969): 35.

[39] *Power Without Property* (New York: Harcourt, Brace and World, 1959), p. 74.

nominal. Moreover, not *all* directors are actually powerful; the majority of *them* hold nominal power. For just as a slight fraction of the population hold the decisive shares of corporate stock, so do a small inner circle of directors hold or represent the critical balance of financial power within a given corporation. Let us look at some figures.

Take, for example, Don Villarejo's study of 2,784 directors in the top 232 corporations.[40] Villarejo found that 99 of these directors with $10 million or more worth of stock in their own firms held as *individuals* $5.2 billion of the total $7.1 billion held by all directors. Adding family members' holdings, trusts not included in individual totals, and stock held in the other 232 corporations in which they were not directors, all these directors' wealth came to $14.4 billion; but the propertied-rich directors— those with $10 million or more inherited or acquired by means other than as employees in one of the top 232 firms, and those with $1 million or more who were members of such wealthy persons' families—accounted for fully $13 billion of this sum. Thus, there are directors and there are directors. All directors' holdings represented over 6 percent of these 232 companies' total common stock, but most of it belonged to a mere 99 persons. Adding holding companies, bank trusts, and other stock held by one of the 232 sample corporations where controlling interest was apparent and identifiable, Villarejo reports that the 6 percent under director control doubles to 12 percent (5 percent is commonly thought to give control, but 10 percent is often used as a safe research figure). In 141 of the 232 firms, directors held enough identifiable stock to give clear control. As an important aside, 520 of the 2,784 directors were propertied rich and the large majority of the remainder of those with $1 million or more in stock were corporation executive officers. This means that the large wealth-holding core of top corporations are not only family inheritors or personal owners, but are also very much directly active themselves. Indeed, as if being key figures on the board of directors were not enough, 197 of the 520 propertied rich were also serving as board chairmen or chief executive officers.

The major stockholders, then, are frequently not only directors but managers as well. Kolko points out that from 1937 to 1957 the proportion of directors occupying a key office in their own company increased from 36 to 50 percent.[41] If directors who were members of management in *some* company are counted, it becomes evident that directors and managers are not two separate groups but greatly overlapped, just as major stockholders and directors are significantly fused. That directors may be pro-

---

[40] "Stock Ownership and the Control of Corporations," *New University Thought* 2 (Autumn 1961 and Winter 1962): 33–77, 47–65.
[41] Gabriel Kolko, *Wealth and Power in America* (New York: Frederick A. Praeger, 1962), pp. 60–61.

hibited from holding a controlling interest in their corporation, as is the case in a large number of firms, in no way modifies the proposition that directors as a group are at once the most powerful and the most highly propertied active sector of the corporate world. The twenty-eight men on the General Motors board in 1966 averaged $6 million in GM shares per family, with key holders such as John L. Pratt receiving up to $60 million. The legion of shareholders with a few thousand dollars assure that those who control a corporation need not hold a very large percentage of the total stock. With an estimated 17 percent of GM shares, the DuPont family has been the chief stockholder in that firm, and family interests need not be directly attended to by a family member on the management team in order to be maximized. For as Mills observes: "Top-level managers are socially and politically in tune with other large property holders." [42]

For top management to be in tune with the propertied rich is not difficult to understand. Chief executives in the leading corporations are often extremely wealthy, even if such wealth is the result of employee status alone; the majority are multimillionaires as a result of the stock-option privilege.[43] Their stock interests in their firms are often many times greater than salary and bonuses combined, though unlike the case of the propertied rich, the salary and bonus are an essential ingredient to the lives of many of the chief executives even in the top two hundred corporations. (In 1971, the seventy-four officers and directors of ITT received over $10 million in pay, for an *average* of $135,500 per person. The thirty-nine leaders of ATT averaged a mere $80,000 per man.) As shareholders run, almost *all* of top management are deeply involved in the ownership of corporate property. As a top Ford manager, one of the geniuses of Vietnam, Robert McNamara, accumulated $1.5 million in Ford property as a result of a $400,000 salary and the exercise of stock options at one-third price (a $350,000 bonus was awarded McNamara when he *resigned* from Ford, but ultimately he cost the taxpayer more than the car buyer). We would agree with Menshikov that being a multi-millionaire is a pivotal turning point in moving from a mere hired manager to manager-capitalist entrepreneur and, finally, to entrepreneur status alone. (Who wants to work the corporate grind when total freedom is possible, or even the enticing option of serving the nation politically? [44]) But money and property alone do not tie hired managers to the oligarchy of wealth. Their backgrounds are typically bourgeois or petit bourgeois

---

[42] C. Wright Mills, *White Collar* (New York: Oxford University Press, 1951), p. 104.

[43] See *Forbes,* May 17, 1972, pp. 205 ff.

[44] S. Menshikov, *Millionaires and Managers* (Moscow: Progress Publishers, 1969), pp. 89–90.

and, as Menshikov notes, "before reaching a leading post in a monopoly corporation a former petty bourgeois or worker undergoes a thorough 're-education' in the spirit of devotion to the financial oligarchy, and this is the only way he can get ahead." [45]

The importance and power of the "technostructure" or top-level management is not in dispute, though J. K. Galbraith's view of the separation of ownership from control is as erroneous as any other.[46] Furthermore, the technostructure has essentially the same interests as the principle capitalists. Obviously, specialized expertise is needed to run a big business (though we can question *how* expert the expertise really is, in view of the losses, overruns, shortages, breakdowns, waste, etc.). Whether good or bad, information specialists and their computers are necessary tools for decision makers, who may even themselves claim specialties of one variety or another which aid the growth of profits. Nor do we dispute Baran and Sweezy's contention that "real power is held by the insiders, those who devote full time to the corporation and whose interests and careers are tied to its fortunes," so long as they add that "the managerial stratum is the most active and influential *part of the propertied class*" (when they are in fact part of the propertied class), and that "managers are *among* the biggest owners" and "function as the *protectors and spokesmen* for all large-scale property." [47] The situation of management within the corporation is summed up by Menshikov: "The power of the top executives is quite real, but only so long as they remain obedient tools of the financial oligarchy" [48] (and of course a sizeable number of top executives are themselves members of this oligarchy).

The financial oligarchy occupy the dominating and controlling positions of the industrial and financial worlds, and this oligarchy and the families it represents constitute the ruling class. While contemporary sociologists more often prefer the term *upper class*, whatever the labels may be they all refer essentially to the same network of fortunes and families. The thesis of the managerial new class has as its corollary that family capitalism is withering or dead—i.e., that a neutral stratum of experts is running things without the interpersonal and intergenerational interests and loyalties of a ruling social class. We have in several contexts observed the high degree of concentration of stock ownership in individuals. These individuals are, of course, members of families. Now, in recent inquiries, it has been found that, in nearly one-third of the top five hundred corporations, controlling ownership is *identifiably* in the hands of an individual or

---

[45] Ibid., p. 95.

[46] John Kenneth Galbraith, *The New Industrial State* (New York: Signet Books, 1967).

[47] *Monopoly Capital*, pp. 34–35. Italics mine.

[48] *Millionaires and Managers*, p. 134.

a single family.[49] This *excludes coalitions* of families and control with less than 10 percent. (For example, Richard K. Mellon, holding some $430 million in Alcoa, GM, Gulf Oil, Koppers, and Pittsburg Plate & Glass, among other firms, was not listed in the data cited above as Mellon family; only Paul Mellon with 11 percent of Carborundum was so listed.)

As alluded to previously, the findings on family ownership also exclude the unidentifiable holdings, those lodged in financial intermediaries such as trusts and nominees. Stocks held by these banks and brokerage houses and other financial institutions totaled about 40 percent of all common stock in 1960, and the figure has probably grown considerably since that time.[50] Commercial banks, for example, held $250 billion in trust assets in 1967, $180 billion of it in privately owned trusts.[51] The point is that there *are* real, live individuals and families behind the "street names" which may cover or obscure identities of the owners of much of this stock. The private brokerage houses which act as fronts for large family holdings may themselves be the largest stockholders and dominant influences in a given bank. Thus, the $70 billion in bank trusts as pensions in the 1967 data end up under the control of the families and individuals whose financial capital controls the banks. And great propertied wealth in a few hands means that few banks will govern an overwhelmingly disproportionate amount of the trust funds; in the mid-sixties ten largest banks had 35 percent of all trust funds, the twenty-seven largest 50 percent, and the hundred largest about 80 percent. But even the few are closely interlaced with one another, and through their trust holdings reach out to dominate large portions of the industrial sector.

In addition to direct ownership, family holding companies, and brokerage house and trust fronts, many families—Ford, Lilly, Rockefeller, Kellogg, Duke, Kresge, and many others—utilize for estate tax purposes foundations as repositories of propertied riches. Whatever the avenues of ownership and control, some new and some old, the ruling class exists and oversees as always the direction of capitalist economy. Heilbroner estimates that as few as two hundred to three hundred families own blocks of stock that ultimately control the top one hundred fifty corporations.[52] Many new-rich oil, insurance, savings-and-loan, real estate, government contract (taxpayer-rich), and speculator tycoons, despite their number and fortunes, are often not in sufficiently advantageous positions of social

---

[49] Robert Sheehan, "Proprietors in the World of Big Business," in Maurice Zeitlin, ed., *American Society, Inc.* (Chicago: Markham Publishing Company, 1970), pp. 79–83.

[50] Villarejo, "Stock Ownership and the Control of Corporations," pp. 33–77.

[51] See Robert Fitch and Mary Oppenheimer, "Who Rules the Corporations?" *Socialist Revolution* 1 (July–August 1970): 93–99.

[52] *The Limits of American Capitalism*, p. 26.

and political power to place them within the boundaries of the established plutocracy of the ruling class.[53] Even their economic power is often strictly dependent upon or controlled by older financial and industrial centers of power, or by the Defense Department or other promoters of state capitalism. Perlo's assessment of fifteen years ago remains largely true today: "For the present, Texas, like the South [and West] as a whole, remains a domestic colony of Wall Street." [54] Nevertheless, the path leading from new rich to old plutocrat remains open; if the route isn't traveled in a generation, there are other generations to follow. Changing and expanding bases of wealth have tended to mean a changing and expanding ruling class.

FINANCE CAPITAL AND CORPORATE POWER

Lenin's economic theory, as well as that of Marx, defined *finance capital* as the merger of financial and industrial interests and assets. *Monopoly capital* is used as an interchangeable term. The potential and existence of conflict between bankers and industrialists is historically factual, just as conflicts of interests exist within banking and industry. The idea of finance capital does not subsume a seemless web of cooperation among capitalists. The point to be stressed is made by Sweezy in his response to the argument that power lies with bankers qua bankers who have emerged victorious in a contest with industrialists over the division of surplus value: [55] "As against the rest of society, the capitalists form a unified class which intuitively understands that its primary interest lies in maximum possible exploitation of the working class. Compared to this, the struggle over the division of spoils is a secondary concern." [56]

Without entering into any of the details of the argument of banks versus industry, we shall only point out that most of the apparent conflicts between finance and industry melt away when it is understood that,

---

[53] For an interesting account of many new-rich tycoons, see Kenneth Lamott, *The Moneymakers* (Boston: Little, Brown and Company, 1969).

[54] *The Empire of High Finance*, p. 250.

[55] See Fitch and Oppenheimer, "Who Rules the Corporations?" *Socialist Revolution* 1, nos. 4, 5, and 6.

[56] Paul M. Sweezy, "The Resurgence of Financial Control: Fact or Fancy?" *Monthly Review* 23 (November 1971): 30. Ralph Miliband would agree: "This 'elite pluralism' does not, however, prevent the separate elites in capitalist society from constituting a dominant economic class, possessed of a high degree of cohesion and solidarity, with common interests and common purposes which far transcend their specific differences and disagreements." *The State In Capitalist Society* (New York: Basic Books, 1969), p. 48.

as O'Connor puts it, "the same people organize the production and realization of surplus value and the appropriation of surplus value." [57] Industrialists, observes O'Connor, become bankers to mobilize capital from the population as a whole and to ensure that they participate fully in the appropriation of surplus value, and bankers have become industrialists knowing in the long run that financial claims are worthless unless surplus value is produced in industry. The question of whether an industrial corporation has a large enough cash flow or has to go to financial institutions for money is not the important one, for the ruling class owns and controls both types of institutions. The venerable banking houses of the nation have been capitalized on industrial fortunes, while industries tap the banking houses for, in Roberts's words, "every penny that they are capable of drawing from the populace for the use of the ruling class." [58] (Pensions are the single most important source of these "pennies.") The Rockefellers, Duponts, Dukes, Mellons, Morgans (originally bankers), and other tycoons capitalized their own fortunes in banks long ago, and the handful of financial centers that dominate the corporate world are or were based in families such as these. Thus, there has been a continual merging of industrial and financial property into finance capital, which has greatly magnified the mass of property controlled by finance capitalists.

The world of finance capital is itself broken down into financial groups, a collective of financially based industrial concerns managed as though components of one corporation, though in name being several separate firms. "A contemporary financial group, as a rule," writes Menshikov "rests on an alliance of several or many families, united by the common striving for further enrichment." [59] When family owners are not directly involved, these financial groups are governed by regents or chief executives hired by the ruling class. An important point to remember with regard to financial groups, and a major reason for their existence, is that the *group* seeks profit and growth to the maximum, not always the individual component firms. Reciprocal agreements, for example, may mean profit stagnation for a given firm but overall profit maximization for finance capital dominating the group.

The financial group is tied together through both common ownership and operating control. At the center of a financial group is one or more of the great banking houses acting as a node of operation and linking together ostensibly competing interests. Increasingly, these linkages take the form of actual controlling ownership of the component firms by the banks. In

---

[57] James O'Connor, "Who Rules the Corporations?" *Socialist Revolution* 2 (February 1971): 126.

[58] Roberts, "The Financial Empires of America's Ruling Class," p. 32.

[59] Menshikov, *Millionaires and Managers,* p. 217.

form, the banks themselves cannot buy industrial stock, but through trust funds they have reached out singly or in combination to gain controlling interests in over one-third of the top five hundred industrial corporations.[60] The forty-nine largest banks account for most of these bank-controlled firms. With the top twenty banks accounting for 43 percent of all bank trust-department assets, it is within this limited circle—and even less than half that number—that the locus of commercial banking power lies. Banks vote the stocks of the centimillionaires' private trusts as well as the pennies of the elderly pensioner; the former group controls the banks, however, while the latter can only hope their money is put to socially constructive uses—which more often than not it isn't. Banks also cream off "promoters' stock" at bargain-basement prices for their financial backing of corporate mergers, another avenue of control and easy enrichment. Direct financial influence in nonfinancial corporations is importantly bolstered through loans or the issuance of corporate bonds.

As an example of banking-industrial financial ties, we might take Morgan Guaranty Trust Company of New York, which in the mid-sixties held approximately $17 billion in trust assets, 6.7 percent of all such assets. At that time, Morgan had in trust 5 percent or more of the common stock of seventy-two corporations, and its officers sat on over a hundred boards of directors. Including its own assets, Morgan's direct connections controlled $70 billion in corporate assets.[61] Among the firms which formed a part of the Morgan financial group were Campbell Soup, National Biscuit, American Can, Atlantic Richfield, Standard Brands, Continental Oil, Procter and Gamble, Coca-Cola, Olin Mathieson, Cities Service, and General Electric. A number of other top firms were controlled jointly by Morgan with other financial groups, including IBM, U.S. Steel, and B. F. Goodrich. Morgan had substantial participation in companies such as General Motors, Standard Oil (N.J.), Kennecott Copper, Burlington Industries, and several major airlines which belonged to other groups. With financial groups such as this in mind, Barber writes: "The unmistakable fact is that, with institutions in control of influential blocks of stock in major corporations, there is a basic risk that our biggest companies can be made to dance the tune of a plutocracy of bank and investment managers who are effectively sheltered from view, let alone having any meaningful notion of public accountability." [62] This is not to imply that trust-department officers are the economic generals, but only a reassertion that finance

---

[60] The Patman Committee, "Investments and Interlocks Between Major Banks and Corporations," in *American Society, Inc.*, pp. 70–76.

[61] See Menshikov, *Millionaires and Managers*, pp. 234–53 for a discussion of the Morgan group, as well as of others.

[62] Richard J. Barber, *The American Corporation: Its Power, Its Money, Its Politics* (New York: E. P. Dutton & Company, 1970), p. 68.

capital, the fusion of bank and industrial assets under the control of the ruling class, reigns supreme in contemporary capitalism.

The other linkage between bank and industry is the human one in the form of interlocking directors. Again from the Patman Committee data of the mid-sixties, the top forty-nine banks had 768 directors that also sat on the boards of 236 of the top five hundred corporations, for an average of three per corporation board. For example, with $7.6 billion in trust assets, Mellon National Bank & Trust Company of Pittsburgh aided their controlling ownership in twenty-one major corporations with seventy-four interlocking directorships. Morgan Guaranty helps glue together the big automobile as well as the major commercial airline "competitors," circumventing the Clayton Anti-Trust Act's restriction on interlocking directorships among corporations in the same field of production. Conglomerates and diversification have made a further shambles of the Clayton Act's intentions. "Public" utilities are especially lucrative targets for the financial groups: twenty-two of the largest utilities averaged four directors apiece compliments of the nation's forty-nine largest banks. And with their investment competitors, the life insurance companies, the big banks counted 146 interlocks with twenty-nine of the largest insurors, an average of five per company (mutual ownership is also widespread). To top off the linkages, the big banking houses own significant shares of one another and are indirectly interlocked with directors. Two hundred of the nation's largest banks reported that 5 to over 50 percent of their own shares were held by other financial institutions.[63] As to directorships, for example, Chemical Bank of New York has ties with twelve other commercial banks plus thirteen insurance companies and ten other financial institutions.[64]

The *tightest degree* of intercorporate linkages, both in terms of ownership and directorship, is found among the *largest* corporations. As one moves down from the top echelons to the second- and third-rank operations, the closeness of connections increasingly fades—logically so—among these very numerous lesser stars and between these and the larger ones.[65] The chief reason is not so much that there aren't enough personnel and assets to go around—although there are not—as because such interconnections just aren't necessary. The direction and control of the economy are determined within the top circles, and the lesser lights must react accordingly.

---

[63] The Patman Committee, "Bank Stock Ownership and Control," in Zeitlin, ed., *American Sociey, Inc.,* pp. 54–62.

[64] Jack Newfield and Jeff Greenfield, *A Populist Manifesto* (New York: Frederick A. Praeger, 1972), p. 54.

[65] See the study by Daniel R. Hoffman, "The Power Elite of Chicago," paper presented to the American Sociological Association, Denver, 1971.

CONCENTRATION AND CENTRALIZATION

In Marxist terms, *concentration* refers to the size and growth of corporations and *centralization* to the process of merger. The latter feeds the former. The fewer the number of entities to govern the easier becomes the problem of communication and control; and monopoly capital as achieved through growth and merger narrows the problem of communication and control. In this context, it should be stressed that concentration, and especially centralization or merger, is no automatic or necessary by-product of sophisticated technology. Understandably, certain heavy industries require a minimal size to be efficient in the use of resources, but in Walter Adams's words: "The facts simply do not bear out the contention that firms have to be big to be efficient, or that they are efficient because they are big." That it is economic control and power which is primarily propelling centralization is attested to by the fact that the merger movement over the past quarter-century has been most active in sectors with relatively simple technologies and low capital intensities such as food, textiles, clothes, lumber, building materials, and personal care and toiletries.[66]

Let us examine first the extent of monopoly among nonfinancial corporations. There were some 1.5 million operating corporations in the United States in 1968. Practically all of these businesses are small fry, suggested by the fact that firms with under $1 million in assets account for 94 percent of the total, but cover only 9 percent of all corporate assets. These smaller firms continue to proliferate and will in the future, as long as they serve needs of the giants—such as, among others, supplying them competitively with odd items and taking the risks of performing innovating functions.[67] Toward the other end of the scale, firms with $250 million or more in assets account for less than 0.1 percent of all corporations but 55 percent of the assets. (Interestingly, 1 percent of the corporations have 82 percent of assets, approximately the same relationship that exists between percentage of the adult population and stock ownership.)

But corporations with $250 million in assets do not bring us all the way toward the other end of the scale. It only represents a beginning. The *end* of the scale has the two hundred largest firms with 60 percent of manufacturing assets in 1969 (up from 48 percent in 1950), and even further,

---

[66] "The Mystique of Bigness," *The Progressive,* November 1972, p. 41.

[67] Paul M. Sweezy and Harry Magdoff, *The Dynamics of U.S. Capitalism* (New York: Monthly Review Press, 1972), p. 71.

the top hundred corporations with 48 percent of the assets (up from 40 percent in 1950). The latter group are the billion-dollar operations. Even the top hundred do not represent the critical end of the scale. Taking total capital assets (land, buildings, and equipment) as well as finances and including joint ventures or companies controlled through less than *majority* ownership, Gardiner Means points out that in 1962 fifty industrials accounted for 36 percent of the total assets, twenty firms for 25 percent, ten firms for 18 per cent, and the 5 largest for 12 percent.[68] In the latter category in 1971, we encounter Standard Oil of New Jersey and General Motors with $20.3 billion and $18.1 billion in assets, respectively. ATT was in a class by itself with $54.5 billion.

In the primary manufacturing markets, such as aluminum, chemicals, glass, copper, rubber, synthetic fibers, foods, electrical equipment, and steel, a few giants dominate three-fourths to nearly all of the field. Under these monopoly circumstances, writes Barber, "price competition is severely restricted, if not eliminated outright." [69]

Monopoly prices mean monopoly profits. The larger the firm—from the smallest to the over-$50-million-in-assets category—the larger the profit rate.[70] The five hundred largest corporations take four-fifths of all after-tax corporate profit in manufacturing, the two hundred largest two-thirds, the hundred largest almost three-fifths, the fifty largest almost one-half, the twenty largest almost two-fifths, the ten largest three-tenths, and the five largest one-fifth of all manufacturing profit.[71] The billion-dollar giants systematically soak up a larger and larger proportion of total surplus value. In 1970, after-tax profits of $44 billion were up over $17 billion from 1960 corporate profits. Undistributed profits of $19 billion and depreciation allowances of $54 billion gave the nation's corporations a cash flow of $73 billion. Chief among the profit takers in 1969 were "public" utilities with $3.2 billion in after-tax profits going to the electrical power companies and $2.1 billion to *the* telephone company.[72] In 1971, four firms scored a billion or more on the profit scale: ATT $2.24, General Motors $1.94, Standard Oil (N.J.) $1.46, and IBM $1.08. With over one-half billion netted were four more oil dealers and another car manufacturer, plus Sears, Roebuck. As for spending money (undistributed profits and depreciation writeoffs), seven companies had more than $1 billion—includ-

[68] "Economic Concentration," in Zeitlin, ed., *American Society, Inc.,* pp. 3–16; see also *Statistical Abstract of the United States, 1972,* p. 467.

[69] *The American Corporation,* p. 24.

[70] Howard Sherman, *Radical Political Economy* (New York: Basic Books, 1972), p. 107.

[71] Williard F. Mueller, "Recent Changes in Industrial Concentration, and the Current Merger Movement," in Zeitlin, ed., *American Society, Inc.,* p. 24; and *Statistical Abstract of the United States, 1972,* p. 467.

[72] *Statistical Abstract of the United States, 1972,* p. 472.

ing five car and oil firms, IBM, and, at the top of the list with about an even $5 billion "the phone company." As to profitability, we might note that corporations selling personal consumer goods reported in 1971 an 18 percent five-year return on equity, with health care (drugs, hospital supplies, etc.) close behind at 17.2 percent. As to 1971 alone, Kellogg reported a 21.6 percent rate of return with a number of other food and drug dealers approaching that figure. Among many of the largest firms, the rate of profit as well as the mass is not falling but rising.

Helping the monopolization of capital along is the merger process. The turn of the century began the large-scale merger movement, the 1920s pushed it much further, and the period since World War II has witnessed another great upsurge. A 1968 peak saw 2,407 mergers, including 206 involving acquired firms with $10 million or more in assets. Though acquisition of competitors and suppliers is not uncommon, as is attested to by mergers in the textile, petroleum, and dairy industries, the predominate form of merger in recent years has been the conglomerate—the linking up of firms in widely diverse fields of production. Of the 206 major mergers in 1968, 173 were of the conglomerate type. Many reasons lie behind the conglomerate merger—immediate financial gain, tax writeoffs, integration of production and distribution, consolidation of market position, spreading of risks, getting in on cost-plus military contracts, entering a fast-growing field, etc.—but growth and profit are the ultimate goals, as in other business activity. With the centralization process having been carried to a nearly monopolistic stage in many areas of the economy, diversification of ownership quite logically becomes necessary for desired growth rates. The pure conglomerate firm (GM is also conglomerate)—Ling-Temco-Vought, Litton Industries, Gulf and Western, National General Corporation, Leasco Data Processing Corporation, and, of course, ITT being among the most successful and best known—owes its advance to a growth reputation and inflated stock values, enabling it to sell its own shares, for example, at a 2-to-1 ratio for those of another targeted firm—an irresistible deal for the many buyers looking for a quick tax-free profit. In this way, new and even smaller firms can attempt to take over large and established corporations, such as LTV did with Jones & Laughlin Steel, and as Leasco Data Processing attempted to do with Chemical Bank of New York, the nation's sixth largest commercial banking house. The threat to the old plutocracy has been met by the Nixon administration with growing opposition, and a renewed interest in the antitrust legislation, though when favorable alignments appear and political contributions are in the offing, even giant conglomerate mergers are permissible (e.g., ITT and Hartford Fire Insurance).

Given the fact that banks serve as the vital centers of financial

groups, it is understandable that banking is more concentrated than industry. In 1970, the fifty largest commercial banks accounted for 48 percent of all banking assets, up from 39 percent in 1960.[73] In 1971, six New
York banks accounted for about one-sixth of all bank assets, and regarding
five of these Fitch and Oppenheimer write: "To a considerable extent the
five banks actually constitute a unified money cartel." [74] If Bank of America's $34 billion is added to the New York group, a sum of around $140
billion is attained, nearly one-quarter of total bank assets. Like industrials,
banks acquire one another, with twenty-three banks worth $100 million
or more being taken over in 1970.

We have already pointed to the high degree of concentration in the
area of trust funds. What must be stressed with regard to corporate concentration is that the pension component of trust funds has already become
one of the chief driving forces behind the monopolization of capital, and
portends to be the single most important factor in corporate concentration. By imposing shares upon the working class in the form of retirement
pensions, the ruling class disperses ownership and concentrates control,
both through their own large blocks of stock and the domination of pension funds. Pension assets in bank trust departments have soared since
1955. Including all private pension and deferred profit-sharing plans,
financial reserves in 1950 totaled $12.1 billion but had jumped to $125.1
billion by 1969. Pension contributions for that year were $6.6 billion more
than payments made to pensioners. At present growth rates, pension funds
will accumulate to staggering proportions. Upward of 28 million persons
in industry are contributing to pension funds, the largest portion of which
goes into stocks and a sizable percentage into corporate bonds. These billions provide massive investment resources for corporate expansion.

The theme of manager-as-civil-servant enters at this point for the end-
of-ideology thinkers. Using Berle's analysis, we read:

> Past rights are collectivized; present capacity is concentrated; future de-
> velopment of economic government will be by relatively few men. These
> men are detached from the conventional workings of the profit system;
> they become, in fact, an unrecognized group of professional administrators
> distributing the fruits of the American industrial system, directing its
> present activities, and selecting the path of its future growth.[75]

The problem with Berle's analysis is that trust-department officials and
hired bank managers he refers to are not the arbiters of power but the
servants of the powerful, well-attuned to the profit system and how to
distribute the fruits of labor so that they yield the highest possible return

---

73 Ibid., p. 435.
74 "Who Rules the Corporations?" part 1, p. 99.
75 *Power Without Property*, p. 18.

for themselves and the ruling class. And all in positions of power are aware of the manner in which pension funds tie the working class into its own exploitation, and more importantly, in Perlo's words, "the ability of the banks to use the funds as a club against labor in time of acute class conflict." [76] This is perhaps the most critical point to be made regarding the size and growth of the pension fund. Nowhere is the capitalist process more clearly at work than in the appropriation of surplus value from the working class in the form of pensions and the narrow class use of these surpluses for further aggrandizement nationally and internationally. These billions in pension funds could be applied to constructive *social* purposes such as middle- and low-income housing, as they are in the government-controlled pension systems of Scandinavia.

A final word must be said regarding a second major financial force in corporate capital, one, as previously noted, in league with the banks: the life insurance companies. The fifty largest operations in this field totaled 83 percent of the industry's $207 billion 1970 assets.[77] But the top ten held almost 60 percent of the total! Yet about eighteen hundred companies are in the field. With a substantial portion of personal net savings flowing into the coffers of the life insurance companies, insurors counted $49 billion in income in 1970; unfortunately for the purchasers, $13 billion of their precious money goes into commissions, expenses, and taxes, and another one-half billion in dividends to stockholders. As in the case of pension funds controlled by banks, life insurance funds represent, in effect, the creaming of surplus value off a large part of the working class for immediate gain of capitalist interests. And as with pension funds, this wealth could be channeled into vitally needed areas of work and production rather than being used for the selective purposes of the financial oligarchy, purposes ranging from posher home office buildings to heavy investments abroad.

In sum, the economic basis of ruling-class power is clear. The concentration of private economic interests is the rule throughout the capitalist world,[78] though the actions of smaller capitalist states are ultimately circumscribed by the actions of the larger ones, the United States in particular. But ruling-class economic power is no longer private in practice, and the economic role of the state looms ever larger in importance. To pluralist or liberal thinking, the increasing prominence of the state may indicate the counterbalancing of private economic power by the public interest. To Marxists, it represents state capitalism under the domination and extensive control of the bourgeoisie, making the latter a ruling class. State capitalism is closely examined in Chapter 10.

---

[76] *The Empire of High Finance*, p. 69.

[77] *Statistical Abstract of the United States, 1972*, p. 449.

[78] For example, on Australia see S. Encel, *Equality and Authority* (Melbourne: Cheshire Publishing, Ltd., 1970).

———————————————

nine

ELITES AND
THE RULING CLASS

POWER ELITE AND RULING CLASS: C. WRIGHT MILLS REVISITED

Although Mills himself footnoted his preference for the term *power elite* as opposed to *ruling class,* and while Marxist critics of Mills have been quick to interpret this minor reference at face value and thus to regard the Millsian thesis as opposing the Marxist view of power, a careful reading of *The Power Elite* offers no such conclusions—as we shall document below. The *power elite* is, in effect, Mills's phrase for Marx's ruling class, and he stands prominently among a few social scientists who have clarified the mechanics of power in the stage of monopoly capital and imperialism. His most important contribution was to bring up to date the principles of Marx, Lenin, and Veblen on the militarization of capitalism in its advanced stages. Oddly enough, it is precisely this important service which has been the focal point of Marxist criticism of Mills, which is that Mills misplaced the locus of power in capitalist society in the military. As we shall see, Mills used the term *military* in a much broader sense than his critics have understood.

First of all, although Mills elevated occupation above property as the key to an understanding of the larger class structure, he left no doubt over what he considered to be the ultimate seat of the higher levels of power: "Power has not been split from property; rather the power of property is more concentrated than is its ownership." [1] Furthermore, and logically enough given this position on the property base of power, Mills

---

[1] *White Collar* (New York: Oxford University Press, 1951), p. 101.

was not taken in by the popular contention that top management had assumed the position of a new and powerful independent class or neutral administrators; this, among other things, aroused the animosity of the liberal
academic establishment against Mills. Mills refused to buy the liberal
rhetoric about the end of ideology. Mills recognized that the corporate elite
are very much a part of the propertied class, either direct participants or
reliable and loyal servants aspiring for full entrance:

> The top man in the bureaucracy *is* a powerful member of the propertied
> class. He derives his right to act from the institution of property; he does
> act in so far as he possibly can in a manner he believes is to the interests
> of the private-property system; he does feel in unity, politically and
> status-wise as well as economically, with his class and its source of
> wealth.[2]

Thus Mills was fully cognizant of the fact that many chief executives
and top corporate officials are themselves richly entrenched in corporate
property, as we outlined statistically in the preceding chapter. At the same
time, he was equally aware that the corporate elite and the propertied class
are not identical, and that where there is no overlap, the former is subservient to the latter: "The executives of the modern corporation in America form an utterly reliable committee for managing the affairs and push-
ing for the common interests of the entire big-property class." [3]

The very rich, then, are the corporate rich, made wealthy through
ownership and control of the property system. Mills goes on to state the
family nature of corporate ownership, a corollary of the ruling-class thesis
as opposed to the concept of all-powerful individual managers: "Every one
of the very rich families has been and is closely connected—always legally
and frequently managerially as well—with one of the multi-million dollar
corporations." [4] More importantly, Mills was emphatic regarding the *class*
orientation of family property interests, and referred to the entrance and
participation of the professional manager into the corporate world as part
of the "reorganization of the propertied class." In a key passage, Mills
writes regarding this reorganization: "By means of it the narrow industrial
and profit interest of specific firms and industries and families have been
translated into the broader economic and political interests of a more
genuinely class type." [5]

Not only do the propertied class recognize their common economic
and political interests, but it has taken the shape of a *social* class as well
—an overlapping network of propertied families who have created sup-

[2] Ibid., p. 102.
[3] Ibid., p. 105.
[4] *The Power Elite* (New York: Oxford University Press, 1956), p. 10.
[5] Ibid., p. 147.

porting social institutions and developed a relatively sharp awareness of class organization: "They form a more or less compact social and psychological entity; they have become self-conscious members of a social class." [6] From a sociological perspective, Mills recognized the existence of a "top social stratum" or "upper class," having its chief social roots in the family, private schools, and, most importantly, the metropolitan men's clubs. And just as their economic base in the corporations is national, so is the upper class more than the sum total of local upper classes; it is a national upper class with a national orientation. The new rich typically find themselves on the outside of established upper-class social institutions and prestige, but in the end—though it may require more than a generation —naked money can usually batter down any obstacles.

The crux of the Marxist criticism of Mills is that his is an elite rather than class interpretation of power, and that this elite consists of corporate, state, and military parts rather than a single ruling class. We have just refuted the notion that Mills was not a class theorist of power. We now turn our attention to the complaint that Mills was an elite "pluralist." Knowing what has been said regarding the complete dominance over corporate wealth by the small capitalist propertied class, and recognizing Mills's stress on the force of sheer economic power in the capitalist system, it would be most illogical for us to expect him to jump to introduce governmental and military elites as co-equals in the power structure. Other unmistakable clues to Mills's rejection of pluralism at the top are his stress on the interchangeability of elite personnel and the coincidence of interests of the dominant institutions. At issue are the three leading institutional areas—corporation, state, and military. First, let us examine Mills's conception of corporate-state linkages.

Mills is unequivocal regarding the domination of the state by corporate interests, though he does state that "the American government is not, in any simple way nor as a structural fact, a committee of 'the ruling class.' " [7] The state is obviously much more, as it must be for corporate capitalism to survive. In *White Collar,* Mills follows the Marxist position of the state being more of a recipient of outside power interests than an independent force in itself: "In short: U.S. politics has rarely been an autonomous force. It has been anchored in the economic sphere, its men using political means to gain and secure limited economic ends. So interest in it has seldom been an interest in political ends, has seldom involved more than immediate material profits and losses." [8] Mills also emphasizes

---

[6] Ibid., p. 11.
[7] Ibid., p. 170.
[8] *White Collar,* p. 342.

the decline of professional politicians at the top and the role of outsiders—
men who bypass local and state government, never serve on national
legislative bodies, are appointed rather than elected, and spend a smaller
proportion of their total working life in politics than do the "pros." Who
are these outsiders? They are "members and agents of the corporate rich
and of the high military." [9] Mills long ago presaged the drastic shift in
the system of checks and balances toward the dictatorship of the executive
branch and the rise to unchallenged and irresponsible power of an inner
circle of self-selected or appointed officials working around and within
the executive branch. The state to Mills is neither a power broker of conflicting interests nor an independent power unto itself, but rather the representative of specific national interests and policies.

Now comes the closing of the circle. Whose interests do those having
real power in the American state today represent? Mills neither splits hairs
nor hedges on this point:

> Not the politicians of the visible government, but the chief executives
> who sit in the political directorate, by fact and by proxy, hold the power
> and the means of defending the privileges of their corporate world. If
> they do not reign, they do govern at many of the vital points of everyday
> life in America, and no powers effectively and consistently countervail
> against them, nor have they as corporate-made men developed any effec-
> tively restraining conscience. [10]

Paul Sweezy writes of Mills that "when it comes to 'The Political Directorate,' he demonstrates that the notion of a specifically political elite is in
reality a myth, that the crucial positions in government and politics are
increasingly held by what he calls 'political outsiders," and that these outsiders are in fact members or errand boys of the corporate rich." [11] How
unhappily satisfied would Mills be today to witness his ideas receive such
open confirmation from the Johnson and especially Nixon administrations!
Among the many recent illustrations of interchangeability between the corporate elite and government is the career of Clark MacGregor, who went
from being a top Nixon aide to vice-president at United Aircraft, the eighth
largest government contractor. In a period of increasing executive power,
the White House aide has become a central figure in government, overriding traditional functionaries of democratic government. [12]

What, then, of the charge that Mills had a warped view of military

---

[9] *The Power Elite*, pp. 231–32.

[10] Ibid., p. 125.

[11] "Power Elite or Ruling Class?" in G. William Domhoff and Hoyt B. Ballard,
eds., *C. Wright Mills and the Power Elite* (Boston: Beacon Press, 1968), p. 124.

[12] George E. Reedy, "White House Aides: Faceless Agents of Power," *The
Nation*, January 1, 1973, pp. 6–9.

power? [13] Critics of Mills have "overmilitarized" Mills's propositions regarding the military. By raising the question, "How did civilians rather than men of violence become dominant?" Mills tells us that the military ascendancy is far from an entirely uniformed one, though with General Eisenhower as president and Admiral Radford as his top advisor when Mills wrote, he surely did not exclude military brass from positions of power and influence. Mills states clearly that the military ascendancy "involves a coincidence of interests and a co-ordination of aims among economic and political as well as military actors." [14] Primarily, the military ascendancy refers to the militarization of the civilian definition of reality—in brief, to the military-industrial complex, or in Mills's language, the permanent war economy. The military includes the Department of Defense, the appointed presidential advisors and committees who draft war policy, the private defense contractors, the "think tank" strategists, the military research network, and the entire cosmology of military thinking that has dominated American life since World War II. "The warlords, along with their fellow travelers and spokesmen," writes Mills, "are attempting to plant their metaphysics firmly among the population at large." [15] To Mills, "the military structure of America is now in considerable part a political structure," and we have already pointed to Mills's economic interpretation of political power. Mills sums it up as follows: "Yes, there is a military clique, but it is more accurately termed the power elite, for it is composed of economic, political, as well as military men whose interests have increasingly coincided." [16]

There can be no other conclusion than that Mills held to the militarization of political thinking, itself dominated by the propertied class in whose worldwide interests militarization acts. Mills leaves no doubt in this regard in *The Causes of World War Three:* "A real attack on war-thinking by Americans today is necessarily an attack upon the private incorporation of the economy" [17] (and not merely an attack on uniformed generals and admirals). Mills argued that political and social democracy cannot be brought about in the United States "so long as the private corporation remains as dominant and as irresponsible as it is in national and international decisions"; and in order to achieve such democracy, "above all, the privately incorporated economy must be made over into a publicly

---

[13] See Herbert Aptheker, *The World of C. Wright Mills* (New York: Marzani & Munsell Publishers, 1960); Kolko, *The Roots of American Foreign Policy;* and Domhoff, *Who Rules America?* (Englewood Cliffs, N.J.: Prentice-Hall, Inc., 1967).

[14] *The Power Elite,* p. 224.

[15] Ibid., p. 219.

[16] Ibid., p. 224.

[17] (New York: Ballantine Books, 1960), pp. 137–39.

responsible economy." [18] Mills, as did Veblen, had a way of stating Marxist conclusions in his own terms, exactly what one would expect from an original thinker of Mills's stature.

Mills comes under fire from others for a number of other aspects of his power theory; one charge is that his is a conspiracy theory, another that he posits an omnipotent elite versus an undifferentiated mass. An objective perusal of Mills's works dispels any such notions. Another misreading of Mills's power theory involves the belief that he overly maligned the morality of powerful men, failing to understand their fundamental integrity and upstanding posture in society. The ruling class is, of course, typically consistent and responsible when it comes to their own ruling ideas, as Marxist theory would suggest and as Mills writes: "The question is not: Are these honorable men? The question is: What are their codes of honor? The answer is: They are the codes of their own circles; how could it be otherwise?" [19] And to adhere to these codes honorably is to perpetuate inequality, poverty, and decay, social and material waste, militarism and war, intense racial hatreds, hunger and disease, and other socially and morally crippling circumstances.

A related theme here is the view that the powerful are exonerated from social problems and injustices, for they themselves are mere observers of the inexorable movement of institutions and, as it were, fate. For example, Livington writes: "Unfortunately the men at the top cannot in any meaningful way be held responsible for the actions the institutions take." [20] Livington may be a brilliant metaphysician, but he is a very poor sociologist. The bombing of Vietnam has, naturally, been carried out by institutions; no one is responsible—not Lyndon B. Johnson or Richard M. Nixon. These unfortunate men have been the unwilling victims of a cruel and mindless set of institutions which willy-nilly trapped them into making massive saturation bombing and burning from on high. Against this, Mills's words offer hope:

> If, on the other hand, we believe that war and peace and slump and prosperity are, precisely now, no longer matters of "fortune" or "fate," but that, precisely no more than ever, they are controllable, then we must ask—controllable by whom? The answer must be: By whom else but those who now command the enormously enlarged and decisively centralized means of decision and power.[21]

---

[18] Ibid., p. 139.
[19] *The Causes of World War Three*, p. 51.
[20] Joseph Livington, *The American Stockholder* (Philadelphia: J. P. Lippincott, 1958).
[21] *The Power Elite*, p. 26.

In the Marxist tradition, Mills recognized that men make history, and modern men make history in a known and determined manner to an unprecedented extent. This is at once the scourge and the hope of mankind.

A final note should be made with regard to the assertion that Mills's power theory offers a static picture of capitalist society and precludes conflict and change.[22] This assertion is a corollary following from the one that Mills portrayed an elite-mass model of society. The point to be informed of here is that Mills's power theory in no way rules out class conflict and change. Mills set forth something of a vanguard theory of change, in which intellectuals, students, and social service professionals formed a potential cutting-edge of historical change toward a publicly responsible economy. Would it not have been poor social science for Mills to write in the fifties of great class conflict, political turmoil, and social change? Simply wishing something, even if a noted social scientist does the wishing, does not make it so. Even today after a decade of turmoil, there is the danger of over-interpreting the extent of class conflict and potential for change. Indeed, the upswing in political mobilization of the 1960s seems to have lost much of its momentum by 1973. But in writing critically and positively, we are following Mills's own advice: that to the extent thought changes the world, it should be oriented toward changing it for the better. Although Mills simply had no grounds for optimism in the fifties, surely his model of power and society closes no doors on optimism.[23]

CORPORATE-STATE LINKAGES

In this section, we examine more fully the Marxist proposition—also a Millsian one, as noted above—that the state is primarily an embodiment and a representative of ruling-class interests. Parkin states the idea well: "Sociologically, the state could be defined as an institutional complex which is the political embodiment of the values and interests of the dominant class." [24] In the United States, we need only look to the Constitution for verification of this point. As Milton Mankoff points out: "The final draft of the Constitution was a masterpiece in terms of the political and economic needs of a highly class-conscious propertied elite." [25]

---

[22] See Isaac Balbus, "Ruling Elite Theory vs. Marxist Class Analysis," *Monthly Review* 23 (May 1971): 36–46.

[23] See the basic themes of *The Sociological Imagination* (New York: Oxford University Press, 1959).

[24] Frank Parkin, *Class Inequality and Political Order* (New York: Praeger Publishers, 1971), p. 27.

[25] Milton Mankoff, ed., *The Poverty of Progress* (New York: Holt, Rinehart, and Winston, 1972), pp. 77–79.

In the ratification process, aside from the total exclusion of women, 40 percent of men were disenfranchised and a bare one-sixth of adult males or 5 percent of the population participated. And of the 160,000 votes cast, 60,000 were registered against ratification. Even then, many of the votes for ratification came only upon the amendment to the Constitution of the Bill of Rights, a move made after concern of some elite and citizenry that the Constitution would not be ratified.[26]

Domhoff has listed four major needs that business has of government: [27] (1) the need for the State Department as the key coordinating agency for overseas operations; (2) the need for the Defense Department to defend the American Way all over the world; (3) the need for self-regulation through commissions and agencies in the hands of qualified experts who understand business viewpoints; and (4) the need to collect money from the populace for defense spending, research and development, and for economy management. These boil down to the twin needs for coordination and economic support. The latter need is easily the most important, and coordination actually is in the service of this need. To quote Mandel: "The bourgeois state becomes the essential guarantor of monopoly profits." [28] More than ever before the state serves as an instrument of shoring up the system of private appropriation of surplus value. State participation has been especially extensive through military spending and re-

---

[26] Now, two hundred years later, the propertied rich see the opportunity to ideologically revive the memory of constitutional independence on behalf of their own further aggrandizement. The American Revolution Bicentennial—with a fifty-member commission board, drawn preponderantly from the Republican business establishment, showing the way—is according to Jeremy Rifkin and Erwin Knoll "a once-in-a-lifetime opportunity to promote the virtues of the domestic status quo in an atmosphere supercharged with emotional 'patriotism.' " ARBC Chairman David J. Mahoney is a personal friend of Richard Nixon, was the key fund raiser for Nixon's 1960 and 1968 presidential campaigns, and is chief executive officer of the billion-dollar conglomerate Norton Simon, Incorporated—a firm with interests in manufacturing, mass media, utilities, insurance, and elsewhere. The top public relations man in the ARBC reported to Nixon communications aide Herbert Klein that "the American Revolution Bicentennial observance should be developed into the greatest single peacetime public opinion mobilization effort in our nation's history." ARBC Director Jack LeVant wrote that the Bicentennial "could be the greatest opportunity Nixon, the Party, and the Government has as a beacon of light for reunification and light within the nation and with the world." Mahoney's wisdom is that "we shall remain the land of the free as long as we remain the home of the brave." "Reminding Americans to be 'brave,' " note Rifkin and Knoll, "—that is, to shoulder the burdens of an endless arms race and an expanding empire, and continue allegiance to the sanctity of the profit system —are the major Bicentennial themes." Americans will be fully familiar with the Bicentennial themes by the time Nixon formally leaves office in 1977, although the Watergate scandal may have some dampening effect upon the operations of the ARBC. See Rifkin and Knoll, "The Greatest Show on Earth," *The Progressive,* September 1972, pp. 14–24.

[27] *The Higher Circles* (New York: Random House, 1971), pp. 292–93.

[28] Ernest Mandel, *Marxist Economic Theory,* vol. 2 (New York: Monthly Review Press, 1968), p. 502.

search and development of weapons systems, though many other kinds of government spending also extend profits and support, as does the structure of the tax system.[29]

The government role of coordination is served abroad by the State Department with the assistance of the Defense Department, though this administrative role is better served by the virtually self-sustaining far-flung private governments of the largest multinational corporations whose overseas staffs dwarf that of the State Department's overseas staff. Domestically, the job of coordination is performed by the regulatory agencies—though here again, government's role, while necessary, is eclipsed by the self-administering intercorporate power structure that ties the core industrial and financial powers together. The chief point to be made regarding the regulatory agencies, beyond the fact that they are largely the creations of the business class itself,[30] is that they do not regulate in the public's interest but very largely in the interests of the private groups and industries under their jurisdiction.[31] As Mintz and Cohen point out with regard to regulatory agencies whose job it is to control charge-rates for utilities and transport industries, government agencies are largely rubber stamps for rate increases set in open collusion by industries or of unreal and wasteful rate bases which yield superprofits after figuring the government-allotted profit percentage.[32] Ex-utility employees sit on state regulatory commissions for utility control and ex-businessmen sit on state regulatory commissions for business control, etc. Little wonder, then, that Kolko can write that "there has been no sustained clash between any federal government agency in existence or created during this century and the industry it nominally regulates." [33] Although it would be difficult to pick out the most perfunctory and collaborative government-industry regulatory tie, the complicity of the FCC (the outspoken Nicholas Johnson aside) with regard to ATT would be a strong candidate.

What are the chief avenues through which the ruling class dominates state policy and activity? The chief avenue is through the executive branch, including the election of the president and, subsequently, a whole array of important appointments, not the least of which involves the high federal judiciary.[34] As the prime example of the latter, Nixon, whose office was

---

[29] See the discussion by J. K. Galbraith, *The New Industrial State* (New York: Signet Books, 1967), pp. 304–31.

[30] Gabriel Kolko, *The Triumph of American Conservatism* (New York: Free Press, 1963).

[31] Jack Newfield and Jeff Greenfield, *A Populist Manifesto* (New York: Praeger Publishers, 1972), Chapter 7.

[32] Martin Mintz and Jerry S. Cohen, *America, Inc.* (New York: Dial Press, 1971), pp. 70–74.

[33] "Power and Capitalism in Twentieth-Century America," p. 219.

[34] See Domhoff, *Who Rules America?* pp. 109–11.

bought very openly by the propertied class, in one term has altered the posture of the Supreme Court with four appointments of conservative judges. The court is on the way to losing even a reasonable resemblance to a body representing a just and democratic interpretation of the Constitution; it has been hand-tailored to meet interests of the propertied class. Cabinet appointments and other high-level administrative and advisory posts, both foreign and domestic, have been overwhelmingly dominated by business and legal interests and personnel of the corporate world—personnel hired by the ruling class and loaned to the government and a large number of ruling-class men who have loaned themselves to the government. The data on this point are hard and unequivocal.[35] Nor does the proposition or the evidence fail to hold for the Democratic presidents of the twentieth century. The Johnson and Nixon administrations have been equally loaded with corporation-groomed and corporation-minded appointees. The main pivot of control, however, is the president himself with his wide-sweeping military, economic, and political powers. A small inner clique of hand-picked aides, accountable only to the president, have reinforced executive fiat. Few modern presidents have proven so accommodating to large business as has Richard Nixon, and few have had the almost total and dedicated commitment of the business elite for their reelection. Republican coffers literally brim over from corporate riches, surplus value stripped from the very working classes who suffer most from Nixon-type policies. Money contributions, then, are among the main levers for getting accommodating politicians into office, including the president, and the ruling class *has* the money, be it for Democratic or Republican purposes.[36] (In 1968, three hundred corporate directors of the top fifty military contractors donated $1.2 million to election campaigns.)

Once in office, or even with mild opponents in office, corporate interests find that money bribes are commonplace solutions to corporate problems. In an election year, money is particularly forceful and useful, as ITT discovered when confronted with antitrust activity or as the dairy monopolies learned when they sought further to inflate their prices.[37] After donating hundreds of thousands of dollars to Mr. Nixon and the Republican party, like magic, ITT and the dairy interests found that the Justice Department and the Wage and Price Commission had altered course. And so democratically oriented taxpayers and consumers are forced to finance the defeat of their own principles and interests. Money bribes at lower

---

[35] Ibid., pp. 97–107; and Kolko, *The Roots of American Foreign Policy,* pp. 3–26.

[36] Domhoff, *Who Rules America?* pp. 87–90. Twelve of the country's richest families gave $2.76 million to the 1968 campaigns, all but $150,000 to Republicans. Newfield and Greenfield, *A Populist Manifesto,* p. 190.

[37] Newfield and Greenfield, *A Populist Manifesto,* pp. 186–87.

levels of government are of classic proportions. (A recently deceased Illinois secretary of state had a lifetime public income of $300,000, but left $3 million, including $750,000 in cash hidden in his closet.)

There are also internal economic influences at work upon the complicity of government officials. For example, many have direct financial investments, assuring their support of legislation favoring the profits of big business; Russell Long of Louisiana as chairman of the Senate Finance Committee has been a staunch defender of the oil-depletion allowance, receiving $1.2 million from oil and gas production—including the $300,000 tax-free depletion allowance—from 1964 to 1969.[38] The case of high-ranking Senate Agricultural Committee member William O. Eastland of Mississippi voting against a $20,000 limitation to the farm subsidy while himself receiving vast sums ($117,000 in 1968) is also illustrative.[39] A very substantial minority of senators, perhaps one-third, are millionaires, an incentive enough to be pro–private capital in the area of subsidy and taxation. The House is stuffed with small businessmen and lawyers, giving it, in Domhoff's evaluation, a National Association of Manufacturers and Chamber of Commerce perspective. Its currently backward stance, outdone only by President Nixon himself, on economic and social programs of all kinds lends support to this view.

A further avenue of ruling-class influence within government, and a most important one, is through the domination of advisory councils and policy-formulating committees. In foreign affairs, the Council on Foreign Relations and the National Security Council have been largely directed by the interests of the propertied rich, as have two domestic advisory groups, the Council on Economic Development and the Business Advisory Council.[40] These variously influential foreign- and domestic-policy-making bodies trace much of their specific supporting information to the foundation-supported research institutes in the nation's most prestigious universities, including Harvard (presidential adviser Henry Kissinger got his start as the head of a CFR study group there), Columbia, and Stanford.

Expensive lobbying is a further method of gaining influence, and business is far and away in the best financial position to succeed along this avenue. But perhaps we can overstate the importance of the process whereby the vested interests set their men and policies to work in the state. The ineradicable fact is that the ruling class controls the means of production in the direct sense, rendering public officials *dependent upon it for their*

[38] Michael Tanzer, *The Sick Society* (New York: Holt, Rinehart & Winston, 1971), p. 46.

[39] Robert Sherrill, "Reaping the Subsidies," *The Nation,* November 24, 1969, pp. 561–66.

[40] See Domhoff, *The Higher Circles,* pp. 111–55.

survival.[41] For if the corporate economy falters in any significant fashion, the political administration standing behind it will fall as well. Government officials, elected and appointed, *know* and *understand* that it would not be realistic for them to seriously challenge and counter the interests of the ruling class. As David Horowitz has observed, "short of committing political suicide, no party or government can step outside the framework of the corporate system and its politics, and embark on a course which consistently threatens the power and privileges of the giant corporations." [42]

There are, of course, diverse opposing views to that which delineates the recruitment and shaping of state officials and policy by the propertied class. Bensman and Vidich contend that "the direct relationship between class and political power as postulated by Marx has been denied by almost all uncommitted thinkers." [43] (*Uncommitted* is a very appropriate term in this context.) Irving Zeitlin would hold open any conclusion regarding the relations between the wealthy classes and the state.[44] Others such as Robert Heilbroner would go to the other side and say that "the distribution of power between business and the state will alter substantially over the future in favor of the state and to the detriment of business." [45] Irving Louis Horowitz argues that political economy is dying and political sociology rising.[46] John Kenneth Galbraith, at least by preference if not interpretation of fact, sees private industry becoming increasingly entangled with government, not as a ruling class imposing its selfish interests, but as an equal partner oriented toward the satisfaction of social needs.[47]

We can agree with none of these positions. Andrew Hacker's summary statement, if taken in the broadest sense, is much closer to the truth: "The government's function is regarded as essentially custodial, tidying up much of the debris created by private pursuits." [48] It should be added, of course, that in the process of cleaning up, the government tends to contribute heartily to the debris and much less to its socially constructive recycling.

---

[41] See Ralph Miliband, *The State in Capitalist Society* (New York: Basic Books, 1969), Chapter 6.

[42] "Corporations and the Cold War," in David J. Colfax and Jack L. Roach, eds., *Radical Sociology* (New York: Basic Books, 1971), p. 281.

[43] Joseph Bensman and Arthur J. Vidich, *The New American Society* (Chicago: Quadrangle Books, 1971), pp. 90–91.

[44] *Marxism: A Re-Examination* (Princeton: Van Nostrand, 1967), p. 106.

[45] *Between Capitalism and Socialism* (New York: Random House, 1970), p. 28.

[46] *The Foundations of Political Sociology* (New York: Harper & Row, 1972).

[47] *The New Industrial State,* pp. 401–6.

[48] *The End of the American Era* (New York: Atheneum, 1970), p. 139. Hacker continues: "While no society can be totally anarchic, the United States has as powerless a government as any developed nation of the modern world" (p. 142).

ELITES AND THE RULING CLASS: RECENT PERSPECTIVES

American social science has been slowly finding its way toward a theoretical and empirical understanding of the ruling class. C. Wright Mills paved the way, and we have studied his contributions in some detail. Floyd Hunter has also made a valuable contribution to the clarification of the links between elite individuals and the power of a social class—that is, to an identification of a ruling class.[49] Two years after Mills wrote *The Power Elite* E. Digby Baltzell published an important study under the innocuous title *Philadelphia Gentlemen,* later to be reissued more appropriately as *An American Business Aristocracy.* Although Mills and Baltzell take almost diametrically opposing views regarding the legitimacy of the capitalist system of class power, their research is entirely complementary. Baltzell's contribution was made through his very careful and detailed examination of the *social institutional* structure of the business elite of one major city, Philadelphia. While the social dimensions of the power elite were incorporated into Mills's analysis, these nonpower aspects of the top stratum occupied a position of relatively minor importance. Baltzell devotes his entire study to an analysis of the history and structure of the upper class as a *social* class, moving from an identification of its economic interests to a full-scale study of its sociological origins and status.

Baltzell's class terminology is clearly defined and fits into the Marxist framework, albeit with fundamentally different intent. Baltzell employs three terms which are of direct relevance here: *elite, upper class,* and *ruling class.* (In a subsquent book, *The Protestant Establishment,* he develops the concept of "establishment" instead of ruling class, but they are largely interchangeable terms.) To quote Baltzell: "The *elite* concept refers to those *individuals* who are the most successful and stand at the top of the *functional* class hierarchy." [50] The most important functional hierarchy is business, though nonbusiness institutions, especially government, may also be included. In Mills's language, we have the corporate elite and political directorate. To continue from Baltzell on the upper class:

> The *upper class* concept, then, refers to a group of *families,* whose members are descendants of successful individuals (elite members) of one, two, three or more generations ago. These families are at the top of the *social class* hierarchy; they are brought up together, are friends, and are

---

[49] *Top Leadership, U.S.A.* (Chapel Hill: University of North Carolina Press, 1959); see also Hunter's *The Big Rich and the Little Rich* (Garden City, N.Y.: Doubleday & Company, 1965).
[50] *An American Business Aristocracy* (New York: Collier Books, 1962), p. 20.

intermarried one with another; and, finally, they maintain a distinctive style of life and a kind of primary group solidarity which sets them apart from the rest of the population.[51]

Mills, too, had precisely the same reference point for "upper class."

Crucial to the understanding of Baltzell's use of the term *ruling class* is the prior understanding of the functions of an upper class. The chief function of an upper class is to exercise *power,* not to pursue social exclusiveness and leisure: "The main function of an upper class [is] the perpetuation of its power in the world of affairs, whether in the bank, the factory, or in the halls of the legislature. Whenever an upper-class way of life becomes an end in itself, rather than a means for consolidating its power and influence, that upper class has outlived its function." [52] In effect, Baltzell is warning the upper class to beware of fulfilling Veblen's notion of a superfluous, functionless, and parasitical leisure class and to maintain a firm grip on the levers of financial, industrial, and political power. So despite his preoccupation with sociological phenomena, Baltzell is fully aware and definitive regarding the indispensability of power for upper-class social status. And quite logically enough, for without the appropriation of surplus value, for which power is required, the upper class could not afford to maintain its "distinctive style of life."

This leads us to Baltzell's concept of ruling class: "A ruling class is one which contributes upper class members to the most important, goal-integrating elite positions." [53] Thus, a ruling class is a financially and politically powerful upper social class; a dominant elite and a social upper class overlap to a great degree if not completely. Baltzell would add that, in addition to their maintaining positions of executive power, the upper class must also be *ethnically representative* of the elite in order to preserve its legitimacy and authority. Thus, his second caution to the upper class is that it must not put up ethnic barriers to all but white Protestant members of the elite. This second prerequisite is actually largely irrelevant. Top members of the functional elites are carefully chosen on social and cultural criteria, making it difficult for various ethnic groups to even get in positions to "qualify" for upper-class status. But even if the upper class were composed of all nationalities, creeds, and colors, it would make very little difference for the respective ethnic groups within the underlying population. The selection and grooming process that accompanies mobility into top

---

51 Ibid., p. 21; Baltzell writes that "the upper class in Philadelphia is the only one which may be spoken of, *qua* class, in terms of a subculture bound together by a common tradition and a consciousness of kind which approximates a primary group; this upper class is a 'we' group in a sense not applicable to any other class in the city" (p. 79).

52 Ibid., p. 405.

53 Ibid., p. 51.

elites assures ideological uniformity and precludes ideological representation of the political and economic interests of ethnic groups. For example, Scandinavian Lutheran in background, I can take no comfort nor lend any greater legitimacy to the ruling class for the fact that William Rehnquist sits on the Supreme Court.

To sum up Baltzell, the United States has had and still has an upper class that is also a ruling class (an establishment), though it has of late displayed a dangerous reluctance to enter into active public and political executive positions and an even greater reluctance to open itself up to non-WASP elites. As a result, we face the problem of declining legitimacy and authority of the upper class and the rise of equally illegitimate elites— illegitimate, according to Baltzell, owing to their uncertified upper-class socialization and status. These elites must resort to more open forms of coercion and to deception to get their way. Baltzell has read the declining legitimacy and authority and the rising resort to coercion and deception by elites correctly. However these developments have little to do with a lack of upper-class activity in and control over financial, industrial, and governmental institutions, or with its unrepresentative ethnic compositon. The fact of the matter is that declining legitimacy and resort to force and lies as a means of rule is due precisely to the perpetuation and predominance of upper-class rule over the means of production, which increasingly includes the partnership of the state. Of course, Baltzell doesn't see things this way, for his utopia is that of the classic conservative—an open aristocracy of wealth and power.

Back in the radical ideological vein, G. William Domhoff forms a direct line of analytical descent from Mills and Baltzell. Employing a systematic social science research methodology, an extremely difficult task with respect to national-elite analysis, Domhoff solidly closes the connection between the power elite and the upper class. In two books, *Who Rules America?* and *The Higher Circles,* Domhoff (a psychologist by academic training) empirically grounds the upper social class within the dominant economic and political institutions of the nation, either directly or through carefully chosen hired employees.[54] Domhoff means essentially the same thing as Mills and Baltzell by the term *upper class.* By *power elite* he means the

> active, working members of the upper class and high-level employees in institutions controlled by members of the upper class. The power elite has its roots in and serves the interests of the social upper class. It is the operating arm of the upper class. It functions to maintain and manage a socio-economic system which is organized in such a way that it yields an

---

[54] These books stem theoretically from *The Power Elite* and *An American Business Aristocracy.*

amazing proportion of its wealth to a miniscule upper class of big business and their managers."[55]

The power elite, then, contains both upper-class people and non-
upper-class people (the latter perhaps future upper-class, given an amass-
ment of wealth as a member of the elite). Looking back at our data on stock
ownership and corporate control, we may conclude that, despite the fact
that the non–upper-class elite occupy important instrumental positions, the
upper class embodies the key power figures of the corporate world—owing
mainly to their ownership of and connections to great masses of property.
In the state too, upper-class members of the elite typically exercise greater
influence and control than mere elite individuals. The studies of Mills, Baltzell, and Domhoff all point in the same direction: to the existence of a
ruling class (Domhoff's conceptual system substitutes the term *governing
class*).[56] They document the earlier theories of Marx, Lenin, and Veblen
regarding the relationships between property, class, and power. The documentation can be and is a laborious process, a process which nevertheless
must be carried out. Yet we are tempted to conclude with Domhoff that
"an upper class exists in American consciousness. *We* know *they* exist"
and *"they* know *they* are members of a privileged social class. *They* also
know *they* have a good thing going, which no doubt sets certain limitations
on the activities and verbalizations of most of *them."* [57] And among the best
things they have going is a property system that enables the transmission
of fortunes from one generation to the next, fortunes that are constantly
expanding virtually on their own from the standpoint of the heirs and recipients, but in actuality are expanding on the backs of the working class.
What of the power of the technicians and intellectuals? Some would
argue that technocracy has arrived. Professors, specialists, journalists, and
politicians, according to Berle, "are thus the real tribunal to which the
American system is finally accountable." [58] Galbraith's "technostructure"
clearly approximates a technocratic interpretation of power. The entire
end-of-ideology argument is, in essence, a pronouncement of the death of
class politics and the ascendancy of technological solutions to purely technical problems. That such a view is a coverup for the perpetuation of
upper-class power and privilege is practically self-evident. Even when an
engineer or scientist makes his way into the higher circles of wealth and

---

[55] *The Higher Circles,* p. 107.
[56] For similar but more limited research studies, see Hoffman, "The Power
Elite of Chicago," and Lynda Ann Ewen, "Economic Dominants and Civic Participation in Detroit," paper presented to the American Sociological Association, Denver,
1971.
[57] *The Higher Circles,* p. 98.
[58] *Power Without Property,* p. 113.

power, he almost always succeeds courtesy of the taxpayer and defense contracts, and his ultimate success is almost always as a businessman, not as a participating member of the scientific community. As Tanzer points out, aspiring technicians and scientists *leave* their practicing fields in order to excel at business rather than remaining technical specialists.[59] But even in their newly acquired technocratic or business capacity, rarely do they go beyond hired subservience. To quote Jean Meynaud: "While they are relatively independent, even those technicians who have turned technocrat are induced by the structure of the system to play the role of administrators —often excellent ones—of the capitalist system." [60]

And what of the "intellectual" or "man of knowledge" summoned by the top executives and powerful bureaucracies, in Mills's words, to "compose suitable myths, about them and it"? [61] There is no question today, after witnessing over a decade of bumbling and tragedy in Indochina and the entire area of foreign policy, and knowing quite precisely the social engineers who helped conceive and conduct these policies, that ex-intellectuals–turned–bureaucrats not only compose complimentary myths about the position and situation of the ruling class and its interests but also take a very active role in formulating and executing policy.[62] As Mills pointed out over fifteen years ago, "persons of power do surround themselves with men of some knowledge, or at least with men who are experienced in shrewd dealings." [63] Yet, to take the political sphere as an example, it is not Harvard professor Henry Kissinger but the ruling-class representative Richard Nixon who "calls the signals" on government foreign policy. Kissinger is rewarded for dressing up and processing the international political designs of the American ruling class, but too much "wrong" advice would land Dr. Kissinger back in Cambridge.

Regarding the role of the intelligentsia, we cannot resist quoting an analogy drawn by M. E. Sharpe: "The genie was able to do marvelous things; but Aladdin held the lamp, and he who holds the lamp tells the genie what to do." [64] In our own terms, of course, the ruling class holds the lamp and the intelligentsia, particularly the technical intelligentsia have evinced little inclination to take over its own lamp and use it for the advancement of the social and material well-being of the underlying population in the sense Veblen once envisaged as a remote future possibility. Undeniably, specialists are indispensable to the limited structural tasks of a

---

59 *The Sick Society*, p. 16.
60 *Technocracy* (New York: Free Press, 1969), p. 188.
61 *White Collar*, p. 154.
62 See Noam Chomsky, *American Power and the New Mandarins* (New York: Pantheon Books, 1969).
63 *The Power Elite*, p. 353.
64 "Tangling With Technology," *Social Policy* 2 (July–August 1971): 60.

technological society, but they are servants and slaves, not free agents, let alone masters of the house.

To recognize that the technical intelligentsia is instrumental rather than powerful is not to deny the predominance of a technocratic *world view*, a world view which nicely suits the interests of the ruling class. The political value of technocratic thinking is that it assumes that conflicts and problems are strictly resolvable and answerable in solely scientific terms. "Scientific" information is held to be available to important people in corporate and state institutions who make decisions objectively on the basis of this ineluctable data. The people are excluded as incapable of deciding such scientific and rational questions, and the people need not be involved anyway, for the intelligence available to the elite enables them to make the right decision benefiting the greatest number (may we take Richard Nixon's private decision—he evidently "consulted" no one besides Henry Kissinger —to carpet-bomb Hanoi and Haiphong with B-52s around Christmas of 1972 as reflecting access to such exclusive intelligence?). Veblen early pointed out that:

> It is to be presumed that, for the good of the nation, no one outside of the official personnel and the business Interests in collusion can bear any intelligent part in the management of . . . delicate negotiations, and any premature intimation of what is going on is likely to be "information which may be useful to the enemy." [65]

Veblen also drew attention to the fact that policy and decision making is replete with "administrative prevarication and democratic camouflage." In Larson's words, technocracy's "ultimate aim is to deny that human will is involved in political decision-making. Crucial decisions are presented as the result of circumstances, which, when carefully and 'scientifically' weighted, necessarily and by themselves yield the answer." She adds that "the function of this ideology is to legitimize the profoundly anti-democratic character of the power structure." [66] In this view, there is no real power elite, only decision makers who carry out the "hard" dictates of social and technological necessity. There is the real danger that a sizeable portion of the population is in the thrall of this technological and scientific fetishism, much to the satisfaction of America's rulers.

---

[65] Thorstein Veblen, *Absentee Ownership and Business Enterprise in Recent Times* (New York: The Viking Press, 1938, 1923), pp. 443–45. Also available as Beacon Press paperback edition, 1967.

[66] Magali Sarfatti Larson, "Notes On Technocracy: Some Problems of Theory, Ideology, and Power," *Berkeley Journal of Sociology* 17 (1972–73): 23–29.

ten

STATE CAPITALISM

THE CAPITALIST SYSTEM

"Production in the corporate economy is consciously oriented solely to what can be sold profitably, rather than what is necessary or desirable for society." [1] This observation by Michael Tanzer hits directly at the essence of the capitalist system, and its truth is the source not only of monumental irrationality in the organization and conduct of human life but also of state capitalism, the compensatory reaction of a ruling class in deep economic trouble. The rationality of planning by the ruling class for its own acquisitive power urges and needs turns out to be destructive irrationality for the society as a whole. Thus, it is not that the system lacks selective rationality and planning, or at least makes serious attempts at such. It is the rationality within the system that makes profit the driving force of investment and production, and the planning that makes the prosperity of the ruling class its guiding and motivating principle, which works such irrationalities upon the masses. As the Marxist theoretical model so strongly portends, every calculation, invention, and cost reduction is carried out not for the good of human or collective social needs, but with the single aim of increasing profits. What is more, the very nature of the capitalist economy *requires* profit rationality, for its components are at constant economic war with one another; not merely greed, but the entire economic *system*

---

[1] *The Sick Society* (New York: Holt, Rinehart and Winston, 1971), p. 21.

234

demands continual pressure for greater profits and expanded sales. The alternative for any given corporation is elimination or slow death.[2]

The criteria of profitability for economic activity and the criteria of human needs are becoming increasingly divergent, and that the former is unable to harmonize with the latter is becoming increasingly obvious. In its early stages, capitalist production at least seemed to be oriented toward the satisfaction of human needs, but in its mature stages the motivation of production is more sharply and painfully visible, leaving diminishing room for the belief that production for profit is also the best method of attaining material security for all and a viable social and physical environment. In producing for profit, capitalism responds in earnest only to money demand, not to the real wants of individuals for food, clothing, medicine, housing, transportation, cleanliness, safety, and free time. "Thus the acquisitive society," writes Robert Heilbroner, "is one that caters to every whim of the rich but that ignores the elemental requirements of the poor. Wants, needs, just deserts . . . play no part in the market's distribution of goods.[3] For a small minority of the population, the system delivers with extraordinary generosity; for perhaps a majority it delivers in amounts capitalists define as necessary for living comfortably within the home, give or take some in either direction; for a solid minority it delivers daily insecurity and even wholesale deprivation. And this is speaking only in private terms. As Hacker so trenchantly observes: "When Americans set foot from their homes, they enter an environment that is physically dangerous, aesthetically repellent, and morally disquieting. The public domain has ceased to be civilized territory."[4]

The persistent market forces exerting pressure on the capitalist class toward greater profits and expansion yield surpluses of goods and services in given profitable areas—a crisis of overproduction. The term *overproduction* within the context of capitalism is not used in the sense that all social and human needs have been satisfied. Production for profit means that only goods and services which yield profit to the capitalist class will be produced, and that if the underlying population or any component part of it cannot yield up the money demand to satisfy the investment "daring" of finance capitalists, then the lords of production will look elsewhere or contrive some profitable artifical demand via psychology or the state.[5] The

---

[2] See Richard C. Edwards, "The Logic of Capitalist Expansion," in Edwards et al., eds. *The Capitalist System* (Englewood Cliffs, N.J.: Prentice-Hall, 1972), pp. 99–106.

[3] *Between Capitalism and Socialism* (New York: Vintage Books, 1970), p. 45.

[4] Andrew Hacker, *The End of the American Era* (New York: Atheneum, 1970), p. 136.

[5] Among other of his works Thorstein Veblen's *Absentee Ownership* early clarified the mechanics of waste under capitalism (New York: The Viking Press, 1938, 1923).

system of class and income inequality which is part and parcel of the capitalist system itself assures, in Tanzer's words, "that production for profit results in a very different range of output than that which would be dictated by real human needs." [6] Beyond individual or class income and wealth inequality, there are a range of collective needs which are by their very nature public in content and satisfaction, and cannot raise their voices to be heard. When these voices are at last heard—such as for medical care, urban reconstruction, environmental protection, poverty alleviation, and public transportation—the ruling class listens via the state, which acts as a money funnel from the taxpayer to the capitalist. Thus, "overproduction" of actual profit-oriented commodities is only part of the total *potential* surplus given the full and rational operation of the forces of production. Baran has rearticulated Veblen's analysis that to realize the potential surplus would require the elimination of excess and superfluous consumption of existing commodities, the application of unproductive subcapitalist labor to productive social tasks, the elimination of irrationality and waste in production, and the utilization of unemployed and underemployed labor due to existing production anarchy and low demand for profitable commodities.[7] It should be noted in this connection that under socialism the extent of the surplus would vary depending upon the development of production and human needs. Under advanced technology and rational needs, socialism would surely not maximize potential surplus; but the nature of things produced would differ significantly from those under a profit regimen, since there would be no class dependent upon profits. Ultimately, socialism would aim for an equally distributed, higher-quality, and less alienating application of economic surplus, even though conceivably smaller than the surfeit productions of advanced capitalism.

Veblen early analyzed how the forces of production are distorted, limited, and wasted owing to an outmoded system of economic relations. As Mandel has more recently phrased it:

> Instead of freely distributing the wealth created by the rise in the productivity of labour; instead of making it the foundation for a free development of the human being, capitalism, wishing to keep profit and the market economy under conditions of semi-abundance, is forced to outrage and mutilate people more and more, at the same time the possibilities for their free development are increasing from day to day.[8]

---

[6] *The Sick Society,* p. 23.

[7] Paul A. Baran, *The Political Economy of Growth* (New York: Monthly Review Press, 1968, 1957), pp. 23–24.

[8] Ernest Mandel, *Marxist Economic Theory,* vol. 2 (New York: Monthly Review Press, 1970), p. 204.

Robert Theobald has written extensively on the same problem, concluding that "so long as the present socioeconomic system is not changed, abundance is a cancer, and the various parts of the system *must* continue to do their best to inhibit its growth." [9]

In talking of abundance, we must remember first that abundance is highly selective and excludes many aspects and components of the society and, even more, the world. Secondly, as André Gorz cautions, much affluence has nothing to do with new and enriched human and social needs but merely attempts to solve or meet very ordinary needs for such things as privacy, safety, relaxation, and clean environments which now demand "rich" means of satisfaction owing to the distortion and impoverishment of the natural milieux.[10] Closely related is the fact that man has created a social system which has trapped him into no-choice corners, forcing him to drive an automobile, for example, in order to get to work; given the fact of a broken-down urban transport system, the automobile is no more a sign of abundance than was a buckboard wagon on a nineteenth-century farm. Indeed, it is clearly a regression in terms of the quality of living— safety, noise level, tension, environment, aesthetics, etc. Thirdly, as Veblen pointed out in calculating the potential of the industrial system, much affluence is purely specious waste and destructive gadgetry.

The last point brings us to a discussion of the manner in which the capitalist class *attempts to deal with overproduction of exchange-values.* Actually, the term *waste* nicely sums up the overall strategy. Veblen was acutely sensitive to the role of waste in capitalism, not just as an inadvertent by-product—which it is as well—but a *consciously contrived* method of maintaining profits. He spoke of the conscientious withdrawal of efficiency and suggested that one-half of the actual industrial output was consumed in wasteful superfluities, not to mention the restriction of potential output.[11] Waste is accomplished by many devices. Most of 1970's $20 billion annual expenditure on advertising (or salesmanship, to use Veblen's term), up from $5.7 billion in 1950 and $11.9 billion in 1960, is not only waste in itself but much worse encourages through artful and crude persuasion massive consumer participation in superfluities and is an important generator of the $127 billion in consumer debt piled up in 1970.[12] And consider

---

[9] *Free Men and Free Markets* (Garden City, N.Y.: Doubleday & Company, 1965), p. 107.

[10] *Strategy for Labor* (Boston: Beacon Press, 1967), pp. 89–91.

[11] Thorstein Veblen, *The Engineers and the Price System* (New York: Harcourt, Brace and World, Inc., 1963, 1921), pp. 45, 120.

[12] The national debt structure, personal, corporate, and public, is rapidly approaching critical proportions; consumer debt payment is 25¢ on the disposable dollar compared to 6¢ in 1946; the liquidity ratio of corporations has dropped from .73 in 1946 to .20 in 1972; and all levels of government are major debtors. Sweezy

the side effects of advertising such as on the consumption of trees for the daily tons upon tons of newspaper, magazine, mail and other advertising media requiring pulpwood—and the aftermath of litter and disposal problems. Advertising has the purpose of stimulating beyond all reasonable limits the desire for goods and services, and is especially urgent at a moment in history when material security promises to take people's minds off consumption and onto less omnivorous cultural pursuits. Marxist theory agrees that material consumption is basic to human development, and is its first prerequisite; but it sharply dissents from the current corporate capitalist tenet that "consumers have a responsibility to accept novelty at the rate corporations produce it, in order to satisfy corporate demands for growth and market expansion." [13] The consumer might ask if he also has the responsibility of paying the higher prices as a result of adding to the costs of production, advertising, and other lavish executive operating expenses.

Tightly intermeshed with advertising is the strategy of planned obsolescence. Advertising tells you that what you have is obsolete in terms of style, prestige, or function; it urges the person on to invidious comparisons and conspicuous consumption. The product itself will tell you of its built-in obsolescence soon after purchase. In the anti-Veblenist words of executive James M. Roche, fabulously rich after forty-two years with General Motors: "Planned obsolescence, in my opinion, is another word for progress." [14] And progress it has been for GM, with cumulative profits of $22 billion from 1947 to 1969; its almost $2 billion in net profits for 1971 placed it second among corporations nationally. On the other hand, fifty-five thousand people were killed in automobile accidents in 1971 and millions injured, a large but unknown proportion of whom were victims of the "progress" of planned obsolescence. With almost four out of ten American-built cars produced between 1966 and 1970 being openly recalled for defects, one wonders if any cars are *not* defective or built in a way which jeopardizes occupant safety. Automobiles, of course, are only one source (albeit an important one) of hazards to consumers arising from planned obsolescence. And certainly, rendering products cheap and short-lived has damaging consequences on environment in terms of waste and disposal.

Waste also takes the form of restriction of output (*sabotage* is Veblen's term) in order to maintain prices and profits. Nearly 30 percent

---

and Magdoff point out that "the debt structure just goes on swelling to the point where even a relatively mild setback in the underlying economy sends tremors through the bloated financial superstructure and threatens to bring it down like a house of cards." See Paul M. Sweezy and Harry Magdoff, *The Dynamics of U.S. Capitalism* (New York: Monthly Review Press, 1972), p. 192.

[13] Donald A. Schon, *Technology and Change* (New York: Delta Books, 1967), p. 44.

[14] See the sad tale by Colman McCarthy, "The Faulty School Busses," *Saturday Review*, March 11, 1972.

of the nation's manufacturing capacity was standing idle in 1971, and manpower unemployment had just reached an eighteen year high. Livestock has been disposed of and crops plowed under over the past 40 years while hungry people of the nation looked on. Produce rots in supermarkets as penny-conscious housewives pass by and the poor fumble in their pockets for food stamps. Able-bodied men sit idle as the cities decay and millions dwell in hovels. Talent and skill abound but the population waits and waits for doctors and plumbers—or at least those who can afford them wait. By contrast, a small minority of the people engage in luxurious consumption and superfluous waste on a variety of fronts, helping to offset the purchasing weaknesses of the lower strata. The system wastes through underutilization and senseless utilization. Horses and dogs of the rich sleep better, eat better, and stay healthier than millions of citizens.

In addition to advertising, credit, obsolescence, and cutback as means of realizing profit duplication, fraud, price fixing, deception, surcharges, and other techniques, legal and illegal, are also frequently employed. Senator Philip Hart (D., Ind.) has estimated that $200 billion a year (almost one in every three cents spent) is stripped from the consumer by what amounts to fraudulent means, including overpricing, substandard goods, and surcharges.[15] In 1968, the total estimated value of property stolen from individuals was less than $55 million, while direct business frauds alone robbed individuals of over $1 billion.[16]

Typically overlooked as a major component of waste and a means of profitably dealing with potential or actual surplus productivity is all the manpower and resources consumed in what we have called subcapitalist pursuits, in particular much of banking, finance, insurance, and real estate. Although these activities are necessary to the capitalist system and are counted as necessary costs of production, they are, along with advertising, specious duplication of products, obsolescence, and other forms of waste, unnecessary and parasitical from the standpoint of a socially rational economy. As Baran and Sweezy observe: "The prodigious volume of resources absorbed in all these activities does in fact constitute necessary costs of capitalist production. What should be crystal clear is that an economic system in which *such* costs are socially necessary has long ceased to be a socially necessary economic system."[17]

Direct foreign investment has been characterized by some as a means of dealing with surplus. However, the very opposite is true. All capitalist investment, and foreign investment in particular, is intended as a means

---

[15] John Rothschild, "The Screwing of the Average Man," *The Washington Monthly*, October, 1971, p. 39.

[16] *The Sick Society*, p. 144.

[17] Paul A. Baran and Paul Sweezy, *Monopoly Capital* (New York: Monthly Review Press, 1968), p. 141.

of *adding* to the surplus; in the case of underdeveloped areas, the advanced capitalist corporations take out far more wealth than they put in, and this equation is worsening. Indeed, the ruling class has come to rely precisely on foreign earnings to offset the global military and political drain on dollars, hoping to substantially increase the direct foreign net profits take from the $4.7 billion of 1971 ($1.9 billion in 1960) by several billions before the decade's end, thus protecting the dollar against a growing trade deficit and costs of empire. The other side, of course, is the sucking of investable wealth from other societies—many of which are underdeveloped countries themselves experiencing payments problems and devaluation.[18] Thus, imperialism taken in its entirety *is* a means of dealing with surplus, for the ruling class requires a vast military operation to back up and enforce its economic exploits around the world. There exists, then, a spiraling cycle whereby foreign investment and profits are required to offset the costs of maintaining world military power and the status quo which, in turn, demands that greater profits be repatriated to protect the value of the dollar and the stability of world capitalism. And we may be assured that the costs of counterrevolution are going to go up, both directly and in support of right-wing dictatorships. But the ruling class doesn't pay the bill for worldwide military operations and the enormous industrial complex required to sustain them. As Marx noted, the working class is sacrificed, both financially and bodily. On balance, the working class is a big loser as a result of imperialism, as it is on all other counts of system strategies for dealing with the contradictions of capitalism.

Military spending is the most glaring aspect of what constitutes a state capitalist approach to dealing with overproduction and the threat of capitalist demise. The aim of state capitalism is to socialize costs and privatize profits, to make the working class pay for ruling-class prosperity. The relations of production remain untouched, but the form of appropriating surplus value is altered; the state enters as an intermediary to assure the survival of the system that funnels power and wealth into the private-property-owning class. As Gorz points out: "Public development is welcome, provided that it is confined *to the public financing of the sources of future neo-capitalist expansion and accumulation;* provided, that is, that it remains subordinate to private enterprise, which must be left with the responsibility of deciding the economy's main orientation." [19] And Michael Harrington observes that "Nixonism [i.e., capitalism] must reconcile increased federal planning and spending with the persistence of private

---

[18] Paul M. Sweezy and Harry Magdoff, "Balance of Payments and Empire," *Monthly Review* 24 (December 1972): 1–12.

[19] André Gorz, "Work and Consumption," in Perry Anderson and Robin Blackburn, eds., *Towards Socialism* (Ithaca, N.Y.: Cornell University Press, 1966), p. 343.

power. It socializes, but only on behalf of part of the society. Its methods are incipiently non-, or even anti , capitalist; its purposes are impeccably pro-capitalist." In noting the blatant use of the state on behalf of the capitalist class—whether it be for government contracts and purchases, research-and-development monies, tax cuts and credits, accelerated depreciation, loan guarantees, overseas investment guarantees, and other mechanisms—Harrington argues that the Republicans (he feels that the Democrats might be better able to use the state for the people) are "dedicated to socialism of, for, and by the rich." [20] The state (the taxpayer) pays the bill for support systems such as education, research, military, highways, utilities, and medicine, but wherever profits are to be had, the capitalist class is on hand to pick them up. The entire welfare system, including that for rich and poor alike, is an essential ingredient of state capitalism—the socialization of costs and the privatization of profits. What the state cannot do is enter into direct competition with private interests in producing socially needed goods and services for nonprofit use or in redistributing wealth and hence power, i.e., it cannot be a socialist state, a working-class state.

The contradictions of capitalism run along other than economic lines. We have already made note of the contradiction between a better-educated working class and the demand for unquestioning adherence to the rules and goals of production as framed by the capitalist managers. Eventually the Veblenist idea of an educated working class coming into conflict with the economic irrationalities of capitalism would seem inevitable; yet we have seen how increasing specialization may work in the opposite direction as well, narrowing the scope and horizon of thought to the point of trained incapacity—something Veblen was equally aware of. Richard Flacks has emphasized a further contradiction relating to capitalism, one related to the cultural value system. The system values of competition, success, individualism, money making, and obedience conflict with the values which would dominate a free society, such as cooperation, self-expression, communalism, and autonomy. Creativity, knowledge, self-expression, and self-determination are blocked by a cultural system which emphasizes money making, military power, and class inequality.[21] Flacks, observing that the economic and political structure of capitalism effectively blocks the realization of new values and cultural styles, avoids the easy trap of thinking that the population at large can liberate their consciousnesses irrespective of the political economy of the society. In effect, then, the cultural contradiction awaits the resolution of the political and economic contradiction.

The status quo cannot possibly permanently obtain. The capitalist

---

[20] "Anatomy of Nixonism," *Dissent* 19 (Fall 1972): 577.
[21] *Youth and Social Change* (Chicago: Markham Publishing Company, 1971), p. 129.

system is being carried forward by its own internal logic. Within its own limits, capitalism may follow two general courses, one carrying it toward the welfare state and the other toward fascism. Scandinavia today represents the leftward limits of capitalism and the welfare state; Hitler's Germany represented its rightward limits and the fascist state. From the left, state capitalism can easily make the transition to socialism; from the right, state capitalism ultimately destroys itself and everything it comes in contact with. The United States wavers between the two poles of capitalist development, now showing the unmistakable signs of militarism, racism, scapegoating, irrationality, and repression so much a part of fascism, then turning a more decent and humane face—though never without careful calculation as to the relevance for profits.

From a discussion of the contradictions of production for profit and types of attempts at their solution, including that of state capitalism itself, we turn next to a closer examination of the role of the state in the advanced capitalist system and what the state can and cannot do.

THE ROLE OF THE STATE

Monopoly capitalism requires for its prosperity an economically active state, something which the majority of the ruling class failed to fully comprehend until the 1940s.[22] On its own in the manner of classical liberal political economy, with relatively minor state intervention, corporate capitalism would command a rapidly sinking ship; indeed, all would have been lost long ago. On its own corporate capital cannot keep the economy running; it needs the taxation and spending powers of the state. With the profit motive only able to keep the forces of production operating at depression levels, it has become absolutely mandatory, as Marxist theory so clearly foresaw, that the state enter the economy to pick up the slack and extend consumption and production to tolerable levels. Through purchases and transfer payments the government creates effective demand, which enables the capitalist class not only to survive, but to reap profits in traditional and new government-subsidized areas. In advanced technological society, government taxation and spending does not subtract from the private sector; quite the contrary: it adds to the economy an amount of surplus which would never appear otherwise. In a rationally planned, socially oriented society, the role of the "state" would be larger than it is today, but its type of involvement would be fundamentally different. "The big question," note Baran and Sweezy, "is not whether there will be more and more govern-

---

[22] See James Weinstein, "The Left, Old and New," *Socialist Revolution* 10 (July–August 1972): 11.

ment spending, but on what. And here private interests come into their own as the controlling factor." [23] It is the *private* appropriation and purpose of government surplus absorption which marks off state capitalism from the socialist transition, which has as its aim the social determination and use of surplus.

With all levels of U.S. government currently accounting for between one-fourth and one-third of economic activity and employment, no one can seriously question the state's indispensability to corporate capitalism. No informed finance capitalist could contemplate life without the economic assistance of the state; only the small businessman still living on the myths of the past talks seriously of eliminating government spending. The finance capitalist only objects to government *business*—i.e., nonprofit production and distribution competing with private enterprise—or government spending for the social purposes of redistributing wealth and security and undermining both the power and profits of the capitalist class. This objection, obviously, covers a very large area, and drastically limits the economic alternatives open to the state. Given the extravagant economic needs of the ruling class, their control of the tax system and the enormous financial demands upon the state, government faces serious fiscal problems.[24] The capitalist class demands billions in subsidies, systematically evades taxes, and unloads the burden of financing state operations upon the working class—all of which creates mounting fiscal pressures upon the public purse.

The state thus finds itself as a buffer for capitalist contradictions and irrationality, desperately trying to preserve the integrity of the capitalist class and its major institutions while at the same time trying to preserve a simulacrum of social stability and well-being for the masses. But in reality this trick can't be carried off indefinitely, for the interests of capital and labor are inherently antagonistic, and glaringly so in the late stages of monopoly capital. Numerous variables are present which the ruling class in conjunction with the state attempts to manipulate in their favor, making only what concessions are required to forestall genuine social upheaval or revolution. Among the inescapable situations the state finds itself in are swings between inflation and recession (though we may witness both of these problems simultaneously). Picking up the cycle at an arbitrary point, say in the early sixties, we find a situation of overproduction and underutilization (recession) being stimulated by deficit government spending. Given the widespread unemployment and correspondingly weak labor position together with the flow of government monies, corporate profits sharply

---

[23] *Monopoly Capital*, p. 151.

[24] See James O'Connor, "The Fiscal Crises of the State: Part I," *Socialist Revolution* 1 (February 1970): 12–54, and "Part II," 2 (April 1970): 34–94; and Thomas Bodenheimer, "The Poverty of the State," *Monthly Review* 24 (November 1972): 7–18.

expanded. But continued spending and accumulation cut unemployment and strengthened the wage position of labor, particularly upon the escalation of war spending after 1965. With an unpopular war being paid for out of deficit instead of taxation, wage pressures from higher employment levels increasing, and military as opposed to consumer goods being produced from the deficit spending, the pendulum swung in the late sixties toward sharp inflation; also, the capitalist class witnessed a relative slowing of profits (cost-plus military contractors held their own or better). Now came time for a reversal of strategies: cut federal spending, raise unemployment, weaken labor, and thus attempt to control the inflation previously set in motion by the attempt to overcome stagnation at home and revolution abroad. On this occasion, the position of the working class was successfully undermined (finally in the blatant form of wage-control policy), but inflation persisted, due partially to 'inflationary psychology" but more to the sheer profit hunger of the monopoly-pricing corporations. As Block and Hirschhorn point out: "Inflation is then a central means by which the capitalist class resists any redistribution of the social production in an era of strong labor unions and rising taxes." [25]

The combination of emphasis on military production and the inflation of U.S. currency has contributed to yet another serious structural problem of U.S. capitalism: an unprecedented (in this century) trade deficit of growing proportions, as productivity in consumer industries declined vis-à-vis world leaders and as inflated U.S. prices placed exports in unfavorable and imports in favorable selling positions. The Vietnam War rapidly hastened these symptoms of economic illness. This, together with the costs of maintaining the empire (the "free world"—as in Brazil, Greece, South Vietnam, South Korea, and dozens of other places), has led to the balance-of-payments problem and devaluations of the dollar—more of which are sure to come, even given continued superprofits taken by U.S. corporations around the world. Thus, the U.S. ruling class, in its actions through the state, is pitted not only against its own working class as it strives to limit wages and increase productivity through speed-ups and automation in order to make its goods more competitive on the world market (and also as it milks the working class for taxes to pay the costs of empire), but also against the bourgeoisie of other advanced nations in the struggle for markets and profits. But nations such as Japan and West Germany are willing to make certain concessions to the U.S. bourgeoisie, such as holding huge amounts of dollars and accepting trade restrictions and tariffs, since they, too, make use of the U.S. military umbrella around the "free world" and

---

25 Fred Block and Larry Hirschhorn, "The International Monetary Crises," *Socialist Revolution* 11 (September–October 1972): 19; see also Frank Ackerman and Arthur McEwan, "Inflation, Recession, and Crises, or Would You Buy a New Car from This Man?" *Radical America,* January–February 1972, pp. 18–60.

find a better outlet for their own goods on an inflated-U.S.-dollar market. Furthermore, although the U.S. international position has been weakened, it is still the center of gravity of world capitalism; serious depression and dollar problems for the United States promise to shake the entire structure of world capitalism to its foundations, something minor partners are willing to sacrifice a lot for in order to avoid.

The consequence of state manipulation of available economic variables, whatever combination might be selected for action, is almost universally destined to be unfavorable to the working class. All actions are calculated to maximize corporate profits, for it is corporate profits which make the system run in the way it does. However, the calculations now current are approaching an impasse: profits cannot be maintained or increased without flagrant violations of the working class and without risking serious destabilizing political unrest and possible upheaval. Temporarily, scapegoats and rationalizations have bought additional time, but the day of more fundamental reckoning cannot be long postponed.

Although the state has assumed other financial burdens, since the beginning of large-scale government economic involvement the alpha and omega of state capitalism has been the military. Eight years of Franklin D. Roosevelt's New Deal, still considered a massive federal financial foray into the economy, raised the federal budget from $4.2 billion to $10 billion. Government spending at all levels totaled $17.5 billion in 1939. The limitations placed upon government by the capitalist system prohibited the kind of involvement required to absorb idle manpower and resources and produce material well-being. Military spending, however, does not offend capitalist interests: *it does not compete,* and production is handed out to the private sector on a cost-plus basis. Indeed, military spending is ideally suited to the ruling class; until recently few people objected to paying taxes for it, and still millions part with their money patriotically while the government funnels the money to private businesses—many of which are entirely dependent for both business and profit upon the taxpayer. Thus it was that federal spending reached $103 billion in 1944, cutting the unemployment rate from around 20 percent of the late thirties to a frictional 1 percent in 1944. Women and previously uncounted minority persons were brought into the labor force on a large and unprecedented scale.

It cannot be overemphasized that war and not welfare now and always constitutes the prime government economic activity. Let Paul Samuelson, eminent M.I.T. economist, tell it like it is: "It needs emphasizing that the bulk of federal expenditure is the consequence of hot and cold war, not of welfare and development programs." [26] Deficit spending for war has been carried on massively and hardly without debate, even for such a travesty as

---

[26] *Economics* (New York: McGraw-Hill, 1970), p. 143.

Vietnam. The federal debt in 1970 was $370 billion, fully 90 percent of it due to military spending. The ruling class can justify in terms of its own appropriation of surplus hundreds of billions for the military but unleashes all of its forces—from within corporate board rooms to the halls of Congress—against socialized production of housing, transport, utilities, medical care, and any other area that threatens its profits. Whether by means of taxes, forced savings, bonds, or simply printing inflationary money, the state can and does raise military funds; the outcome is a hard-pressed working class and an enriched bourgeoisie. One of the magnificent feats of legerdemain has been for the latter to convince the former that militarism is a blessing for all.

In adding up the military bill for 1970, we count $82 billion for defense, $8 billion for veterans, $16 billion for interest, $4 billion for international affairs and finance (Senator William Proxmire—D., Wisc.—estimates the true cost of foreign aid to be $10 billion, the bulk of it straight military spending), $4 billion for space, and $3 billion for atomic energy (primarily military-oriented). Three-fifths of federal spending is thus devoted to military and quasi-military pursuits. In 1971 and 1972 the defense budget officially dropped slightly, but interest on debt (over $20 billion) and veterans costs (over $10 billion) have compensated. In 1972 the secretary of defense requested $8 billion additional military dollars, and the 1973 budget included a substantial increase. As in spending so in property assets, the military has the lion's share—$274 billion out of a $400 billion 1968 federal total. Besides the 2.8 million uniformed military personnel, the Department of Defense pays the salaries of 1.2 million persons compared to Health, Education, and Welfare's 110,000 and Housing and Urban Development's 15,000. Such are the spending values of state capitalism, typified by the fact that federal spending for the *interest* on militarily incurred debt is greater than the combined *spending* for education and manpower, community development and housing, natural resources, and peace-oriented foreign aid.

Another important way of evaluating the direction of investment and the spending thrust of state capitalism is to examine the manner in which research funds and manpower are used. In 1971 the federal government spent $15.3 billion for R & D—research and development (mostly development in this case)—of which $7.5 billion went to the Department of Defense, $3.7 billion to NASA, and $1.3 billion to the Atomic Energy Commission, for a military and quasi-military total of $12.3 billion or 80 percent. Health, Education, and Welfare had $1.4 billion to work with in that year. In less than a decade's time, well over $100 billion has been poured into military R & D. Needless to say, the large majority of federally supported scientific and technical manpower works with military-related projects. In fact, of all federally funded research conducted three-fifths is military research, and almost half of all scientists and engineers do military related work. Aircraft, missiles, and electronics, the bastions of military R & D spending, account for over half of *total* research done by industry, though these areas account for only a small fraction of manufacturing production.[27] Thus, the economy of capitalism is a permanent war economy, and the technology of capitalism is preeminently a military technology. Housing construction is primitive, the merchant marine founders, power sources fail, telephone communications break down, public transit withers, the environment is destroyed, and life expectancy shortens; where are the research and development funds for life's real needs? Both material and human resources are potential and available for application to these and other pressing needs, but the capitalist class is not interested in nonprofitable social and cultural development.

State capitalism does spend for things other than military. In 1971 some $11 billion was distributed in direct subsidies, half to agriculture and most of this to large farmers and agribusinesses; in addition, "business" got $2.6 billion. Homeowners and tenants received $399 million, most of which ended up in the hands of real estate agents and private financial interests such as banks and loan associations; conservatives complain that the poor are getting "free housing" when in fact they are being swindled in the classic sense by the pillars of the financial community, and the taxpayer again is left holding the bag. Billions upon billions are spent on highways and freeways and a pittance for mass transit, much to the delight and bidding of the gas and oil complex. To prevent beggary and social unrest on a large scale, the government pays marginal sums to dependent women, children, and the elderly—money which again feeds into private financial coffers. Other so-called welfare programs such as Social Security, Medicare, and unemployment compensation are social insurance funds paid for out of sharply regressive payroll taxes. Also proudly chalked up to welfare spending is public education, paid for by the underlying population but absolutely indispensable to the operation and growth of corporate capitalism. In point of fact, the public schools are starved for funds. Portland, Oregon was forced to close its schools a month early in 1972, despite voluntary salary freezes and cutbacks by teachers; Nixon's response in 1973 was to reduce federal aid to education. State capitalism is a system which can afford anything to pulverize a distant peasant population or send men to the moon, but it cannot accommodate the welfare of its own people.

Since the state is a big spender and cannot enter into productive enterprise to earn revenues, it must tax. With the ruling class in charge of the state, we may naturally expect fiscal operations to be exploitative

---

27 Richard J. Barber, *The American Corporation* (New York: E. P. Dutton & Company, 1970), pp. 136 ff.

of the working class and supportive of the capitalist class. Inasmuch as the general objectives of state capitalism are the socialization of costs and the privatization of profit, we may translate this into tax terms by saying that the working class is taxed much more than it is subsidized and the capitalist class is subsidized much more than it is taxed. The working-class poor pay an overall rate of federal, state, and local income taxation comparable to those reporting income of over $50,000.[28] Including capital gains, tax-exempt bonds, depletion, and other loopholes, persons with incomes of $200,000 or more actually pay an effective federal income tax rate of only 30 percent, about 15 percent less than the official statement and 40 percent less than the IRS rate for this bracket! [29] Excluding such unearned income, the overall rate for the $2,000–$4,000 bracket is 35 percent and for the $25,000–$50,000 bracket 33 percent. The middle American pays about 30 percent overall.

The tax cards stack up against the working class, mechanically speaking, owing to the sharply regressive nature of the Social Security, sales, and property taxes [30] and the loopholes in the federal income tax structure. The federal income tax loopholes are worth approximately $77 billion a year, accruing almost entirely to the rich. Chief among the loopholes are those for capital gains (the official 25 percent rate is far under the legal rate for income of the wealthy and the actual payment is very far under), inheritance of capital gains ($22 billion is lost to the Treasury in capital gains passed on to heirs untaxed), tax-exempt bonds (Mrs. Horace Dodge, Sr. has had $56 million in such bonds, yielding $1.7 million of tax-free income annually [31]), depletion allowances (Standard Oil of California paid a tax rate of 1.6 percent in 1971, Conoco 2.1 percent, and Gulf and Texaco each 2.3 percent [32]), and inheritance trusts (William Randolph Hearst left hundreds of millions in 1951 to a family trust which probably won't be taxed for a hundred years [33]). There is also philanthropy, expense accounts, gifts, estate dividing, deferred compensation, and so on. The single annual biggest chunk of capitalist rake-off in the tax system is accounted for by capital gains. Law Professor W. David Slawson calculates that the wealthiest 1 percent of adults receive income of upward of $30 billion a year from capital appreciation, but this income

[28] Bodenheimer, "The Poverty of the State," p. 14.

[29] Jerry J. Jasinowski, "Mr. Nixon's Tax Mythology," *The Nation,* October 30, 1972, pp. 399–404.

[30] See data in Bodenheimer, "The Poverty of the State," pp. 12–14.

[31] Kenneth Lamott, *The Moneymakers* (Boston: Little, Brown and Company, 1969), p. 275.

[32] *The Progressive,* December 1972, p. 12.

[33] Joseph A. Ruskay, "Tax Reform: The Loopholes Still With Us," *The Nation,* March 22, 1971, pp. 268–71. The Rockefeller fortune also makes use of generation-skipping trusts.

produces only about $1 billion in tax—"a rate of only 3.3 percent despite the income's being received by persons most of whom are (or should be) in the 70 percent bracket." [34]

Corporations themselves paid $36.7 billion in 1969 income taxes on profits of $136 billion, amounting to a 27 percent rate. However, it is common knowledge and understandable logic that the majority of this tax is passed on to consumers in the form of higher prices; one would be exceedingly generous to estimate corporate taxation at 15 percent of profits.[35] Running close competition with the 122 individuals who earned over $200,000 and paid no 1971 taxes (millionaires can do the trick, too) were 43 percent of the nation's corporations, who paid less than 5 percent. Perhaps top loophole prize should go to nine of the largest eighty-six industrial corporations who in 1970 paid nothing but made $682 million.[36] Under the loyal leadership of Nixon, corporate tax has steadily declined both in terms of official rates and share of tax paid. Supposedly, the bonanza tax credits and allowances promote economic efficiency, but the simple fact that in a given period in the past $1.4 billion worth of oil subsidies generated only $150 million in petroleum reserves disproves this notion. The Joint Economic Committee of Congress further found that seven subsidies worth $23 billion a year produced nothing at all or actually lost money in the end.

Robert Lekachman calculates that a recovery of only one-third to one-half of the over $70 billion lost through tax benefits to the wealthy plus a reduction in military spending could obtain $100 billion for public programs, and that it would be feasible to directly transfer $43 billion of this to those with incomes under $12,000.[37] The McGovern fiscal proposals of the 1972 presidential campaign stood to accomplish roughly the same thing. (Did he fail to communicate or is the working class that falsely conscious of its objective interests? Perhaps cynicism has temporarily triumphed.) The cost of state capitalism, regardless of how many social programs Nixon cuts or vetoes, is going to go up; the military alone will see to that. Nixon the economizer had run up unprecedented deficits in 1972; tax increases in some form must come soon, and with a dedicated servant of the capitalist class heading the government, the hard-working working class will just have to dig a little deeper. For the tax structure is an essential component of ruling-class power and dominance, and it will not be changed to any fundamental degree within the capitalist system, even though it could be substantially reformed.

---

[34] "Moves to Patch the Loopholes," *The Nation,* June 16, 1969, p. 763.
[35] Bodenheimer, "The Poverty of the State," pp. 12–13.
[36] Jasinowski, "Mr. Nixon's Tax Mythology," p. 401.
[37] "Toward a Reordered Economy," *Dissent* 19 (Fall 1972): 585.

Why is it that capitalism as a system, despite accompanying social ideologies of progress, reform, and equality, tolerates so little in the way of actual redistributive social and economic justice? Why is it, aside from the great military expenses demanded by empire building, that a business-man's president such as Richard Nixon has in one term of office vetoed congressional money bills for the Office of Economic Opportunity, health, hospital modernization, general hospitals, aid to students, housing, urban development, veterans' benefits, veterans' hospitals, education, job pro-grams, family doctor training program, public works program, legal ser-vices, child development and nutrition, and other similar social measures? [38] Is it because Richard Nixon has little concern for schoolchildren, college students, the poor, veterans, the unemployed, the ill and untreated, the undernourished, the poorly housed, and the undefended and confused? In the case of this particular president, yes; yet the structure of capitalism and the collective power of the capitalist class would themselves set limits—though nowhere as stringent as Nixon sees them—on the extent of social developmental programs by the state. The more advanced seg-ment of the ruling class would in its greater liberalism and foresightedness apply a more constructive hand to the sick society, though considerably short of introducing any real structural social change. Right now, however, the troglodytes seem to be largely in charge of state matters.

The antagonism to structural change displayed by the capitalist class is simply an involuntary reflex for keeping the system operating according to its dictates and desires. Genuine social equality, secure employment and income, quality education and medical care for all, an end to poverty and unemployment, quality low-priced housing and transportation, and genu-ine social security in the larger sense would certainly put an end to the greater part of ruling-class power over the masses. Social security would undermine capitalist control of the labor market and severely limit its capacity for exploitation.[39] Capitalism champions "the necessity of social inequality," and *for capitalism* this is indeed true; by definition, the ruling class requires inequality in order to exercise its power and accumulate its profits. It requires mass insecurity, scarcity, and uneven privilege in order to maintain labor force control, to keep the masses sweating uncom-plainingly and apathetically. Capitalism needs dirty workers, a hierarchy of education and status, a stratification system in which people know their place and the dedicated servant is elevated to the feet of the powerful.

C. Wright Mills sounded the appropriate message almost fifteen years ago regarding the essence of state capitalism:

---

[38] See A. Q. Mowbray, "Negative Evidence: Knowing Nixon by his Vetoes," *The Nation,* November 6, 1972, pp. 426–29.

[39] Baran, *The Political Economy of Growth,* pp. 101–9.

> The sort of government programs that would be necessary . . . to re-
> place the defense economy—to maintain prosperity without arms—are
> exactly the sort that are the most distasteful, politically and economically,
> to those who in the name of free enterprise now benefit politically and
> economically, from the arms race. Imagine the uproar were it proposed
> to launch a 50 billion dollar "socialistic" program of urban renewal,
> valley development, school construction! [40]

Senator George McGovern was carried to the Democratic presidential
nomination in 1972 on the force of his peace platform, intention of cutting military spending, and a proposed alternative reconstruction economy.
Richard Nixon has always been the epitome of the state capitalist militarist. The voters chose, albeit in the face of monumental corporate money
and propaganda at all levels of society, which type of ideological leadership they preferred. It was a critical decision for the future of state capitalism in the United States as to whether it was to move toward the
liberal left and the welfare state or toward the conservative right and
the military-police state.[41] Not long after the president was sworn in for
another four years, the AFL-CIO hierarchy began to glimpse the beginning of the anti-working-class policies which they helped put into power
by their implicit and open support of Nixon.

THE PERMANENT WAR ECONOMY

The military-police state is already the dominant fact, if not the exclusive fact, of American life today. Since 1945 the military has consumed one trillion three hundred billion dollars, a sum exceeding the
value of all commercial and residential structures that now exist in the
United States. The U.S. military can deliver many tons of TNT for every
person on earth. For years the United States spent a small fortune every
time it killed a single Vietcong. Over the span of a few days at the end
of 1972, Nixon demonstrated a part of this capacity by ordering the Air
Force to bomb North Vietnam with the equivalent of forty pounds of
bombs per every inhabitant (at a cost to the taxpayer of $500 million).
While "winding down" the Vietnam War in 1970, the Department of
Defense spent $25 billion on military destruction in that unfortunate land,
and continued to spend over $15 billion in 1972; the several billions in
"savings" since the peak ground assault goes into other facets of military

---

[40] *The Causes of World War Three* (New York: Ballantine Books, 1960),
p. 77.
[41] See the important article by Joseph C. Goulden, "Tooling Up for Repression: The Cops Hit the Jackpot," *The Nation,* November 23, 1970, pp. 520–33.

operations around the globe. In the decade from 1960 to 1970, heedless of President Eisenhower's warning of the potential for the disastrous rise of misplaced power in the military-industrial complex, federal military spending increased from $46 billion to $80 billion, excluding the additional billions for veterans, foreign military assistance, space, etc. We are a nation which sees fit to devote almost 10 percent of our gross national product to military and quasi-military purposes and to spend over $379 per capita on military goals—by far and away the largest per capita military allocation among the major powers and nearly the same as per capita outlay for public health and education combined. Illustrating the distortion and imbalances within the U.S. economy is the .53 ratio of military expenditures to gross domestic fixed investment (1967–69) compared to .14 for West Germany and .02 for Japan—the basic reason why we are losing ground in consumer trade. Excluding Indochina since 1964, we have generously given (officially) $35 billion in military aid to other nations between 1950 and 1970; military and right-wing dictatorships are, naturally, the chief beneficiaries of today's foreign military assistance. The large majority of federal employees are on the military payroll, and roughly one-quarter of national economic activity and employment relies directly or indirectly on the permanent war economy. Approximately 10 percent of jobs are directly generated by the Department of Defense. Even at that, as Yarmolinsky points out, "while it seems possible to define and measure the population of the military establishment, the fact is that the list of persons ultimately connected with the military is almost infinitely extensible." [42] We noted above how technological research is dominated by military goals and how the technical intelligentsia is heavily reliant upon military make-work. With approximately 7 percent of the world's population, the United States accounts for one-third of world military spending. Not surprisingly, the United States was the lone abstainer in a 1972 United Nations General Assembly Political Committee vote of 110 to 0 to examine prospects for a world disarmament conference.

"The price of building a colossal military power, and endlessly adding to it," writes Seymour Melman, "has been the depletion of American society, a process now well advanced in industry, civilian technology, management, education, medical care, and the quality of life." [43] The hundreds of billions consumed on military purposes are permanently lost to society for use toward goods and services that would form part of the standard of living; it is a cost of man-hours, materials, and wealth for

---

[42] Adam Yarmolinsky, *The Military Establishment* (New York: Harper & Row, 1971), p. 15.
[43] *Our Depleted Society* (New York: Holt, Rinehart, and Winston, 1965), p. 4.

nonproductive goods and services and a loss of these factors for the standard of living and future production.[44] One *Polaris* sub with missiles cost the country 331 elementary schools, or 6,811 hospital beds, or 13,723 low-rent public housing units. One TFX airplane cost the country 13 schools, or 278 hospital beds, or 570 dwelling units.[45] This is what is meant by permanent loss, depletion, and the deterioration of the quality of life. Every B-52 bombing raid over Indochina could have been an important start toward the reduction of property taxes for schools in hundreds of communities across the nation. Yet new and more expensive weapons systems float through Congress with every passing session.

The Vietnam War has proven incredibly costly. Its annual cost could have *doubled* Social Security benefits across the board; its monthly cost could have financed the annual food bill for ending hunger among 10 million Americans. Vietnam spending, estimated to be $144 billion to date and estimated eventually to cost $352 billion, has sharply reduced the purchasing power of the consumer dollar, raised interest rates to century-high levels, and produced huge budget deficits and interest-bearing debts even with tax increases and surtaxes, grossly distorted the labor force and made employment rates fluctuate, greatly inflated food prices and generated serious all-round inflation, and badly exacerbated a growing balance-of-payments problem which has destabilized the international monetary situation and threatens to disrupt the entire world capitalist structure.[46] The human cost has been staggering, while American society has and will continue to pay dearly the psychological, social, and moral costs. Fifteen years ago Paul Baran wrote the following lines on militarism:

> A spiderweb of corruption is spun over the entire political and cultural life of the imperialist country and drives principles, honesty, humanity, and courage from political life. The cynicism of vulgar empiricism destroys the moral fibre, the respect for reason, and the ability to discriminate between good and evil among wide strata of the population.[47]

Vietnam was the inevitable outcome of the militarization of the United States since World War II and the government's foreign policy of backing corporate imperialism in the Third World. The Vietnam War and the military-industrial complex—and there will be more Vietnam-type wars—

---

[44] See Seymour Melman, "Pentagon Bourgeoisie," *Trans-Action* 8 (March–April 1971): 4–12.

[45] Melman, *Our Depleted Society*, p. 37.

[46] See Seymour Melman, *Pentagon Capitalism: The Political Economy of War* (New York: McGraw Hill, 1971), pp. 190–91.

[47] *The Political Economy of Growth*, p. 130.

threaten to destroy the American experiment in democracy, although the reaction to Vietnam may assist in making some inroads into ruling-class power.

The obstacles, however, are imposing. The ruling class has two substantial reasons for insuring the preservation of the military-industrial complex and all it stands for. First, as we shall discuss in the following chapter, the military is required to protect and cover foreign threats to imperialism. Vietnam was intended as a prime lesson to anti-imperialist forces in the Third World, though the reverse has come about. The ruling class requires foreign economic intervention to maintain its expansion of growth and profit, and militarization is essential to these aims. Baran early recognized the essence of this militarization: "The larger and more permanent the military establishment, the greater the temptation to 'negotiate from strength'—which means to serve ultimata to smaller and weaker nations and to back them, if need be, by force." [48] Secondly, the ruling class depends heavily upon the permanent war economy to maintain a semblance of economic prosperity at home, i.e., to deal with the problem of surplus absorption. The ramifications of military waste, however, can have major destabilizing effects throughout the system, and, as Baran has noted, "as with many other narcotics, the applicability of this shot in the arm is limited, and its effect is short-lived." [49] For every immediate need that military spending meets, larger difficulties are created in the process. There are, of course, other means of constructive surplus absorption. Military absorption is, in fact, not only wasteful but inefficient: dollar for dollar, military spending generates only *half as many jobs* as does civilian spending.[50] This point should be made clear to people such as the utility worker who was quoted as saying, "It's a helluva thing to say, but our economy needs a war. Defense spending should be increased to make more jobs for people." [51] The working class should be made to understand that military spending is an instrument to preserve the existing balance of inequality and prevent any redistribution of wealth. Furthermore, military spending is ideally suited to capitalist needs insofar as it is noncompetitive, has built-in obsolescence, and has an indefinite consumption limit. Social spending on the scale of military spending would radically transform the structure of power and wealth, and would have surplus absorption capacities under the long-term needs of corporate capitalism (social spending

---

[48] Ibid., p. 133.

[49] Ibid., p. 121.

[50] See Michael Reich and David Finkelhor, "Capitalism and the Military-Industrial Complex," in Richard C. Edwards et al., eds., *The Capitalist System,* pp. 392–406.

[51] Cited in Seymour Melman, "Who Needs a War Economy?" *The Nation,* November 20, 1972, pp. 487–88.

could, however, absorb all surplus in the immediate future given the
enormous neglect and need).

We might also note with Veblen that militarization is also psychologically supportive of the capitalist class. The psychological-support
factor should not be underestimated: hierarchy, authoritarianism, obedience, superpatriotism, and conformity, are important components of
ruling-class wealth and power in their relationship to the underlying
population.

In assessing the obstacles to modifying the permanent war economy,
Reich and Finkelhor remind us that the military-industrial complex is
not an isolated enclave tucked away in a corner of the economy, but
resides at the very core.[52] Two-thirds of the top hundred corporations are
significantly involved in the military market, and all but five of the top
twenty-five corporations in 1968 were among the top hundred Department of Defense contractors. Financial and board interlocks involve even
those firms which do not directly deal with the Defense Department in
the permanent war economy, while ownership of defense industry resides
firmly in the hands of one and the same group: the ruling upper class.
Thus, the militarists are not some band of outsiders or narrow interest
group of the capitalist class, but are virtually one and the same with that
class. After all, the so-called liberals within the establishment have long
been the chief builders of the militarist-imperialist system which rules this
country and many others. The development of the military-industrial complex and imperialism would have in all likelihood followed a very similar
course in the sixties had Richard Nixon won in 1960 instead of 1968.
One must look outside the upper or capitalist class to find true opponents
to the military-industrial complex and imperialism, and then one is looking today only at the relatively powerless.

The billions in prime weapons contracts constitute the heart of the
military-industrial complex. Many firms are largely or virtually entirely
military contractors, and many others depend upon defense spending for
their profit margins. From 1961 to 1967 Lockheed received $11 billion
in defense contracts, constituting 88 percent of its total sales; General
Dynamics received $9 billion for 67 percent of its sales; McDonnell-
Douglas $7.6 billion for 75 percent; Boeing $7.1 billion for 54 percent;
and Ling-Temco-Voight $8 billion for 70 percent. Other large firms rep-
resent themselves as civilian producers but are big military contractors
as well: General Electric received $7 billion during this period, ATT $4.1
billion, General Motors $2.1 billion, and Sperry Rand, General Tire,
Western Electric, Ford, RCA, Bendix, Textron, ITT, IBM, Standard

---

[52] "Capitalism and the Military-Industrial Complex," pp. 394–96.

Oil, Kaiser Industries, Honeywell, General Telephone, Chrysler, and Litton each over $1 billion in military contracts.[53] In 1968, a very good year for war industries, five firms held over $1 billion apiece, with General Dynamics topping the list at $2.2 billion. Since then, defense profits have slackened, "dropping" to an industry average of approximately 10 percent. The war contractors are undaunted, however, and one business magazine surmises that "the hopeful side to this prospect of lower but stable total volumes in defense is the heightened recognition that only increased profitability will make the defense industry stronger and more stable" [54]—good news for the taxpayers naturally. The billion-dollar cost overruns (and presidential authorization of firing the Defense Department employees who disclose them) and the bailing-out process which follows are all too commonplace to detail here.

Helping to keep things going profitably between the hundred largest defense contractors and the state were, as of February 1969, 2,072 retired military officers of the rank of colonel, Navy captain, or above. The top ten contractors list the largest number of ex-military officers in their employ, though technically retired brass do not act as liaisons between their firms and the Defense Department.

Who runs the military-industrial complex? The military brass? The civilian military? Big business? Kolko argues that "the 'military-industrial complex' that exists in the United States is a lopsided phenomenon in which only businessmen maintain their full identity, interest, and commitment to their institution, while the military conforms to the needs of economic interests." [55] Heilbroner takes the opposite view: "There is little doubt that a military-industrial-political interpenetration of interests exists, to the benefit of all three. Yet in this alliance I have seen no suggestion that the industrial element is the dominant one. It is the military or the political branch that commands, and business that obeys." [56] Galbraith and Melman both locate the source of power within the civilian and military departments of government.[57] Yarmolinsky does likewise.[58] Through-

---

[53] Ibid., pp. 77–78; see Victor Perlo, *Militarism and Industry: Arms Profiteering in the Missile Age* (New York: International Publishers, 1963); and Raymond G. Hunt and Gregory W. Hunt, "Some Structural Features of Relations Between the Department of Defense, the National Aeronautics and Space Administration, and Their Principal Contractors," *Social Forces* 49 (March 1971): 414–31.

[54] *Forbes,* January 1, 1972, p. 183.

[55] Gabriel Kolko, *The Roots of American Foreign Policy* (Boston: Beacon Press, 1969), p. 31.

[56] Robert L. Heilbroner, *The Limits of American Capitalism* (New York: Harper & Row, 1966), p. 51.

[57] John Kenneth Galbraith, *How to Control the Military* (New York: Signet Books, 1969) and Melman, *Pentagon Capitalism.* Melman writes: "Government is business. That is state capitalism" (p. 2).

[58] *The Military Establishment;* for the classic documentation of the historical development of the military-industrial complex, see Fred J. Cook, *The Warfare State* (New York: Collier Books, 1964, originally published, 1962).

out these debates there is, in the final analysis, a single, definite answer to the question of power. As on other questions concerning the forces of production, we must look to the ruling class, to the financial groups and financial oligarchy for the answer. Further, the state occupies a decisive role in the military-industrial complex, while the military brass does not, except for erroneous advice and mechanical obedience to the dictates of real power.

The military-industrial complex is simply the most blatant and monstrous face of state capitalism, which we have already defined as the socialization of costs and the privatization of profits. The ruling class has its interests so deeply involved in the state that the two are in this case indistinguishable. As Gottleib has pointed out: "Part bureaucratic, part industrial, the complex is a network in which even the closest observers fail to detect where government ends and the corporation begins." [59] Or from Mills: "An attack on war-making is also an attack on the U.S. power elite." [60] The debate is really academic. The ruling class controls the military-industrial complex, through the state, which itself makes many important autonomous decisions but none which can run counter to the interests of finance capital for very long. Indeed, no military master plan or major military-industrial investment can be long pursued without the full consent of the ruling class, for if its own members are not always present for the decision making, its hired hands know the rules of the game. In short, the Pentagon is *used* by finance capital for whatever immediate or long-range interests it might have.[61]

THE WELFARE STATE

In the preceding section, we examined the ugly face of state capitalism. In this section, we examine another face of state capitalism, its welfare face, which is at times hardly less ugly than its militarist one. ("Welfare" must here be sharply distinguished from "socialism.") In America, welfare is inadequate to the point of callous indifference to hunger, poverty, disability and illness, and wretched living conditions; in its operation it is often degrading, humiliating, and destructive of self-respect; in its funding it is woefully inadequate to the needs of those receiving it. Welfare in the limited sense of providing support for the helpless and dependent is a failure in the United States; it is a self-perpetuating, self-defeating bureaucratic monstrosity. It is a system designed to cover up and decon-

---

[59] Sanford Gottleib, "A State Within a State," *Dissent* 18 (October 1971): 493.
[60] *The Causes of World War Three*, p. 140.
[61] See Lawrence Ross, "The Pentagon: Master or Servant?" *Monthly Review* 23 (September 1971): 62–73.

taminate the worst, most glaring aspects of corporate capitalist society, while assuring a negative example and warning to those who are working of what will be their fate should they stop. It is a strategy for deradicalization of the working class, and a tool for manipulating the labor force, and is so used with disregard for any consequent human suffering and misery. "The 'Welfare State,'" writes Mills, "attempts to manage class chances without modifying basic class structure." [62] As Gouldner points out, the welfare state is the managing of the useless—it functions to take care of the uselessness produced in the private sector. Moreover: "It is the nature of the Welfare State to be a counterpuncher, acting only after and in response to the undeniable emergence of a 'problem.'" [63]

Ulmer defines the welfare state in the following terms: "In a welfare state it is assumed that a democratically elected government, *together* with a business system dominated by private enterprise, can and should work *in consonance* to achieve certain economic objectives." [64] This definition is satisfactory as long as we recognize that not only is the business system dominated by private enterprise but the "democratically" elected government is so dominated as well, and that the consonance that is attained between them is due to the nature of certain economic objectives, i.e., the perpetuation of the wealth and power of the ruling propertied rich.

Historical scholarship has documented the leading role taken by the forward-looking component of the propertied classes in shaping the outlines and strategy of the American welfare state. [65] The deradicalization and placation of the working class has been welfare's cardinal achievement, beyond succeeding in holding the system together as such. More recently, the salience of welfare spending for aggregate demand and corporate profits has occupied a more prominent role, and, with the threat of popular revolt against excessive militarization, welfare spending is the logical alternative in expanding the socialization of cost and the privatization of profit—though the welfare route is replete with a variety of political dangers which militarization avoids. Now that the propertied rich have left the society in extensive squalor and disarray, it should be expected they will capitalize on its "reconstruction." Barber has pointed out, along with numerous others, that "social problem solving will be one

---

[62] C. Wright Mills, *White Collar* (New York: Oxford University Press, 1951), p. 299.

[63] Alvin Gouldner, *The Coming Crises in Western Sociology* (New York: Basic Books, 1970), pp. 77, 80.

[64] Melville J. Ulmer, *The Welfare State* (Boston: Houghton-Mifflin, 1969), p. 3.

[65] See Gabriel Kolko, *The Triumph of Conservatism* (New York: Free Press, 1963); and James Weinstein, *The Corporate Ideal in the Liberal State, 1900–1918* (Boston: Beacon Press, 1968).

of the biggest new industries in the United States. It is the basis for planning by the nation's most technologically hep and most aggressive companies.[66] But as in the pre-Progressive and New Deal eras, there are nineteenth-century capitalists who see their mission as blocking neo-capitalist advance; the reactionaries, however, are likely to lose again, for their wealth, influence, and brain power are no match for the liberal sophisticates. Should the latter lose or alter course—a distinct possibility under sufficient pressure—the social and economic crises of capitalism would be greatly sharpened and intensified.

The larger meaning of the welfare state, beyond that of preventing misery and death from exposure and starvation for the helpless and dependent, is to extend social and economic benefits to everyone as a right of citizenship, and to accomplish these ends in a just, egalitarian, and humane manner. This is the kind of welfare state Michael Harrington has asked socialists to promote and defend.[67] It is the kind of welfare state which the Scandinavian countries have gone a long way toward achieving. The fully developed welfare state in this larger sense—not that of managing uselessness but one designed throughout as a socially responsible and socially administered system of socioeconomic cooperation—must be a working-class state or socialist state, for these collective purposes cannot be promoted or achieved under the domination of finance capital, state capitalism, and imperialism. Only if the forces of production are firmly in the hands of the working class is it possible to utilize society's resources for the pursuit of material security and economic liberation for all on an equal footing.

The social democracies of Europe were initially powered by a working-class ideology, the Scandinavian countries in particular. In these latter nations the working class has fared comparatively well and has been largely spared the destitution, humiliation, and physical neglect endured by the severely alienated sectors of the American working class and industrial reserve army today. A few modest measures, perhaps the most important being a system of social medicine, have made the difference. Yet, as Parkin has pointed out with regard to Great Britain and Scandinavia, "the efforts of Social Democratic governments to undermine the structure of privilege generated by the market and private property have not been impressive." [68] Working-class governments have been deradicalized over the years and, failing to pursue a thoroughly socialist course with regard to property relations, have operated under vast limitations in the area of

---

[66] *The American Corporation,* p. 201.
[67] *Socialism* (New York: Saturday Review Press, 1972), p. 272.
[68] Frank Parkin, *Class Inequality and Political Order* (New York: Frederick A. Praeger, 1971), Chapter 4.

political economy. Gradually, these working-class governments have re-defined themselves as protectors of the national interest, even dropping so much as a working-class rhetoric from their platforms and programs. The result has been aborted socialism, welfare-state capitalism, and the perpetuation of class inequality. This is not to underestimate the differences between the Scandinavian countries and the United States. The socioeconomic differences are large and significant.

Let us return to the nature and extent of welfare in the United States. Welfare in the narrow sense, so-called giveaway programs for the financially impoverished, is very small potatoes in the U.S. economy. Since 1950, public assistance payments as a percentage of both total personal income and average or mean income have declined. There are two major federally funded public assistance programs: Old Age Assistance (OAA) and Aid to Families with Dependent Children (AFDC). In 1960 OAA was the largest, transferring $1.9 billion to elderly persons needing survival funds beyond Social Security, itself a regressively purchased social-insurance program which paid a fabulous $118 a month to the average retired worker in 1970. OAA payments were still at $1.9 billion ten years later in 1970, with some 2 million recipients averaging $78 a month. In other words, a 1970 elderly population counting 4 million more persons than in 1960 were receiving public assistance having about 30 percent less purchasing power. Meanwhile, Social Security benefits were also fighting a losing battle against inflation generated by excessive military spending (perhaps this is one reason why the elderly have consistently shown even greater opposition to the Vietnam War than the youth). Given the total inadequacy of state financial support for the elderly, it is understandable how private pension and retirement programs have succeeded in enrolling those able to participate. The starvation levels of state pensions and assistance intentionally force the working class to funnel surplus into the hands of finance capitalists; the alternative—adequate public pensions—is anathema to the ruling class, for such a system would compete with the corporate insurors.

The other major public assistance program, AFDC, has experienced sharp growth from $1.1 billion in 1960 to $4.9 billion in 1970, and the figure continued to rise through 1972. The program serviced some 9.6 million persons in 1970, including 7 million children, the large majority in father-absent families—a common prerequisite for qualification and thus an incentive to family break-up. One-half of the recipient families are white, and three-fourths are urban. It is a "counterpunching" program which picks up the clutter left by an irrational job market, a sop put into full use since the mid-sixties to "cool off" the central cities. However, nothing should be taken away from the efforts and accomplishments of welfare rights organizations and the pressure they have placed upon the welfare bureaucracy to increase eligible recipients. Like OAA, AFDC varies in payments from state to state; $46 a month goes to Mississippians who are fortunate enough to make the rolls and $292 to New Yorkers. The national average was $187 in 1970. In addition to the blind and permanently disabled on the public assistance rolls, these elderly persons, mothers, and children form nearly all of the welfare recipients.

In addition to Social Security, another social-insurance program worthy of mention, and the only federal program of any relevance for nondependent adults, is federal unemployment insurance. The program is totally inadequate; out of approximately 80 million persons in the labor force—not to mention the millions who do not even begin to qualify— only 53 million were covered in the average month of 1970.[69] What the other 27 million workers have for security is their own business—and it is these who are most likely to face unemployment. The "fortunate" worker who is covered can look forward to an average weekly benefit of $50.31, or 38 percent of his average wages. Of 1.8 million persons who on the average week in 1970 were receiving unemployment compensation (financed by a payroll tax), one-quarter exhausted their benefits before returning to work. After that, these people could fend for themselves no better than the millions of other jobless workers who were never covered in the first place. It is of telling significance that the unemployed are treated so harshly by the ruling class; for as unemployeds these people cannot contribute to the creation of surplus value and are therefore irrelevant to the propertied rich, except as a means of leverage against higher wages among the employed and a back-up force in the event additional labor is needed. Even more telling is the fact that disabled workers, who average 57 years of age and shall never be of *any* direct use to the capitalist class, received an average of only $131 a month in 1970, some 60 percent of that of the potentially active worker.

A final major insurance type program of the contemporary welfare state tied in with the regressive Social Security tax structure, Medicare is a typical state capitalist operation for the socialization of cost and privatization of profit. Even at that, Medicare is not a completely developed state capitalist program, for in 1970 the patients themselves picked up 23 percent of in-patient hospital charges and 27 percent of physician charges (Nixon's economizing will have the elderly picking up a larger percentage). Total physician charges to the elderly were $2.2 billion in 1970 (inflated from $1.7 billion just two years earlier—like defense contractors, the medical profession caught on to the cost-plus nature of state capitalism very

---

[69] *Statistical Abstract of the United States, 1972* (New York: Grosset & Dunlap, 1972), pp. 286–87.

quickly after dropping their massive lobbying campaign against it [70]); thus, the elderly were assessed $500 million in physician charges out-of-pocket.[71] Medicare has proven so successful for the medical-industrial complex that such diverse interests as the American Medical Association and New York Governor Nelson Rockefeller are setting forth some variety of "national health insurance," both programs having in common the socialization of expense and the privatization of control and profit. The insurance companies view it as another method of forced appropriation of surplus value from the working class, while physicians and medical suppliers tend to be positive toward the prospects of greater profits all round.[72]

The medical-industrial complex occupies an important position in corporate capitalism and portends to play an increasingly prominent role in both private and public sectors. Americans devote 7 percent of their gross national product to health, for a total of $67 billion in 1970, $25 billion of this being public expenditures. In 1969, $24 billion was spent for hospital services, $17 billion for physicians' and dentists' services, and almost $7 billion for drugs. Yet, as Barbara and John Ehrenreich remark, "for more and more people, middle-class as well as poor, health care is not a right, and not even a privilege—as the A.M.A. would have it—but a luxury." [73] In their comprehensive study of American health empires, the Ehrenreichs observe that, while hospitals are expensive for a number of nonmedical reasons, among the more important is that "they have become outlets for the greed and ambition of some of the most profitable private businesses and some of the most grasping private businessmen in the

---

[70] The rapid inflation of physicians' fees following passage of Medicare is common knowledge. While thousands of physicians receive over $25,000 a year from Medicare payments, and many over $100,000, most make an effort to remain within the letter of the law. Some don't, as the 1,884 cases of Medicare fraud pending trial or under investigation in late 1972 suggest. One conviction was obtained on a former chief of psychiatry at Philadelphia General Hospital (thirty-nine other doctors have also been convicted) who provided "music therapy" at nursing homes. The doctor, who collected $47,000 in payments over the first six months of 1971, was accompanied by a violinist or other musician and a female assistant to the homes where the music would draw the elderly out of their rooms to listen. Urging the "patients" to clap, the doctor instructed his assistant to go around the room and obtain the Medicare number of each person, then sent in bills for "psychiatric treatment." When caught, the doctor offered the government agent $15,000 a year as director of a "music therapy" corporation which would minister to additional nursing homes. The bribe attempt failed and the doctor was fined $40,000 and placed on probation for five years. (What sentence would a blue-collar worker have been given for stealing at least $47,000 from an insurance company and offering a bribe to a federal agent?) See Rose Dewold, "Medicare: The Easy Swindle," *The Nation,* November 6, 1972, pp. 429–31.

[71] Ibid., p. 281.

[72] See John Ehrenreich and Oliver Fein, "National Health Insurance: The Great Leap Sideways," *Social Policy* 1 (January–February 1971): 5–9.

[73] *The American Health Empire: Power, Profits, and Politics* (New York: Vintage Books, 1971), p. 136.

United States—drug and hospital supply companies, physicians, and hospital administrators   From an economic point of view, hospitals are on their way to being little more than conduits, places where consumer and taxpayer money is funneled into private profits." [74]

Look at the 1971 returns on total equity of health-care industries, among the highest in the corporate world: American Home Products, 33 percent; G. D. Searle, 30 percent; Merck, 27 percent; Smith, Kline & French, 23 percent; Sterling Drug, 22 percent; Eli Lilly, 20 percent; Johnson & Johnson, 19 percent; Pfizer, 18 percent; Miles Laboratories, 19 percent; Squibb, 18 percent; and Upjohn, 13 percent.[75] These firms alone netted $800 million in profits in 1971.[76] We have pointed previously to the high incomes of physicians. The insurance companies, as third-party participants, are also prospering. Mail-order health insurance companies, such as the Combined Insurance Group of major Nixon-campaign donor W. Clement Stone, are prospering by paying out a mere 40 cents in benefits out of each dollar collected (1970). The big sales pitch of these operations, boosted by such personalities as Art Linkletter, is that they pay claims up to $50,000; in fact, they average only $150.[77] More and more people are aware of these facts, and growing numbers of people are disconcerted-to-angry about the state of medical delivery. Despite large government expenditures of taxpayers' money on "health," the average man gets little or nothing in return; 25 million persons have no health insurance of any kind, and those that do never find out really what it covers until they get sick and have to pay the balance. By now it is commonplace to point out the highly questionable quality of the health care received, a point easily backed up by data.[78] "Health," write the Ehrenreichs, "is no more a priority of the American health industry than safe, cheap, efficient, pollution-free transportation is a priority of the American automobile industry." [79]

For all the money spent, Americans are not a particularly healthy population. Six out of ten people have at least one chronic health condition. Males have an acute incidence of illness at the rate of 144 per 1,000 population, and chronic incidence at the rate of 119; females count 182 and 149, respectively. Fifteen days per person are lost to restricting illnesses yearly. One-quarter of the population requires yearly medical attention or restricted activity due to bodily injuries. On the average, an American

---

[74] Ibid., p. 146.
[75] *Forbes,* January 1, 1972.
[76] *Forbes,* May 15, 1972.
[77] Herbert S. Denenberg, "Those Health Insurance Booby Traps," *The Progressive,* September, 1972, pp. 29–33.
[78] See Ehrenreich and Ehrenreich, *The American Health Empire;* and Martin Gross, *The Doctors* (New York: Dell Publishing Company, 1967).
[79] *The American Health Empire,* p. vi.

must call for a physician four times a year, and this varies significantly by social class or income level. Over 150 out of every 1,000 persons is a general hospital in-patient for an average length of stay of ten days. Amid these health requirements, the American people in 1969 had 163 physicians at work for every 100,000 population, up an entire 14 doctors from twenty years previously; they had eight hospital beds available for every 1,000 population, *down* a bed from a decade earlier (and in 1973 Nixon was busy slashing hospital construction funds). This is on the average. For the majority the ratios are worse, in many cases incredibly bad—such as the 1 physician per 100,000 in Brooklyn's Bedford-Stuyvesant area, or the nearly one-half of all black births in Mississippi not occurring in a hospital, or the thousands of rural and small-town locations in which a physician can only be reached by a long-distance telephone call (there is no money or prestige in doctoring rural folk). Despite the volume of propaganda to the contrary, an increasing number of people would agree with the Ehrenreichs that "most people who have set out to look for medical care eventually have to conclude that there *is* no American medical system—at least there is no systematic way in America of getting medical help when you need it, without being financially ruined, humiliated, or injured in the process." [80] Now consider the following:

> In child after child we saw: evidence of vitamin and mineral deficiencies; serious, untreated skin infections and ulcerations; eye and ear diseases; also unattended bone diseases; secondary to poor food intake; the prevalence of bacterial and parasitic disease, as well as severe anemia, with the resulting loss of energy and ability to live a normally active life.[81]

A report from India? Paraguay? Mexico? Nigeria? It could be, but it's not. It's a report of four doctors to the United States Senate in 1967 concerning some of the country's own citizens.

This sort of neglect is the extreme, but not an untypical and rare extreme. And the extremes, including the opposite one of health care unlimited for the rich, tell us much about the situation of the average man, woman, and child. An effective and humane system of health care can never be realized as long as decision-making power, control, and profit incentive remain in private hands for private purposes. The only alternative is a socially owned and operated system. The Scandinavian health systems are socially operated and largely socially owned, though hospital supply and drug needs are purchased at a loss to the taxpayers from largely foreign corporations. A fully owned social system of medicine must include

[80] Ibid., p. 17.

[81] *Hunger and Malnutrition in America,* Hearings before the Subcommittee on Employment, Manpower, and Poverty of the Committee on Labor and Public Welfare, United States Senate, 90th Congress, 1st Session, July 1967, p. 46.

these medical supplies, and Sweden is taking steps in this direction such as the creation of a national drug manufacturer. And contrary to adverse propaganda about "socialist medicine," none of the Ehrenreichs' conclusions or evaluations concerning medical care in the United States could stand up in the Scandinavian context (save where the state is dependent upon private medical suppliers). As to cost, the Swedes like the Americans spend approximately 7 percent of their gross national product on health care; unlike the Americans, the Swedes receive for their tax dollar free and complete medical coverage, in quality and availability second to none.

Adequate health care is the center of any genuine social welfare state, whether it be primarily state capitalist or socialist in structure. It would be difficult or impossible to build a fully socialized system of health care within a state capitalist economy, as the Scandinavians have found out. The health industry is inextricably linked with practically every other major producing and financial sector, not just medical supply as such. Of central importance is banking, whose loans to hospitals constitute a part of the patients' expense and which holds massive investment funds needed for medical development. There are also the utilities, construction and building supply, textile, food, and innumerable other more or less closely related supportive industries which direct or indirectly feed off health needs.

While health care is at the center of a humanistic society, education permeates the entire structure. We shall not enter into a discussion of education here; suffice it to say that in both quantity and quality, there are far-reaching changes which must be effected if we are to claim a genuinely social system of learning and training for life and work. And the ties between medicine and education are also extensive, suggesting, for one thing, that medical education must be opened up to all qualified candidates on a free basis and with long-term, low-interest loans or clear stipends, particularly for those students promising to enter public service upon graduation. There are other crucial areas to which a working-class state must assign high priority—for example, housing. As Engels observed long ago: "The housing shortage from which the workers and part of the petty bourgeoisie suffer in our modern big cities is one of the innumerable *smaller, secondary* evils which result from the present-day capitalist mode of production." [82]

We have one further dimension of ruling-class power and interest to discuss: foreign policy and economic investment. We thus turn next to a discussion of imperialism, a logical extension and an integral part of finance capital as discussed in the previous chapters and of state capitalism as discussed in this one.

---

[82] Frederick Engels, *The Housing Question,* in Karl Marx and Engels, *Selected Works,* vol. 2 (Moscow: Progress Publishers, 1969), p. 305.

eleven _____

IMPERIALISM AS
ADVANCED CAPITALISM

Marxist theory contains within it the prognosis of concentration of production, monopoly, the creation of finance capital, the internationalization of capital, and international conflict among the most powerful capitalist bourgeoisie. (Marx's own commentary on the less developed nations was limited and, of course, was restricted to the colonialist stage of international capitalist development—the era of more blatantly outright plunder and territorial conquest and feuding among capitalist powers for such global dominance.) Only a theory holding immense validity could even dimly presage these developments in the middle of the nineteenth century. Yet worked through to its logical conclusion, Marxist economics prefigures these historical developments. However, it would by necessity have to be left to later Marxist thinkers to fill out the empirical truths generally presaged by or contained within Marxist economics. Lenin was the best known for this effort, and did so from within a personal world of revolution. Not long before the October Revolution of 1917 Lenin completed what many consider his major contribution to Marxist economic thought—*Imperialism: The Highest Stage of Capitalism*.[1] In it he traced through from a Marxist base the significance of monopoly, finance capital, and imperialism —terms having great overlap and common references. To Lenin, monopoly capital was at once imperialistic. It is the ultimate and final outcome of the capitalist mode of production.

_____
[1] V. I. Lenin, *Imperialism: The Highest Stage of Capitalism, Selected Works*, vol. 1 (Moscow: Progress Publishers, 1970), p. 737.

The starting point of Lenin's analysis of imperialism is the point where all Marxist economic thinking must start: the labor theory of value. The working class produces a value (wealth) considerably greater than that which it costs capital to reproduce or to hire labor-power. The result is the accumulation of surplus labor, surplus value, and capital. As has already been discussed, the characteristic crises in capitalism stem from overproduction. Even with the rise of a surplus class, a class that consumes much more than it produces, the crises of overproduction cannot be avoided. For this class, too, is typically exploited in the sense that it saves the capitalist an amount of surplus value greater than it itself is hired for.

Thus, behind the accumulation of capital is a powerful force driving it toward potentially profitable reuse or investment. The force drives it out of the national and into the international economy, first as trade and later as the export of capital per se. Trade is not as such a capitalist economic act, though under capitalism profit through trade is a major underlying motive and can be very succesfully accomplished when the trading partner is no partner at all but a desperate and exploitable victim. The under-developed countries of the Third World are such victims of trade with heavily capitalized nations, having to sell their raw materials and food cheaply and paying dearly for industrial imports.

But the essence of the new imperialism does not lie in this kind of exploitation; rather, it lies in the export of capital from the more advanced capitalist countries to the less developed ones. The international investment of accumulated capital offers the finance capitalist a vast and profitable outlet for the surplus produced by his own working class. The imperialist does not have to rely solely or even in small part on direct trading of goods, for through the export of capital he is able to bring under his own control the very source (both labor and raw material) of the goods he previously had to trade for. His exploitation of surplus value can be much more direct and profitable, even more profitable than with respect to his own working class. Owing to such things as a relatively high subsistence-wage level in the advanced capitalist society compared to the less developed area, and to the high use of machinery compared to labor and the subsequent lower rate of profit in advanced as compared with less developed areas, the return on monopoly capital is significantly higher in the Third World than domestically. Lenin captures the idea well in his own statement:

> As long as capitalism remains what it is, surplus capital will be utilised not for the purpose of raising the standard of living of the masses in a given country, for this would mean a decline in profits for the capitalists, but for the purpose of increasing profits by exporting capital abroad to backward countries. In these backward countries profits are usually high, for capital is scarce, the price of land is relatively low, wages are low, raw materials are cheap.[2]

---

[2] Ibid., p. 716.

Not only does the building and buying up of productive capital around the world have its rationale in higher profits and the avoidance of stagnation in the metropolitan economy, but also at stake is the *control* of the international market. Just as monopoly is the key to the control of domestic exchange-values, so is international monopoly important to the realization of profits on the world level. Not only control of prices, but the control of raw materials as such, and especially the control of *potential* sources of raw materials, figures crucially in the plans of international capitalism. As Lenin points out: "Finance capital is interested not only in the already discovered sources of raw materials but also in potential sources, because present-day technical development is extremely rapid. . . . Hence, the inevitable striving of finance capital to enlarge its spheres of influence and even its actual territory." [3]

In brief, not only had the separate capitalist countries divided themselves along class lines of exploiters and exploited, but capitalism had also divided the world into rich and poor. And much like the capitalist countries themselves, Lenin writes, "the world has become divided into a handful of usurer states and a vast majority of debtor states." The usurer states, while competing with one another wherever possible throughout the world, tend to divide up the world into general spheres of influence so as to lower the intensity of competition for the spoils of less developed areas.

Finally, we might note that Lenin's analysis of imperialism does not seek to reduce it to a single, rigid formula of explanation such as overproduction in the advanced capitalist countries. The foregoing discussion should make clear that there is a complex of economic, political, and ideological factors involved. There are many conditions and details which we cannot enter into here. Nor has Lenin said all that must be said about the new imperialism, not to mention its era of decline. But the line of thought from Marx to Lenin to the present day is both logical and empirical.

THE IMPERIALIST SYSTEM

Imperialism is a system of international exploitation designed to deal with the internal contradictions of developed capitalism, a means of postponing and diffusing the crises of domestic capital. From the perspective of Marxist theory, Paul Sweezy could in 1949 make the ominous and now-validated prediction that "the greatest danger to world peace, and indeed to much that is best in human civilization itself, is that the rulers of America will seek to put off the day of reckoning by embarking on

---

[3] Ibid., p. 733.

a career of unlimited militarism and imperialism." [4] A quarter-century later we are reaping the deadly harvest of this career.

Imperialism is, in both theory and practice, an essential aspect of capitalism. In the United States' capitalist system, imperialsm is so closely enmeshed in the overall economic structure that it would be erroneous to conceive of two separate phenomena called capitalism and imperialism. In Lenin's view, we have imperialism as international finance capitalism, the most advanced and final stage of capitalist development. Imperialism constitutes the extranational perspective of the ruling class, and the implementation of this perspective necessitates state capitalism. The tax resources of the state are employed economically and militarily as a protective shield for ruling-class interests abroad as well as domestically.

Imperialism is international capitalism in all of its economic, political, and social aspects. All of the exploitative relations found to exist between ruling and working classes within the capitalist economy are reenacted on an international scale. It is of utmost importance to recognize that imperialist relations do not obtain between nations as such, but between the ruling class of an advanced capitalist society and the people of an unequal, underdeveloped society, in particular those of Asia, Africa, and Latin America—or Third World peoples. The working class of the advanced capitalist society is structurally a party to imperialist exploitation of the Third World, as are the lesser advanced capitalist states; but this advanced working class is itself the loser in the process—in terms of taxes, prices, jobs, and lives. As Victor Perlo cogently observes: "The decisive fact we must recognize is that imperialism is a system of super-profit and plunder first and foremost of the working people in the home country." [5] It is another facet of the socialization of costs and privatization of profits, a cost to the working class which Perlo calculates to be twice the total profit taken; of that total profit the working class itself receives an insignificant amount compared to that appropriated by finance capital. The ruling class is not concerned that the American people should come out on top within the imperialist system, but only that ruling-class profits and gains should exceed ruling-class deficits and losses. The American people pay the cost of militarization and war, costs which each year exceed the total of all investments abroad; yet both military spending and investments abroad support ruling-class profits and property expansion. The $10 billion foreign aid expenditure is yet another face of imperialist mechanisms, the majority going toward military purposes and most of the rest toward tightening the economic grip on Third World governments,

---

[4] *The Present as History* (New York: Monthly Review Press, 1953), p. 73.

[5] "U.S. Imperialism Today," *Political Affairs* 45 (June 1970): 22. Stated otherwise: "Today the socialized costs of imperialism exceed the private profits" (p. 26).

i.e., toward putting them in our debt and paying off accumulation of interest on such debt. Money is thus taken from the working class and ultimately shifted to finance capital via the route of foreign aid—no more foreign than Wall Street.

The home working class pays also in the form of lost jobs, as imperialists see the opportunity to return a higher rate of surplus value in a backward country without social legislation or an organized labor force. Imperialists can exploit unskilled labor in an absolute manner through long working days for the same low wages; they can exploit labor relatively as well, by introducing machinery without having to pay higher wages from the increased productivity.[6] The home working class further pays the costs of imperialism through inflation rates set in motion by heavy spending for military goods. The working class pays for imperialism by picking up the costs of foreign payments imbalances caused by world policing and financial activity of the ruling class; gold flows outward, other capitalist countries refuse to absorb losses on our behalf, the dollar is devalued, the home working class pays higher prices for imported goods, and the nation's monopolists raise their prices to match imports. As taxpayers, the working class pay indemnities to corporations which have lost property through nationalization.

The list of costs could be extended, but the point has been made. Each military and political act undertaken by the corporate state is not based on strict cost-accounting rules, especially from the standpoint of the working class and taxpayers. These often incredibly expensive acts are carried out to control as much of the globe as possible for international expansion by finance capital; there is, then, an economic reason behind ostensibly uneconomic actions. They are an expression, to borrow a term from Mills, of "imperialist gambling."[7] The aim of the economic and political policies that constitute "imperialist gambling" is to extend the control, power, resources, and profits of the financial oligarchy which dominates U.S. foreign affairs. In foreign policy, the bourgeoisie seeks to control as much as possible of the known and potential sources of raw materials, to maintain open doors to safe and profitable investments, to wield decisive influence over "conquered" countries in the politico-economic sense in order to maximize a favorable investment and profit environment, to cream off local surpluses for investment and ease the problems of exporting home capital and balancing payments, to limit state or national industrial development which would compete with imperialism, to block national reform movements threatening to pass social

---

[6] See Ernest Mandel, *Marxist Economic Theory,* vol. 2 (New York: Monthly Review Press, 1968), pp. 455–58.

[7] C. Wright Mills, *The Causes of World War Three* (New York: Ballantine Books, 1960), p. 74.

legislation and organize labor, and to assure dependence on capitalist nations and development along capitalist lines.[8]

The chief enemy of these aims, and the reason behind the biggest imperialist gambles, is socialism—or whatever the ideology may be called that stands for the nationalization of the development process. Self-determination and independent development, even if it is *not* socialist, cannot to tolerated by the imperialist bourgeoisie. All reform movements are labeled communist (i.e., "evil"). As Eakins points out: "The corporate demand for government spending that avoids redistribution by servicing the external empire has been maintained, justified, and buttressed by the ideology of the anticommunist mission of the cold war." Once the major champion of democracy and self-determination in an era of its own push for autonomy against older colonial powers, the American bourgeoisie, writes Eakins, "now stand exposed as the main opponents of their own articulated principles."[9] In the process, Heilbroner observes, we "have ranged ourselves against nearly every movement that might have led men toward a better life, on the grounds of our opposition to communism."[10] "All revolutionaries," write Baran and Sweezy, "are automatically suspect; no regime is too reactionary to merit all-out United States backing."[11] From John Hay's description of the Spanish-American War as "a splendid little war" to Hubert Humphrey's characterization of Vietnam as a "glorious adventure," the United States has persisted in its aggressive imperialism around the world. Perceiving the essence of foreign aid and military assistance, Senator Frank Church (D., Ida.) stated to his colleagues in 1972 that "a government may torture and terrorize its own population but—from the standpoint of our policy makers—as long as it remains anti-communist, provides 'stability,' generally supports American foreign policy and is hospitable to American investment, it qualifies, for purposes of aid, as a 'free country'." (Church also pointed out that foreign aid is presently designed "to serve private business interests at the expense of the American people," suggesting that one need not be a Marxist economist to decipher the nature of state capitalism.)

Vietnam has proven to be the biggest and most costly imperialist gamble ever taken in the Third World. As David Horowitz has remarked, "While not entirely unique among U.S. actions in the cold war decades,

---

[8] See Fred Block, "Expanding Capitalism: The British and American Cases," *Berkeley Journal of Sociology* 15 (1970): 138–65.

[9] David W. Eakins, "The Modern American Empire: A Review of Its Origin and Ideology," *Socialist Revolution* 1 (September–October 1970): 59–60.

[10] Robert Heilbroner, *Between Capitalism and Socialism* (New York: Vintage Books, 1970), p. 78.

[11] Paul Baran and Paul Sweezy, *Monopoly Capital* (Harmondsworth, England: Pelican Books, 1968), p. 201.

. . . this savage aggression showed more vividly than anything previously the lengths to which Washington was prepared to go to defeat a social revolution that threatened to breach its international system." [12] Or in Arthur MacEwan's words: "What is at stake in Vietnam is not just a geographic area but a set of rules, a system." [13] Heilbroner captures well the intended and actual lessons of Vietnam:

> The ultimate purpose of our intervention in Vietnam was . . . to beat a *revolutionary force,* to demonstrate beyond a doubt that "wars of national liberation" would end in disaster for the revolutionaries. Now, by a supreme irony, we have shown just the opposite. The prospect, in other words, is one of worldwide upheaval in which, retrospectively, the Vietnam war will have been only the first successful campaign.[14]

But let us hear the imperialists' side of the story on Vietnam, as told by a vice-president of Chase Manhattan Bank in charge of the Far Eastern area:

> In the past, foreign investors have been somewhat wary of the over-all political prospect for the [Southeast Asia] region. I must say, though, that the U.S. actions in Vietnam . . . —which have demonstrated that the U.S. will continue to give effective protection to the free nations of the region—have considerably reassured both Asian and Western investors.[15]

Or from another of the vice-presidents of one of the big New York banks, First National City: "We believe we're going to win this war. . . . Afterwards, you'll have a major job of reconstruction on your hands. That will take financing, and financing means banks." [16] Needless to say, the "free nations" of the region will be unreservedly thrilled to have finance capitalists swarming around. And by "we" winning the war, the latter writer means the cannon fodder out in the field, not himself, and by "you" doing the financing he means the taxpayers, not the finance capitalists of the American oligarchy—who are only on hand to collect

---

12 *Imperialism and Revolution* (London: Penguin Press, 1969). Reprinted in David Horowitz, ed., *Radical Sociology* (San Francisco: Canfield Press, 1971), p. 286.

13 "Capitalist Expansion, Ideology, and Intervention," in Richard C. Edwards et al., eds., *The Capitalist System* (Englewood Cliffs, N.J.: Prentice-Hall, 1972), p. 417.

14 *Between Capitalism and Socialism,* pp. 57–59.

15 Cited in Claude Julien, *America's Empire* (New York: Pantheon Books, 1971), p. 226.

16 Ibid., p. 33. See Nicholas P. Philip, "Southeast Asia: Investment and Development," *Columbia Journal of Business* 6 (November–December 1970): 63–68. Heavy emphasis is placed in this article on "a political climate acceptable to investors" and "an acceptable political accommodation" as a prerequisite for domination of the Southeast Asian market in coming decades.

the interest and profit. How long can the imperialist system stand up, asks Baran, in the face of the "staggering contrast between the terrifying human and material costs of imperialism and its yields—lavish profits to a handful of large-scale businesses"? [17]

The billions poured into Third World reactionary forces are often not enough in themselves to quell revolutionary threats and assure the maintenance of the status quo. Vietnam is only one of many American military and CIA interventions in underdeveloped nations. Since 1945 the list is long; among the several countries included are Greece, Korea, Guatemala, Lebanon, Cuba, Iraq, Iran, Syria, Peru, Indonesia, and the Dominican Republic. Before 1940 U.S. troops intervened in China twelve times! Interventions in Latin America are too numerous to recount in full here. But even since 1962, U.S. "mobile training teams" of the Special Forces have intervened in every Latin American country except Cuba, Haiti, and Mexico.[18] Not only through military and secret agencies does the United States intervene in Latin America and elsewhere, but as the aborted political intelligence-oriented Project Camelot suggests, social science is drawn into service as well. Nor is the United States the sole perpetrator of armed intervention in the Third World; Great Britain, France, Holland, and Portugal have also been involved in counterrevolutionary warfare in the Third World since 1945. These latter four nations plus South Africa stood by themselves against ninety-nine other United Nations members who in 1972 voted to recognize the legitimacy of anti-colonial armed struggles. Beyond military intervention, economic warfare is another option the United States has chosen to use, against Cuba in full and against Chile in part. If ITT were in complete charge, Chile probably would be victimized by full-scale economic sabotage by the United States.[19] Indeed, the Nixon administration permitted significant economic maneuvering by U.S. financial interests against the elected Marxist President Salvador Allende to prevent him from assuming power. Only fear of strong popular support for Allende has held the forces of military reaction at bay in Chile.

A further word is in order regarding the U.S. intervention in the Dominican Republic, since it typifies the post-Cuban Revolution U.S. military strategy in Latin America. The magnitude of American action in the Dominican Republic should not be lost in the time passed since 1965; a truly massive invasion force of some forty to fifty thousand personnel were involved, and the treachery and firepower employed against the

---

[17] Paul A. Baran, *The Political Economy of Growth* (New York: Monthly Review Press, 1968, 1957), p. 118.

[18] Julien, *America's Empire,* pp. 284–85.

[19] See Dale L. Johnson, John Pollock, and Jane Sweeney, "ITT and the CIA: The Making of a Foreign Policy," *The Progressive,* May, 1972, pp. 15–17.

rebels and Santo Domingo's rebellious sections were large-scale. Three to four thousand Dominican lives were lost in the brief violence. The Dominican Republic represented a situation where a moderate reformist, constitutionally elected president faced a U.S.-backed right-wing military force dedicated to preserving the political and economic status quo for the benefit of U.S. investors and the national bourgeoisie, whom James Petras defines as export-importers, commercial agrobusinessmen, and pirate capitalists in the military caste.[20] Those fighting to preserve the legally elected government consisted largely of the poor, unemployed, workers, students, and a small faction of the regular army. The conflict was quickly constricted to Santo Domingo as the reactionaries succeeded in isolating nationalist activity and communications. Had President Juan Bosch openly and determinedly armed the working class, and surely had not the U.S. military invaded the island, the military rightists would have been defeated and limited reforms undertaken.

As it stands today the Dominican Republic is a U.S.-advised police state concentrating on anti–working-class and antireform political measures, with one-third of the urban labor force unemployed, over three-fifths of the population illiterate, and the face of poverty everywhere. But never mind such sentimental aspects of Dominican life, for "in the next five years," recently stated an eager American businessman to Petras, "this will be the best country in Latin America to make a fortune in." [21] It was for this gentleman and others like him that the United States raised its flag of counterrevolution over the Caribbean, sacrificed lives, and spent the taxpayers' money. There will be no more Cubas, where the masses are employed in national construction, educated for modern political and economic life, hospitalized and treated for illness and disease, and fed, housed, and entertained as well as collective resources will allow—at least not if the U.S. ruling class has anything to say about it. And throughout most of Latin America, they are proving convincingly that they have very much to say.

Whether imperialism assumes the form of unmitigated oppression and colonialism, trade exploitation, or economic ownership, it is an intractable ingredient of advanced capitalism. Finance capital *needs* the imperialist avenue to sustain its inherent driving forces of expansion and growth, power, and wealth; it cannot survive confined to its own soil, for its own soil and own people cannot deliver the expansion and growth which comprise its lifeblood, despite all of the counteracting strategies

20 *Politics and Social Structure in Latin America* (New York: Monthly Review Press, 1970), p. 289.
21 Ibid., p. 280.

corporate capital has pursued on the domestic front. In Pierre Jalee's words: "This is the key to the problem: imperialism does not pillage the Third World diabolically or for fun, but because of *vital necessity,* because it could not survive otherwise." [22] Or from Harry Magdoff: "Imperialism is not a matter of choice for a capitalist society; it is the way of life of such a society." [23]

Who directs U.S. affairs and intervention abroad? "If there is one issue-area truly and solely the domain of the power elite," writes Domhoff, "it is foreign policy." [24] Lenin observed that imperialism expands state power at the expense of elected legislative bodies. The president acts as a virtual dictator in pursuing the foreign policy interests of the ruling class. To the extent that the national legislature dissents, it is increasingly helpless to do anything about the situation except allow legislators to ask more questions and express their personal opinions. The big foreign investors, the multinational corporations, make foreign policy, and they see to it that their policy is carried out either directly or by proxy.

The interlacing of government decision-making personnel with the multinational corporations is an established fact. [25] Typical and classic is the case of chief cold warrior John Foster Dulles, influential secretary of state under Eisenhower, who had been a stockholder, director, and lawyer for Latin America plantation operator United Fruit. Under Dulles the CIA engineered the overthrow of reformist, constitutionally elected Guatemalan President Arbenz after he had dared to do such "unfriendly" things as nationalize 234,000 acres of United Fruit property. [26] Former CIA director John McCone is on the board of directors of ITT and Standard Oil of New Jersey. The Rockefeller financial interests are second to none as exploiters of Latin America, and are extremely instrumental in shaping American foreign policy. Not the least of their instruments include Rockefeller Foundation international research grants and Chase Manhattan Bank president David Rockefeller's chairmanship of the policy-shaping Council on Foreign Relations, under whose auspices such study groups as spawned Henry Kissinger are conducted. Ultimately, Kissinger received the chance to put his theories into action, as did Walt Rostow, whose research for the bourgeois saga *Stages of Economic Growth* (an ironic title for a book

---

[22] *The Third World in World Economy* (New York: Monthly Review Press, 1969), p. 131.

[23] *The Age of Imperialism* (New York: Monthly Review Press, 1969), p. 26.

[24] G. William Domhoff, *The Higher Circles* (New York: Vintage Books, 1971), pp. 111–12.

[25] See Gabriel Kolko, *The Roots of American Foreign Policy* (Boston: Beacon Press, 1969), pp. 17–19; Domhoff, *The Higher Circles,* Chapter 5.

[26] Michael Tanzer, *The Sick Society* (New York: Holt, Rinehart, & Winston, 1971), Chapter 3.

written by an advisor on the destruction of Vietnam) was funded by the Carnegie Foundation.[27]

Certainly there are disagreements within the ruling class as to how imperialism should be practiced with maximum effect, just as there are disputes regarding the operation of corporation capitalism at home. There are also lesser corporations that suffer as a result of imperialist activities, or at least lose as a result of the financial disturbances which follow in the wake of rising taxes, inflation, and reduction in effective consumer spending for their products. But lesser corporations do not make policy. The largest corporations make it, and the largest corporations are very much multinational operations. Disagreements and disputes among the giants regard means and the division of spoils, never the overall aims of what is to be accomplished abroad. The same fact holds true with respect to conflicts of interests between major imperial powers, though these international capitalist clashes tend to be more clear-cut than the interlaced conflict of American financial groups. In days past, these international differences led to wars; this is an unlikely development in the future given the mutually confronted threat of socialist powers and national revolutionary movements in the Third World. There will be jockeying for spheres of influence, favorable terms of trade, and currency valuations— all to the advantage of imperialists and to the disadvantage of the imperialized.

FOREIGN INVESTMENTS AND PROFITS

The magnitude of the foreign orientation of the U.S. economy is documented by the fact that foreign markets absorb the equivalent of two-fifths of U.S. production of moveable goods (agricultural, manufacturing, and mineral), "foreign markets" including domestic exports and output of U.S.-owned foreign firms.[28] Of the some $200 billion in deliveries of U.S. products to foreign markets, only one-sixth of these come from U.S. exports; the rest is made and sold abroad by foreign workers employed by American-owned subsidiaries.[29] We have already alluded to some of the reasons for the preference for such foreign production i.e., lower wages, tax privileges, avoidance of tariffs, declining dollar values, improvement for balance-of-payments problems, lower transport costs, etc. over domestic production and export. The end result is normally higher

---

[27] Domhoff, *The Higher Circles,* pp. 114–27.
[28] Jalee, *The Third World in World Economy,* p. 132.
[29] Richard J. Barber, *The American Corporation* (New York: E. P. Dutton & Company, 1970), p. 8.

profits, which have averaged better than 15 percent but reach 20 percent
in oil (oil accounts for over 40 percent of foreign investment but at least
60 percent of profits).

Long-term direct private investments abroad have increased in value
from $12 billion in 1950 to $32 billion in 1960 and to over $71 billion
in 1970.[30] The private total, including all types of portfolio investments,
exceeded $110 billion in 1970, between five and six times that of 1950.
Of the long-term direct investments, nearly 30 percent is located in Third
World countries, half of this being in Latin America. Direct foreign
investments yield profits amounting to approximately one-fifth of all
after-tax profits of nonfinancial corporations. Adding together U.S. trade
profits and military profits used to "defend U.S. interests," Sherman points
out that up to 30 percent of all corporate profits derive from foreign
sources.[31] Investment and profit are highly concentrated within a few
large firms, basically the same firms that dominate the domestic economy.
Fewer than fifty multinational corporations account for the large majority
of U.S. foreign assets, and in Western Europe only twenty firms account
for two-thirds of direct investment.[32] Esso, General Motors, and Ford
have predominated, having as much as 40 percent of the total in West
Germany, France, and Great Britain. As to profits, a mere 1 percent
of foreign operations take 60 percent of the earnings.[33] The United States
alone held three-fifths of all foreign-invested capital in 1960, and more
importantly, the majority of this was direct ownership of branches and
subsidiaries rather than stocks and bonds of the portfolio type—the usual
form of foreigners' holdings in the U.S. economy.

Oil, transport equipment, steel, electrical equipment, chemicals, and
aluminum are among the dominant producers with major foreign interests.
Many firms depend from 20 to 90 percent upon foreign-based, export,
and military sales for markets, and from 80 to 100 percent for clear
profits. The foreign sales, assets, and earnings of the top twenty-five
corporations comprise almost one-third of their total operations. ITT,
operating in sixty countries with more than $3 billion in foreign assets,
had 47 percent of assets and sales abroad in 1971, and 59 percent of its
profits flowed from foreign operations.[34] In banking, foreign assets have
soared from $1.5 billion in 1959 to $7.2 billion in 1965 to $30 billion

---

[30] *Statistical Abstract of the United States, 1972* (New York: Grosset & Dunlap, 1972), p. 754.

[31] Howard Sherman, *Radical Political Economy* (New York: Basic Books,
1972), p. 169.

[32] Magdoff, *The Age of Imperialism*, p. 62.

[33] Howard J. Sherman, "Concentration of Foreign Investment," in Maurice
Zeitlin, ed., *American Society, Inc.* (Chicago: Markham Publishing Company, 1970),
p. 42.

[34] Johnson et al., "ITT and the CIA," p. 15.

in 1970. These assets are also highly concentrated within a few giants; First National City, Chase Manhatten, and Bank of America are top rankers, accounting for 70 percent of foreign deposits, while nine New York banks hold three-fourths of the $30 billion in foreign banking assets. Bank of America's foreign profit flow amounted to 20 percent of its 1969 total profits.[35] By any criteria, finance capital in the United States has a very prominent foreign orientation.

The greatest exploitation conducted by U.S. finance capital lies in the Third World, though the exploitation of developed countries such as Canada is no less real. Underdeveloped areas account for less than 30 percent of long-term direct private investment but for *two-thirds* of the net income derived from such investment.[36] In developed countries, the repatriated profit has averaged only one-third of the rate for the Third World. Latin America and the Middle East returned net income considerably greater than Europe and Canada combined, despite the fact that U.S. assets in Europe and Canada came to almost four times that for these two Third World regions.[37] American imperialism takes three dollars out of the Third World for every one dollar invested; Canada also comes out as a relatively serious loser, though Europe balances out if all private investments are counted. (Europeans are extensive short-term and portfolio investors and speculators in the U.S. corporate economy, which returns to them interest, dividends, and capital gains that help partially to balance out the direct corporate profits taken by U.S. multinational firms from Europe.) Minerals and petroleum account for the bulk of profits taken from the Third World, whereas manufacturing far outweighs everything else as a profit producer for U.S. firms in other advanced capitalist countries. On a per capita basis of exploitation, oil from Venezuela, Iran, Iraq, and Saudi Arabia has easily returned the highest yields on equity. On the basis of foreign control of the economy, Canada now finds approximately 60 percent of its corporate capital in the hands of American imperialists (Canada is itself an active Third World capital investor, thus being on both ends of exploitation), greater even than Mexico's 55 percent.

The economic battle for Europe has only begun, but the size and volume of U.S. profits, financial resources, state research-and-development subsidies, and operations puts smaller European firms at a disadvantage. The latter are beginning to redress the balance of power

[35] Rick Wolff, "The Foreign Expansion of U.S. Banks," *Monthly Review* 23 (May 1971): 29.

[36] See Thomas E. Weisskopf, "United States Foreign Private Investment: An Empirical Survey," in Edwards et al., *The Capitalist System*, pp. 426–35.

[37] *Statistical Abstract of the United States, 1972*, p. 755.

through inter-European mergers, though this process has just begun. American corporate *growth* in Europe is illustrated by the leap from fifty companies operating in Switzerland prior to World War II to 640 in 1966, and the *size* of industry investment by the fact that foreign U.S. chemical investment was alone greater than all British and German investments in this field in 1965. However, financing is largely European, for from 1962 to 1966 U.S. branches invested $2.2 billion through local self-financing compared to $5.5 billion depreciation allowances and $9 billion from European capital market banks. Like Third Worlders, the Europeans tend to be paying the bill for their own exploitation. Multinational European firms can be expected to fight current trends, but this raises problems for the national working classes, since each may be played off against the other by a firm's national branches. The only answer to this, Mandel argues, is the formation of international unions to counter international capital.[38]

But if any area of the world were to be singled out as the chief victim of U.S. imperialism, it would have to be Latin America. As Boorstein has remarked:

> For the United States, Latin America is a gigantic plantation, the most valuable part of its world empire. Latin America is by far the biggest supplier to the U.S. of tropical agricultural products. Together with Canada, it supplies most of the U.S. mineral–raw material imports. Nowhere in the world is U.S. penetration and domination as great as in Latin America.[39]

Every year U.S.-controlled enterprises in Latin America deliver well over $1 billion in earnings, most of which assumes the form of repatriated profits.[40] The relationship is largely one way; from 1953 to 1968 U.S. mining and smelting operations in Chile (90 percent copper) earned well over $1 billion, whereas new investments and reinvestment of profits totaled only $71 million.[41] Should it come as a surprise that Chile elected a Marxist president intent on nationalizing the copper industry?

The Third World weighs heavily in the imperialist nations' raw materials needs, especially the United States as the world's leading user. Leading Latin American investor Nelson Rockefeller asserted in 1951 that "with critical shortages developing rapidly, a quickened and enlarged

---

[38] See Ernest Mandel, *Europe vs. America: Contradictions of Imperialism* (New York: Monthly Review Press, 1970).

[39] Edward Boorstein, *The Economic Transformation of Cuba* (New York: Monthly Review Press, 1968), pp. 234–35.

[40] *Statistical Abstract of the United States, 1972*, p. 754.

[41] Johnson et al., "ITT and the CIA," p. 16.

production of materials in the underdeveloped countries is of major importance." [42] In metal after metal, the U.S. shifts an increasingly greater dependence on imports. Not only such metals as bauxite, nickel, manganese, chromium, tin, zinc, and cobalt are in major part or totally import-dependent, but iron ore, copper, lead, and oil are progressively enlarging in the proportion being imported.[43] Especially in military production is the United States dependent upon foreign supplies; for over half of the sixty-two strategic industrial materials listed by the Department of Defense, imports account for 80–100 percent, and for five-sixths they account for at least 40 percent.[44] Three-fourths of these important materials come from the Third World. Many foods and fibers of importance must also be largely or entirely supplied by Third World economies. Whatever the product—oil, mineral, agricultural—the Third World in its underdevelopment is the exporter of raw materials and semifinished products and the importer of manufactured goods; it produces bauxite but must import aluminum, it produces iron ore but little steel, crude oil but few refined-oil products, and so on. The Third World is the unskilled component of the international capitalist division of labor, creating much surplus value but appropriating very little, selling cheap and buying dear. But it is not an international division of labor and trade per se which perpetuates underdevelopment, for the division *could* be applied so as to increase productivity and development; the problem today is that one partner specializes in poverty and the other in profit making.

Corporate capitalism thus needs the world as a resource and a market. It seeks to expand into new and less competitive markets having cheaper labor rather than enlarge the domestic market with lower prices and higher wages. Of great importance is the control of *potential* resource areas—as, for example, oil reserves in the western Pacific and Southeast Asian shorelines. David Rockefeller estimated in May 1970 that $35 billion would be spent in this area by American oil firms (with Rockefeller interests at the center, no doubt) over the next dozen years.[45] Petroleum investments in the Third World are likely to reach three-fourths of all U.S. investments there should this prediction come true. Oil monopolists, like others, must strive to gain control of known and potential reserve resources in order to protect their monopoly prices and profits. An extra 5 percent world supply of oil outside monopoly control could drive down prices by a much greater proportion.

---

[42] Cited in Baran, *The Political Economy of Growth,* p. 192.

[43] Jalee, *The Third World in World Economy,* pp. 41–47; Julien, *America's Empire,* p. 229.

[44] Tanzer, *The Sick Society,* p. 72.

[45] See Barry Weisberg, "South East Asia: Offshore Oil Boom," *The Nation,* March 8, 1971, pp. 294–95.

This brief review of the data unmistakably confirms the dependence of the dominant financial groups not simply upon equal terms of trade but upon imperialist domination and exploitation of the world's resources and markets in order to sustain acceptable levels of expansion and profit. Not all corporations, but only a small fraction are so dependent, though many of the nonforeign enterprises are indirectly involved through their links with multinationals. The point is, however, that the largest and most powerful businesses are imperialist, and it is the propertied rich behind these firms who are the prevailing influences over the domestic economy and the virtual dictators of foreign policy. Who else has so compelling a reason to intervene permanently on the world stage and in the conduct of U.S. foreign policy? And does the ruling class so intervene for the well-being of their own working class? Clearly not, for we have already added up some of the costs of imperialism the latter must pay. And it is fully erroneous to contend, as many do, that international capitalism accrues to the benefit of an underdeveloped country.

twelve ———————————————————————

SOCIAL CLASS
AND
SOCIAL CHANGE

In this chapter our task is to delve into the prospects for radical change in the existing class system and to assess the actual and potential class forces working toward such change. Marxist theory views the urban working class as the driving force in the radical reconstruction of bourgeois society. Without in any way being "Dead Marxists" or "Sophisticated Marxists," we may reassert in the 1970s that the urban proletariat, in both its advanced technological and traditional components (new and old working classes), remains the central force in the socialist revolution. Working-class radicalism is at present more visible and marked in countries such as France, Italy, and England than in the United States, Canada, and West Germany, but there is no absence of militance even in these latter countries. In France and Italy working-class radicalism is rooted in socialist principles and assumptions; the same might be said but to a lesser degree for Great Britain and the Scandinavian countries. In the United States, earlier conflict generated within the proletariat frequently had a socialist underpinning, but after 1920 the larger labor movement ceased to be radical.[1] Even the Great Depression could not restore socialism as a vital issue, though the working class participated fully in the first major reform political movements which laid the foundations of the existing welfare state. Today that same welfare state is rapidly reaching its outer

———————

[1] For a history of the U.S. Socialist party see David A. Shannon, *The Socialist Party in America* (Chicago: Quadrangle Books, 1967).

limits of operation, and again the working class must not only become involved but lead the way to postwelfare socialism if it is to overcome the many existing and potential traps of the existing order.

Logically enough, there tend to be three broad and mutually exclusive views on working-class radicalism: (1) the working class is no longer exploited and is neither radical now nor likely ever to become so; (2) the working class continues to be exploited but has so far acquiesced to the status quo; and (3) an exploited working class is growing increasingly radical and is likely to become more so in the future.

Let us examine the first view, which is, of course, a full rejection of Marxism. The chief assumption here is that the capitalist system no longer exploits labor and has made life comfortable or even affluent for the vast majority.[2] Take it from Zweig: "The idea of the working class as an oppressed or an exploited class . . . is fading from [the worker's] mind and is more and more replaced by the idea of the working class as a class well established and well-to-do in its own right." Zweig goes on to argue that "it took the employer a long time to imbue the worker with his own values and to turn him into a full and willing partner in the acquisitive society, but he has finally succeeded." [3] Daniel Bell contends that the labor problem has become "encapsulated" within a specifically economic context and is related to "the sociology and culture of the society, and less so [to] the polity." [4] Hacker writes that "the contemporary working class, no longer exploited and no longer at a subsistence level, has been a grave disappointment to socialists and radicals," [5] i.e., there are few or no socialists or radicals in the contemporary working class. The gist of what these writers are saying is that the worker in capitalist society is individualist rather than collectivist, privatized and home-centered rather than class-oriented and socially minded, and thus basically satisfied rather than discontented and desirous of change. From these arguments it would follow, then, that G. Rose is correct in arguing that "while some conflict undoubtedly exists between strata, it is diffuse, and bears no relation to the Marxist analysis of class conflict." [6] Two such sociologists entitle their research article "Class Conflict: Forget It." [7]

---

2 For example, John Goldthorpe et al., *The Affluent Worker in the Class Structure* (Cambridge: Cambridge University Press, 1969).

3 Ferdynand Zweig, *The Worker in an Affluent Society* (London: Heinemann, 1961), pp. 209–11.

4 "Labor in the Post-Industrial Society," *Dissent*, Winter 1972, p. 189.

5 Andrew Hacker, Introduction to *Towards Socialism*, edited by Jerry Anderson and Robin Blackburn (Ithaca, N.Y.: Cornell University Press, 1966), p. ix.

6 Gordon Rose, *The Working Class* (London: Longmans, Green and Company, 1968), p. 8.

7 Richard T. Morris and Vincent Jeffries, "Class Conflict: Forget It," *Sociology and Social Research* 54 (April 1970): 306–20.

Secondly, we may take note of the co-opted view of the working class, which holds that, even though the proletariat has been ingratiated to the capitalist system, exploitation of labor and class oppression is as much if not more a part of capitalism as before. The exponents of this view tend to be Marxists, though not all Marxists hold to this view.[8] Nicolaus, for example, has written that "the most industrially advanced capitalist nations typically have the most quiescent, noninsurrectionary proletariats—witness the United States."[9] (After the 1968 demonstration of working-class radical activism in France, Nicolaus amended this stance by noting that the working class is "alive and kicking" and that "he who writes off the working class, writes off."[10]) Nicolaus attributes the nonradicalism of the working class to the step-by-step improvement and the continual promises of further improvement in their material position. In a similar vein, Kolko sees the United States as a class society with measurable oppression, "but also without decisive class conflict at this time"—an oppressive class society "with the consensual support or apathetic toleration of the dispossessed classes."[11] "At no time in American history in this century," writes Kolko elsewhere, have "the labor movement or the dispossessed translated their struggles for specific demands into a larger demand for fundamental change."[12] Finally, from Aronson we have the contention that "for a long time it has been all too obvious that the key sectors of the American working class are integrated into the capitalist system. This is a fact: proletarian class-consciousness does not exist in the United States."[13] Herbert Marcuse and C. Wright Mills are other Marxist-oriented scholars who follow the integration thesis, though Mills once embraced the idea of an alliance of class forces which included radical labor.[14] In a recent statement, Marcuse, too, has suggested that blue-collar labor may be one element in the revolutionary equation.[15] In some instances, as with

---

[8] Quite mistaken, then, is Martin Nicolaus's assertion that "the body of Marxist thought has implicitly or explicitly given up on the industrial working class as an agency of socialist revolution." "The Crisis of Late Capitalism," in George Fischer, ed., *The Revival of American Socialism* (New York: Oxford University Press, 1971), p. 5.

[9] Nicolaus, "Proletariat and Middle Class in Marx," *Studies on the Left* 7 (January–February 1967): p. 29.

[10] "The Crisis of Late Capitalism," p. 20.

[11] *The Roots of American Foreign Policy* (Boston: Beacon Press, 1969), p. 11.

[12] "The Decline of American Radicalism," *Studies on the Left* 6 (September–October 1966): 18.

[13] Ronald Aronson, *Studies on the Left* 6 (September–October 1966): 52.

[14] See Ralph Miliband, "Mills and Politics," in I. L. Horowitz, ed., *The New Sociology* (New York: Oxford University Press, 1965), pp. 76–87.

[15] "The Movement in a New Era of Repression: An Assessment," *Berkeley Journal of Sociology* 16 (1971–72): 1–14.

Mills, those leftists who can discern no radical ideological spark within the blue-collar working class see the emerging agent of change in the intelligentsia and professional class—the service sector of the new working class, in our own class terminology. We shall return to a discussion of this stratum in a subsequent section.

The position that the working class is exploited but nonrevolutionary and nonradical is Veblenist; it is the "full dinnerpail" idea so pointedly phrased by Veblen in *The Engineers and the Price System,* though Veblen had primarily in mind the new working class of the technically trained production sector. It is also Veblenist in not closing the door to a change in working-class tone, in adding "at present," "to date," or as Veblen put it, "just yet." This is an interpretation difficult to refute, and certainly impossible to reject out of hand—something which cannot be said regarding the end-of-exploitation, happy-worker thesis. Implicit or explicit in this second view is that the working class has not been genuinely absorbed into the affluent society, as the first view posits, but has been manipulated and propagandized by the ruling class and the ruling ideas—i.e., the proletariat has been unable to escape the false consciousness of the bourgeois period. Indeed, this is an interpretation which fails to identify any real, serious oppositional efforts and tendencies within the working class.

At this point we may pick up the third view—the position which envisages an increasingly aware, informed, and radicalized working class. The position may be Marxist or populist, but it tends to include the idea that, although radicalization has indeed failed to materialize on schedule because of unforeseen developments within capitalism which mitigated the full impact of economic cycles, significant pressures are building up within the system which involve not only employment and wages but larger social demands and contradictions as well. It is precisely these social contradictions and needs, in addition to the work-specific problems of alienation and exploitation, which are, in this view, generating contemporary working-class radicalism. An important ingredient in this new radicalism is the rising level of education and skill within the working class, particularly the new working class. We have previously discussed the emphasis placed by such writers as André Gorz (and Veblen much earlier) on the contradiction between worker knowledge and ability and worker routinization and simple repetition, between rational control and irrational obedience, and between a sense of social purpose and blind labor for private accumulation. Gorz, Harrington, Mandel, and others point to the increasing awareness of the waste and irrationality in capitalism and to the growing recognition that the market is unable to deal with social demands in the areas of education, health, housing, transportation, environment and recreation, urban planning, and, above all, with the twin phenomena of poverty and flagrant inequality throughout the system.[16] These Marxists and socialists are saying that the ruling ideas are crumbling, that bourgeois rationalizations are falling apart, and that capitalist economics are totally inadequate in dealing with the structural problems of advanced industrial society.

Special attention has been drawn to the younger workers' high potential for radical change. Edelman notes that "there is a new mood of militancy, anger, and readiness to struggle among many of today's young workers. . . . Significantly, there is a new interest in and openness to advanced political ideas, to Marxist-Leninist concepts, among many young workers." [17] Widick observes, as have a number of executives themselves, that younger workers are less concerned about losing their jobs, less willing to put up with "dirty" and uncomfortable work, less likely to accept an unvarying pace on moving lines, and less willing to conform to arbitrary rules or defer to higher authority than their elders.[18] In Widick's words: "Observe the picket lines of teachers, policemen, other municipal workers, auto workers, electrical employees, truck drivers, anywhere in the country and the new impression is the young brashness. The specter of unemployment haunts older workers; many of the young don't give a damn." Rank-and-file movements within labor are heavily represented by under-thirty people, who make up over one-third of the work force. There is reason to suspect that older workers are equally concerned about the irrationalities of the status quo, but that owing to their higher stakes are less willing to risk antiestablishment activity. Yet there are no age lines which can be safely drawn on the new radicalism. What Charles Flato writes about the British working class is hardly less true for the American: "The voice of working-class resentment against the Establishment is so strong and clear today that even politicians may get the message." [19]

A study by Hamilton of French workers as long ago as the 1950s attests to the depth of opposition to the status quo in France. Almost one-half sought revolutionary changes, while one-fourth would adopt noninstitutional means if necessary.[20] Workers at the larger plants, those who had experienced unemployment, and union members were more radical than other workers. Neither did an improving standard of living or wage in-

---

[16] André Gorz, *Strategy for Labor* (Boston: Beacon Press, 1967); Michael Harrington, "Old Working Class, New Working Class," *Dissent,* Winter 1972, pp. 146–62; Ernest Mandel, "Workers Under Neo-Capitalism," *International Socialist Review* 29 (December 1968): 1–16, and in Fischer, ed., *The Revival of American Socialism,* pp. 169–87; and George Novack, "Can American Workers Make a Socialist Revolution?" *International Socialist Review* 30 (February 1969): 41–64.

[17] Judy Edelman, "Young Workers: A Force for Change," *Political Affairs* 50 (November 1971): 13–16.

[18] B. J. Widick, "Labor's New Style," *The Nation,* March 22, 1971, p. 358.

[19] "Very Un-British Miners," *The Nation,* March 20, 1972, p. 366.

[20] Richard H. Hamilton, *Affluence and the French Worker in the Fourth Republic* (Princeton: Princeton University Press, 1967), pp. 48–59, 122, 189, 213, 249.

creases appear to mitigate radicalism. Four-fifths of the sample sensed many injustices within the system, and almost one-half engaged in political participation such as attending meetings, donating money, and persuading others. White-collar workers were as prochange as were blue-collar. The French general strike of 10 million workers in 1968 confirmed the discontent Hamilton had found earlier.

British workers have voiced strong discontent with the rate of surplus value appropriated by capital, including foreign capital;[21] socially paralyzing strikes by coal miners and longshoremen, and the broad social support strikers have received, back up these complaints. In Italy, some 70 percent of a sample of blue-collar workers were identified as liberal to radical on the political spectrum;[22] the strike activity in that country has attained disruptive heights. All over the capitalist world, the number of strikers climbed from 36 million in 1965 to 70 million in 1970. Over 3 million U.S. workers walked off their jobs in 1970. Plant administration and union organization and security are becoming prominent issues. In discussing white workers, union leader Gus Tyler points out that "our white worker is ready for battle. But he does not quite know against whom to declare war."[23]

The ruling class and their political representatives do what they can to confuse the issues. It goes without saying that in its political thinking the bourgeois state is far behind the working class. When worker radicalism rises to the surface, politicians supposedly elected to represent the interests of labor avert their eyes and block up their ears. Historically, we have seen how Scandinavian Social Democrats made their peace with private capitalism. We have recently seen how so-called labor leadership clung to the political status quo when power was within the grasp of the French working class. Our own history is replete with labor militance and popular-change movements that have been undermined or viciously suppressed by the ruling class and political elites.[24] The political articulation of labor militance during the first quarter of the twentieth century is suggested by the fact that in 1912 one-third of the unions in the American Federation of Labor had elected Socialists as leaders.[25] Denied duly elected

[21] Goldthorpe et al., *The Affluent Worker in the Class Structure*, pp. 87–88.

[22] William H. Form et al., "The Accommodation of Rural and Urban Workers to Industrial Discipline and Urban Living: A Four Nation Study," paper presented to the Seventh World Congress of Sociology, Varna, Bulgaria, 1970.

[23] "White Worker/Blue Mood," *Dissent*, Winter 1972, p. 195.

[24] See, for example, Norman S. Cohen, ed., *Civil Strife in America* (Hinsdale, Ill.: Dryden Press, 1972); Maurice Zeitlin, ed., *American Society, Inc.* (Chicago: Markham Publishing Company, 1970), pp. 423–501; Guido Baldi, "Theses on Mass Worker and Social Capital," *Radical America* 6 (May–June 1972): 3–21.

[25] See James Weinstein, "The IWW and American Socialism," *Socialist Revolution* 1 (September–October 1970): 3–43.

seats in legislative bodies, deported, jailed, and otherwise harassed, radical
labor leaders were systematically repressed. Typical of the manner in
which the ruling class deals with major demonstrations of labor protest
was the reaction to the 1932 march of the unemployed on Ford's Dearborn
plant, where police opened fire on the protesters, killing four and wound-
ing many more. Typical of the manner in which politicians view working-
class demands for income security was the congressional reaction in the
1930s to the Townsend old-age pension plan, petitions for which had been
signed by *25 million* petitioners: two hundred representatives didn't even
bother to attend the session to vote, and those in attendance voted it
down without a rollcall.[26] Senator Huey Long, popular leader of "Share
Our Wealth" movement which demanded a five-thousand-dollar guaranteed
family income thirty years ago, ended up the victim of assassination.

Nor has working-class militance and establishment repression been
confined to the first half of the century. From 1945 to 1968 fourteen different industrial disputes occasioned the mobilization of some 11,451
National Guard troops—actually a small number compared to the hundreds of thousands of troops called out to deal with essentially class-based
racial disorders and riots, not to mention the repeated thousands called
out to deal with antiwar protestors (largely new working class in our
terms).[27] Skolnick convincingly argues that mass uprisings and protests outside of specifically labor contexts are not to be dismissed as aberrations
or deviant behavior, but are politically motivated and oriented toward
structural change.[28] Political conventions must be removed to the isolated
resorts of the bourgeoisie and turned into armed camps so that the protectors of the status quo can assemble for mutual accolades and self-
congratulations. The president of the country cannot freely walk the streets
of its cities, nor openly mingle with his own laborers on the floor of steel
and auto plants, nor stand comfortably before the faculties and student
bodies of the nation's greatest universities. The ruling class and their top
political representatives must live in plastic cubicles, walled off from the
barbarities and anger their own civilization has produced. Police arsenals
are stocked with sophisticated antiriot equipment and the National Guard
is trained more and more to deal with mass confrontations and civic counterrevolution. Surveillance and sabotage of reform and radical political
activities goes to the police state lengths of wiretapping and disrupting in
diverse ways against the mildly critical Democratic party in 1972. In

---

[26] Francis Fox Piven and Richard Cloward, *Regulating the Poor* (New York:
Pantheon Books, 1971), pp. 100–11.
[27] Adam Yarmolinsky, *The Military Establishment* (New York: Harper Colo-
phon Books, 1971), pp. 162–72.
[28] Jerome H. Skolnick, *The Politics of Protest* (New York: Ballantine Books,
1969), pp. 1–24.

Chapters 5, 6, and 7, we variously made note of the considerable discontent, protest, and criticism among workers themselves in their attitudes regarding work and inequality.

Social unrest, we all know, does not always inspire constructive policies of change. More often than not, the immediate response of many people—and not just those within the dominant classes—is to favor repression. Neither is the working class, many critics argue, immune from this reaction to social disorder and social discontent. Irving Louis Horowitz, whose social observations are characteristically objectively critical, has written recently: "The working class has turned to the Leviathan with a vengeance. Not the liquidation of the state, but its celebration, has become of crucial importance. The working-class demands legitimacy, law, order, and a ruling class willing and capable of exercising full authority." [29] We have noted before that the working class is not a uniform entity in political and ideological orientation. But the results of the 1972 presidential election may be interpreted to grant Horowitz's contention a degree of validity—perhaps even a greater degree than a progressive's limits of comfort allow. Socialist scholar Michael Harrington suggests that the "middle masses" (read "white, stably employed salaried and wage workers") have gotten "uptight" over permissiveness with regard to drugs, welfare, government spending, bureaucracy, youth culture, and other currents of protest, change, and discontent and have allowed Nixon to freely associate all these phenomena with George McGovern and his supporters. [30]

But what, then, can be said of the state of class consciousness of a working class that is distracted from pursuing its own interests by such items as amnesty, bussing, abortion, pot, and welfare "chiselers"—and which has not been able to discern the easily verified fact that Nixon is *the* government spender and bureaucracy builder par excellence, except where broad social needs are at stake? (Nixon has had by far the biggest White House staff in history, greatly exceeding that of his immediate predecessors.) Where is the class consciousness of a working class that failed to respond adequately to the first democratic breakthrough in U.S. political party history and to a candidate whose economic proposals could have favorably altered (though not structurally changed) the balance of class power? Regarding such policies as McGovern's proposed tax on inheritances larger than $500,000 at 77 percent, economist Robert Lekachman wrote that "taxes at McGovern levels would in a generation wholesomely diminish the power of money over elections and legislation." [31] Surely a substantial

---

[29] *Three Worlds of Development*, 2nd ed. (New York: Oxford University Press, 1972), p. xvii.
[30] "Negative Landslide: The Myth That Was Real," *The Nation*, November 27, 1972, pp. 518–21.
[31] "Counter Brookings," *Social Policy*, September–October 1972, p. 33.

proportion of the working class were largely under the sway of ruling-class ideology, were frightened by the liberalism and magnitude of change represented by McGovern, and were easy prey for the "law and order" themes of a distinctly procapital, antilabor man such as Nixon. Four more years of Nixonism may do much to rectify the cloudy political thinking of that segment of the working class which failed to distinguish between a friend—not a savior—and an enemy.[32] (It is difficult to imagine, though not entirely impossible, that a candidate to the left of McGovern—say, someone representing Michael Harrington's views rather than James Tobin's—could at this point in history have carried the working-class vote in 1972. After all, was McGovern not considerably closer to a Harrington perspective than Nixon was?)

Nevertheless, the view that the working class as a whole is apathetic or integrated, though perhaps appealing on the surface, fails to take full cognizance of the depth of opposition feelings within the broad working class—as well as of their activities. This is not to say that class consciousness is widespread; it is to say that the conditions are ripe for its full development, and that a growing minority of the working class is class conscious and aware of its opponent. The labor movement of today is largely on its own; to fully materialize it needs to cultivate men and women of inspirational and imaginative organizational talent and leadership ability working within the union, the political party, and the government, whether within traditional or entirely new forms. Workers themselves must provide the bulk of this inspiration and leadership. A major source of this inspiration and leadership has and will continue to come from minorities, especially blacks.

BLACKS AND CAPITALISM

The inequalities and discrimination which confront blacks in the United States have been pointed up on a number of previous occasions. Our chief concern in taking up the racial question here is to review the position of black people vis-à-vis capitalism and social change. Blacks and other non-white minorities have without question been subject to personal and group prejudice and discrimination in varying degrees of intensity. The critical point which must be made, however, is that the social and material condition of blacks is due primarily to capitalism as such, and only secondarily to intergroup bigotry. Many peoples of the Third World are more deeply colored than those of the advanced capitalist nations, yet it is not their

---

[32] See Ronnie Dugger, "George McGovern: A Jeffersonian for our Time," *Progressive*, November 1972, pp. 14–19.

color which induces imperialists to behave in the manner they do, but the laws of capitalist development. Without question, imperialism and capitalism have dealt with nonwhite peoples in a racist manner that has markedly exacerbated the direct economic exploitation they have undergone. Black and brown laborers can be driven harder, cared for less, and paid less by racists than can white laborers; their enslavement can be more easily rationalized if need be. Yet it is proletarian status or colonial status and not racial or ethnic status which is the pivot of inequality, exploitation, and underdevelopment. As Baran and Sweezy have emphasized: "It was capitalism, with its enthronement of greed and privilege, which created the race problem and made of it the ugly thing it is today. It is the very same system which resists and thwarts every effort at a solution." [33]

The black population in America, from the time of slavery to the great wartime and postwar migrations and down to the present day, has always found its location and situation determined by the labor requirements of capital.[34] Under the popular guise of emancipation, according to Eugene Genovese's Marxist analysis, northern capital crushed the independence movement of the Southern planter aristocracy, who feared a strong urban bourgeoisie and a politically unpredictable white working class. Northern capital, on the other hand, required an open and mobile labor force and a market for the consumption of industrial products, neither of which conditions a rural aristocratic slaveholding system could meet.[35] Then after attaining its economic ends and assuring its own continued power, the bourgeoisie allowed the same rural elite to renew its full exploitation of black labor. Upon the introduction of advanced mechanization into the rural South and with the increasing availability of cheap migrant labor power in the industrial sector, the ruling class permitted the nativist restrictionists to have their way and stemmed the heavy tide of immigration—itself a long-time necessary source of unskilled labor ripe for exploitation. And in the recent period of expanding automation, the unskilled and even semiskilled labor of blacks in both the North and the South have become increasingly irrelevant to the interests of finance capital. Thus, Sidney Willhelm has recently written persuasively on *Who Needs the Negro?* comparing the situation of the black man to that of the Indian.[36]

Nevertheless, despite the sharp slackening of demand for industrial and agricultural labor, blacks are very far from being an unnecessary part of the work force. Quite to the contrary; they bear a heavy burden in both

---

[33] Paul A. Baran and Paul M. Sweezy, *Monopoly Capital* (New York: Monthly Review Press, 1966), p. 271.

[34] See Sidney Willhelm, *Who Needs the Negro?* (Cambridge, Massachusetts: Schenkman Publishing Company, 1970), pp. 37–79.

[35] *The Political Economy of Slavery* (New York: Pantheon Books, 1965).

[36] Willhelm, *Who Needs the Negro?*

production and service sectors. The overwhelming majority of the approximately 9.5 million blacks in the labor force are working-class and are especially heavily concentrated in blue-collar production jobs. Almost 3 million may be counted as working within the basic industries such as steel, chemicals, rubber, auto, shipping, and transport. There is still much unskilled and semiskilled work to be done in this society, and there will continue to be so as long as it is cheaper for human beings to perform the work than machines.

It might be well here to summarize the particular importance of blacks to the capitalist class. First, inasmuch as black labor is cheaper, the higher rate of surplus value for black labor yields higher profits. Secondly, an industrial reserve army heavily staffed by blacks applies relatively greater downward pressure on wages and upward pressure on surplus value. The racial composition of the reserve army is important in that blacks as a group constitute a highly visible threat to white jobholders. And who could harbor any illusions regarding the willingness of capital to utilize cheaper black labor over more expensive white labor—at least as far as social peace will allow? As Edna Bonacich points out: "White capitalists would gladly dispense with and undercut their white working-class brethren if they could, and have done so whenever they had the opportunity." [37] Jeffrey Prager is not entirely correct, then, when he argues that "white people have arranged 'to take care of their own' at the expense of the non-whites who are relegated to subordinate positions." [38] As a corollary of this second function, a society with racist values and overtones can find a high rate of unemployment among blacks and other nonwhite minorities entirely acceptable from a moral standpoint, thus holding welfare and income redistribution to a bare minimum (even though whites constitute the majority of the unemployed!).

A third function performed by black labor for capitalism is that its presence offers the opportunity to employ human labor in the place of full installation of technological capital ("niggermation," as a black critic has put it), thus holding down capital investment relative to labor (the organic composition of capital) and maintaining the rate of profit. As a corollary to this function, blacks are frequently used to perform the dirtiest dead-end jobs, thus partially mitigating one potential source of white frustration and resentment against the modern industrial system. Frequently, this black dead-end labor supports very cheaply the bourgeois life styles of the more affluent middle mass. Finally, and most important of all, the presence of working-class blacks, whether they be employed union members or entirely

---

[37] "A Theory of Ethnic Antagonism: The Split Labor Market," *American Sociological Review* 37 (October 1972): 547–59.

[38] "White Racial Privilege and Social Change: An Examination of Theories of Racism," *Berkeley Journal of Sociology* 17 (1972–73): 139.

withdrawn from the labor force, creates and feeds the kinds of divisions within the underlying population which allow the capitalist class to perpetuate its full and unchallenged power. With thinly veiled racist slogans concerning work, welfare, bussing (44 percent of U.S. public school children ride a bus to school, but less than 1 percent is attributable to integration), and crime, the 1972 Nixon campaign took full advantage of racial fears and cleavages within the underlying population and diverted white attention from the wholesale failings of the economic system.[39]

What, in fact, does the white working class gain from the racial division within the underlying population? The only palpable gain to the white middle or working mass is that *within* the capitalist system, racist practices in hiring, housing, education, selling, politics, medicine, or whatever give "first-choice" preferences to whites. But what pitiful gains these are for most working-class people compared to the tremendous losses they face within a system in which capital holds undisputed control over the nation's wealth and material resources! So-called status gains from simply being white are even more pathetic. The working class, whether it be white or black, pays a high economic, psychological, cultural, and moral cost for living in a racially divided society. The only minority which gains is the capitalist class and its peripheral circles which prey upon the restricted and helpless choices of the ghetto population. In brief, the evidence disputes Willhelm's conclusion that no one needs the Negro and that the ruling class has decided it can afford to lock them up on ghetto reservations or exterminate them in a genocidal race war (although the most brutal kind of repression of black opposition movements or uprisings has and will be employed). More acceptable is the view that blacks perform key and crucial functions in the profit equations of the ruling class and will continue to do so as long as the capitalist system persists.[40]

We have alluded to the similarities between the blacks' economic position within U.S. capitalism and that of Third World peoples within world imperialism. This parallel has received due attention in the literature and should be further explored at this point. As it has been developed, this parallel goes considerably beyond the problem of labor as such, encompassing the entire institutional complex of the urban ghetto. Robert Blauner has termed the domestic phenomenon "internal colonialism." [41] William K. Tabb has probed the analogy extensively and writes that "the black ghetto is best viewed from the perspective of development econom-

---

[39] See Richard A. Long, "Scapegoat Victory: The President's White Mandate," *The Nation,* December 4, 1972, pp. 555–57.

[40] A similar conclusion is drawn by Prager, "White Racial Privilege and Social Change," p. 143.

[41] "Internal Colonialism and the Ghetto Revolt," *Social Problems* 16 (Spring 1969): 393–408.

ics. In its relations with the dominant white society, the black ghetto stands as a unit apart, an internal colony exploited in a systematic fashion." [42] Tabb enumerates the following traits, found in colonial societies, that find analogies in the ghetto: low income, small middle class, low increase in labor productivity, low rate of capital formation, import of expensive goods and export of cheap ones and a consequent balance-of-payments problem, small modern sector owned by outsiders, unskilled labor, native business lacking capital resources and markets, credit defaults high, export of unskilled labor cheaply, high unemployment, important jobs held by white outsiders, foreign army of occupation (police), indigenous leaders dependent on outsiders for help, and the cultivation of capitalist values and enterprise.[43] In the case of the last point, there is the idea of unequal partnership through which external powers can control the flow of profits from the ghetto, but through which also might be developed a native bourgeoisie to give pride, stability, and integration. But black capitalism has never gotten beyond small secondary and tertiary exchange and service operations within the black community itself. And rather than expanding, it is being systematically squeezed very much like the world of small business in general.

Blacks held in ownership only 18 percent of ghetto businesses in 1968, the majority of these being in the area of personal services.[44] At the same time they owned a mere 3 percent of other central-city business establishments and less than 1 percent of suburban. As the data of Reiss and Aldrich indicate, absentee white owner managers of ghetto businesses reap substantial profits, while at the same time having little or no interest in the community per se. Though smaller and somewhat more understanding of ghetto economic life, whites who themselves own and operate ghetto businesses, typically smaller than absentee-managed firms, are scarcely more sympathetic to ghetto problems. The least profitable and most cooperative of the white businesses are those owned and operated by inner-city residents. Within the ghetto (as well as outside it!), black businesses earn less income, pay out relatively lower wages, and serve proportionately fewer customers than white businesses, while the same relationships hold

---

[42] *The Political Economy of the Black Ghetto* (New York: W. W. Norton and Company, 1970), p. 21; see also Tabb, "Race Relations Models and Social Change," *Social Problems* 18 (Spring 1971): 431–44.

[43] *The Political Economy of the Black Ghetto,* Chapter 2. For an analysis and discussion of a prototypical urban "colony" see Joseph M. Conforti on Newark, "Ghetto or City?" and Clark Taylor, "Parasitic Suburbs," *Society* (September–October 1972): 20–34 and 35–41, respectively.

[44] *The Statistical Abstract of the United States, 1972* (New York: Grosset & Dunlap, 1972), p. 462; see especially Albert J. Reiss, Jr., and Howard Aldrich, "Absentee Ownership and Management in the Black Ghetto: Social and Economic Consequences," *Social Problems* 18 (Winter 1971): 319–39.

true for local as opposed to absentee-owned firms. Significantly, it tends to be the locally oriented white businessmen, frequently Jews and other European ethnics, who enter into the most direct conflict with the ghetto population rather than the more profitable absentee-managed firms. Cashing in on ghetto weaknesses in a major way are the pillars of the white establishment in banking, insurance, and real estate. The subcapitalist net of financial appropriation is cast into every inner-city corner, sometimes within the letter of the law, sometimes in clear violation of its intentions.

Typical of capitalist operations in the ghetto have been the recent profit machinations of financial speculators on housing purchases by low-income people under the Federal Housing Act of 1968. Speculators bought old houses for a few thousand dollars, made superficial renovations, and sold them for three and four times the purchase price to the unsuspecting poor—all with the approval of the Federal Housing Administration, which had insured the mortgages. Faced with crumbling houses and expensive repairs, the new but poor owners can very frequently do nothing but allow the FHA to foreclose, pay off the private speculators with taxpayers' money, and see the rotten hulk go into the public domain.[45] This is state capitalism at its degenerate "best." Meanwhile, many well-meaning but naive politicians investigate to see what went wrong.

Of the opponents to the ghetto-as-colony argument, Nathan Glazer recognizes the troubling fact that, if blacks are not just another ethnic group on their way up the American dream-ladder but represent a separate case, then "profound political and economic adjustments will be required." [46] Anyone as infatuated with the existing system as Glazer is would find such radical change singularly unnerving. What Glazer neglects to see is that it is the experience of the working class as such—with all ethnic groups included therein—which negates the American dream; blacks simply stand out as the most conspicuous and glaring example of the failure of capitalism to create a humanistic democracy. But since a humanistic democracy is not even a goal of capitalism, it can scarcely be charged with failure. Glazer and other social analysts [47] are often preoccupied with ethnic groups, an effort harmless enough in its own right but damaging when utilized to divert attention away from class relations.[48] The study of ethnic and racial groups becomes genuinely salient only when these groups are examined for their distinctive roles and positions within the capitalist

---

[45] See Erwin Knoll, "Fellow Slumlords," *Progressive* 36 (July 1972): 26–28.

[46] "Blacks and Ethnic Groups: The Difference and the Political Difference It Makes," *Social Problems* 18 (Spring 1971): 444–61.

[47] See also Andrew M. Greeley, "New Ethnicity & Blue Collars," *Dissent,* Winter, 1972, pp. 270–77.

[48] For a related criticism of the above, see Dennis Wrong, "How Important is Social Class?" *Dissent,* Winter, 1972, pp. 278–85.

division of labor (or any system of inequality and exploitation). The hoped-for parallel between the mobility and assimilation of European ethnic groups and black Americans breaks down when one considers the fact that the latter were resident here in large numbers well over a century before the waves of European "ethnic" immigration even started—and emancipated decades before the bulk of immigrants arrived. As Willhelm argues: "If there is any analogy in America's racial history relative to the Negro, it is with the Indian, not the immigrant." [49] Glazer's recent warm and overt embrace of rightist ideologies suggests that he actually has no illusions about the black population riding the time-machine up the ethnic ladder of success. He may be bracing himself for the reaction of the ghetto-as-colony and the verification of Willhelm's thesis that "the state of suspension cannot remain forever; the insurrections by the despairing Negro are the prelude of a forthcoming race war, just as Indians finally took the warpath to defend themselves from white hostility."

While the many parallels between the black ghetto and the Third World are obvious, the analogy may be overworked or misinterpreted when taken as a guide to a strategy for effecting social change. If we take as the objective of both black ghetto and Third World peoples economic independence and liberation, two quite different courses of action are indicated. The Third World has small enclaves of development surrounded by a mass of underdevelopment; the ghetto is a small enclave of underdevelopment surrounded by a mass of technology and wealth. The problem of the former is development as such; the problem of the latter is integration into an already developed technological society. These two cases represent opposite ends of capitalist development—or quite nearly so. The direction of progressive change for the Third World is to sever those relations that perpetuate their underdevelopment with imperialist economies, while the direction of progressive change for the ghetto is to become incorporated on a full and equal basis within the developed society. Control of their own land and resources would provide the initial leverage for economic liberation for Third World peoples; control of ghetto territory would not carry its population very far along the road to material security and financial independence. The ghetto sits on the fringe of a society capable of building a highly developed socialism, while the Third World must focus on building the very economic foundations for socialism.

Unlike the masses of the Third World, the black proletariat is a highly class-conscious, or at least economically and politically conscious, industrialized sector of the U.S. working class. It not only has a relatively high level of formal education by world standards, but is rather advanced in social and political awareness and information in the broadest informal

---

[49] *Who Needs the Negro?* p. 210.

sense of the terms. Quite the opposite of the agrarian peasant mass of the Third World, the black proletariat in the United States may readily be conceived of as standing in the forefront of working-class consciousness. The road leading out of economic necessity to liberation for the black ghetto is socialism; the road leading out of Third World underdevelopment has been and always will be national liberation movements. In brief, the concept of the ghetto-as-internal-colony may be an aid in understanding certain aspects of the nature of economic exploitation, but it offers little in the way of indicating a way of throwing off that exploitation.

That the large majority of black Americans desire democratic participation and material justice *within* the larger society rather than some sort of separate territorial sovereignty or national independence *from* the larger society has been confirmed by numerous pieces of survey research.[50] Feagin's data, for example, suggest that only 5 percent of the black population consider a separate state, states, or country for blacks a "good idea." Rather chilling is the fact that 26 percent of Feagin's nationwide sample (N = 551) of whites favored separate states for blacks in the United States; and 36 percent (over 40 percent of blue-collar workers and 56 percent of southerners) favored a separate country for blacks. The white separatist attitude correlated with an antiblack attitude, but far from perfectly. Many whites, even sympathetic ones, would prefer to wish the racial issue away, whereas nearly all blacks realize the issue must be squarely faced. The Fendrich and Axelson data on black veterans also indicate a preference for integration and political action within the institutional framework of the larger society.

Some observers would interpret such data as indicating that the nation's blacks are essentially conservative. Harold Cruse feels that black militancy actually conceals an essential flabbiness of purpose (yet paradoxically enough, he also believes that blacks are misled by Marxist socialism and a class analysis such as our own, which views the large majority of blacks as an exploited and oppressed proletariat).[51] Irving Louis Horowitz and William H. Friedland raise the important argument that blacks "are more nationalist than revolutionary in that they are concerned with developing black expression, not with changing the entire social system. The black militancy is restrained by blacks' social aspirations; most want to make it within the existing system, perhaps slightly 'blackwashed' but fundamentally untouched."[52] Horowitz and Friedland, speaking of black

---

[50] For example, Joe R. Feagin, "White Separatists and Black Separatists: A Comparative Analysis," *Social Problems* 19 (Fall 1971): 167–80; and James M. Fendrich and Leland J. Axelson, "Marital Status and Political Alienation Among Black Veterans," *American Journal of Sociology* 77 (September 1971): 253.

[51] *The Crisis of the Negro Intellectual* (New York: William Morrow, 1967).

[52] *The Knowledge Factory* (Chicago: Aldine Publishing Company, 1970), pp. 198–99.

students, go on to argue that blacks can be more easily bought off than white radicals, who tend to be revolutionary rather than simply militant in the manner of blacks. Horowitz elsewhere contends that "the black movements tend to be anti-liberal, dogmatic, sectarian in their direction." [53]

J. K. Obatala, in attempting to explain the demise of black student activism, writes that "there was militancy, as well as anger, hate and racial frustration, but—except for radical rhetoric—never much of a genuine revolutionary conviction on the part of most black students." [54] Obatala makes the further point that black power meant different things to the masses than to the black student elite: "For the masses, the struggle for power had truly revolutionary implications, in that such a struggle must necessarily concern itself with a redistribution of goods and income and a change in the ownership of productive capacity. . . . On the other hand, when the Afro-American middle-class—including the black student elite—spoke of power, it was, with few exceptions, speaking mainly in terms of social recognition and social mobility within the present system." Obatala perceptively argues that black student unions, black capitalism, Miss Black America, black homecoming queens, and other mirror images of white America were nothing more than deferred dreams of the integrationist movement and that such provocative symbolism tended to obscure "the essentially conservative political and institutional outlook of the Afro-American nationalist movement on campus."

Cruse, Horowitz, Obatala, and others are raising crucial points here, particularly regarding black professionals and students who could play such vital leadership roles. There is the slim possibility that the black intelligentsia is even more poorly articulated with the needs and aspirations of the black working class than the white intelligentsia is with the white working class, which would constitute a wide gap indeed. For as Proctor has cautioned, "it must be recognized that all of the major class divisions existing within the U.S. capitalist society are to be found among Black people." [55]

The fact that most blacks seek material and social justice within the larger society rather than as a separate nation is simply being realistic on their part; but to seek material and social justice within U.S. society cannot be interpreted to mean that blacks wish to make it within the *existing* system, "fundamentally untouched"—at least so far as the black proletariat is concerned. Conceivably, the black middle class has indeed been bought off or is too remote and unrealistic to see that the mass of work-

---

[53] *The Struggle is the Message* (Berkeley: Glendessary Press, 1971), p. 29.

[54] "Black Students: Where Did Their Revolution Go?" *The Nation,* October 2, 1972, pp. 272–74.

[55] Roscoe Proctor, "Black Workers and the Class Struggle," *Political Affairs* 51 (January 1972): 16.

ing-class blacks and poor cannot possibly make it within the existing system; further, no one wants to buy *them* off, but only to keep them quiet. There is strong evidence to suggest that *working-class* blacks are more *radical* than they are *militant*—that is, they seek fundamental change, but have thus far not engaged in much heated rhetorical attack. For example, fully 94 percent of a sample of urban, blue- and lower-white-collar blacks agreed with the statement, "Our country is in bad shape and needs a lot of changes." [56] (Significantly, 68 percent of the whites agreed with the same statement.)

The same research as above, conducted by Kahl and Goering, indicates that a majority of blacks—as well as of whites—conceive of "the good life" as having the material resources to obtain what our culture has defined as necessities (Marx's subsistence level) such as an operable mode of transportation, a decent home, adequate funds for food and clothing, and enough money for a modicum of recreation—i.e., rational consumption. With "the good life" placed on a seven-point scale, blacks on the average scored over two points short and whites almost two points short of this rather simple definition of "the good life" (the ruling class as well as the rest of the bourgeoisie would consider such a level of living as deprivation levels, and to fall two points below that level as destitution). Though both blacks and whites were rather satisfied with their jobs, they were obviously dissatisfied with their material resources, and they explicitly envisaged the need for much social change. This would confirm the arguments of Harrington, Gorz, and others that the strategy for labor should be expanded from the work place proper to include all of the surrounding relevant social institutions.

Significant in terms of the prospects for orderly change were the further findings of Kahl and Goering that, far from feeling powerless, the large majority of both black and white workers felt that individual votes can make a difference and that ordinary citizens can influence government decisions. With this in mind, one would think that the working class would vote for politicians who speak a language of change, who see things to be in "bad shape" and "in need of a lot of changes." The black working class is largely consistent in this regard, the white working class is much less so. Proctor points to one of the chief reasons for what inconsistency there is within the white working class: "Without a doubt, one single most powerful weapon in the arsenal of the ruling class used to cause division in the ranks of the working class is racism." [57] Another weapon, of course, is nationalism—chauvinism, which diverts attention from political economy to militarism and patriotism.

---

[56] Joseph A. Kahl and John M. Goering, "Stable Workers, Black and White," *Social Problems* 18 (Winter 1971): 315.

[57] "Black Workers and the Class Struggle," p. 17.

The black proletariat, whatever black professionals and students might be, are *primarily* motivated by class rather than racial symbols. In one of the few researches which broach this important issue, Leggett discovered that 51 percent of black auto workers in his sample used both class and race symbols in social analysis, 38 percent class symbols, and only 7 percent race symbols only.[58] Zeitlin discerned a predominantly class rather than race orientation among black Cuban workers, though in both the United States and Cuba the racial factor adds considerable impact to that of class. In addition to the disprivilege confronting the black worker in the United States, the collective ethnic influence is in all likelihood a decisive factor in the greater degree of class consciousness and radicalism found among blacks in comparison to whites. Yet, black liberation cannot be achieved apart from the emancipation of the entire working class.[59] The threat confronting the various forces and movements for change, fired by the ruling class, is succinctly stated by Harrington: "There are reasons to fear that these different groups, all with a practical interest in the transformation of society, will war with one another rather than coalesce in a new radical majoriy and eventually into a socialist movement." [60]

There is no reason to believe that the black proletariat is not ready for socialism; while their radicalism or perception of needed change may not yet have been transformed to socialist thought and practice, it would seem only a matter of time before it is so defined. For this to be accomplished requires additional determination among blacks, for the ruling ideas already have them portrayed as something less than "100 percent Americans." On the other hand, in view of their second-class citizenship, what have they to lose? Although the American Socialist party of the early twentieth century shared the racial bigotry of the rest of the society, socialism today must actively seek black leadership and support. The black proletariat has its own independent rationale in socialist construction.

The 1960s witnessed the first black organization to take a formal socialist position. Although the police and local authorities were primarily aroused by the Black Panther party's militance, the ruling class has been much more concerned with its ideology and potential political appeal to the black masses in the ghetto. In formulating Panther doctrine, Huey Newton once stated that "we see a major contradiction between capitalism in this country and our interests." [61] In seeking self-determination, full

---

[58] John Leggett, *Class, Race, and Labor* (New York: Oxford University Press, 1968), p. 106.

[59] "Black Workers and the Class Struggle," p. 17.

[60] Michael Harrington, "Why We Need Socialism in America," *Dissent* 17 (May–June 1970): 280.

[61] Philip S. Foner, ed., *The Black Panthers Speak* (Philadelphia: J. B. Lippincott, 1970), p. 51.

employment, guaranteed income, collective ownership of the means of production, housing, education, and other social goals, the Black Panther party, wrote Eldridge Cleaver, feels that "the only safe guides to action are the revolutionary principles of Marxism-Leninism." [62] Newton has envisaged his party as a vanguard party, and "the main purpose of a vanguard group should be to raise the consciousness of the masses." In establishing early Panther goals, Newton wrote that "the means of production should be taken away from [the ruling class] and placed in the people's hands, so that the people can organize them in such a way as to provide themselves with a livelihood." [63] Newton, Cleaver, and other Panther spokesmen—now warring on many of these same points—argued that a minuscule black bourgeoisie is identified with the white power structure and its interests (Adam Clayton Powell was a "Jackal from Harlem," and Farmer, Young, and Wilkins are "enemies of black people"). Stokely Carmichael came under attack for his racial approach to change, acceptance of all blacks as friends and whites as enemies, and refusal to form alliances with white radicals.

The Panthers have also attacked, as any class approach to change must do, the propensity among black militants toward cultural nationalism and the elevation of ethnic symbols to ends in themselves. Linda Harrison viewed cultural nationalism as "a universal denial and ignoring of the present political, social, and economic realities and a concentration on the past as a frame of reference. . . . Cultural nationalism offers no challenge or offense against the prevailing order." She quoted Fanon: "A revolutionary culture is the only valid culture of the oppressed." [64] Or from Newton: "We believe that culture itself will not liberate us. We're going to need some stronger stuff." [65] In working in black communities for free meals, liberation schools, medical care centers, legal defense, etc., the Panthers have stimulated revolutionary consciousness among the people. Thus, it has been the threat of a contagious economic and political *ideology* which frightens the ruling class, rather than the modest self-help programs of a minority political party. (That Panther representatives enter actively into electoral politics in no way necessarily deradicalizes them. After all, the Panthers are organized as a political party in the first place.) As in all other cases of repression, the ruling class has had other willing men conduct the dirty work of systematic and violent attack on the Black Panther party, men who have seen the party not so much as an economic and ideological threat but as a threat to uncontested local power and control over the black community.

---

[62] Ibid., p. 110.
[63] Ibid., pp. 41, 43.
[64] Ibid., pp. 151–52.
[65] Ibid., p. 50.

Black protests, disorders, and violence have never in the past alarmed the ruling class so much as have incidents within the past decade. The reason for this is that the temper of racial confrontations has shifted from specifically white-black hostilities of a largely apolitical nature to more or less articulate expressions of opposition to the very structure of the society. Contrary to the beliefs of many social scientists regarding a relationship between improving conditions and protest activities, the ruling class itself knows that it is not improvement and hope that has led to violence, but rather depression and despair. Whether in the streets, on the campuses, in the factories, or in the prisons, specifically racial and civil rights issues have become political and economic ones having to do with the distribution of power and material reward. White liberals within the establishment are so desperate to placate the black community before its militance and discontent turn to explicit and conscious political radicalism that they have shunted their own working class aside in the process, a process which itself generates resentment among white workers against both established liberals and blacks. This is precisely the outcome the centers of ruling-class power hoped for. There is no questioning the fact that a certain amount of this kind of resentment toward blacks exists within the white working class.[66]

But the resentment which does exist among white workers, in any event, is not mainly against blacks qua blacks or even against the social and economic programs designed for blacks. The resentment is chiefly over what is perceived as social security programs for blacks only, however inadequate these programs might actually be. The message from such white resentment is not necessarily that the white working class is entirely racist or still under the influence of the Protestant work ethic, but perhaps rather that the white working class itself is to some degree searching for an economy which would provide the kind of social security the forces of production are, in fact, capable of rendering.

CLASS RADICALISM, STUDENTS, AND THE NEW LEFT

The concept of the *"new* left" as opposed to "left" refers here to the fact that the traditional forces seeking social reconstruction in American society have been injected with a profound catalyst in the form of college-

---

[66] See Angus Cambell, *White Attitudes Towards Black People* (Ann Arbor, Mich.: Institute for Social Research, 1971).

educated youth, many of whom belong or will belong to the new working class. In the late fifties and early sixties, the number of socially aware and politically concerned left-leaning student youth reached a sociologically relevant threshold and began taking organizational shape around such groups as the Students for a Democratic Society and the Student Non-Violent Coordinating Committee. Neither these nor any other given set of youth-dominated organizations could have been or can be said to encompass the new left; they simply represent its tangible structural origins.[67] Thus, it was not then and certainly is not now possible to give organizational definition to the new left. If one chooses to identify the new left with SDS, SNCC, or any other organization or given mobilization effort, then certainly we could say that there is not much left of the new left.[68] Radically oriented persons, groups, and political mobilizations may all be taken as manifestations of what might be referred to as the new left—or simply of the left if the "new left" label now bears too many specific historical connotations. (For many, it may be easier and/or more accurate to refer to forces seeking radical change simply as the left, a more open and inclusive term.) There are no age, occupational, or educational limitations to new-left orientations. In this larger sense, then, the new left is very much alive and growing, branching out from its original student base into the larger society by means of both ex-students and the working citizenry.

In its initial manifestations, the new left was leftist only by comparison to the prevailing political stupor of the 1950s; it was not radical, revolutionary, socialist, Marxist, or anything else which historically might be classified as leftist. Mainly, early student political activists were liberal reformers who in their educated idealism sought to rectify the glaring contradictions between democratic values and social practice in the areas of civil rights and race relations, poverty and inequality, decision making and control, and military spending and the arms race. As Richard Flacks points out, the earliest activists envisaged, not a mass student movement per se, but rather integrated working support of and alliances with other liberal reformers in the civil rights movement, labor, government, the churches, and so on.[69] Many of these older liberals were veterans of political ferment in the 1930s, and certain others could be linked with the "old left" of that period—purportedly a more dogmatic, doctrinaire, and

---

[67] On the development of the new left, see James O'Brien, "Beyond Reminiscence: The New Left in History," *Radical America,* July–August 1972, pp. 11–46.

[68] See Michael Walzer's discussion, "Notes For Whoever's Left," *Dissent* 19 (Spring 1972): 309–14.

[69] *Youth and Social Change* (Chicago: Markham Publishing Company, 1971), p. 78; see also Flacks, "The New Left and American Politics After Ten Years," *Journal of Social Issues* 27 (Summer 1971): 21–34.

narrow-minded group than the new group of student activists (predictably, "old leftists" frequently see the new activists in the same terms).[70]

Increasingly, younger reform-oriented thinkers and activists began to perceive, through practice, the lessons so cogently presented by C. Wright Mills concerning the irrelevance of established liberalism to the kinds of reforms sought. Not only did change-oriented efforts through alliances with the liberal establishment fail to yield palpable results, but one could see, under the rule of liberal rhetoric, the growth of corporate power, the expansion of the military-industrial complex, escalation of the arms race, new schemes of Third World counterinsurgency, and the makings of full-scale war in Indochina. The new left, continually growing in absolute numbers, turned away from this distorted, inverted liberalism and began to perceive it as the chief enemy of the democratic, egalitarian goals it sought to achieve. Still largely without a consciously articulated political ideology and theory of change, the student left began to move outside traditional legalistic, institutionalized methods of change and toward mass protest, civil disobedience, and calculated confrontation.

The concept of student power and mass student movement crystallized, as the university itself assumed the medium through which the student left began to act. This exacerbated the growing tensions between the new left and the liberal establishment, especially within the university. Particularly explosive was the issue of university involvement in the arms race and the Vietnam War, a war conducted according to policies that were proving to be entirely unresponsive to the opposition tactics of any sort of politics. The war proved to be the grand awakener and the great divider on the American political front. The war delivered to the masses of students and nonstudents alike their first fundamental education in political realism, something which the power structure has always striven to obstruct. It laid bare, despite frantic attempts to cover it up, the essential nature of the "new American society" of the post–World War II period. Political sides shifted and sorted themselves out, as innocent conservatives moved leftward and many established liberals and "old leftists" moved to the right.

The new left of today is thinking in increasingly socialist or Marxist terms, that is, in more classical leftist terms as opposed to the atheoretical reformist terms of the early student movement. (Although many speak a populist language as well, it is difficult to imagine how turning back the clock of history to small-scale capitalism is possible, much less a feasible mode of attaining a humanistic democracy.) And critics of today's left

---

[70] For a comparative effort of new and old left, see Armand L. Mauss, "The Lost Promise of Reconciliation: New Left vs. Old Left," *Journal of Social Issues* 27 (Summer 1971): 1–20.

who charge it with theoretical immaturity and analytical chaos fail to take note of the substantial and growing body of theoretical socialist literature produced in this country.

Although many movements of cultural dissent are first and foremost concerned with states of individual consciousness and essentially apolitical aspects of behavior thought to deliver liberation, the left is only secondarily—if at all—preoccupied with such "cultures of awakening." [71] Granted that the values of Marxism pertaining to equality, material distribution, rational consumption, and collective control frequently overlap with countercultural values, just as often Marxist ideological underpinnings are in direct conflict with the culture of awakening.[72] Whereas the communal orientation of the counterculture is virtually preindustrial or tribal, the communal orientation of Marxist socialism is postindustrial or advanced-technological. The counterculture would "live off the land," while the socialist would to a considerable extent "live off machines." The distinctions between the left and the counterculture are frequently vague and confused for many, regardless of how real these distinctions indeed are. We shall have more to say regarding the counterculture below; suffice it to note here that the ruling class benefits greatly from this confusion and seeks to co-opt youthful discontent both for commercial and political reasons into "hip" or "green" life styles in contradistinction to serious opposition politics and culture.[73] Even authentic opposition life styles cannot withstand the emasculation and co-optation power of the system, for as John Anson Warner has noted: "The system has demonstrated that it is capable of draining the meaning out of many forms of symbolic protest and gutting counter culture life styles of their radical content in order to absorb them into the normal youth culture norms of organizational society (and even that can seep upwards into middle age). Even in a political sense, the system has proven that it can take radical slogans and employ them for the most conservative purposes." [74]

In their analysis of the student movement, Horowitz and Friedland argue that the movement has not been a means of achieving sexual freedom, a reaction against anonymity, or any other largely psychological or

---

[71] See Joseph Downing, "The Tribal Family and the Society of Awakening," in Herbert A. Otto, ed., *The Family in Search of a Future* (New York: Appleton-Century-Crofts, 1970), pp. 119–35.

[72] Karl Klare, "The Critique of Everyday Life, Marxism, and the New Left," *Berkeley Journal of Sociology* 16 (1971–72): 15–45.

[73] On the policy of co-optation, see Richard Flacks, "Young Intelligentsia in Revolt," in Norman R. Miller and Roderick R. Aya, eds., *The New American Revolution* (New York: Free Press, 1971), p. 191.

[74] "Alienated Post New Left Youth: Secular Marxism and Religious Mysticism," paper delivered at the Canadian Sociology and Anthropology Association 1972 Annual Meeting, Montreal, p. 10.

cultural search—that "the student movement is a genuinely *political* one." [75] Flacks observes that "to assume that basic change can occur outside the political system is a gross error." [76] In a definition which seems to capture rather well the goal of the radicalism of today's left, Flacks writes:

> It is a vision of a society in which *technological development and economic investment* are guided not by imperatives of profit, economic growth, and empire, but rather by imperatives to eliminate "alienated" labor and to promote public happiness and personal self-actualization. It is a *culture* that values cooperation and love over competition and dominance, self-expression over self-denial, and equality over materially based status differentiation. It is a quest for a *political order* in which the nation-state is replaced by self-governing communities.[77]

Much debate has taken place over the roots or causes of new left activity. Some of the literature in this area is utter nonsense—such as that tracing the movement on the left to "primordial facts of human nature," i.e., historical universals deep in the Freudian psyche.[78] Other, more serious analyses search for the gestation of the new left in such aspects of contemporary life as impersonal relationships and bureaucratization, crass materialism and technological gadgetry, middle-class competitiveness and status hierarchies, the clash of idealistic socialization and contradictory realities, authoritarianism and the narrow demands of work, the obstruction of career aspirations, artificially prolonged education and adolescence, and other conditions characteristic of advanced capitalist society.[79] This "reaction against bourgeois culture" approach suggests that the children of the bourgeoisie are at the forefront of the new left, that the new left is a reaction to the conditions of our particular brand of security and affluence rather than a product of insecurity and deprivation. Flacks has been most

---

[75] *The Knowledge Factory*, p .104.

[76] *Youth and Social Change*, p. 120.

[77] "Strategies for Radical Social Change," *Social Policy* 1 (March–April 1971): 10.

[78] We refer mainly to Lewis A. Feuer's attempt to devalue the political and social causes of student radicalism in his *Conflict of Generations* (New York: Basic Books, 1969). For example, he considers Vietnam merely as a medium or vehicle through which youth rebel against their elders rather than as the greatest moral tragedy in U.S. history and an issue which catalyzed democratic radicalism or anti-establishment political activity (p. 414). This book may be viewed as a "sour grapes" attempt to strike back at politicized students by a man who departed from Berkeley after the first major student revolt.

[79] For discussions of the roots of student activism, see the following sources: Horowitz and Friedland, *The Knowledge Factory*, pp. 1–65; Flacks, *Youth and Social Change*, pp. 1–46; Skolnick, *The Politics of Protest*, pp. 25–175; and S. M. Lipset, *Rebellion in the University* (Boston: Little, Brown and Company, 1971), pp. 3–37; on the origins of cultural dissent, see Theodore Roszak, *The Making of a Counter Culture* (Garden City, N.Y.: Doubleday & Company, 1969).

closely associated with this interpretation.[80] To the extent that student dissentions have been spawned by middle-class affluence and are reacting against bourgeois culture per se, the movement tends toward awakening or counterculture preoccupations; to the extent that the left consists of class-conscious defectors from the capitalist system of political economy, the movement tends toward socialist politics. The two strains may be combined.

While this affluence thesis may be valid for the first small circles of new leftists—especially when their family backgrounds are liberal—it has ceased to be of any explanatory value for some time now. The student left is much too large to be encased within specific strata or family backgrounds, a fact which empirical research bears out.[81] "In sum," writes Kirby, "student activism can no longer be treated as the behavior of a rather small number of students with particular social-psychological characteristics." [82] It is not so much class or family *background* which is correlated with activism, but *current* occupational and peer orientations.[83] (We shall discuss below the notion of students as a class.) Activism also tends to be correlated with academic achievement and libertarian attitudes. Finney can thus write of his research that "all told, the evidence suggested that the students of the New Left appear to number among our most capable, most serious, and most idealistic youth." [84] In a related vein, Goertzel interprets student political activism "as an inherent result of the *educational* process, not as an aberration or as a result of some failure of the university." [85]

The radical left is virtually by definition a class-conscious political stratum. The ultimate roots of the new left are in the growing awareness of the social, economic, and political contradictions and irrationalities within the capitalist system. This consciousness knows no class or family background limitations, though it may follow the classical Marxist pattern of crystallizing theoretically among the defected intelligentsia and finding its mass outlet among the children of the working class.

While many events and government policies might be singled out as

---

[80] Richard Flacks, "The Liberated Generation: An Exploration of the Roots of Student Protest," *Journal of Social Issues* 23 (July 1967): 52–75.

[81] For example, Henry C. Finney, "Political Libertarianism at Berkeley: An Application of Perspectives from the New Student Left," *Journal of Social Issues* 27 (Summer 1971): 35–61; Douglas Kirby, "A Counter-Culture Explanation of Student Activism," *Social Problems* 19 (Fall 1971): 203–16; and Lipset, *Rebellion in the University*, p. 86.

[82] "A Counter-Culture Explanation of Student Activism," p. 215.

[83] Harold C. Meier and William Orzen, "Student Legitimation of Campus Activism," *Social Problems* 19 (Fall 1971): 181–92.

[84] "Political Libertarianism at Berkeley," p. 59.

[85] Ted Goertzel, "Generational Conflict and Social Change," *Youth and Society,* March 1972, p. 345.

catalysts of student awareness and radical consciousness—the arms race, the civil rights movement, the rediscovery of poverty, and so on—there can be no doubting the chief catalyst, without which the course of development of the left in the United States would have been profoundly slower and weaker. That prime catalyst was the Vietnam War. The war was the chief starting point for a much broader comprehension and understanding of the ossification and decay of U.S. political economy, as it brought into sharp relief the unresponsiveness and ineffectuality of operating political institutions.[86] If the ruling class could not be reached on such a specific and unpopular matter as Vietnam, how could the institutions it controls be expected to deal with the larger problems of marked social inequality, unemployment and poverty, urban decay, housing and medical shortages, environmental destruction, waste and the cheap commercialization of life, and other systemic aberrations, not to mention the Vietnam-related theme of imperialism and the military-industrial complex? Vietnam was the real beginning of the delegitimation of ruling-class authority and the ruling ideas. And an end to the hostilities in Indochina, far from signifying the loss of a raison d'être for the left, will only permit theory and action to get down to more concentrated, undeflected attacks on the social and material needs confronting the nation.

In referring to the contemporary left as a class-conscious political stratum, further words of clarification are in order. In terms of culture, material interests, property and power position, group association and interaction, and social-psychological awareness, much of the left constitutes a social class as we have defined it.[87] To the extent that left radicals have accepted the Marxist theory of society and social change, either intellectually or practically, the criterion of working-class consciousness could be added as well—working-class consciousness not in the narrow sense of identification with the interests of factory workers, but a consciousness of the interests of propertyless and powerless people as an entirety. Furthermore, as to students, professionals, and technicians, many on the left are what we have termed new working class. Like their lesser-educated counterparts in blue-collar production and service jobs, the college-educated working class has also been defining interests in much larger terms than job-specific ones alone. And it is precisely these larger social interests and concerns common to all positions of propertylessness and powerlessness that bind together the various sectors of the working-class population.

---

[86] See the evidence presented by Robert B. Smith, "The Vietnam War and Student Militancy," *Social Science Quarterly* 52 (June 1971): 133–56.

[87] For discussion of the class nature of the student population, see Horowitz and Friedland, *The Knowledge Factory,* Chapter 5, and Charles H. Anderson, *Toward a New Sociology* (Homewood, Ill.: Dorsey Press, 1971), pp. 122–26.

Although the fact of a common age grouping has lent internal solidarity to the new left and may continue to play some role, this generational factor will in all likelihood lose the great part of its force as youth itself more sharply polarizes for and against progressive change and as the new left merges into a larger stratum of radical class interests.[88] Equally important, so long as the new working class maintains its close ties to the central institutions of bourgeois society, it can marshal both the social power and the organizational ability to effect fundamental change, especially when taken in conjunction with the blue-collar proletariat.

A brief look at the student population today, and the empirical data derived from it, will attest to the absence of a distinctly generational definition of class radicalism on the left. Despite the progressive energy which has flowed out from the student population, it is highly doubtful that young people, taken as a group—and this includes the college population as such—are significantly more radical than older generations. The student left has simply had greater time and personal and information resources to act out their opposition than has the employed working class. Conservative and right-wing students have generally been apoliticized, floating along with the status quo; this situation cannot long continue, for as they see the interests of their own class background and class orientation threatened, they will come to the political surface to act. This should help clarify the division-of-interests problems as they are perceived by blue-collar college students and working-class youth in general. The establishment has done what it can to define minority and radical students as the opponents or enemies of the blue-collar white youth, student or working; but as conservative students begin to take their stand against change, this myth cannot be upheld at all. Class interests will override ethnic and educational labels. The process is already underway.[89]

Survey data suggest that approximately one-half of college students consider themselves liberal-reformist or radical, with about 10 percent in the latter category.[90] Surveys also indicate that a radical movement could mobilize about one-third of the students on major university campuses. (Horowitz and Friedman point out that one-third of the population were active participant supporters of the American Revolution, with 5 to 10 percent in the leadership group).[91] In 1970, one-third of students could be

---

[88] On the convergence of political positions of new leftists and liberals see David R. Schweitzer and James M. Elden, "New Left as Right: Congruent Themes of Political Discontent," *Journal of Social Issues* 27 (Summer 1971): 141–66.

[89] See Alan Wolfe, "Working with the Working Class," *Change,* February, 1972, pp. 48–53.

[90] For example, data presented in Lipset, *Rebellion in the Universities,* p. 49, and in Michael Miles, *The Radical Probe* (New York: Atheneum, 1971), pp. 17–18.

[91] *The Knowledge Factory,* p. 147.

considered neutralized and 15 to 20 percent conservative or right. The neutrals and conservatives roughly balance the change-oriented students.

If we may take opinions on Vietnam as an indicator of political orientation, it becomes evident that students have been no more critical of the power structure than the rest of the population. Not until the spring of 1968 did more students favor a reduction of military activity in Vietnam than favored escalation, a decision reached considerably earlier by people over 50 years of age.[92] Since the early years of the war, for example, people over 50 have considered it a mistake in greater proportion than students. In the previous section of this chapter we noted a study which found that the large majority of both white and black workers felt that the country was in bad shape and needed a lot of changes; compared to this, surveys of students about the same time found a significantly more sanguine reading of things, with the majority feeling the system was basically sound and not in need of fundamental overhauling.[93] The majority of the students expressed confidence in the policies of banks and financial institutions and in big corporations, though unlike the workers they largely lacked confidence in the political parties and organized labor. Forty-seven percent favored no substantial change, and 37 percent moderate change only. Three-fifths opposed a guaranteed income. At the same time, however, there was ample sentiment for some degree of economic and political reforms, 20 percent favoring change to the point of socialism. Any number of other studies indicate both broad divisions within the student population and changes on basic attitudes toward economics and politics, compared to an earlier student generation, of far less significance than is frequently thought to be the case.[94]

The point to be made, in brief, is that although students have contributed greatly to radical consciousness, students cannot be taken to be a class as such either subjectively or objectively speaking. They are as much future members of the ruling class and bourgeoisie as they are of the new working class and proletariat. They come from and enter into different classes, even while large numbers of them are in a transitional state. In an increasingly state capitalist economy, students must look toward government in ever-larger numbers for work and economic security. Whether their interests be intellectual, professional, technical, or business, the manner in which they view their relationship to the power structure and the manner in which the power structure reacts to them in turn will determine the quality of their political consciousness. They could be ignored (at a peril) or bought off through expanded state capitalist programs, or they

---

[92] Lipset, *Rebellion in the University*, pp. 39–41.
[93] Ibid., pp. 58–60.
[94] Dean R. Hoge, "College Students' Value Patterns in the 1950's and 1960's," *Sociology of Education* 44 (Spring 1970): 170–97.

could become part of a movement seeking social rationality and well-being through democratic self-control.[95]

The new left has had more than its share of critics. Criticism from the right is expectedly strident, attempting as it does to portray the student left as wild-eyed and wholly un-American, bent on wrecking everybody and everything in sight. Yet the most abrasive denunciations are as likely to come from establishment liberals as from right-wingers. Proving that the liberal intelligentsia are as divided as the student bodies they instruct, some college professors tend to be among the sharpest critics of the new left. Criticisms of the new left ranging from caustic sophistry to smug ridicule may be found in the writings of Nathan Glazer, S. M. Lipset, Daniel Bell, Lewis Feuer, Sidney Hook, and many other, lesser lights of the academic establishment. Their criticisms emanate mainly from fear— fear of loss of their intellectual authority, fear of a disruption of the status hierarchy in which they occupy top slots, and fear of unsettling social change. These fears are real enough. They also fear what they consider a lowering of intellectual standards and a loss of academic freedom through an acceptance of the values of the student left—another way of saying that they fear the debunking of their own pet theories and rationalizations of the status quo and the replacement of them by radical critical analyses of the inequities and injustices of the system which supports their own affluence. Dedicating one of his books to Irving Kristol, Daniel Bell betrays the true nature of his fear of the new left by writing that "their politics thus becomes . . . the tearing down of all authority." [96] Kristol echoes in a subsequent piece: "Indeed, it is my impression that, under the strain of modern life, whole classes of our population—and the educated classes most of all—are entering what can only be called, in the strictly clinical sense, a phase of infantile regression." [97]

Expectedly enough, support of student activism by faculty varies inversely with the instructor's income, rank, and situation regarding tenure. For example, 64 percent of professors with 1968 incomes of $10,000 or less expressed a high degree of support for student protest, compared to 39 percent of those with incomes of $20,000 and above.[98] Similar differences obtain between professors and assistant professors, tenured and

---

95 The notion of students being "bought off," in this case black students, is challenged in Charles V. Hamilton, *They Demand Relevance: Black Students Protest* (New York: Random House, 1970), and in Harry Edwards, *Black Students* (New York: Free Press, 1970).

96 *Marxian Socialism in the United States* (Princeton: Princeton University Press, 1967), p. xi.

97 " 'When Virtue Loses All Her Loveliness': Some Reflections on Capitalism and 'the Free Society,' " *The Public Interest* 21 (Fall 1970): 13.

98 Stephen Cole and Hannelore Adamsons, "Professional Status and Faculty Support of Student Demonstrations," *Public Opinion Quarterly* 34 (Fall 1970): 389–94.

untenured faculty. Over half of the sixty thousand faculty members interviewed in the Carnegie Commission Survey on Higher Education disapproved of the "emergence of radical student activism in recent years." [99] Even among self-defined liberals, about six in ten favored the suspension of students disrupting the regular operations of the university, and seven in ten declared such activity a threat to academic freedom.[100] Of this sort of intellectual and professorial withdrawal from responsibility and defense of the status quo other intellectuals and professors have written much criticism.[101] Suffice it to cite the remark of C. Wright Mills that "the American university system seldom if ever provides political education; it seldom teaches how to gauge what is going on in the general struggle for power in modern society." [102]

Other critics of the new left, many themselves part of the movement, have offered a variety of items of constructive criticism and advice. For example, Klare warns against too much rejection of organization, too much emphasis on a new life style that can cut off the new left from contact with the larger working class, the lack of a systematic theoretical analysis of political power and change, and the neglect of a strategy of how diverse groups can come together to work out their differences.[103] Michael Walzer has written an incisive analysis of problems for new-left politics and organization.[104] Christopher Lasch cautions that "the Left today should be concerned not only with the long-range problem of creating new institutions of popular democracy but with the immediate problem of saving what remains of liberalism—free speech, safeguards against arbitrary authority, separation of power—without which further democratic experiments of any kind will come to an end." [105] Such are the nature of sympathetic and constructive criticisms of new-left activity coming from concerned academics and intellectuals.

Critics of the new left who charge that it is counterrevolutionary in that it seeks to escape through the adoption of pastoral values and life

---

[99] Miles, *The Radical Probe,* pp. 42–43.

[100] S. M. Lipset and Everett C. Ladd, Jr., "The Divided Professoriate," *Change,* May–June, 1971, p. 60; see also Douglas Dowd, "Campus Disruptions and the Liberal-Left," *Monthly Review* 21 (September 1969): 28–39.

[101] See the essays in Charles H. Anderson and John D. Murray, eds., *The Professors: Work and Life Styles Among Academicians* (Cambridge, Mass.: Schenkman Publishing Company, 1971), pp. 305–50, and Theodore Roszak, ed., *The Dissenting Academy* (New York: Random House, 1968).

[102] *The Sociological Imagination* (New York: Oxford University Press, 1959), p. 99.

[103] "The Critique of Everyday Life, Marxism, and the New Left."

[104] *Political Action: A Practical Guide to Movement Politics* (Chicago: Quadrangle Books, 1971).

[105] *The Agony of the American Left* (New York: Random House, 1969), pp. 161–62.

styles and is rejecting or uncomprehending of technology confuse the left with the counterculture or "hippie" aggregate. Conversely, many of those who consider the counterculture as revolutionary, such as Charles Reich in his *Greening of America,* are equally confused in thinking that symbolic and life style changes among "hip" individuals will somehow alter the political economy of capitalism.[106] A counterculture of any sort cannot be established within the larger society, beyond small groups of isolated and dependent people,[107] as long as the ruling financial oligarchy holds power over the sustaining resources of the nation. As Flacks points out: "to have a new culture—and hence new life styles, new identities and new freedoms—requires a new social organization," something which can only be achieved through the political activity and support of the great majority of people.[108] Even such an "individual liberationist" as Marcuse recently writes that there can be "no individual liberation without a political struggle on a social scale against the prevailing unfreedom." [109] *Societal* change can only be accomplished, logically enough, from within the society, by a dismantling of existing institutions which perpetuate exploitation of labor, powerlessness, poverty and gross inequality, waste, militarism, urban decay, and human services shortages, and the reconstruction of democratic and people-oriented ones. Phrasing it in the skeptical sense, David Horowitz declares that "it remains to be shown that the values of the Woodstock Nation will lead in practice to a sustained revolt against the dominant culture and its power structure." [110] Even with the ruling class itself involved in hip life styles, observes Kopkind, "it still has the power to fragment our lives, kill our brothers and sisters, and do an inordinate amount of damage all over creation." [111]

Just beneath the façade of long hair, exotic dress, drugs, sexual experimentation, and religious mysticism may very well lie the most bourgeois political morality of all time as anything resembling revolutionary ways of life. Many adults uptight about today's youth have not taken the time to probe beneath surface extravagances. J. A. Warner has looked more closely: "Most youth still are in a mode of consciousness that can

---

[106] For another optimistic appraisal of the cultural approach to social change, see Jürgen Habermas, *Toward a Rational Society* (Boston: Beacon Press, 1970).

[107] For the most part, the culture of awakening has not demonstrated its ability to be materially self-sustaining or very adept at learning survival skills of a pre-advanced technological kind. Perhaps if greater numbers of farm and working-class youth entered the counterculture, these kind of fundamental manual survival skills would be acquired in larger proportions.

[108] *Youth and Social Change,* pp. 129–30.

[109] "The Movement in a New Era of Repression," p. 11.

[110] "Revolutionary Karma vs. Revolutionary Politics," *Ramparts* 9 (March 1971): 28.

[111] Andrew Kopkind, *"The Greening of America:* Beyond the Valley of the Heads," *Ramparts* (March 1971): 52.

be termed 'traditional' or 'organizational.' " [112] Goertzel has published data which confirm the continuity of social values among college youth since the late fifties, though there has been a noteworthy increase in sensitivity to ethical behavior and a decrease in interest in established religion.[113] (The latter trend has probably been more than compensated for by the current interest in nonestablished religious and quasi-religious movements such as "Transcendental Meditation," the "Jesus freak" movement, imported forms of Buddhism, astrology, and other similar security-granting pursuits adopted by young adults politically adrift in an alienated world. Characteristically, the unarticulated political values of these mystical enthusiasts are, like those of the typical religious fundamentalist, hard right-wing.)

In his book *The Making of a Counter Culture,* Theodore Roszak has cogently summarized many of the trends and tendencies of advanced technological society which have generated a cultural reaction among many youth.[114] The major generating forces noted by Roszak include overrationalization, overbureaucratization, overmechanization, and overinstitutionalization—in general the forces heralding the emergence of a Brave New World as seen by a Huxley or Orwell. The direction of the counterculture's thrust, according to Roszak, is not against capitalism or state capitalism, but against the technological society. It is in this connection that Bell, Lipset, and other organizationally and technologically oriented social scientists attack the youth movement as counterrevolutionary. But the left is not, in fact, antiorganization or antitechnology; it is anticapitalist. It aims toward a democratic social organization and a humane application of technology—that is, toward Marxist socialism. By his essentially apolitical interpretation of the roots of social problems and the origins of youthful opposition, Roszak is led into making further assertions regarding the merger and identification of the cultural and political aspects of rebellion and dissent. Although a certain degree of countercultural and left-political orientations are mutually compatible and overlapping, they are also to a large degree antithetical and incompatible—particularly in view of the widespread reliance upon drugs within the counterculture. As Kenneth Keniston astutely observes:

> Sustained engagement in an effort to change the world is rarely compatible with the kind of self-absorption and inwardness that results from intensive and regular drug use; conversely, however strongly the com-

---

[112] "Alienated Post New Left Youth," p. 8.
[113] Ted Goertzel, "Changes in the Values of College Students: 1958 to 1970–1971," *Pacific Sociological Review,* April 1972, pp. 233–44.
[114] See also Lyman T. Sargent, *New Left Thought: An Introduction* (Homewood, Ill.: Dorsey Press, 1972).

mitted drug user may feel about the inequities of American society, his primary efforts are usually directed toward self-change, rather than changing the world around him. Although some individuals alternate at different times in their lives between activism and alienation, it is very difficult to be an active social reformer and a "head" at the same time.[115]

Cultural and symbolic orientations to fundamental social change are strongly reminiscent of Pitirim Sorokin's apolitical theories of ideational and sensate cultures.[116] As with the more recent cultural interpretations, ideational cultures may be as authoritarian, class-ridden, and militaristic as sensate ones; political economy can be ignored only at the luxury of ignoring a powerless and exploited mass.

WOMEN'S LIBERATION

Women's liberation is an essential ingredient of Marxist theory and the socialist transition.[117] The economic, political, and social inequities endured by women are fundamental, and we have taken note of certain of these on several previous occasions.[118] While American history has not been without its feminists and feminist movements, their accomplishments have fallen far short of sexual equality.[119] Taken by itself, women's liberation thought and activity of the contemporary period is no more likely to succeed in achieving equality between the sexes.[120] Although some token gains for middle-class women may be realized, much as the black bourgeoisie have made tenuous gains through the civil rights movement, the condition for the large mass of working-class women, blue- and white-collar, remains substantially unchanged and will not change so long as the predominant thrust of women's liberation is sexually rather than class defined. The disinterest in women's liberation on the part of working-class women attests to its strategical failure. Women have indeed been exploited in a variety of ways by men, and sex roles have been established which tend to undermine the dignity and status of the female.

---

115 "Heads and Seekers: Drugs on Campus, Counter-Cultures, and American Society," *American Scholar* 38 (Winter 1968–69).

116 *The Crises of Our Age* (New York: E. P. Dutton, 1957, originally published 1941).

117 "Women: The Fight for Equality," *Political Affairs* 50 (March 1971).

118 See further Jessie Bernard, *Women and the Public Interest* (Chicago: Aldine Publishing Company, 1971), and Cynthia Fuchs Epstein, *Woman's Place* (Berkeley: University of California Press, 1971).

119 Mari Jo Buhle, Ann G. Gordon, and Nancy Schrom, "Women in American Society: An Historical Contribution," *Radical America* 5 (July–August 1971): 3–66.

120 See the radical collection *From Feminism to Liberation,* edited by Edith Hoshino Altbach (Cambridge, Mass.: Schenkman Publishing Company, 1971).

Profound changes in the realm of sexual social psychology are pre-requisite to male-female equality.

But the liberation of women rests no more on the elimination of attitudes of male supremacy than black liberation rests on the elimination of racism. Both male supremacy and racism must go, but neither in it-self can account for the exploited position of women and minorities. Without either male supremacy or racism, the large majoriy of women and blacks would still occupy positions of marked inequality. But this is utterly hypothetical, for male supremacy is a carefully cultured component of bourgeois society, and the exploitation of sex an indispensable compo-nent of commercialized corporate capital. The capitalist system relies in many ways upon sexual inequality and sexism for maximum appropriation of surplus value. It relies upon, for example, the unpaid labor of house-wives, the underpaid labor of unskilled females, the lowered wage and salary expectations of educated and skilled females, the inability of female labor to assert itself through unionization and militance, and sexism in advertising and marketing on almost every conceivable item of personal consumption. Especially important is the exploitation of female labor, owing to its largely individualist, unorganized, supplementary, unskilled, and highly fluid nature. As Coser and Rokoff note, women tend to be mainly in occupations or jobs in which each individual worker is replace-able or is defined as replaceable.[121] When justification for this tenuous rating is needed, there is always the self-fulfilling reason of potentially disrupting home and family obligations. Female labor is often cheaper than machinery; as Agassi correctly argues, "as long as women are willing to fill these demanding, high-speed, mind-dulling, and nerve-racking dead-end jobs for wages lower than those of most male workers, management will not invest in modernization."[122] The waste of female labor and productive capacity is incalculable, certainly greater than the given level of labor waste among males.

The right to equal pay for equal work, and the right *to* equal work for women, must be central to any kind of equality between the sexes and movements to attain such equality. We have already drawn attention to the relatively major strides the various state-controlled economies have made in these directions, both in terms of their own past and in com-parison to capitalist systems. There remain enormous obstacles from the old order defining sex roles and relations which must be overcome if equality is ever to be achieved. But the economic groundwork is being laid, at least in part. With attention to socioeconomic opportunities, child-

---

[121] See the seminal article by Rose Laub Coser and Gerald Rokoff, "Women in the Occupational World: Social Disruption and Conflict," *Social Problems* 18 (Spring 1971): 335–54.

[122] Judith Buber Agassi, "Women Who Work in Factories," *Dissent,* Winter, 1972, p. 235.

care centers, sex education and birth control, maternity leave, communal dining, and other egalitarian-oriented social policies, inroads may be begun to be made into traditional sex-role inequities.

The point we are driving at is that women as such are not a class.[123] Women are members of families, families of the ruling class, the working class, the lumpenproletariat. The family is the social-unit basis of the system of class inequality, not individual men, women, and children. Like the youth discussed in the previous section, women suffer specific discriminations because of their status; but also like these youth, women divide along much more crucial lines in the area of class relations. As opposed to a class-based approach to women's liberation, notes Marlene Dixon, "sisterhood temporarily disguised the fact that all women do not have the same interests, needs, and desires. Working-class women and middle-class women . . . have more *conflicting* interests than could ever be overcome by their common experience based on sex discrimination." [124] She justifiably observes that bourgeois women have as much at stake in the class appropriation of surplus value, nationally and internationally, as do bourgeois men. By the same token, working-class men are as proletarianized as their wives, and their wives identify their interests with those of their families and husbands, not with those of the women of the bourgeoisie. Quite to the point is Dixon's statement that "only very privileged women can in the security of their class status and class earning power create a little 'manless Utopia' for themselves." [125]

Parkin has succinctly summarized the issue:

> If the wives and daughters of unskilled labourers have some things in common with the wives and daughters of wealthy landowners, there can be no doubt that the *differences* in their overall situations are far more striking and significant. Only if the disabilities attaching to female status were felt to be so great as to override differences of a class kind would it be realistic to regard sex as an important dimension of stratification.[126]

A viable women's liberation movement can make what use it can of sex-specific mutualities of interests, just as black liberation can with regard to race; but where black liberation is almost entirely tied into class considerations, the issue of women's liberation hardly runs along class lines

---

[123] Henry Winston, "Women's Liberation: A Class Approach," *Political Affairs* 50 (July 1971): 1–10.

[124] "Public Ideology and the Class Composition of Women's Liberation," *Berkeley Journal of Sociology* 16 (1971–72): 154–56.

[125] "Why Women's Liberation?—2" in Milton Mankoff, ed., *The Poverty of Progress* (New York: Holt, Rinehart, and Winston, 1972), p. 263.

[126] Frank Parkin, *Class Inequality and Political Order* (New York: Frederick A. Praeger, 1971), p. 15; for a stratification approach to sex, see Randall Collins, "A Conflict Theory of Sexual Stratification," *Social Problems* 19 (Summer 1971): 3–20.

at all. The radical female activist will have much greater relevance if she approaches women's liberation through the larger perspective of social class, particularly in relations with lower-white-collar, and low-income persons and groups, strata which must be the chief focus of the liberation movement.

The class approach to women's liberation does not exclude the possibility of there being wide variation in the status of women within different capitalist societes. For example, the degree of freedom and equality in Scandinavian and Japanese women is quite markedly different, with the former enjoying a condition of equality and material security perhaps unparalleled among women in industrial nations and the majority of the latter continuing in an almost classic state of female subservience. Yet the differences here can only in small part be accounted for by women's liberation values and ideology per se. The Scandinavian states have highly developed social welfare systems built by the political parties representing organized labor; women live in an economic environment which offers them independence and personal security. Japan has nothing of the sort, but rather a paternalistic and atomized economy which makes men heavily dependent upon their employers and women dependent upon their men. Egalitarian ideologies can and do contribute greatly to the building of social welfare systems in the first place. Nor are state welfare systems in themselves, even if highly developed, any assurance of sexual equality; for example, if Cuba eventually attains economic development and social welfare, the traditional value of *machismo* could stand in the path of equality between the sexes.[127]

While it follows logically from the preceding arguments, we might make explicit the point that Marxist socialism does not view the family as such as an oppressive institution. It is family life under the regime of capital which erodes its relationships and heaps indignities upon family members. As Fern Winston has pointed out, abolishing the family as we know it today would not change women's relation to production, household status, male supremacy, material inequality, child care, etc.[128] Marx would not eliminate the family; it can be an important support system in the class struggle. If "wife" and "marriage" are taken literally and strictly, then Dixon is quite mistaken in her assertion that "the institution of marriage is the chief vehicle for the perpetuation of the oppression of women; it is through the role of wife that the subjugation of women is maintained."[129] (Conversely, then, we should expect that single and

---

[127] Petur Gudjonsson, "Women in Castro's Cuba," *Progressive,* August, 1972, pp. 25–29.

[128] "The Family: Is it Obsolete?" *Political Affairs* 50 (August 1971): 56–69.

[129] Marlene Dixon, "Why Women's Liberation?" in *Divided We Stand,* by the editors of *Ramparts* (San Francisco: Canfield Press, 1970), p. 35; Dixon's approach to sex inequality is, as noted previously, a class approach.

divorced women are free to escape oppression, and that Las Vegas and Sun Valley are bastions of female emancipation.) The point made by Anne Farrar and Peggy Somers is well taken that raising children and keeping a home are not in themselves inescapably degrading and super-fluous activities, but rather are made to be so under capitalist regimens and bourgeois demands and expectations.[130]

Talk of abolishing the family may turn on members of the counter-culture, but it's a sure means of turning off the working class, current divorce rates notwithstanding. Mariarosa Dalla Costa may simply "walk out" on house, family system, and market jobs, and advise all women to do so in an effort to bring down the whole structure of oppression; but where, pray tell, is our working-class wife to walk to and what life-support system is she to enter?[131] Many working-class women, though probably not a very large proportion, would indeed like to walk out of house, family, and job (if they have one), but they know it is "easier said than done." The importance of family and kinship within the working class is among the most extensively documented facts of sociology.[132]

---

[130] See Evelyn Frankford and Ann Snitow, "The Trap of Domesticity: Notes on the Family," *Socialist Revolution* 10 (July–August 1972): 83–99, including critical "Comments" by Farrar and Somers.

[131] "Women and the Subversion of the Community," *Radical America,* January–February 1972, pp. 67–102.

[132] For example, Elizabeth Bott, *Family and Social Network* (London: Tavistock Publications, 1957); Mirra Komarovsky, *Blue-Collar Marriage* (New York: Vintage Books, 1964); and Lee Rainwater et al., *Workingman's Wife* (Chicago: Oceana Publishing Company, 1959).

thirteen ———————————————————————————

TOWARD SOCIALISM

Marxist theory assumes that the full realization of socialism—or communism, in Marx's terms—requires permanent revolution; that is, socialist society cannot be completely achieved simply by socializing the means of production or by performing any other given set of political and economic acts. The attainment of full socialism requires objectively an economy of relative abundance and subjectively a society of men and women who feel secure and engage in free and creative labor not for the aggrandizement of self but for the well-being of everyone. Both objective economic and subjective social-psychological goals require a transitional period during which birthmarks of the old society and the "nightmares" of the old culture are overcome and erased. Unlike bourgeois culture and economy which grew within the old feudal order, socialist culture and economy must await its growth until after the proletarian revolution. Under collective ownership of the means of production and the political power of the working class—a workers' state—the dual goals of abundance and voluntary labor are pursued.

The central problem of socialism is not nationalization of production and a higher standard of living, but surmounting and overcoming the cultural priorities and forms of the old order.[1] Production and material well-being are, nevertheless, crucial to the attainment of a new social

---

[1] See Paul M. Sweezy, "The Transition to Socialism," *Monthly Review* 23 (May 1971): 1:16.

order; there is, in fact, a need for the constant interaction of objective
and subjective factors, and empirically the two are increasingly fused.
For the goal of socialist economy is the elimination of dehumanizing and
forced labor and the satisfaction of all rational social and individual material needs through technologically produced abundance. The full attainment of this economic goal presupposes parallel changes in social values
and value priorities regarding the elevation of human needs over private
profit, seeing people as ends and not as means to the accumulation of
capital, feelings of social security as opposed to threat and anxiety and
acquisitiveness, and working freely rather than out of fear and necessity.
Yet these values cannot be fruitfully cultivated without the commensurate
reality and promise of corollary objective economic changes.

Socialism is first and foremost a system of people who are liberated
from the oppression of wage labor and forced production, and who are
as free workers in collective control of the definition of their needs and
the forces of production designed to meet them. In Eugene Kamenka's
words, socialism "is a vision of freedom, of spontaneous cooperation, of
men's conscious self-determination once they are freed from dependence
and need. It is not merely a vision of economic plenty or social security." [2]
Ernest Mandel makes the interesting observation that the ruling class has
a large degree of socialism for itself within capitalism; they are free from
material necessity, have control of their lives and the means of production, have essentially free goods and services since they have so much
money as to make it immaterial, and they utilize the social surplus for
themselves.[3] Little wonder that they should oppose any fundamental
changes in the system.

The socialist transition is also a democratic political transition. It
is a process whereby people progressively take charge of the organization
of their own lives and social institutions. It is a revolution in initiative
and control which transfers responsibility from elites to producers, producers motivated not by profit or hierarchic authority but by an awareness of social needs and goals. People become masters of their social
and technological machinery rather than appendages to it. This is among
the most difficult aspects of the socialist transition, for the old order has
deeply ingrained the feelings of helplessness and dependency and the
values of unthinking subservience and compliance to hierarchical authority.
In order for people to take charge of the institutions they live and work
within, these destructive mental states must be overcome and the knowl-

---

2 "Marxian Humanism and Crisis in Socialist Ethics," in Erich Fromm, ed.,
Socialist Humanism (London: Penguin Press, 1967), p. 112.

3 *Marxist Economic Theory*, vol. 2 (New York: Monthly Review Press, 1970),
Chapter 17.

edge and skills necessary for full participation and responsible work acquired. Difficult experimentation will be required to build new democratic forms of administration which, in turn, interact with and reinforce personal feelings of confidence, participation, and control. Beneficent elites, if there are such, may engineer a society of plenty, but never a socialist society. As Norman Thomas has pointed out:

> If by socialism one understands a highly collective economy with a great deal of government planning and control, sweetened by much welfare legislation, then it is virtually inevitable. It is the logical extension of present developments—always assuming that we do not destroy ourselves in war. If by socialism one understands a fraternal society of free men, managing for their common good the natural resources and the marvellous tools at their command, socialism is far from inevitable.[4]

By the same token, socialist transition is an egalitarian transition, a movement from a class-stratified, highly unequal society to a classless, equal one. This is not a metaphysical proposition, but a hard economic one importantly tempered by social values and psychology. Economic or material equality can never be achieved within the context of bourgeois assumptions regarding scarcity and material incentives, and is, therefore, quite chimerical to the bourgeoisie. But we are not speaking of bourgeois assumptions of scarcity and material incentives; we are speaking of abundance and free labor as possible within a democratic socialist society. The transition is all-important here, as the system of distribution moves progressively away from monetary remuneration for work done toward increasing free distribution of goods and services to individuals out of the social fund. As people come to feel that personal well-being and freedom depend on social production as a whole, the system of wage labor and wage inequality loses its reason for being.[5] Personal possessions may grow, but they become a smaller and smaller proportion of total consumption as goods and services received free by all citizens from the social fund, or social wage, increase. The social fund of goods and services, especially of services, is itself increased as production is turned away from the profit rationale to one based upon human needs; overproduction crises are rendered impossible and use-values are multiplied at the cost of exchange-values. Good by good and service by service, from milk to medicine and transportation to education, the steady accumulation of universal use-values undermines social inequality (beyond, of course, the initial major step of expropriating the means of production and eliminating propertied wealth).

---

[4] "Humanistic Socialism and the Future," in *Socialist Humanism,* p. 323.
[5] A. S. Makhov and A. S. Frish, eds., *Society and Economic Relations* (Moscow: Progress Publishers, 1969), pp. 140, 197.

As socialist society moves from the proposition "to each according to his work" to the proposition "from each according to his ability, to each according to his needs," and as elites and hierarchy are replaced by workers' control and democracy, inequalities of wealth and power fade. At the same time, inequalities of personalities and individualities *increase*, for security and liberation from economic necessity have the potential of allowing full self-development, a naturally diversifying process given the variety among people. As Mandel observes: "Paradoxically, it is the full development of *inequality* among men, of the inequality of their aspirations and potentialities, the inequality of their personalities, that emerges as the aim of socialism." [6] It is not full socialism that would drown individuality, but the scientific paternalism of a managed-welfare-state capitalism. The latter seeks individuality through superficial fashions and slick gadgetry, all part and parcel of specious need creation and waste so necessary to corporate profits in an age of overproduction.

Marxist theory rejects any unilinear or straight-line development of history and socialism. Thus, that Russia was the first country to carry out a socialist-oriented revolution is no guide to an assurance of the Soviet Union being the first developed socialist society. Thus far it has succeeded only in being the first state-controlled economy to industrialize. The Soviet Union clings steadfastly to a hierarchical system of unequal wage labor, utilizes money bonuses for fulfillment of plans, single-mindedly pursues the accumulation of capital, and organizes production around elites of professionals, specialists, and managers. Although unequal material rewards are widely applied as work incentives, the social wage is large and growing. Moreover, the use of prices and profits in economic planning and organization does not, as some ethnocentric observers would believe, represent a return to the capitalist market mechanism. Prices are instruments for state allocation of resources and redistribution of wealth. Industrial profits and sales are tools of quality control and cost-accounting, as well as incentives to realize a piece of a production unit's profit-sharing fund. There is no market which is utilized as a means of private appropriation of surplus value. In the words of Shiryaev: "The socialist state retains control of the main levers of management, and enterprises and trusts are run in the interests of the whole society." [7] Return to the capitalist market would lead to anarchy and production crises, mass unemployment, greater inequality of income—in short, all the consequences of rejecting Marxist principles.

Those who contend that material inequality, individual acquisitiveness,

---

[6] *Marxist Economic Theory*, vol. 2, pp. 672–73.

[7] Y. Shiryaev, *Effectiveness of Socialist Production* (Moscow: Novosti Press Agency Publishing House, n.d.), pp. 60–65.

profit-oriented markets, and organizational elites are forever universal necessities of a technological society display their inability to overcome the encrusted forms of the past.[8] They are unable to visualize with Marx and Veblen a truly *socially* efficient productive system planned and controlled by the workers themselves, a system where pride and satisfaction in the quality and social contribution of labor overrides wage labor, private appropriation, and emulation of unearned wealth and consumption. In the realm of status, they fail to grasp that achievement and workmanship may produce differential prestige without correlating class and economic inequalities, that the money economy can itself be eliminated.[9] Bourgeois theorists choose to write off socialist visions as violating the nature of man rather than recognize the manner in which the existing system warps and bends human beings for its own purposes.

Finally, a comment is needed here concerning the nature of anarchism and the extent, if any, to which it differs from socialism as we have defined it. The emphasis within anarchist theory is on strict libertarianism and simple communications linkages of administrative bodies larger than local productive and social units. Contrary to many impressions, anarchism does not stand for chaos and disorder, but rather for the natural self-imposed order of the group as opposed to order imposed from without.[10] Anarchism in fact largely shares the main principles of Marxist socialism, such as worker self-control, democratic forms and process, collective ownership by producers, and material rewards based on productive labor. Further similarities include the recognition of the need for intermediate bodies between communes and the state (the state being the federation of communes) and the need for certain national services of a public nature administered by the state or national federal organ. The consistent direction of social organization is from the local level up, with the higher levels being instruments of the lower. To the extent that anarchism and socialism differ it is largely in socialism's tendency toward accepting greater centralized or state power during a transitional period to liberation or fully attained socialism.

The Soviet Union very early arrived at a form of state socialism which lacks a great deal—some would say almost totally—in Marxist socialism, whereas China has moved rapidly from early centralization toward producers' and local self-management. China has moved along the socialist transition toward communism and today embodies many of

---

[8] For example, Robert Heilbroner, *Between Capitalism and Socialism* (New York: Vintage Books, 1970), pp. 79–114.

[9] See the important discussion by Hans Blumenfeld, "Incentives to Work and The Transition to Comunism," *Monthly Review* 19 (November 1967): 71–84.

[10] For an extended discussion of the nature and background of anarchism, see Daniel Guerin, *Anarchism* (New York: Monthly Review Press, 1970).

the above principles shared by Marxist socialism and anarchism. The United States, and most other advanced capitalist states, has the material means to soon achieve full socialism. But to date the political consciousness necessary for the transformation remains insufficiently developed. Growing contradictions within the national and world capitalist systems will contribute to the maturation of a socialist consciousness.

SOCIALISM AND SOCIAL CHANGE

Thomas Jefferson once wrote:

> But I know also that laws and institutions must go hand in hand with the progress of the human mind. As that becomes more developed, more enlightened, as new discoveries are made, new truths disclosed, and manners and opinions change with change of circumstances, institutions must advance also, and keep pace with the times. We might as well require a man to wear still the coat which fitted him when a boy, as civilized society to remain ever under the regimen of their barbarous ancestors.[11]

In Marxist terms, as the forces of production continue to develop, the relations of production must change if a society is to avoid perpetual crises and disruptive difficulties. To cling to outmoded institutions is an exercise in futility and danger. As the foundation of other social institutions, economic organization and relations must be the first to be modernized if a society expects the best from its other social and cultural endeavors in family, education, work and leisure, medical care, and intergroup relations. Model communities and experimental classrooms will lead nowhere so long as economic resources are controlled largely by a small power elite concerned mainly with expanding its own influence and wealth.

In the last analysis, Marxist socialism is concerned with individual liberation and human creativity. It assumes that these are *socially* possible only within the supporting context of a participant-oriented, democratically controlled, advanced industrial society—that is, a socialist economy. A class-dominated, elitist, or authoritarian system, no matter what its intentions, is bound to fail in the task of liberation. The immediate problem, then, is how to construct this democratic, person-oriented economic context. In this final section, we shall examine some possible concrete measures calculated to move us in that direction. We shall assume at the outset that

---

[11] *Jefferson Himself,* edited by Bernard Mayo (Boston: Houghton-Mifflin, 1942), p. 324.

if democratic, person-oriented economic institutions are not soon created, it is highly unlikely that the system can "muddle through" the present crises and emerge looking anything like an open democracy of the kind envisioned by Jefferson. The alternative society is one dominated by centralized authoritarianism, a growing and hostile lumpenproletariat, the decivilizing of public existence, the loss of individual liberties and rights, coercion and repression, decline of organized labor and pervasive antiunionism, costly counterrevolution abroad, continuing inflation of the currency and stagnation or even decline of living standards and quality among the masses, and, above all, the continued growth of violence and militarism both privately and publicly. Anyone with a passing knowledge of political history recognizes that such a complex of traits looks much more like fascism than anything else.

Liberals and reformists propose the kinds of changes which are intended to enlarge the welfare state within the capitalist political economy. These proposals typically have to do with establishing a minimum income, enlarging pensions, creating a socially paid-for and privately controlled fee-for-service national medical insurance system, federal subsidies for public transport, federal grants to states for environmental clean-up, government job training and retraining programs, the use of government as employer of last resort, tax reforms, income redistribution, dispersal of stock ownership, closer federal regulation of corporations, consumer-protection legislation, elimination of the huge federal subsidies to the rich, family allowances, federally subsidized low-income housing, and many other such measures aimed at reducing poverty, inequality, unemployment, and public neglect.[12] Nearly every one of these measures involves action by government. While the goals are laudable, and while a few of the measures may to various degrees be put into effect under a liberal administration, it is highly unlikely that such measures could ever achieve the goals of democratic liberation and equality to any significant extent.

Could such an array of praiseworthy measures be fully enacted and would they be adequate to the tasks posed by poverty, inequality, unemployment, and public neglect? The answer is largely negative. The

---

[12] For example, Patricia Cayo Sexton and Brendan Sexton, *Blue Collars and Hard-Hats* (New York: Random House, 1971), pp. 285–311; Herbert J. Gans, "The New Egalitarianism," *Saturday Review,* May 6, 1972, pp. 43–46; and James Farmer, "Strategies for the '70s: A Ten-Point Public Service Program," *Social Policy* 2 (July–August 1971): 3–5. Farmer's proposals, and those found in *Social Policy* generally, are among the most substantive liberal recommendations to be found, in that they stress massive government job-creation programs which are designed to deliver *quality* services and pay union wages, the elimination of credentialism, participatory management, and the transfer of military funds to civilian production. How Farmer expected to achieve these ends by making overtures to a Nixon White House is puzzling.

capitalist class in the United States holds such enormous powers over the governmental process that the introduction of any measures which would *fundamentally* alter the balance of power and wealth would never be allowed passage in anything but watered-down form if at all. Further, given the fact of ruling-class power, the kinds of state-capitalist measures sought by liberal reformers and permitted passage by the power elite could only be expected to ultimately feed greater wealth and control into existing centers of power; as long as the seats of economic power are privately held and controlled as tenaciously as they are in the United States, state welfare capitalism is bound to accrue to the advantage of the bourgeoisie rather than its intended beneficiaries in the working and lower classes. The United States has slight chance of building the kind of people-oriented welfare state found in Scandinavia or even West Germany; corporate power is simply too overwhelming. And let it never be seriously thought that this power can be circumvented so as to achieve one's measures and aims outside of government and economy proper by taking them directly to the intended target groups and institutions. The ruling class could effectively block any such serious attempts. The resources required and the jobs to be done are too big to accomplish without state power. Many of these tasks must by definition be achieved through collectivism. They are social and political tasks, not alternatives for isolated groups. As Birnbaum declares: "If men make their history, they do so because they possess sufficient political will and political vision to alter their circumstance." [13]

The political will and political vision which this country must develop if it is ever to approximate its professed traditional ideals of democratic justice and equality is socialism, a working-class state. It follows from the preceding discussion of the obstacles to welfare reform that the first step on a socialist agenda must be the elimination of corporate power and irresponsibility. Given this fact, state capitalism could begin the transition to socialism in an open and untrammeled way. This does not refer to stock ownership by all corporate employees, or the distribution of stock to more people, either of which would fail to touch corporate power and would perhaps even enhance it. The elimination of corporate power and irresponsibility can only be achieved by, at the least, state ownership and social control of all of the largest corporations, including all basic industry, advanced scientific-based industry, transport and utilities, and finance. Public ownership of a few of the supporting sectors such as rail and power would achieve little, since the U.S. corporate oligarchy is sufficiently powerful to capture any such public operations for its own sub-

---

[13] Norman Birnbaum, "Late Capitalism in the United States," in Fischer, ed., *The Revival of American Socialism*, p. 152.

sidization and aggrandizement. By scientific-based industry is meant the field encompassing computers, electronics, chemicals, pharmaceuticals, scientific instruments, and so on. Public control here is as important as it is in the primary sectors of mining, petroleum, steel, aluminum, rubber, glass, lumber, and other raw material and building supply, for in an age of synthetics it becomes increasingly difficult to clearly separate natural from manmade primary materials. Furthermore, the electronic and chemical industries are the growth fields of the future.

Communications and utilities such as telephone, natural gas, electrical power, television, rail, and aerospace are so clearly publicly essential services that for any to be held by private stockowners is an abridgement of collective rights. The same applies to medical care and all of its major supporting industries. If education, including medical education, is considered a public domain, why isn't the more basic domain of health care removed from the greedy hands of private individuals? The profit motive destroys what should be the *most* human-oriented, use-value–determined, compassionate sphere of existence; universal health care is at the foundation of an egalitarian and just society. Private capitalists have taken advantage of human need in medical care to the point where it is the most profitable of industries and includes the most highly affluent of professions; the time has come to put an end to the exploitation of personal suffering.

The large agrobusinesses have moved far beyond the structural and psychological factors which operate on the family farm; their collectivization would not only reduce the cost of food, but save the taxpayers billions of dollars in subsidy money. These large agricultural industries produce the bulk of food goods which appear on supermarket shelves. And on what grounds should a handful of private stockholders in the big food corporations and conglomerates profit from human nutritional requirements? Why should the working class pay $500 million in higher milk prices because the big dairy interests contributed $300,000 to reelect a probusiness president and other Republicans. ("Whether we like it or not," answers a spokesman for big dairy interests, "this is the way the system works." [14]) Because the big agrobusinesses must have their profits to produce, the taxpayer pays for "soil bank" land, storage, and subsidies and shells out ridiculously high prices for a simple loaf of plain bread. Wheat is so abundantly produced on the fertile fields of the Great Plains with the century-long help of state-supported agricultural research and the advanced machinery produced by generations of laborers that it must be traded to such historic enemies of the United States as the Soviet Union and China in order to keep many family farmers alive and working and the big grain dealers prospering. Obviously, in the United States capitalism stands be-

---

[14] Editorial "Milk and Money," *The Nation,* September 11, 1972, p. 164.

tween the population and free bread—and any number of other food staples as well, including potatoes, soybeans, milk, eggs, margarine, and probably most kinds of meat. Capitalists and corporations would lose control of supply and demand and surplus value, but the farmers and workers who produce the food would enjoy security and a much higher standard of living.

This is not the place to enter into a detailed blueprint for social ownership and control. The chief point to be made is that if a public economy is the goal, it cannot successfully function without control of the basic and most advanced industries; for government to take over, piecemeal, failing sectors of old or infrastructure industries is to invite trouble for both the taxpayer and the acceptance of public ownership. As Mandel observes: "An economy can no more be 'a little bit socialist' than a woman can be 'a little bit' pregnant." [15] However, it is not an all-or-nothing proposition at a given point in time; rather, essential and leading sectors must come under social control at the beginning and lead the way toward further production of use-values as opposed to exchange for profit.

Socialist principles would assume that workers' control stresses local autonomy in innovation, initiative, and operation, while linking together individual operations through a democratically designed general national plan. In heavily capital-intensive sectors, fewer separate firms and more centralization would perhaps be desirable, whereas lightweight, labor-intensive kinds of production would tend toward greater proliferation and looser interfirm articulation. Schwartz, Theobald, and others have suggested the value of small "consentives" or "creatories" in which production would be more organic and craft-oriented, where labor would be a "prime want," voluntary, self-developmental, and self-satisfying, and tied into recreation and education in an integrated and unfragmented manner.[16] Certainly small-scale, communal production would not be the core of the alternative society, though it may appeal to growing numbers of people, especially young people who have not been fully habituated to individuated lives. It would certainly render the ecological problem more manageable.

The goal of production would be to trim off all purely and largely waste expenditures designed to increase private profit and to increase expenditures on what are necessary and culturally necessary human and social needs. Whether on balance a *trimming off* of commercial trash and porkbarrel spending and an *increase* in socially necessary production

---

[15] Ernest Mandel, *Marxist Economic Theory,* vol. 2 (New York: Monthly Review Press, 1968), Chapter 17.

[16] Robert Theobald, *Free Men and Free Markets* (Garden City, N.Y.: Doubleday & Company, 1965), pp. 143–45; and Eugene S. Schwartz, *Overskill: The Decline of Technology in Modern Civilization* (Chicago: Quadrangle Books, 1971), pp. 303–4.

would result in a statistical rise in GNP is uncertain, although when one considers the enormous environmental, housing, transport, medical, recreational, and other needs and shortages, an immediate increase in labor and service consumption would definitely seem likely. In time, rational production and consumption would result in a marked lowering of labor time and energy consumption, as the labor theory of value would be replaced by that of free time. The problems posed by free time have been provocatively dealt with by Theobald.[17] With the growth of free goods and services, money would have to be progressively reduced through lower payments and wages and prices, or the cost of remaining purchased goods and services would inflate.[18]

Problems inherent in the socialist transition would be plentiful and persistent, but the pains of experimentation required in working them out would amount to but a small fraction of the accumulation of misery and unnecessary alienation harbored within the existing system and the even less desirable turns possible in the future.

In the international arena, the transition to socialism would mean the return of U.S. foreign-held corporate property to the respective countries in which they now operate and a return to trade as the means of obtaining foreign commodities. The gains in employment and consumption to the U.S. working class would be significant; only the ruling class would stand to lose anything. By the same token, foreign capital in the United States would be limited to government-controlled investment pools, and Third World bourgeois investors would be excluded on the grounds that their own economies need the resources more urgently. Anyway, without U.S. corporations paying off the national bourgeoisie of the Third World, these kinds of monies would dwindle in any event. As to the development of the Third World, a socialist transition in the United States would find its new kind of investments to be long-term, low-interest loans, equal terms of trade, grants, and technical assistance—all stripped of compromising ties and strings. The political influences of a socialist America would be used to promote popular democracy and development, rather than military dictatorship and counterrevolution. Trade with the Soviet Union, Eastern Europe, and China would reach large proportions, as the international division of labor renders them useful to us and us to them. Given the cooperation of these nations, gradual demilitarization of much if not all of the Third World would be a possibility, and economic development

---

[17] *Free Men and Free Markets.*

[18] For discussions of economic problems and policies of the socialist economy as it would appear in advanced industrial society, see Mandel, *Marxist Economic Theory*, vol. 2, Chapters 16 and 17; and Paul Sweezy and Charles Bettleheim, *On the Transition to Socialism* (New York: Monthly Review Press, 1971).

would be a certainty. On the international front, the U.S. ruling class stands as the chief threat to peace and the chief obstacle to economic development.

The dilemma involved, however, is this: if the ruling class has within itself the power to subvert such minimal reforms as those pushed by liberals, how is it possible to take the first and necessary step of socializing the key sectors of production? There are two broad avenues which may be taken: (1) via the legislative process by virtue of cycles of economic crises and progressive radicalization of the electorate in its unwillingness further to tolerate such insecurities and disruptions; and (2) via direct revolt of the production sector of the working class and the institution of industrial democracy, which would then carry forward into the governmental and legislative process. Whether either of these two developments could transpire peaceably is open to question. It is not at all characteristic of ruling classes to step aside gracefully, even within the structure of democratic and constitutional processes. Yet no ruling class can prevent change for long solely through the use of force. Furthermore, U.S. capitalism is incapable of reforming itself. As Michael Harrington has written: "In education, housing, agriculture, welfare and every other area of social life it is necessary to attack the systematic concentration of economic power in order to achieve serious reform. . . . We insist . . . that the fundamental solution of these problems requires measures that go beyond the limits of the capitalist economy." [19] So, too, must the same conclusion be drawn for problems of counterrevolutionary war, military waste, consumer waste, poverty amid wealth, and the erosion of nature and natural resources.

We are realistically aware, as was Paul Sweezy over three decades ago, that "every capitalist nation, in the period of imperialism, carries within it the seeds of fascism." [20] And no less must we come to conclude with Sweezy that "ultimately it will be found that the *only* way to combine peace and prosperity is through socialism, and that it would be much better for us all if this discovery were made sooner rather than later." [21] Over fifty years ago Veblen made it clear that:

> So long as no such change of base is made [to socialism], what is confidently to be looked for is a regime of continued and increasing shame and confusion, hardship and dissension, unemployment and privation,

---

[19] *Socialism* (New York: Saturday Review Press, 1972), pp. 279, 291.
[20] *The Theory of Capitalist Development* (New York: Monthly Review Press, 1968, 1942), p. 346.
[21] *The Present as History* (New York: Monthly Review Press, 1953), p. 369.

waste and insecurity of persons and property—such as the rule of the Vested Interests in business has already made increasingly familiar to all the civilized peoples.[22]

Half a century after this prognosis for capitalism, the factuality of such wisdom has not yet made a fully sufficient impact upon the working classes of America. How much later it will be before it does make an impact is uncertain, but we suspect that the time is not too far distant. The radical choice is certain to present itself with greater clarity and force in the immediate decades.

---

[22] Thorstein Veblen, *The Engineers and the Price System* (New York: Harcourt, Brace and World, Inc., 1963, 1921), p. 147.

INDEX

Power (*cont.*)
elite, 216-22, 228-33, 256, 275
of executive branch, 219, 225-26
militarization of, 220
political vs. economic, 79
student, 304
theories of, 120, 190-94
and wealth, 12-13
Price fixing, 239
Production
under capitalism, 234
and employment, 155-61
and exchange value, 16-17
forces of, 10, 46-48, 173, 177
and inequality, 78, 86-87
machine stage, 26-29, 33
and Marxist theory, 6-7, 9-11
and state ownership, 14
and wages, 155-61
Professionals
and bourgeoisie, 55
income of, 103-6
proletarianization of, 168, 172
radicalization of, 285
Profits, 22, 40-41, 183, 208
and black labor, 293
under capitalism, 234-36
from foreign investment, 276-81
and federal agencies, 224
monopoly, 212-13
sharing, 214
in Soviet Union, 323
state guarantee of, 223
and surplus value, 17-19
Proletariat
vs. bourgeoisie, 46-49, 171
composition of, 125
dictatorship of, 66-68
expansion of, 51
impoverishment of, 23-24
in Marxist theory, 52-56
and New Left, 309-310
and new working class, 171-74
radicalization of, 282, 284-86
revolution of, 64-65, 320
and wages, 20-22
white-collar membership, 168
vs. working class, 142
Property class, 47, 116-41, 216-18

Race
and income, 92-94, 96, 101-2, 106
racism, 290-302 *passim*
See also Blacks
Radicalism, 282-90, 302-15
Real estate industry, 54, 144-45, 206-7, 238, 247
Religion
and alienation, 43

Religion (*cont.*)
of lumpenproletariat, 130
of New Left, 313-14
Revolution, 12, 26-27, 271-73
in Asia, 75
and class consciousness, 135
vs. legislation, 331
and Marxist theory, 46-75
of middle class, 174
of peasantry, 59, 75
in Soviet Union, 323
Revolutionary class, 48, 61
Ruling class, 13, 141, 169, 173, *190-215*, 310, 327
and class consciousness, 59-62, 136-39
in Marxist theory, 56-59
foreign earnings of, 240
occupations, 102-3
power elites, 216-22, 228-33
and poverty, 148, 160, 189
socialism, 321
technology of, 157-58
women, 317
Ruling ideas
on blacks, 300
on inequality, 76-77
of power elite, 221
radicalization of, 285-87
on Vietnam War, 308

Scandinavia
capitalism in, 115, 242, 287
health care in, 264-65
pension system in, 215
and welfare state, 259-60, 327
and women's liberation, 318
working class radicalism, 282
Scarcity, 85-86, 88
artificial, 152
Servant class, 131, 142, 146
Social class
and class consciousness, 134-40
foundations of, 46-49
inequality of, 76-89
as property class, 116-41
and revolution, 63-66
and social change, 282-319
and social mobility, 140-41
study of, 1-5
stratification variables, 121-23
Weber's concepts of, 116-21
See also entries for individual social classes
Social Democratic Parties, 259, 287
Socialism, 320-32
European, 259
and imperialism, 271
inequality in, 72, 323, 326

Value
   and automation, 29-32
   exchange. *See* Exchange-value
   labor theory of, 16-17
   surplus, 17-19. *See also* Surplus value
   use, 14-16, 31, 41, 69
Veblen, Thorstein
   on inequality, 80, 95
   on leisure class, 205, 229
   and Marxism, 2, 221, 234, 324
   on new working class, 173, 241, 285
   on overproduction, 236-38
   pessimism of, 136, 161, 331-32
   on power elite, 216, 222, 231-33
   on underlying population, 142
   on unemployment, 152
   and Weber, 116, 118
Vietnam War
   attitudes toward, 170, 260, 310
   and class consciousness, 2, 138, 139
   cost of, 244, 251, 253-54
   and imperialism, 271-73, 276
   and New Left, 192, 304, 306, 308
   union support of, 164
Violence
   black, 302
   and power, 191-93, 195

Wages, 28, 53, 155-61
   abolition of, 34
   black labor, 294-95
   of bureaucracies, 195-96
   control of, 244
   distribution, 92, 322
   in Soviet Union, 323
   and status, 122, 126
   subsistence level, 18, 19-22, 181-89
   of women, 316
Waste, 237-39
Wealth
   vs. contribution, 87
   and corporate power, 201
   distribution of, 71, 111-15
   as leisure time, 32
   and state power, 12-13
Weber, Max
   on bureaucracy, 194-96
   class concepts of, 3, 79, 116-21
   on democracy, 199
Welfare state, 257-65
   and alienation, 175
   foundation of, 282

Welfare state (*cont.*)
   Scandinavian, 242
   and women's liberation, 318
West Germany
   and imperialism, 277, 279
   and state capitalism, 244, 252
   worker radicalism in, 178, 282
White-collar workers
   income of, 103-6
   and Marxist theory, 168
   and proletariat, 54
Women, 315-19
   class consciousness, 137-38
   employment of, 28, 143-47, 245
   franchise, 223
   income of, 97-99, 102, 106-7
   and poverty, 109-11
   unemployed, 149, 150
   and unions, 166
Working class, 19-22, 64, *167-89*, 258,
      269-70
   alienation of, 176-81
   black, 290-300
   vs. capitalist class, 46-47
   class consciousness, 136-40
   composition of, 125, 310
   egalitarianism, 91
   and employment, 142-66
   and finance capital, 207, 214-15
   new, 124-25, 171-74
   and New Left, 303
   political power of, 13, 200
   psychology of, 168-70
   and radicalism, 282-90
   revolution of, 331
   and social mobility, 140-41
   taxation of, 38-39, 243, 244, 248
   violence, 64
   Weber's theory of, 119
   women, 317

Youth
   child labor, 152
   class consciousness, 137-38, 313-14
   employment, 143-44, 146
   income of, 97-98
   and lumpenproletariat, 130
   and poverty, 109
   radicalization of, 286
   unemployed, 150
   See also Students